Christian Engagement in Social Change

Christian Heritage Rediscovered

The Series, as the name suggests, is meant to focus on Christian Faith & Living vis-à-vis topics like Literature & Poetry, Indigenous Philosophizing, Ethical Response towards Agriculture, Health & Healing, Science & Technology, Eco-Feminist Theology, Sociological Approach towards Human Rights, Law & Politics, Arts, History of Ideas, Ancient Civilizations, Cultural Contiguity, Religious Cosmologies & Mysticism, Footsteps of Famous Theologians, World Peace & Harmony, Global Capitalism, Network Marketing, Cybertheology, Population & Demographics, Epigraphic Studies, Contextualized Education, and many others. We welcome a Mss. on any topic/s mentioned, whether they are original works, scholarly monographs, collections of conference papers, revised dissertations, or translations of historical documents. Through the Series we, the Publishers, are striving to put forward published works that may help Institutions, Academic Bodies, Researchers, Scholars and the World at large in furthering their respective knowledge and understanding on the concerned subject. We welcome your comments on our efforts and further suggestions on how we can foster the upcoming thought provoking theologically grounded books.

Christian Heritage Rediscovered - 57

Christian Engagement in Social Change

The Role of Theological Education

Editors
Muthuraj Swamy
Wilson Paluri
Asish Thomas Koshy

CWI
Christian World Imprints™

First Published in 2018 by

Christian World Imprints™
Christian Publishing & Books from India
H-12 Bali Nagar, **New Delhi-110015**
info@christianworldimprints.com
www.ChristianWorldImprints.com
Phone: +91 11 25465925

ISBN: 978-93-5148-225-3 (HB) ISBN: 978-93-5148-226-0 (PB)

Cataloging in Publication Data--DK
Courtesy: D.K. Agencies (P) Ltd. <docinfo@dkagencies.com>

Postgraduate Interdisciplinary Seminar (2015 : Union Biblical Seminary)
Christian engagement in social change : the role of theological education / editors, Muthuraj Swamy, Wilson Paluri, Asish Thomas Koshy.
pages cm. -- (Christian heritage rediscovered ; 57)
"Earlier versions of a good number of essays in the book were presented in the Postgraduate Interdisciplinary Seminar at the Union Biblical Seminary (UBS), Pune, in 2015, on the theme 'Christian Engagement in Social Change'"--Acknowledgement.
ISBN 9789351482253 (HB)
ISBN 9789351482260 (PB)

1. Church work--Congresses. 2. Social change--Religious aspects--Christianity--Congresses. I. Swamy, Muthuraj, editor. II. Paluri, Wilson, editor. III. Koshy, Asish Thomas, 1971- editor. IV. Title. V. Series: Christian heritage rediscovered; 57.

LCC BR517.P67 2015 | DDC 303.49 23

Printed in India.

Contents

Part 3
Philosophical, Theological & Religious Perspectives

Part 4
Missiological & Ministry Perspectives

Foreword

It is matter of great joy to know that this collection of select papers, many of them originally presented at a seminar by the 2014-2016 batch of Master of Theology year students at the Union Biblical Seminary (UBS), is being published now. The writers are now teaching faculty members in various theological institutions in India and at different ministry positions of leadership in church and missions, and they have taken sincere efforts in revising and updating their papers. Included are also some select papers from professors in the teaching faculty from UBS and other theological institutions. The theme, 'Christian Engagement in Social Change,' was chosen with a view to bringing to light the historically strong social commitment of the Christian church which unfortunately seldom figures in the Indian public discourse. The fact however, remains that Christianity in India has attracted many from the excluded, deprived and marginalised of the religiously organised Indian society and polity because of one of Christianity's fundamental tenets which is social inclusiveness. Consequently, the Indian church continues to have a robust social engagement in the upliftment of its poor and disadvantaged, and equity in society despite the many odds and oppositions the church faces in doing so.

The essays published here comprehensively project range of perspectives from major areas of the theological discipline over the issue of Christian engagement in contemporary India. The writers are drawn from all over our country representing a wide spectrum of socio-cultural realities, as well as various sections/denominations of Christianity: therefore are uniquely placed in terms of their experience, observation and understanding of social change. Here they have been true critics who both authenticate and critically comment on the role of the church and Christianity as a whole as catalysts and agents of social development.

It was my good pleasure and privilege to watch over this process of academic exercise and contribution of thoughts of this academic community as a facilitator and fellow faculty member in position of the Dean of Postgraduate Studies. These essays surely would be useful to both theological students and the general readers in terms of information about and insights into the complex issues of social change and the change agent. A good addition, no doubt, to individual and institutional knowledge and libraries.

Jagat R Santra
Associate Professor
Union Biblical Seminary
August 2017

Acknowledgments

More than ever, Christians in India and all over the world today are in the need of serious thinking and articulating Christian participation in the public sphere, and overcoming the creation of boundaries between 'religion' and 'public' (or other similar categories) for which they too are responsible to a great extent. In other words, while there are forces which continue to argue for privatizing religion, Christians themselves continue to harbor discourses that isolate 'religion' from other aspects of life which have dangerous potential for leading to ghettoization. The theme of the book, which has been chosen and reflected against this context, is only a continuation of many directions that have been already initiated by many Indian Christian thinkers but have still a long way to go in a society like India.

This book would not have been possible without the help of many people. We thank all the contributors of the book who quickly came back whenever contacted. We thank them for patiently waiting for several months through the editing process. Richie Varghese and John Fredrick David have been immensely helpful in proofreading the text and our thanks are due to them. Earlier versions of a good number of essays in the book were presented in the Postgraduate Interdisciplinary Seminar at the Union Biblical Seminary (UBS), Pune, in 2015, on the theme 'Christian Engagement in for Social Change,' and our thanks are due to Rev. Dr. Jagat Santra, the Dean of Postgraduate Studies, for his encouragement in choosing this theme and his many interactions with us. We are also grateful to the UBS administration. Most of the essays in this book were specifically written for the above-mentioned seminar on the theme of this book and they are published here for the first time unless mentioned otherwise.

The cover for this book has been designed by Robin Matthew and we record our sincere gratitude to him for his excellent and evocative work.

We might have tested the patience of Christian World Imprints, our publisher, a lot, as there was a delay in the submission of the manuscript. We thank Mr. Sudhanshu Kanda for his reaching over to us tirelessly in spite of our extensions.

Muthuraj Swamy
Wilson Paluri
Asish Thomas Koshy

March 2017

Part 1

Introducing the Theme and the Book

1

Christian Engagement in Social Change
The Need of the Hour

Muthuraj Swamy, Wilson Paluri and Asish Thomas Koshy

Christians today find themselves in a world of several and ongoing changes. Scientific and technological advancements, political, social, cultural, economic and other changes in our society have become rapid and inevitable. Generally these changes can be defined as and classified under social change, and the reality of this change cannot be ignored by any right thinking human being.

Social change is primarily the restructuring of human social institutions and social conditions: family, community, consciousness, religion, political systems, financial institutions (economics), culture, science & technology, organizations, settlement systems, and structures of authority, power and decision making and many more. Some of the aspects of social change such as science, technology and development have greatly accelerated in recent times, and this creates new problems as people take various efforts in adapting to and resisting change.

The above mentioned various forms of social change have direct impacts on our life affecting and influencing our individuality, rights, livelihood, community formation and human relations and interactions. The very reality that social change is either initiated or resisted means that it requires human responses. In such a context Christians as responsible human beings cannot be blind and ignorant to these changes and the challenges they bring to the whole of human life and earth.

One of the fundamental principles of Christian life and spirituality is the need to engage with our environment or context. In fact it is an unavoidable task. We may cease to be Christians when active engagement in all aspects of our social life is lacking. We have several examples in the Scripture including in the life of Jesus Christ who always enthusiastically engaged with the people and the situations around him. Through the centuries several committed theologians and church leaders also have insisted this aspect of Christian engagement in social change.

However still, detachment rather than engagement has become the actual reality of living in many Christian circles in the contemporary context. Christian spirituality becomes closed rather than engaged when we are concerned only with the life yet to come. Against such a context we have to widen the horizons in our understanding of Christian life and spirituality in order to engage with social change. Of course, we do not engage to compete with other groups or other religions in controlling the process of social change, rather to engage in it along with them. We engage in order to responsibly address the problems and prospects of social change for all God's creation.

Christian engagement in social change has stronger applications for us Christians in India. Like other societies Indian society too is undergoing changes, and these changes have many concerns for our life. Among them, identity, justice and human rights concerns are important, especially for minorities including religious minorities in India, and these cannot be ignored as if Christianity does not have any stake in them. Especially, the increasingly hostile environment towards Christians in India invites us to engage actively rather than withdrawing or detaching from these realities. It is through engagement in social change that we make the Christian message more relevant and significant.

This book is both an exploration of various issues connected with social changes and an assessment of Christian responses to factors affecting and effecting social change, as well as an invitation to Christians in India and worldwide to actively participate in issues concerning all aspects of human life. The important aspect here is the participation, and not a power struggle to compete with other religions or political systems to take over control. In fact while one laments about the limitations of Christians in actively participating in issues concerning social, political and other aspects of life, nevertheless, it is true that Christianity has often been comfortable with aligning with powerful forces or accommodating into power systems. What happened with Constantinianism in the early fourth century CE is an historic example. By participation what I mean here is to overcome the discourses of separation between Christianity and culture, church and state, religion and sate and similar other binaries which dominate the everyday lives of millions of Christians and cooperate and to coordinate with people from other walks of life. All essays in this book are written within this framework but discuss specific cases, examples and texts to illustrate the importance of Christian engagement in social change and to invite Christians for an effective engagement particularly in the contemporary Indian context.

Richie Varghese sketches out some basic principles to be kept in mind while engaging as Christian individuals or institutions towards the end of social change. These principles are important in setting the tone for any such engagement and determine its course. Four principles are suggested. Firstly, the local community must be seen as the primary locus to bring about social change. Secondly, all strict sacred-secular binaries must be overcome in order to be fruitfully engaged in society. Thirdly, the use of voice must be seen as a very important means of social engagement and this must effectively counter passive and oppressive silences. Fourthly, all Christian social engagement must be carried out with a posture of utmost sensitivity rather than one of misplaced moral certainties and pontification. These principles can constructively inform all concrete attempts towards Christian engagement in social change

Asish Thomas Koshy's essay, 'Breaking the Power of Silence and Espousing Engagement' explores the intricacies of the power of silence that obstructs the experience of the fullness of life and how Jesus undoes it by breaking the fetters of the power of silence. He uses narrative criticism and historical-critical method to explore the concepts dealt in the narrative of Mark 3:1-6. Jesus breaks the silence of Pharisees which is seen as a tool to actively safeguard an oppressive status quo by giving a physical and symbolic invitation for the withered man to move from the 'periphery' to the 'center' and experience wholeness. Koshy takes this incident as the basis of forming a theology of engagement where the kingdom of God engages us in the suffering of those who have been silenced and continue to be silenced. The theology of engagement brings social engagement within the purview of spirituality and provides healing and restoration to those who are rejected and denied their identity by the evil social structures.

In her essay "Prophetic Intervention for Social Change," Rachel Katty explores the issue of land conflict between Naboth and Ahad-Jezebel in the 9th century BCE and prophet Elijah's role in bringing justice and reconciliation in such conflicting situation. Through socio-rhetorical analysis she identifies the plot in the passage where faulty means and power is used to steal and grab Naboth's land. She argues that similar issues of land conflict like land encroachment, boundary tempering, power abuse and injustice could be witnessed in Sumi Naga Society and that these issues should be addressed from the perspective of human rights, social justice, and freedom to have one's own land. The church can play a prophetic role by practicing justice and bringing peace in such conflicting situation where land is treated as important part of Sumi life and society.

Malsawmlien Gangte's study on "You are the Light of the World (Mt. 5:14-16)" is an attempt to analyse the significance of this beatitude from the social, ethical and missional perspectives. He uses missiological, ethical and postcolonial approaches to explore the role of a disciple of Jesus in bringing social change through integrity in word and deed, moral living, communitarian ethics and challenging the socio-political structures around us. 'Being light', for disciples, imply an active engagement and participation in dispelling the 'darkness' of socio-political structures and systems and not a complacent, selfish and greedy attitude. Passivity is not an option as the very nature of light suggests.

Reji George, in his essay "The New Commandment in the Farewell Discourse (Jn. 13:34)", points to the inclusive nature of the love commandment of Jesus. He argues that the commandment to 'love one another' should be seen in relation to Christ's *agape* love, foot-washing episode, and in the context of universality of love expressed in the Johannine Community. The 'new commandment' of Jesus indicates that Jesus' love for his disciples and their love for one another have a universal intention; it is not exclusive, but expansive. For George, Jesus' special concern for the poor in John's gospel should challenge the believers today to open the doors of the church for the marginalized and to endorse freedom, justice and equality at all levels.

Holika uses socio-rhetorical method in exploring Paul's teaching on moral and social ethics in the context of sexual immorality in 1 Corinthians 5:1-8. She identifies the corporate responsibility, holiness, discipline, judgment, repentance, salvation and sincerity as the motives of Paul's writing to the Corinthian Church. It is a strong reminder to the present church of its responsibility to promote the renewal and discipline of good moral life within its fold and its commitment to participate in socio-political changes in the wider society.

Mary Grace Pangamte examines Paul's rhetoric of persuasion in the book of Philemon. Paul persuades to evoke in the heart of Onecimus, the owner of the slave, a voluntary humane attitude and Christian responsibility through love in Christ. Slavery in the Greco-Roman society was commercial where slaves had little or no access to justice. The slaves had no voice in the society and their owners had exclusive rights over them. Her contention is that taking the cue from Paul's intervention in this issue, The church today could provide voice to the voiceless and helpless babies killed mercilessly through female infanticide and inspire the community of faith to speak up and make each life count.

John Jebaseelan's essay draws lessons about the use of rhetoric or the art of persuasion from Plato and Paul to apply in the context of the church today. Plato in his work *Gorgias* talks about the misuse of rhetoric in the hands of politicians of his time. Paul in his letter to *Corinthians* talks about the obsession of his contemporaries to hear oratory filled with rhetorical techniques and in that process fails to understand the truth and power of the gospel. These works show the limitations of using persuasive words to manipulate, to entertain and to accumulate status. Based on these observations, Jebaseelan argues that pulpit cannot bring substantial change by mere rhetoric – empty words which are based on lack of knowledge or based on the non-truth. Change can happen only when thoughtful sermons are preached interpreting the events of the world in the light of the eternal word of God.

Nicky Sangma's "Towards a Dialogue of Subjectiveness" is a reflection on the plight of homosexuals and the response of the church towards homosexuality in India. He uses Hegel's dialectical method of thesis, antithesis and synthesis to form a model of dialogue between homosexuals and the church. The hostility, suspicion and hatred towards each other could only be minimised through openness in dialogue. Nicky is honest in accepting that such dialogue may not be completely fruitful, however, will open the doors of mutual respect and willingness to listen to each other.

Paluri Wilson uses Social Philosophy as a methodological tool to analyse the religious commitment towards social change in India. He attempts to formulate a Christian model of social philosophy that is based on morality which synthesizes the knowledge of 'revelation theology', 'rational theology' and the 'empirical social sciences'. 'Spiritual humanism' developed by the modern Indian thinkers directs us to the fact that human problems are both spiritual and social; spiritual awareness and social efficiency are not only consistent but also complementary. He proposes that the social philosophy based on religious humanism encourages Christians to recognize the metaphysical conception of oneness of life and equality of all living beings and to consciously uphold human dignity in bringing social change.

Muthuraj Swamy focuses on the growing menace of religious fundamentalism in the global context, and particularly in the Indian context. Hindutva fundamentalism is growing especially after its political party has been able to form a government at the centre with a majority in 2014, and it is threatening the lives of minorities, particularly religious minorities. Christian engagement in such context is very limited barring a few responses. Even in those responses, there are very few approaches to address the problem in a holistic manner. Discussing the limitations in such approaches, Swamy proposes some possible ways for strengthening the Christian responses to Hindutva fundamentalism in India. These include properly understanding religious fundamentalism, the need for Christians in India to overcome isolationism and to move towards engagement and openness towards other groups, the importance of critical scholarship from Christian communities in India and working with Hindu moderates in India and outside.

James Wesly discusses the problem of development which has become a catchword today. People have voted for development and political parties have come to power in the name of development. Development is often measured in terms of material abundance and technological advancement. But the ethics of development is rarely taken into consideration. Sacrificing the livelihood of indigenous and marginalized communities, destruction of valuable natural resources at the altar of development is often seen as the inevitable sacrifice for greater good called development. Within the larger global debate on sustainability and protection of environment the use of bio-fuel and solar electricity and other clean mechanisms are seen as answers to the problems of global warming and climate change. However, the use of clean development mechanism such as bio-fuel and solar electricity rarely question the larger energy consuming lifestyle which is very unhealthy and which is at the core of recent ecological crises. This essay critiques the usefulness of clean development mechanism as an alternative means for sustainable development. Since the present ecological crisis cannot be addressed effectively by just planting more trees, creating more national parks or even by bringing to stop all the development projects. Even alternative Clean Development Mechanism, no matter how clean and green it will be, will be inadequate unless and until our unethical, un-spiritual, unjust, selfish energy consuming lifestyle is transformed by a more simple, sustainable just living based on sharing, preserving and equitable use of resources.

Lalnunmawia's essay is an analysis of the mission work of Mizoram Presbyterian Church towards HIV/AIDS infected patients. He argues that the three departments of the Mizoram Presbyterian Church; Synod Rescue Home, Family Guidance and Counselling Centre and Grace Home that are concerned about the social issues have neglected the needs of this big section of our society. He employs two methods of Hoekendijk's *World Centric Paradigm* and M. M. Thomas' *Humanization* to remind the Mizoram Presbyterian Church that its participation in mission also involves participation in the struggle for a just society. The church today needs to realize that it is not 'church' but the 'world' that is the focus of God. Along with soul saving activities love and care for our neighbours should also be given importance to accomplish the expectations of Christ in the life of the church. His proposal of church's involvement in giving importance to Home Mission towards HIV/AIDS persons, running awareness programmes to eliminate negativity towards them, providing sex education and equipping counselling centres has a strong message that these needy, desperate and stigmatized members our society should no longer be neglected by the body of Christ.

Watirenla Jamir's essay on missional engagement among Differently-Abled children is an exploration of the possibility of DABA (Dimapur Ao Baptist Arogo) engaging in mission towards such neglected children. By highlighting the struggles of Differently-ables children and their family members in the area of social isolation, stigmatization, inferiority complex, medical facilities and other, she challenges the families, churches and the society to change their attitude towards the Differently-Abled children. Jesus often responded to the Differently-Abled people with compassion. He himself participated in their suffering by accepting the cross. Therefore, the missional engagement includes the active involvement of the church (including DABA) in spreading awareness among people to change their mindset and attitude towards them.

Saraswati Koirala has done a study on the 'positive and negative impact of BPO work culture on Indian families especially the Christian families'. For her, such technological advancement is a major factor affecting some core family values.

The work culture of BPO sector is composed of odd timing of work schedule and in comparison to their counterparts, BPO employees experience burn-out due to extreme work demand. Moreover, they get into serious health issues like chronic fatigue, insomnia, nausea, irritability and even depression. In order to cope with the psychological and physical stress, BPO employees develop poor eating habits, smoking, excessive drinking of coffee and so on. The work stress has also led to the breakdown of marital relationships. Due to the odd working hours, the employees' personal and social life gets totally disturbed. However, the response of the church has been very poor in such situation. Pastors and church leaders have not fully addressed these concerns from pastoral care and counselling perspective. Koirala proposes the Conjoint Family Therapy developed by Don Jackson and others in addressing this issue. This therapy is the simultaneous treatment of more than one family member. It provides resources for understanding client problems, gather information about their difficulties, and ultimately treat them. It develops healthier balance between their need for togetherness and their need for autonomy, providing more room for the later. She is of the opinion that in the fast changing scenario of our society, the church should come out of its conventional way of ministry. There should be new ways and means of providing pastoral care through weekday worship services, support groups, counselling, producing recorded church sermons, conducting seminars and creating awareness among the other church members about the struggles of BPO employees.

Lipoklemla Pongener discusses the issues faced by sexual minorities (LGBT) in her essay. She argues that the sexual propensity of these people is misunderstood by the society as well as the church, which further raises medical, constitutional, legal, societal and psychological issues. She proposes that counselling methods like Erik H. Erikson's Psychosocial model, Sigmund Freud's Psychosexual model, Albert Ellis' Rational Emotive Behavior Therapy, and Thomas C. Oden's Empathetic Counselling method can be helpful in defining adolescence identity confusion, in clearing their irrational thinking and in approaching in a non-judgmental way through therapeutic techniques. The church needs to recognize that at the heart of LGBT struggle there is a deep loneliness, the natural human hunger for mutual love, a search for identity and a longing for completeness. Therefore, a Christian environment of love, understanding, acceptance and support is needed.

Lochumi Ezung identifies the rapid changes taking place in Indian society which has its serious implications on senior citizens. Factors like the emergence of nuclear families, greater longevity, physical separation of parents from children and the changing values of the younger generation are affecting the lives of the senior citizens. Over two-third of elderly people in India are neglected by their family members while one-third of them claimed to have suffered physical or verbal abuses. Other major problems they face today are malnutrition, lack of shelter, depression, isolation, non-productivity and financial incapacity. Increasing urbanization has led to a rise in crime against the elderly and the criminals pick on them because they are easy targets. To address these socio-psychological problems faced by senior citizens today, she proposes that the church should not think primarily of ministry for or to the elderly but ministry with the elderly and even ministry from the elderly. Senior citizens deserve our respect, recognition, love and care in their life, and the church and society should create this awareness among young people in our country.

Nukshijungla suggests Paulo Friere's method of Critical Consciousness and Thomas Groome's method of Shared Praxis to combat and suppress human trafficking, which is kind of modern day slavery and exploits human beings by treating them like commodities. Human trafficking constitutes one of the greatest human rights challenges of our time. Nukshijungla's approach to the issue deepens the critical awareness of the situation and aims at bringing liberation and transformation. One of the strong reasons for the church to be concerned about this social issue is that every life is of great value and God loves all individuals. Her contention is that Church should join hands with some of the organizations such as End Child Prostitution in Asian Tourism (ECPAT), Action against Trafficking and Sexual Exploitation of Children (ATSEC), Action Aid, etc., which are actively working towards rescuing children and women from this trade and providing them rehabilitation and a means of living a dignified life. Along with other initiatives, The church should also work towards organizing training programmes and activities to promote gender equality through gender sensitization. A study like this draws our attention towards illegal prostitution, slavery, sexual abuse, forced labour and other kinds of violence acted upon innocent children and women, and to engage actively in bringing social change in this area.

Marian Susi Dharamraj discusses the feeling of loneliness and isolation among migrant families in Mumbai. Today, the socio-economic, political, cultural and psychological problems arising out of the large and uncontrollable migration throughout the world are increasing, and the psychological stress, anxiety, frustration, uncertainty and loneliness faced by them cannot be denied. Apart from their social isolation, they also face health problems, legal conflict or financial issues in work places. From the Christian Ministry perspective, Dharmaraj suggests that the church should be open and welcoming to the migrants, and should create small support groups and provide educative counselling to them. To address this issue, he advocates Logotherapy and other therapeutic methods developed by scholars like Viktor Frankl, which can help the victims to face the challenging situations and redirect them to find meaning in life.

2

Christian Social Engagement
Some Guiding Principles

Richie Varghese

Introduction

We live today in increasingly tumultuous times with social cleavages growing wider and political fault-lines deepening and becoming exceedingly hostile. The situation clearly demands a social change, which is required urgently. Fear, hatred, xenophobia and 'othering' are becoming the characteristic features of human relations, naturally leading to unending cycles of violence. Poverty, growing inequality, political instability, weakened democratic and social institutions, and corruption have become the norms in the prevailing social order. Unfettered capitalism and the resulting conspicuous consumption as well as other heavy social demands that it places on people have not only begun threatening the physical, emotional, psychological, social and spiritual well-being of individuals, but have also frayed the social fabric of human society and placed us within a full-blown ecological crisis. India is certainly no exception to these trends and challenges – in fact, we are witnessing a time when many of these challenges are more pronounced in our country. These huge problems that face humanity are of gigantic proportions, signaling nothing short of an existential crisis. Thus, the social change that we talk of must also be radical and undertaken with urgency if we are to tide over this crisis – a transformation of the individual human soul, communities, social institutions and political establishments.

Even as we list out the many problems facing us as done above, it is important for us not to become pessimistic or fatalistic in our general disposition. As we talk about and strive towards social change, we must carry a posture of hope. Christian individuals and communities can be a part of the process of change, with the Christian message of hope molding such a posture. Christian hope is not something that merely points us to an eschatological glory, thus pushing us away from dealing with present realities. It rather is something that compels us to positively and receptively engage with those realities. And such an engagement is exactly what this book is about – forgetting what lies in the past and the dire present that it has created and straining forward to what lies ahead (to borrow an expression from Paul) with hope and a determination to change as well as bring change. But before we look at different ways in which such changes can be concretely brought about, it is important to look at some principles that may guide the contours and manner of Christian engagement in the social and political scenario.

1. Immediate/Local Community as the Primary Locus of Engagement

Very often, what goes amiss about attempts on the part of civil society to bring about social change is that issues are attempted to be dealt with primarily at the macro level. This sort of approach is pervasive in most Christian theological discourse about social issues today. What this does is to ignore the complexities infused into any social issue by unique characteristics of smaller communities. Especially in a diverse country like India, any given social issue would take on a different dimension in most places depending on their culture, language, customs, beliefs, etc. This obviously precludes any piecemeal approach to bring about social change in any area through a uniform national or even regional strategy. This is lucidly propounded by E. F. Schumacher in the area of economic policy. He says that any fight against poverty or economic injustice must be undertaken within smaller political units where intimacy is possible. "Therefore, we must learn to think in terms of an articulated structure that can cope with a multiplicity of small-scale units."[1] Thus, any sustainable social change has to be brought by treating the local communities as the primary loci of meaningful engagement.

This tendency of communitarian engagement obviously must not descend into a narrow regionalism – this is certainly not what I am proposing. A focus on the local community does not discount the larger picture and neglect it altogether – the latter simply forms a less immediate locus. This simply means that a number of different local community-oriented initiatives can be brought together to form the whole – a bottom-up approach as opposed to a top-down one. Understanding this is especially important in an age of grand unifying theories and one-size-fits-all modes of social action. Engagement for social change must be seen more as a sort of quilt work – bringing patches together to form a whole – rather than stitching a shirt with a single piece of cloth.

[1] E. F. Schumacher, *Small is Beautiful: Economics as if People Mattered* (New York: Harper and Row, 1973), 75.

2. Overcoming the Sacred-Secular Divide

In order to have a fruitful and impactful engagement in society, Christian theological discourse and community praxis must overcome the huge sacred-secular binary that has become entrenched within them. Especially, we see this divide very strongly embedded in the ethos of evangelical Christianity in India. It is necessary to clearly recognize the fact that no clear lines of distinction can be drawn between the church and the world, the spiritual and material, the eternal and temporal, etc. All these are mutually intersecting and held together in a balance within Christian faith and a full expression of it. To put this into the words of M. M. Thomas, "Every theology has an anthropological content inherent in it and derivable from it; and every anthropology is based on theological presuppositions either explicitly or implicitly."[2] Any clear distinctions drawn between the sacred and secular that make them seem mutually exclusive or even contrasting are purely arbitrary. These must be jettisoned if we are, as Christians, to engage fully with society. A serious engagement also cannot come if social change is considered as a less immediate or purely secular (as opposed to religious) agenda. Our discourse must be a "theology intertwined with a series of social upheavals and political changes."[3] Such a discourse can effectively guide and drive a vital Christian social engagement.

The breaking down of this divide in order to engage with social change must flow out of a clear recognition of the fact that God is in action in the world and Christian communities are called to be partners with Him. This would imply allowing our faith and its expressions, our discourse and praxis, to be "broken and reshaped continuously by God's continuous action."[4] Thus, a breaking down of the sacred-secular divide means abandoning comfort zones and venturing forth bravely towards ever-widening horizons of the outward expression of faith that extend towards social realities. This would include, in the Indian theological context, letting go of our preoccupations with the abstract – cultural, philosophical and religious aspects – and embracing the concrete socio-economic and political realities of the lives of common people.[5] Of course, an embracing of the political does not imply an attempt to Christianize the political or social order and this dangerous tendency must be avoided at all costs. Thus, a Christian political or social engagement is a delicate balancing act in this regard.

---

[2] M. M. Thomas, *the Secular Ideologies of India and the Secular Meaning of Christ* (Bangalore: CISRS, 1976), 193.

[3] Harvey Cox, *Religion in the Secular City* (New York: Simon and Schuster, 1984), 262.

[4] Harvey Cox, *the Secular City* (New York: Macmillan, 1965), 105.

[5] Felix Wilfred, *Asian Public Theology* (Delhi: ISPCK, 2010), 151.

3. Choosing Voice over Silence

Over centuries, silence has been glorified and proverbial wisdom often states propositions along the lines of an understanding that silence is the most important marker of a wise person. While this insight has important implications, it can be disastrous if applied in situations of systemic social injustice or evil. This is exactly what Bonhoeffer meant when he said "Silence in the face of evil is itself evil. God will not hold us guiltless. Not to speak is to speak. Not to act is to act."[6] Silence does not always mean a neutral abstinence from speaking. In fact, in a situation of grave injustice, one cannot be neutral at all. In the words of Desmond Tutu, "If you are neutral in a situation of injustice, you have chosen the side of the oppressor. If an elephant has his foot on the tail of the mouse, and you say you are neutral, the mouse will not appreciate your neutrality."[7] To carry this analogy a bit forward to make a related point, voicing out or opposing the elephant's action in any way, however, may come at huge risks and personal costs.

A good example of the contrast between voice and silence can be seen in the Bible in Mark 3:1-6, where Jesus heals a man with a withered hand. Jesus chooses to voice out the injustice of a status quo that prohibits "doing well" – an oppressive status quo. This voicing out to question the injustice of the legalism of the Pharisees precedes the eventual act of healing. On the other hand, the silence of the Pharisees, as expressly described by the writer of the gospel, provides a striking contrast. It is not a simple silence whereby they are persuaded by the argument of Jesus. It signifies a deliberate choice to uphold the unjust status quo. This is further interpreted as the "hardness of their heart."[8] Their silence is not a neutral position but one of siding with oppression. Further, it becomes clear that Jesus' speech brings him bitter opposition from these upholders of the oppressive order – to the extent that they plotted to kill him. Reading the rest of the gospel would tell us that they eventually succeeded in this mission. Jesus' choice of voice as opposed to silence – a choice he made not only in this instance but consistently throughout his public ministry – came at a huge personal cost, i.e., death. When we talk of Christian engagement for social change, it will very often entail running into very powerful vested interests, situations of systemic injustice or oppression, or long entrenched status quos at least. Attempting to change any of this would primarily involve breaking the deafening silences that may indirectly consent to the continuation of status quo. But this obviously would come with huge risks, and this risk of voicing out must be the cost any Christian must consider before hoping to get involved in bringing about social change.

---

[6] This quote is commonly attributed to Bonhoeffer, though it remains unclear where it comes from exactly.

[7] As quoted in Robert McAfee Brown, *Unexpected News: Reading the Bible with Third World Eyes* (Philadelphia: Westminster, 1984), 19.

[8] Robert A. Guelich, *Mark 1-8:26,* vol. 34A of WBC, Ed. Ralph P. Martin (Dallas: Word, 1989), 137.

4. Sensitivity as against Misplaced Moral Certainties

All Christian social engagement must be undertaken with a posture of sensitivity and solidarity rather than one of moral pontification. Rather than holding on to a dogmatic moral certainty in all matters, we should be able to conscientiously struggle with moral dilemmas that often come as an inextricable part of social engagement. In other words, this would mean rejecting all sorts of legalistic understandings of moral laws and be more sensitive towards the situations and contexts of the people towards whom social action is directed. This by no means implies a giving in to utter relativism or subjectivism, but simply that one's praxis is driven by compassion for the other and the unconditional love of Christ. John A.T. Robinson describes this fittingly when he says that the Christian ethic is one where there is "nothing prescribed – except love."[9] This goes very well in line with Jesus' summation of the entire law into loving God and loving one's neighbor. Very often, Christian social engagement in India has come short of bringing about real change because of failing in this area. Any change tried to be effected without high sensitivity towards contextual realities is bound to fail. Even when contextualization has been attempted, it has often stayed in the cosmetic areas, rather than dealing with the everyday life of people and its realities.

As we engage to bring about social change, we must make painstaking efforts to fully grasp the social fabric of the communities where we try to do this. Any problem or social issue is imbued with great complexities by the local context and the moral worldview and culture of the people in question, as we have already discussed. If these issues are to be dealt with, these complexities must be fully taken into account. This may sometimes mean that we let go of certain dearly-held moral imperatives and struggle with the grey areas that may exist, without compromising the moral core of our Christian ethos. It would make us very vulnerable and would often compel us to change ourselves in the process of bringing change. This is indeed challenging and demands a high level of intellectual and emotional energy. But this sort of posture must be developed nevertheless. Even if one must bring about certain cultural or moral changes, this must not be done aggressively, but in a spirit of love and solidarity. Change can only come about gradually and organically, and any engagement must be infused with a high dose of sensitivity and patience.

Conclusion

The terms of engagement put forth here attempt to forcefully bring out some aspects of Christian social action. Firstly, such an engagement cannot merely be external to us but rather must be internalized in such a way that it compels us to change ourselves in the process. These two aspects of changing ourselves and changing the society around us must always be held in a dialectical tension

[9] John A. T. Robinson, *Honest to God* (London: SCM, 1963), 116.

to ensure a fruitful engagement. Secondly, another balancing act that must be handled deftly is that of being sensitive towards contextual realities but at the same time refusing to be silent supporters of unjust status quos. These sort of dialectics and nuances illuminate the fact that engagement for social change is not a simple proposition, but one that involves utmost care and skill. It also requires a huge amount of intellectual, emotional and practical flexibility. Any attempt towards a Christian engagement for social change must be tempered by an understanding of these factors.

Part 2

Biblical Perspectives

3

Breaking the Power of Silence and Espousing Engagement (Mark 3:1-6)

Asish Thomas Koshy

Introduction

Social engagement is not a new trend in biblical studies. Its origins can be traced to the corporate dimension of the Jewish faith, which saw the involvement of the Israelite community with the other communities, embracing the widows, orphans and the aliens. However, this corporate dimension of faith was marred by the socio-political and economic realities of the first century Palestine. Double taxation, resurge in sectarianism, debt, and stifling economic realities were rampant in such a context. Jesus, in his engagement with events, situations and people, brought out the quintessence of the dynamic aspect of faith, which sees the other, who is despised and disregarded, in relation to the self. The other is not outside of oneself but is part and parcel of the self. By stating this, one is not diminishing the importance of the other but rather redefining the importance of the other; it is seeing the interconnectedness between self and the other. When the other is part of oneself, relating with the other becomes unavoidable as it relates to oneself. In other words, the other is to be valued, if the self is to be valued. An important issue of addressing the other is to confront the issue of silence. Silence is often the dominant tool to curb the voice of the diminished other and a legitimate excuse against social engagement.

Silence is commonly welcomed and given its loftiest place, particularly in a religious setting. It is primarily seen as a profound and intelligible way of expressing one's feeling to God. But, at times, when silence is deliberately chosen to garner support for oneself, it assumes the role of hoarding power. Here, silence overrides its neutral categories and shelters the hidden motives of the oppressors; it dampens and hinders fullness of life. In this regard silence is gruesome, oppressive, and inhuman with its sole aim of keeping the status quo. Thus, silence is not always neutral and does not mean the same in all contexts. Rather, it is a language of communication that is veiled and discreet expression of dislike and hatred. This article explores the intricacies of the power of silence that obstructs the experience of the fullness of life and how Jesus undoes it by breaking the fetters of the power of silence. Thus, Jesus defines the engagement with the other as the profound expression of religiosity.

1. Method

The Markan narrative is chosen as it is the shortest and probably the earliest,[1] even though the setting is the same in all three,[2] i.e., all narrate the incident immediately after the incident of plucking of grain on the Sabbath. This article primarily makes use of narrative criticism for the following reasons: firstly, because it is a healing story, giving a better scope for narrative reading wherein the possibilities and challenges are intertwined; and secondly, because there are not many words used by the speaker, which is Jesus himself (approximately 18 words in the Greek text) and the rest are by the narrator; thus reinforcing the predominant role of the narrator. However, historical-critical method is also used to help in exploring the concepts dealt in the narrative. Thus, a multiplex approach is used to interpret the text.

2. Structure

The structure of the narrative can be seen in terms of interplay between possibilities and challenges. The narrative can be broken into several segments: a) Setting: possibilities of and challenges to breaking the silence (3:1-2); b) Initiative for and opposition to breaking the silence (vv. 3-4); c) Breaking the silence through action (v.5); d) Consequences of breaking the silence (v.6).

3. Analysis

(a) Setting: Possibilities of and Challenges to Breaking the Silence (3:1-2)

The entire narrative is set in the context of five conflicting stories starting at 2:1[3] and this one is part of the second argument relating to Sabbath, the first being

---

[1] Stein opines that the Markan account deals with the early stage unlike Matt. 12:9-14 though the narrative features Makan redaction in vv. 5a-6. Robert H. Stein, *Mark*, Baker Exegetical Commentary on the New Testament (Grand Rapids, Michigan: Baker Academic, 2008), 152.

[2] Mark 3:1-6; Matthew 12:9-14; Luke 6:6-11.

[3] The section from 2:1-3:6 deals with questioning of Jesus' authority. Stein, *Mark*, 152.

2:23-28.[4] The present narrative takes up the two aspects of the earlier narrative (2:23-28, especially v.27) i.e., τὸ σάββατον διὰ τὸν ἄνθρωπον ἐγένετο and κύριός ἐστιν ὁ υἱὸς τοῦ ἀνθρώπου καὶ τοῦ σαββάτου. This is set in the form of miracle but lacks one of its vital elements, the applause from the gathering.[5] Rather, the pericope ends with the plot to kill Jesus. The whole pericope is couched in contrasts of entry and exit[6] – the entry of Jesus into the synagogue (v.1) and the exit of the opponents in v.6.[7]

The setting of the narrative presents both the possibilities of and challenges to disturbing the silence. The narrator has balanced these by presenting different routes the narrative can take, i.e., either affirming the status quo or opposing it. The course of action would depend on the primary character, Jesus, who takes the focus at the very beginning of the narrative.

Further, there are several indicators of the setting. The location of the narrative is set in the synagogue, a revisit by Jesus;[8] this is significant because it gives room for the suffering person to be present, a human being with a withered hand, unlike the Jerusalem temple which offered restricted access. The narrator also introduces in v.1 the characters that will be playing significant part in the narrative, namely Jesus and the person with a withered hand. Jesus possibly enters the synagogue at Capernaum[9] and this is not his first visit. The previous visit to the synagogue, in the introduction to the first part of the gospel, was an instance revealing his power.[10] The mention of the person with the withered hand opens the possibility of healing and restoration. The person remains anonymous; he is not described by a name but rather by the limitation that he carries, i.e.,

---

[4] Joel Marcus, *Mark 1-8: A New Translation with Introduction and Commentary*, The Anchor Bible 27, New York: Doubleday, 2000, 250.

[5] Marcus, *Mark 1-8*, 250. Stein describes this narrative in terms of "controversy-pronouncement story." Stein, *Mark*,

[6] Marcus, *Mark 1-8*, 251.

[7] Marcus, *Mark 1-8*, 251.

[8] Most scholars would attribute the use of πάλιν by Mark as redactional. Marcus, *Mark 1-8*, 250. The singular reference to Jesus devoid of the disciples is taken by Marcus to suggest "...the progression from the question of the disciples' Sabbath observance in 2:23-28 to the question of Jesus' own Sabbath observance here." Marcus, *Mark 1-8*, 251.

[9] Stein states that the concluding statement of Jesus going with the disciples to sea in 3:7 affirms the location as Capernaum. Stein, *Mark*, 153. Broadhead seems to disagree with Stein when he states, "The introduction relates no specific synagogue experience, but instead casts the story in a general way within the ongoing plot line of Jesus' activity." Edwin K. Broadhead, *Teaching with Authority: Miracles and ChristoOlogy in the Gospel of Mark*, JSNT Supplement Series 74, edited by Stanley Porter (Sheffield: JSOT Press, 1992), 80.

[10] John R. Donahue and Daniel J. Harrington, *The Gospel of Mark*, Sacra Pagina Series, vol. 2, edited by Daniel J. Harrington (Minnesota: The Liturgical Press, 2002), 114.

ἐξηραμμένην ἔχων τὴν χεῖρα.[11] Donhaue and Harrington observe that the use of perfect passive participle (ἐξηραμμένην) indicates that his suffering commenced at birth.[12] Ironically the Pharisees do not see this as a threat to fullness of life. They view him not as person requiring healing on the Sabbath, thus remaining victims of their perception. Therefore, the narrator presents the possibilities in the description of various terms- Jesus' entry (εἰσῆλθεν), synagogue, and the presence of the man (ἦν ἐκει) with the withered hand.

Unlike the previous verse, in v.2, the antagonists, the Pharisees, are now introduced in the narrative. They too, like the healed person, are not named at the beginning but only at the end of the narrative (v.6) probably to hold the readers in suspense.[13] The narrator presents a window to the nature and purpose of their presence with the help of two revealing verbs: παρατηρέω,[14] which probably highlights their religious scrutiny;[15] and κατηγορέω,[16] which defines the purpose, not noble, of maligning Jesus; a moralistic stance taken by the narrator.[17] France[18] notes in this regard, "… the 'watching' of Jesus is not out of neutral interest, but, as the sequel shows clearly, marks a hostile search for further evidence of Jesus' unorthodox stance with regard to the sabbath."[19] The narrator chooses not to describe the Pharisees by their words but by their looks. The nature of their silence cannot be comprehended only by the mere absence of words. In effect, their silence is anything but passive. Instead they use it as a tool to actively safe guard an oppressive status quo.

Taken together, vv. 1 and 2, balance the opportunities for healing with the challenges that seem to obstruct their progression. The challenge to Jesus performing the healing and thus asserting he is the Lord of the Sabbath is

[11] The use of the passive in the man's sickness (ἐξηραμμένην) implies that it was a long standing problem, presumably occurred at birth. Donahue and Harrington, *The Gospel of Mark*, 115.

[12] Donahue and Harrington, *The Gospel of Mark*, 115.

[13] Stein is of the view that Mark might have deliberately left the opponents unnamed in order to mention it at the end. Stein, *Mark*, 153.

[14] The verb does not lend to a neuter connotation. The use of the same verb in Psalm 36:12, where it describes those who look for the righteous person in order to kill him, does convey a negative understanding. Marcus, *Mark 1-8*, 252. Stein notes that the use of the verb in the plural relates the present pericopae with 2:24, where the subject is identified as Pharisees. Stein, *Mark*, 152.

[15] The term could refer to both medical scrutiny and religious scrutiny. Donahue and Harrington, *The Gospel of Mark*, 115.

[16] Luke adds the verb to find and Matthew leaves out the description of the opponents (Luke 6:7) but instead puts the question on the mouth of the opponents asking Jesus whether it is lawful to heal on the Sabbath (Matthew 12:10).

[17] Stein states, "This event was to be used to be used to garnish evidence in order to bring their plans to fruition." Stein, *Mark*, 154.

[18] R. T. France, *The Gospel of Mark: A Commentary on the Greek Text* (Grand Rapids, Michigan: William B. Eerdmans Publishing Company, 2002).

[19] France, *The Gospel of Mark*, 148.

intensified in this pericope, unlike the previous one (2:23-28), as it occurs in an open setting and in a situation where there is a growing opposition.[20] Thus, opportunities to heal coexist with visible hindrances to healing.

Both the verbs (παρετήρουν and κατηγορήσωσιν) find their significance in juxtaposition of the time at which the event takes place- the Sabbath day- and the act expressed in the verb θεραπεύω. Earlier the narrator indicated the place, i.e., the synagogue which permitted the man with the withered hand to be present, but now the time seems to be an obstruction to healing. Was Sabbath really a hindrance to healing?

Beilner states, "The sanctification of the seventh day of the week (the Sabbath) was the source of decisive religious behavior and customs in Israel."[21] There are sixty eight occurrences of it in the New Testament, of which 24 are plural.[22]

Mishnah Šabbath[23] 7:2 states thirty nine prohibitions on the Sabbath:

> The main classes of work are forty save one—viz.: Sowing, ploughing, reaping, binding into sheaves, threshing, winnowing, fruit-cleaning, grinding, sifting, kneading, baking, wool-shearing, bleaching, combing, dyeing, spinning, weaving, making two loops, weaving two threads, separating two threads (in the warp), tying a knot, loosening a knot, sewing two stitches, tearing in order to sew together with two stitches, hunting a gazelle, slaughtering or flaying or salting it or curing its skin, scrapping it or cutting it up, writing two letters, erasing in order to write two letters, building, pulling down, putting out a fire, striking with hammer, and taking out aught from one domain to another. These are the main classes of work forty save one.

In this list, healing is not mentioned as a prohibition but taken as so except when life is in danger.

Mishnah Yoma 8:6 gives allowance for activities on Sabbath based on cases where there is doubt on whether one's life is in danger or not: "...Moreover, R. Mattihian b. Heresh said: If a man has a pain in the throat they may drop a medicine into his mouth on the Sabbath, since there is a doubt whether life is in danger, and whenever there is doubt whether life is in danger this overrides the Sabbath."[24]

---

[20] Marcus, *Mark 1-8*, 252.

[21] W. Beilner, "σαββάτον," in *Exegetical Dictionary of the New Testament*, edited by Horst Balz and Gerhard Schneider, vol. 3 (Grand Rapids, Michigan: William B. Eerdmans Publishing Company), 220 (219-222).

[22] Beilner, "σαββάτον," 220.

[23] Herbert Danby, *The Mishnah: Translated from the Hebrew with Introduction and Brief Explanatory Notes* (Oxford: Oxford University Press, 1964).

[24] Danby, *The Mishnah*. France notes that helping in childbirth was permitted as one could not wait.

The man with the withered hand does not come in the category of exceptional cases that are allowed on Sabbath.[25] Therefore, healing, though good in itself, incites a negative reaction when done on the Sabbath.[26] But for Jesus, the yardstick, as his act signifies, was not whether there is or not a threat to life rather whether this person could be disallowed from experiencing fullness of life on the Sabbath. This is a much broader way of seeing the person as well as the meaning of Sabbath. Moreover, the presence of the Lord of the Sabbath (Mark 2: 28) and Sabbath as instituted for human beings override any restriction on the Sabbath (Mark 2: 27).

(b) Initiative for and Opposition to Breaking the Silence (vv. 3-4)

The narrative takes a turn towards breaking the oppressive atmosphere. This is done so by the central character of the narrative, Jesus. The phrase, "ἔγειρε εἰς τὸ μέσον, which can be literally translated as "rise into the centre,"[27] is both an invitation and preparation for healing. These are essential as they pave way for the healing to take place. The invitation extended to the withered man physically moves him from the periphery to the center. More importantly, this symbolically represents a movement from the position of a mere observer to that of a significant participant in breaking the silence. Thus, it not only challenges the silence but the very silencing of the person, which has taken place due to his physical deformities. Jesus in calling attention to the man presents an open face-off with the Pharisees.[28] It also suggests that Jesus is aware of what the opponents are considering.[29] The focus shifts from the opponents of Jesus to the person to be healed; a situation which the person was not used to. In the narrative, there is a movement from the private sphere to the public sphere, a movement from postponement to immediate action, a movement from reluctance (on the part of the Pharisees) to being involved - "...public display both of his healing power and of his status as κύριός τοῦ σαββάτου."[30]

Even though, calling the man to the centre opens up the possibilities for healing, as far as the narrative is concerned, it results in the beginning of conflict.

---

[25] France, *The Gospel of Mark*, 149-150. Lohse mentions some more exceptional cases that were allowed, namely, in the case of mortal danger (in that case taking arms on the Sabbath was allowed), fire, circumcision." E. Lohse, "σαββάτον," in *Theological Dictionary of New Testament*, edited by Gerhard Kittel, Gerhard Friedrich, translated by Geoffrey W. Bromiley, vol. 7 (Grand Rapids, Michigan: William B. Eerdmans Publishing Company, 1971), 14-15.

[26] Beilner, "σαββάτον," 221.

[27] Donahue and Harrington note that the term "ἔγειρε is commonly related with healing as in 1:31; 2:9, 11, 12; 5:41 and 10:49. It also carries with it aspects of restoration of health and life. Here it is used to draw attention to the readers to the healing event. Donahue and Harrington, *The Gospel of Mark*, 115.

[28] Marcus, *Mark 1-8*, 252.

[29] Stein, *Mark*, 154.

[30] France, *The Gospel of Mark*, 150.

However, one tends to disagree with Stein who views the absence of request for healing from the person as indicating Jesus' desire to purposefully run into conflict with the opponents.[31] It is rather Jesus' concern for the not so able bodies that results in conflict. Instead of seeing this in terms of conflict turned into healing, one could look at it as healing turned into conflict.

This conflict, now, which forms the hindrance to healing, i.e., the narrow interpretation of Sabbath, is removed by Jesus in the form of a question: ἀγαθὸν ποιῆσαι ἢ κακοποιῆσαι, ψυχὴν σῶσαι ἢ ἀποκτεῖναι. Though, the choices are present, in actuality it affirms the synonymous aspects of doing good (κακοποιῆ σαι) and saving life (ψυχὴν σῶσαι) as the only viable course of action. This aspect was agreed upon by all in relation to the Sabbath.[32]

As Marcus puts it, "...the necessity of saving life overrules the imperative of Sabbath observance."[33]

What was the problem? It had to do with interpretation of doing good in terms of saving life. For the opponents of Jesus, the person with a withered hand could wait for some more time and the action of Jesus could take place after the Sabbath ended. This is because they viewed saving life merely as negating death. But for Jesus, postponing the healing is on the level of killing the person and administering healing is equivalent to saving life; and this is seen from the perspective of God's reign,[34] which affirms fullness of life, not just an absence of death. France notes, "Certainly, it leaves no scope for the rabbinic enterprise of building a fence around the sabbath law."[35] Schweizer, "... failure to do good is the same thing as doing evil; failure to save life is the same as destroying it. When good ought to be done there is no neutral ground where one neither does good or evil."[36] The options do not give room for neutral ground and therefore the silence on the part of the Pharisees takes on the representation of evil within the given contrast.

The use of δὲ is significant here as it shuts out their choices and highlights their opposition. The opponents prefer the deafening silence (σιωπάω) instead of revealing their motives. Why were they silent? In effect throughout the narrative they remain silent. The only character who speaks is Jesus, who breaks the power of silence. France is of the view that silence could be seen as a deliberative step not to get into useless argument but more so reflecting the Pharisees dilemma: if the answer is positive then it would nullify their approach and foundations of their

---

[31] Stein, *Mark*, 154.

[32] France, *The Gospel of Mark*, 150.

[33] Marcus, *Mark 1-8*, 252.

[34] Marcus, *Mark 1-8*, 252.

[35] France, *The Gospel of Mark*, 150.

[36] Eduard Schweizer, *The Good News according to Mark*, translated by Donal H. Madvig (Atlanta: Westminister John Knox Press, 1970), 75.

objection; and if response is negative then it would go against the understanding of the Sabbath and also lose favour with the synagogue congregation.[37]

How could one read their silence? Did it have to do with their own perception that was a part of their identity? Was it an unsaid approval of what Jesus was emphasizing – doing good and saving life? Probably not, as in v.6 they seek to destroy Jesus. Or was it a case where their understanding of the Sabbath ran contrary to what they did on the Sabbath, which is doing harm and destroying life? Probably their stand on Sabbath reflected their identity as a group; boundaries they created could not be toppled over. Marcus states, "The Pharisees cannot either disavow their principle of saving life on the Sabbath or go along with Jesus' radicalization of it. They were silent – ominously so…"[38]

The challenge comes in the form of silence; the silence of the opponents of Jesus. Σιωπάω is limited to the synoptics and Acts of the Apostles.[39] It means to stop speaking and keeping absolute silence.[40] The narrative does not stop with silence but goes on to capture Jesus' determination to break the silence emerging from his own reaction to the situation.

(c) An Act of Breaking the Silence and Bringing Transformation (v.5)

Jesus' response to the crippling effect of silence is not only through an emotional reaction but also by the tangible action of restoration of the person's withered hand. There seems to be a deliberate time lag between Jesus questioning the Pharisees and the act of healing. Marcus notes, "One might now expect Jesus to perform the cure, since he has cleared the way for it by silencing the Pharisees; but instead Mark raises the narrative tension further by a delay that also provides a rare insight into Jesus' inner state."[41] Jesus responds to the silence of the Pharisees with anger (ὀργη) and grief (συλλυπούμενος[42]).[43] This is explained by the narrator

---

[37] France, *The Gospel of Mark*, 150.

[38] Marcus, *Mark 1-8*, 253. Marcus also draws the comparison between Pharaoh in the Exodus narrative and the Pharisees. He says that in both cases the salvific aspects are highlighted. For Pharaoh the hardening results in reception of God's glory (Exodus 10:1-2) but for the latter, the plotting of Jesus' death leads to God's disclosure on the cross (15:37-39).

[39] Matthew 20:31; 26:63; Mark 3:4; 4:39; 9:34; 10:48; 14:61; Luke 1:20; 19:40; Acts 18:9. W. F. Moulton and A. S. Geden (eds.), *A Concordance to the Greek New Testament* (Edinburgh: T & T Clark, 1957).

[40] W. Radl, "σιωπάω," in *Exegetical Dictionary of the New Testament*, edited by Horst Balz and Gerhard Schneider, vol. 3 (Grand Rapids, Michigan: William B. Eerdmans Publishing Company), 247.

[41] Marcus, *Mark 1-8*, 253. Both Matthew and Luke exclude the mention of Jesus' anger and grief.

[42] France notes that the intense form of the verb is best rendered as "grieved at" rather than "grieved for." France, *The Gospel of Mark*, 151.

[43] The participial (συλλυπούμενος) recurs only here and "…is the intensive form of the verb "to be sorry or grieve."" Donahue and Harrington, *The Gospel of Mark*, 116.

as being caused by the antagonists' hardness of heart. The phrase is a common way of describing those who are not able to understand the truth – in the case of Israel's rejection of Jesus (Romans 11: 7, 25)[44] and also disciples' limitations to comprehend the meaning behind Jesus' miracles.[45]

The focus of Jesus' response is not just on the opponents but primarily on the person who was silenced, the man with the withered hand.[46] Thus, Jesus commands him to stretch out his hand and restoration takes place when he obeys the command. Here, λέγει breaks the silence of oppression and paves a path for the experience of the fullness of life. Broadhead notes, "...with the repetition of λέγει τῷ ἀνθρώπῳ. This command reverses the plot transition created by 3.4-5b and leads to the actual healing."[47] Jesus does not touch the affected portion but only speaks. Marcus makes an insightful comment, "He does so in a clever way that eludes the charge of performing work on the Sabbath; rather than touching the affected limb (cf. 1:31. 41), he commands the man to stretch it out himself, and when he does so, it is miraculously healed ..."[48] The effect of Jesus' words on the restoring the hand is put in the passive (ἀπεκατεστάθη, the divine passive). This suggests that the person participates in God's eschatological act of restoration and fullness of God through Jesus.[49] Jesus only commands and does not use a word for healing nor is there a positive public reaction to the healing, unlike the several miracle stories of Jesus.[50]

The restoration was not merely a restoration of his hand but also experience of fullness of life because his limitation that stigmatized him is removed. The boundaries that stifled his living and identity are now squashed; the outsider of the religious community is turned into an insider.

(d) Consequences of Breaking the Silence (v.6)

The Pharisees continue their role in creating conflict as in the earlier stories (2:16, 18, 24). The use of εὐθὺς, a favourite term of Mark, notes "...both the departure of the Pharisees and their almost concomitant conspiracy with the Herodians."[51] The act of breaking the silence steam rolls into the plot to kill Jesus and gets wider attention. Stein states in this regard, "The accusers of Jesus detail his death for doing the noble thing on the Sabbath."[52]

---

[44] It could also mean those who have refused to hear God's word (Ezekiel 3:7; Acts 28:27; Romans 2:5). Donahue and Harrington, *The Gospel of Mark*, 116.

[45] France, *The Gospel of Mark*, 150-151.

[46] Marcus, *Mark 1-8*, 253.

[47] Broadhead, *Teaching with Authority*, 81.

[48] Marcus, *Mark 1-8*, 253.

[49] Marcus, *Mark 1-8*, 253.

[50] Donahue and Harrington, *The Gospel of Mark*, 116.

[51] Donahue and Harrington, *The Gospel of Mark*, 116.

[52] Stein, *The Gospel of Mark*, 156.

The opposition takes on a larger dimension with the inclusion of the Herodians. The text presents a strange combination of Pharisees and Herodians; they are seen again in 12:13. The Greek word Ἡρῳδιανοί refers to the followers of a prominent figure.[53] Josephus utilizes alike terms in *War* 1.319 and in *Antiquities* 14.451 in the sense of supporters of Herod Antipas. Later on, the leader of Herodians (Herod Antipas) puts to death John the Baptist (6:17-28), which Jesus views as a foreshadowing of his own fate (9:12-13).[54] However, the merging of religious and political factors was not unusual in the first century context and thus a likely meeting of Pharisees and Herodians.[55] Edwards comments, "The reasons for their resolve are not stated, but the evidence against Jesus is compounding: Sabbath violations (1:21-24; 2:3-28), fraternizing with sinners (1:40; 2:13-17), disregarding rabbinic custom (2:18-22), and presumption to forgive (2:10-11)."[56]

The phrase συμβούλιον ἐδίδουν need not to be taken as a well thought out plan of action to execute Jesus as the following narrative do not seem to suggest so (14:1-2; 10-11).[57] But there is a propelling of the plot and puts forth two opposite reactions to Jesus' act (chapters 3-4).[58] The portrayal of characters fits into the larger depiction of Jesus' opponents.[59] There is also a note of irony, the Pharisees and the Herodians though looked at Sabbath on promoting life plan to kill Jesus on the Sabbath and thus breach the profane and the deepest significance of Sabbath.[60]

The narrative was, thus, analyzed into four sections that brought out clearly the possibilities and challenges to breaking the silence. One should note that in interpreting the story, one must refrain from an "antinomian" and "supersessionist" perspective, putting Christianity over against Judaism as suggested by Kurt Quelller.[61] However, this narrative can be seen in a larger perspective of social engagement, which would involve relating the self with the other rather than

---

[53] France, *The Gospel of Mark*, 151.

[54] France, *The Gospel of Mark*, 152.

[55] France, *The Gospel of Mark*, 151.

[56] J. R. Edwards, *The Gospel according to Mark*, Pillar New Testament Commentary (Grand Rapids, Michigan: William B. Eerdmans Publishing Company, 2002), 101.

[57] France, *The Gospel of Mark*, 152.

[58] France, *The Gospel of Mark*, 152.

[59] Marcus views 3:6 in relation to 8:15; 11:18 where there is a similar description of the opponents of Jesus and thus views it as redactional. Marcus, *Mark 1-8*, 250.

[60] Donahue and Harrington, *The Gospel of Mark*, 117.

[61] "Antinomian" and "supersessionist" are terms used by Queller. Kurt Queller, ""Stretch out your hand!" Echo and Metalepsis in Mark's Sabbath healing controversy" *Journal of Biblical Literature*, 129/4 (Winter 2010): 737-758, 737. The article is an in-depth intertextual reading of Mark 3: 1-6, especially looking into the connection between haggadic midrash on the narrative of Reed Sea crossing and the aspects of Sabbath release (Deuteronomy 15:1-15) with the Markan story. Though, these texts can be seen in the background, yet, following the Markan narrative sequence

distancing the self from the other. What has this narrative to do with the theology of silence and disengagement with the other?

Movement from Silence to a Theology of Engagement

It is common to distance issues concerning faith and practice from social involvement. The former is usually seen as relating to concerns of God and self while the latter as what is outside the purview of the self or the other. James H. Evans brings out the lacuna in such a position, "Human problems or social problems are theological problems because they bring us face to face with the ultimate question of human existence. In seeking to have life and to have it more abundantly, we are not only concerned with activities of getting and spending. We are also concerned with meaning of life itself."[62] This quote from Evans highlights the need for a theology of engagement.

What is engagement? Engagement can be defined as "involvement," "participation," "commitment."[63] It carries with it the connotation of opposition and also sometimes constructive change without opposition. Therefore a theology of engagement would mean an engagement that redefines the contours of theology itself.[64] It enables one to relook at the very root of how theology is constructed. Volf rightly notes, ""For me, as for many others, especially outside the West and its cultural sphere of influence, love of God (spirituality) and love of neighbor (social engagement) are not alternatives to each other. Love of God entails love of neighbor; and love of neighbor is an index of love of God. The task of theology is primarily the struggle for the proper vision of God and the proper shape of human love for God. That is also true of theology's public engagement."[65] Theology of engagement brings the social engagement within the purview of spirituality; not as distinct phenomena but as one.

On the flip side, silence disconnects spirituality from social engagement; it disconnects the self from the other as though the other did not matter to the self. Looking at the narrative, there are two responses to the plight of the man with the withered hand. First, the Pharisees who chose to take the route of silence and this had to do with their inability to embrace a theology of engagement. The reasons could be many: it had to do with their own identity markers; their distancing from the one who was suffering; or the resistance to redefine the understanding of God's involvement in the mundane human affairs of healing a person, especially

---

and narrative world enshrined in the Sabbath controversy, there seems to an affirmation of Jesus' authority and a resistance to boundary making that crippled fullness of life.

[62] James H. Evans, *We Shall All Be Changed: Social Problems and Theological Renewal* (Minneapolis: Fortress Press, 1987), 11.

[63] Ian S. Markham, *A Theology of Engagement* (Oxford: Blackwell Publishing House, 2003), 10.

[64] Markham, *A Theology of Engagement*, 10.

[65] Miroslav Volf, "Faith, Pluralism and Public Engagement: A Response" *Political Theology* 14/6 (2013): 813-834.

on a Sabbath. Silence usually comes from those who are termed as good. Friedrich Nietzsche in a philosophical novel, *Thus Spoke Zarathustra,*[66] very clearly presents the relation between negative side of the good and silence.

> My brothers! In whom does the greatest danger lie for all of future humanity? Is it not in the good and the just?– is it not in those who speak and feel in their hearts: "We already know what is good and just, and we have it too; woe to any who still search here!"
>
> And whatever harm the evil may do, the harm of the good is the most harmful harm!
>
> And whatever harms the world slanderers may do, the harm of the good is the most harmful harm!
>
> My brothers, there was a man who once looked into the hearts of the good and the just, and he spoke: "They are Pharisees." But he was not understood.
>
> The good and the just themselves were not permitted to understand him: their spirit is imprisoned in their good conscience. The stupidity of the good is unfathomably clever. But this is the truth: the good *must* be Pharisees – they have no choice! The good *must* crucify the one who invents his own virtue! This *is* the truth!
>
> The second one, however, who discovered their land, the land, hearts and soil of the good and just: he was the one who asked: "Whom do they hate the most?"
>
> The *creator* they hate the most; he who breaks tablets and old values, the breaker – him they call the lawbreaker.
>
> Because the good, you see – they *can* not create: they are always the beginning of the end — they crucify the one who writes new values on new tablets, they sacrifice the future to *themselves* – they crucify all future humanity!
>
> The good – they were always the beginning of the end. –

Also, Jesus redefines the understanding of God; and brings wholeness and fullness of life through engagement. For him, the kingdom of God engages in the suffering of those who have been silenced and continue to be silenced. Jesus' engagement breaks the silence of oppression through words – asking the person to stretch out his hand. Speech is an important tool in social engagement as it clearly defines the one who is suffering. It also brings to focus the intentions behind the

[66] Fredrich Nietzche, *Thus Spoke Zarathustra: A Book for All and None, Third Part On Old and New Tablets*, Cambridge Texts in the History of Philosophy, edited by Adrian Del Caro and Robert B. Pippin, translated by Adrian Del Caro (Cambridge: Cambridge University Press, 2006), 26.

conflict, especially in the case when it is not stated, as like the Pharisees here. Their own religious affiliation warranted a theology of silence and probably supported it. Thus, they preferred silence over against speech to Jesus' questions in order to affirm boundaries; boundaries to keep their identity going. More importantly, speech lends identity to the one who is suffering. Jesus in asking the person to come to the centre of the synagogue and healing the person in public was not just healing and restoration but granting identity. Violence done through silencing is overcome by speech.

In this regard, Evangeline Anderson-Rajkumar notes that the 'triadic concept' 'Silence-Voice-Speech' "... emphasizes the immense potential as an analytical tool to study the experiences of power-powerlessness, patriarchy, violence, caste, class, race, Hindutva, Empire and other dominant ideologies and issues in our society."[67] She also states, "A Theology of Engagement demands that we are engaged consciously, concretely in context and experience that we are living beings, called to live as a community on earth. Theology of Engagement necessarily involves a readiness to immerse in the issues and challenges in our context that are actually life-death matter for our sisters/brothers."[68]

Conclusion

How is this incident in the gospel related to Christian involvement in social engagement? This particular narrative presents several possibilities. Firstly, Christian social engagement is not an option but rather imperative for defining Christian involvement. Secondly, it counters the intense resistance against social engagement because it often leads to altering the defined group values and ideals of those opposing it. Thirdly, it rightly describes the relation between faith and praxis; praxis lends the dynamic aspect to faith. By presenting the dynamic aspect of Sabbath, Jesus brings out the fuller dimension of faith that is fuelled by praxis. Fourthly, religious places and time need to become places and periods of social engagement. The synagogue and Sabbath which were often seen only in terms of worship is also seen as a place of healing and restoration by Jesus.

---

[67] Evangeline Anderson-Rajkumar, "Decoding 'Silence-Voice-Speech' As An Epistemological Tool for a Theology of Engagement" in *God of Life, Lead Us to Justice and Peace: A Theological Reflection in the Context of India Today*, edited by H. Vanlaluva (West Bengal: Department of Research/SATHRI), 76.

[68] Evangeline Anderson-Rajkumnar, "Decoding 'Silence-Voice-Speech,' 83.

4

Prophetic Intervention for Social Change
A Study of Prophet Elijah's Intervention in Land Conflict (1 Kings 21) from the Sumi Naga Context

Rachel Katty

Introduction

The world that we live in today has always been changing since time immemorial. Our society is changing economically, socially, politically, spiritually, psychologically and in many other ways. There are many good and bad changes that take place each having a great impact on society and changing the structure of society different from what it was before. Therefore, the question is this: how are Christians engaging in the problems of the world today to bring change? How are we being and becoming the agents of change? There are many Christians who believe that the Church's main concern is with the spiritual and religious life of the people and so it is not supposed to intrude in matters, which are of no concern to the church. But to be a true church, the church must speak for the promotion of good citizenship which depends on the attainment of liberty, equality and justice.[1] For an effective change to take place, the individuals, the church and the society should be engaged in issues that bring down the society. For change to take place, effective participation becomes extremely important.

With the intention to learn how Christians can engage in social issues to bring change in the society, this study focuses on the chapter 21 of 1 Kings: the

[1] Alfred J. Shaw, *Christianity and Social Change in India* (Lucknow: Lucknow Publishing House, 1983), 169-170.

story of land conflict between Naboth and Ahab and Jezebel in the 9th century which has insights for reflecting on change. In this story, one can see a great change evolving from a single person participating in the issue on land. It has the power to bring one's mind how an effective change can be brought if the society at large involves in an issue. A large participation is hundred fold more effective than a single participation to change something grotesque into something beautiful. 1 King 21 is usually seen as a small story, possible to be quickly dismissed and not taken as a conflict resulting from land. So, by subjecting this story to a full socio-rhetorical analysis (to understand the language, accusations and sentence), this study attempts to argue that 1 King 21 is a serious issue of land conflict between Ahab and Naboth and bring out the effectiveness of Elijah's participation in the issue to bring change in the conflict situation. This study also attempts to address the issue of land conflict among the Sumi Nagas by employing Tribal theological reading to understand the present situation of understanding land issue in the contemporary Sumi society. It finally focuses on what and how the Sumi Nagas must learn to confront and engage in land conflicts to bring change in a society by relating their context to the story in 1 King 21.

1. Land in the Old Testament

In the Old Testament, there are two Hebrew words for land, i.e., ארצ *erets* and אֲדָמָה *adamah.* The noun *erets* refers to a specific geographical area or the territory of a specific people. While *adamah* designates the agricultural land, ground, field, soil. It is also connected with fertility and blessing, a land property as in 1 Kings 21:3 and a dwelling place.[2] W. Janzen is of the opinion that "land" is identified as the land to which Israel has a claim. Israel's relationship to land is characterized by the nouns "inheritance" (*nahala*), "possession" (*ahuzza*) and "rest" (*menuha*).[3] According to Volkamer Fritz, "inheritance" does not mean inherited land only but also used to describe the land given by Yahweh as inheritance and so it is significant as it is connected with Yahweh. Thus, its owner cannot offer it for sale (Lev 25:33),[4] unless the person is too poor to do anything else.[5] The second thing is that, the land of Canaan was given by God to Israel as its "possession." Like *nahala* it can refer to the land holding of Israel as a whole or of individual tribes, clans and households. In most instances, it refers to the land and real estate that is handed down through the generations and should not be sold. In Israel, "land" was not a private possession and commercial commodity but a gift and trust held

---

[2] Laiu Fachhai, *The Land must be Distributed Equally: The Promise and Covenant Aspects of Land in the Old Testament* (Delhi: ISPCK, 2009), 1.

[3] W. Janzen, "Land" (*ABC*; New York: Doubleday), 143–145.

[4] Volkamer Fritz, *1 & 2 Kings* (ACC; Minneapolis: Fortress Press, 2003), 211.

[5] Peter Leithart, *1 & 2 Kings* (BTCOB; Grand Rapids: Brazos, 2006), 154.

by God, the real owner (Leviticus 25:23), for the sake of the family (Numbers 27:1-11; 36:1-12).[6]

2. Land Conflicts in the Old Testament

The primary social structural issue raised in the story of 1 King 21 is the importance of the land, the vineyard that Ahab wants, but Naboth refuses to give up and Jezebel takes it by force at the end. Land use and possession is an extremely important issue in an agrarian society, especially one like ancient Israel.[7] Joseph Blenkisopp as cited by P. P. Thomas states that since Israel was an agrarian society, a majority of population from seventy to ninety percent were peasant cultivators. Therefore, land was a major feature of an Israelite family household.[8] As opposed to modern understandings of private ownership of land, ancient Israel apparently understood land to be held by a kinship group, a clan based in a village or villages. Individual extended families of the clan were granted the holding of plots of land for their use but ultimately the land belonged to the clan or family inheritance and could not be given or sold out from inheritance.[9] Richard Hess says that the book of Joshua 13-21 presents the land as a divine gift, given to Israel through Joshua.[10] Thus, according to the theology of the ancient West Asia, the land of Israel belonged to Yahweh, who as landlord and head of household gave it out to the twelve tribes. It was this theological idea that was used to justify and explain the inalienability of patrimonial area (Lev. 25:23).[11]

However, with the advent of monarchy, the new pattern of distribution and administration of land replaced the old system of land tenure.[12] The vast territorial expansion necessitated major changes in the governmental system which had far reaching consequences for the systems of land tenure[13]. The king acquired the land through various ways through conquest, by confiscating heirless land as seen in possessing vacant land as in the story of Shunamite woman in 2 kings 8:1-6, through purchase as in 2 Samuel 24:24, through exchange of commodities as in 1 kings 9:11-14,[14] and through forced possession as in Naboth issue in 1 kings 21. Therefore, in the centuries after Solomon's reign, i.e., 9th and 8th centuries, the

[6] Gene Rice, *1 Kings: Nations under God* (Michigan: Eerdmans, 1990), 176.

[7] Patricia Dutcher-Walls, *Jezebel: Portraits of a Queen* (Minnesota: Liturgical, 2004), 116.

[8] P. P. Thomas, *Jeroboam II and Amos the Prophet: A Social-Scientific Study on the Israelite Society during the 8th Century BCE* (Delhi: ISPCK, 2003), 174.

[9] Dutcher-Walls, *Jezebel: Portraits of a Queen*, 117.

[10] Richard Hess, *Joshua* (TOTC; Leicester: InterVarsity, 1996), 47.

[11] P. P. Thomas, *Jeroboam II and Amos the Prophet: A Social-Scientific Study on the Israelite Society during the 8th Century BCE*, 174.

[12] Thomas, *Jeroboam II and Amos the Prophet: A Social-Scientific Study on the Israelite Society during the 8th Century BCE*, 182.

[13] D. N. Premnath, *Eight Century Prophets: A Social Analysis* (Danvers: Chalice, 2003), 21-31.

[14] D. N. Premnath, *Eight Century Prophets: A Social Analysis*, 21-31.

land became the focus of constant struggle between the forces of dispossession, greed, exploitation and land grabbing on the one hand, and the protest of the prophets on the other.[15]

Then, in the exilic period, Israelites failed to live according to the covenant and requirements concerning the land and needy people and so they were exiled.[16] Amos' prophecy in the 8th century that the Lord would throw his people from the land, putting them and their king into exile were fulfilled when northern kingdom was destroyed by the Assyrians in 721 BCE. The same warning was given by Micah, Isaiah and Jeremiah. Such threats when set against Israel's faith in God's promise and God's gift of land must have sounded like a treason but it remained a constant feature of the message of all pre-exilic prophets until the destruction of Jerusalem and exile of Judea in 587 BCE. The pain of the experience of exile is felt in Psalm 137 and Lamentations because life without the land was scarcely life as God's people.[17]

3. Land Conflict in 1 King 21:1-16

The text describes that Naboth had a vineyard in Jezreel beside the palace of king Ahab of Samaria which the king wanted, a clear sign of covetousness breaking the tenth commandment "*Thou shall not covet*" (Ex.20:17).[18] Here, the object of contention is the "vineyard" כֶּרֶם of Naboth (a free citizen)[19] of which A. Graeme Auld says that, "A vineyard is not just land that may have been in the family for a long time," but, "it represents a high investment."[20]

In v.2, similar to the approach of some pre-state Jewish settlers, Ahab presents Naboth with a reasonable deal offering in exchange for the land "*a better vineyard*" or payment for "*its value in money.*"[21] However, Naboth refuses to sell King Ahab his vineyard[22] with a strong rhetorical reply, "*The Lord forbid that I should give you the inheritance of my father's*" (v.3). Naboth claims the right to keep his land because it was the inheritance (*nahalah*) of his ancestors,[23] his link with his ancestors, source of his identity, livelihood and position in the community.[24]

---

[15] Christopher J. H. Wright, *Old Testament Ethics for the People of God* (Leicester: InterVarsity Press, 2004), 81.

[16] J. L. Helberg, "Land in the Book of Lamentation," *Zeitschift fur die Alttestamentliche Wissenchaft* 102/3 (1990): 372-385.

[17] Christopher J. H. Wright, *Old Testament Ethics for the People of God*, 82.

[18] Warren W. Wiersbe, *The Bible Exposition Commentary: History* (Secundrabad: Om Books, 2003), 485.

[19] Fritz, *1 & 2 Kings*, 211.

[20] A. Graeme Auld, *I & II Kings* (DSBOT; Philadelphia: The Westminster, 1986), 137.

[21] John W, *Envisioning the Congregation, Practicing the Gospel*, 21.

[22] Fritz, *1 & 2 Kings*, 211.

[23] Rice, *1 Kings: Nations under God*, 176.

[24] Rice, *1 Kings: Nations under God*, 176.

Simon J. DeVries says that Naboth refused to part with his land on the ground of ancestral law of Leviticus 25. It is evident that the loss of land could result in the loss of position.[25] Gray also remarked on Naboth's refusal saying that the attitude of Naboth towards his ancestral land reflects the strong family solidarity and ties among the Palestinian peasants. Accepting the proposal would have made Naboth jeopardize his own status and that of his family, putting them to the status of royal dependents.[26]

Ahab accepts Naboth's refusal,[27] but becomes sullen and angry and refused to eat. When Jezebel inquires about the reason for his mood, rather than relating the truth of Naboth's faithfulness to the Lord and his land, Ahab makes Naboth appear unreasonable and stubborn by saying, '*But he said, "I will not give you my vineyard."*' (v.6)[28] This action of Ahab provokes his wife to act upon the issue of land as the main section (vv 5-13) shows Ahab's wife Jezebel plots against Naboth to take his land.[29] The status of land changes when Jezebel enters the scene as from her point of view and according to her rhetorical strategy, the land in question is simply a vineyard that the king wants and Jezebel gets for him.[30] She exceeds her powers, as she has no governmental authority, in manipulating the two classes (elders and nobles of the city) who had a voice in judicial proceedings and arranging for two false witnesses to swear that Naboth had cursed God and the king.[31]

When Jezebel arranged for false witnesses along with the elders of the city, they clearly broke the ninth commandment of Ex.20:16. The elders conducted their illegal trials by taking Naboth and his sons (2 Kings 9:26) outside the city and stoned them to death. As nobody was alive in the family who could inherit the land, Ahab felt he was free to take it but it did not belong to him as the law says, "*Thou shall not steal*" (Ex. 20:15).[32] Thus, in the study of the land conflict in 1 king 21:1-16, one can clearly see that greed for a neighbor's land (v1-4) led to wrong action, i.e., abusing one's power by producing false witness (v5-10) to steal the land (v14-16) and it had a disastrous end with murder of Naboth (v11-13). The next section will discuss on what happens after injustice is done.

---

[25] Simon J. DeVries, "1 Kings" (*WBC*; Texas: Word Book, 1985), 256.

[26] Gray, *I & II Kings,* 439.

[27] Rice, *1 Kings: Nations under God,* 176.

[28] John W, *Envisioning the Congregation, Practicing the Gospel,* 21.

[29] DeVries, "1 Kings," 257.

[30] Dutcher-Walls, *Jezebel: Portraits of a Queen,* 47.

[31] DeVries, "1 Kings," 257.

[32] W. Wiersbe, *The Bible Exposition Commentary: History,* 485.

4. Prophet Elijah's Intervention in Land Conflict and Ensuing Change (1 Kings 21: 17-29)

Elijah was a prophet who was active in Northern Israel around the middle of the 9th century BCE. In 1 Kings 21: 17-29, the important role played by Elijah will be discussed to show how he intervenes in the land conflict of King Ahab and Naboth by confronting and condemning injustice, murder and abuse of power through powerful and effective speech. It will also bring out the consequent change brought through his prophetic ministry.

(a) Elijah Confronts Ahab and Jezebel (vv 17-20)

In vv 17-20, the word of the Lord comes to Elijah, charging him to meet Ahab with a word of judgment. Gray remarks that Elijah is introduced suddenly and he confronts Ahab while the Ahab was formally taking possession of Naboth's vineyard.[33] So, just as Ahab is about to satisfy his greedy desire and the success of injustice,[34] Elijah is introduced as the organ of Yahweh's condemnation of Ahab and Jezebel.[35] Elijah confronts Ahab by employing a rhetorical question in v19 כֹּה אָמַר יְהוָה הֲרָצַחְתָּ וְגַם יָרָשְׁתָּ "*Thus says the Lord, Have you killed and also taken possession*?"Ahab and Jezebel are condemned for the violation of the two basic laws in Israelite society, i.e., those condemning murder and forced possession.[36] Then, in v20, the King greets Elijah oddly, "*Have you found me, o my enemy*?" Jerome T. Walsh says that in only two words in Hebrew, "Ahab still has his style for powerful, concise rhetoric in which multiple levels of meaning resound." Here, Ahab knows that Elijah seeks him with condemnation and that he (Ahab) deserves it. Ahab is not happy to be found and Ahab's defensiveness betrays his guilty conscience. Elijah's response begins by repeating the first significant word of Ahab's question, "*I have found you,*" which is the standard Hebrew fashion for saying "yes." It not only answers Ahab's question but also implies that Ahab's description of Elijah as his "enemy" is accurate.[37] The use of the word מָשָׂא *masa* 'to overtake in pursuit of' indicates that Ahab regards Elijah as the punisher of blood, who pursues his victim uncompromisingly.

(b) Elijah Pronounces Judgment for Sin(vv 21-26)

The content of Elijah's accusation and prediction of doom at the command of God is pronounced by the word הִנְנִי מֵבִי "*behold I shall bring*," a formula introducing imminent judgment. Elijah directly points out that the grabbing the vineyard is

---

[33] Gray, *I & II Kings*, 442.

[34] Fritz, *1 & 2 Kings*, 178.

[35] Gray, *I & II Kings*, 434.

[36] Gray, *I & II Kings*, 442.

[37] Jerome T. Walsh, *Ahab: The Construction of a King* (Minnesota: Liturgical, 2006), 55-56.

Ahab's sin.[38] In vv 21-24, a shameful end is predicted for Ahab and his family. The rhetorical statement employs the imagery of dogs licking his blood.[39] So, it is seen that firstly, Ahab will suffer a similar fate like Naboth, i.e., the dogs will lick his blood in the place where the dogs had licked Naboth's blood.[40] Secondly, Ahab's dynasty will be completely cut off like the dynasty of Jeroboam and Baasha, his predecessors in idolatry. Then in v.23, Jezebel's punishment is that, the dogs would eat her flesh by the wall of Jezreel.[41]Ahab and his family will be left unburied. In Israelite society, leaving a corpse unburied was a very shameful end.[42]

(c) Ensuing Change(vv 27-29)

Vv 27-29 explains why the fulfillment of the prophecy concerning Ahab's end was delayed after a genuine repentance from Ahab showing regret, sorrow and humility expressed by the word "*humbled himself*" in v29.[43] Henry says that Ahab's humiliation under the judgment passed upon him and the message delivered by Elijah in God's name put him into a fright that he "*tore his clothes*" and "*put on sackcloth.*"[44] On this, John Gray says that the tearing of one's garment and the wearing of sackcloth and the refusal from food and normal exercise were all part of normal activity practiced at periods of social crisis. In v29, God says, "*Have you seen how Ahab has humbled himself before me? Because he has humbled himself before me, I will not bring disaster in his days*", which indicates that God's final word is not one of judgment but of grace as God in a private communication to Elijah postpones the end of Ahab's dynasty into the next generation.[45] Thus, in vv 27-29, a change in Ahab is seen which results from Elijah's powerful confrontation. So also, a change in God's judgment is seen as God forgives Ahab, which results from the change in Ahab's attitude. Marvin A. Sweeney states that YHWH's decision demonstrates mercy and accounts for the fact that the dynasty was overthrown only during the reign of his son Jeroboam/ Joram ben Ahab (2 Kings 9-10).[46]

---

[38] Gray, *I & II Kings*, 442.

[39] Marvin A. Sweeney, *I & II Kings: A Commentary* (Louisville: Westminster John Knox, 2013), 251.

[40] Kenneth L. Barker and John R. Kohlenberger III, "1 Kings" (*EBC*; Grand Rapids: Zondervan, 1994), 534.

[41] Rice, *1 Kings: Nations under God*, 179.

[42] Fritz, *1 & 2 Kings*, 214.

[43] Donald J. Wiseman, 1 & 2 Kings (Leicester: InterVarsity, 1993), 184.

[44] Mathew Henry, *Mathew Henry's Commentary in one volume: Genesis to Revelation* (ed. Leslie F. Church; Michigan: Zondervan, 1960), 395.

[45] Rice, *1 Kings: Nations under God*, 180.

[46] Sweeney, *I & II Kings: A Commentary*, 252.

5. Land Conflicts in Sumi Naga Society

The Sumis are one of the many Naga tribes of Nagaland, who point to the South as the direction from which they originate,[47] which point to the Khezakeno Village in the South as the center point of Sumi history.[48] Today, Sumis are scattered in different directions including Assam and Arunachal Pradesh.[49]

(a) The Concept of Land

To the Sumis, the "Land" forms an important part of life, like the rest of the Nagas who are known for their intimate link with nature and land. Land forms an inalienable part of their life and is considered much more than a property as it is part of their identity and life.[50] According to Wati Longchar, the land is to the tribal people,[51] "a temple, university, hospital, market, the vast hall where one congregate and celebrate, one's parent, one's life. If the land is lost, the family, clan and village and the tribe's identity will be lost."[52] The Sumis regard the land as a gift from God and so they give every tenth of the land produce to God as offering. God is the real owner of the land,[53] and so the land is not a disputable property as people believe that dishonesty in the land boundary is a fatal sin against the land and against God. So also, the land cannot be commercialized, exploited or abused.[54]

L. K. Achumi in his book, "*Sumi Lhoyezah*: *Sumi Customary Practices and Usages,*" states that some Sumi clans in the past practiced a system of gifting property to others like high ranking persons and to other families to extend ties of friendship. Today exchanges of such materials have diminished. Landed properties such as jhum land, terraced fields and "asukhalis" which are divided among the kith and kin, cannot be given to others, be it common property or individual property. So also, the ancestral properties and community properties cannot be gifted.[55] A person cannot gift his property to other third parties during his lifetime but he can bequeath property to his daughter or his wife. If other persons are given property, proper examination is done as under what circumstances the property was given, before arriving at a settlement to the dispute.[56] Sale or transfer of land

[47] Zhekugha Assumi, *The Sumi Ahuna* (Dimapur: Heritage, 2009), 6.

[48] http://www.nagalandpost.com/PostMortem/PostMortemDetails, 15th August.

[49] Zuheto K. Swu, *Sumi Xu Ghili* (NP: The Sumi History, 2003), 33.

[50] Lanusashi Longkumar and Toshimenla Jamir, *Status of Adivasis/Indigenous Peoples Land Series-6: Nagaland* (New Delhi: AAKAR Books, 2012), 18.

[51] Here, Tribal people refer to the Sumis also.

[52] Wati Longchar, "Eco-Theology: Resources from Primeval Traditions," in *A Living Legacy* (eds. Shimreingam L. Shimray & Yangkahao Vashum; Jorhat: Barkataki, 2014), 186-187.

[53] Interview with Hojevi Kappo, 26th August, 2015.

[54] Wati Longchar, "Eco-Theology: Resources from Primeval Traditions," 186-187.

[55] L. K. Achumi, *Sumi Lhoyezah: Sumi Customary Practices and Usages,* 94-97.

[56] Achumi, *Sumi Lhoyezah: Sumi Customary Practices and Usages,* 98-102.

from one individual to another or from one clan to another is possible within the village prescribed norms, but selling and transfer of any of these lands outside the villages is strictly prohibited with dire consequences.[57] Regarding inheritance, in case the person dies, only the natural children can inherit the deceased's properties and if he has no natural children, his relatives can inherit it. If he has no relatives, then his clan can inherit it but the illegitimate cannot claim inheritance.[58]

(b) Land Ownership and Issues

The Sumis follow the chieftainship system in their social and political set up and practice hereditary form of succession to the seat of power and responsibility.[59] In western Sumi areas, the man who proposes to establish the village first surveys the land and its boundaries and then approaches the government for permission. When the village is settled, the man who establishes the villages approaches the government for recognition of his village. The man who established the village automatically becomes the village chief and his position is hereditary.[60] So, the system of land ownership among the Sumis falls under village chief (*akukau*) who has an autocratic system of governance and thus enjoy wide range of control over the land within the village jurisdiction.[61]

The individuals, clans and community enjoy ownership over their land,[62] as the Sumis have common land, clan land and individual land.[63] Yet, regarding those villages formed by clans, the village authority has the sole power to seize or take over any of those lands within the village jurisdiction either for purposeful reasons or as a disciplinary measure to the defaulting citizens.[64]

Shimreingam Shimray states that in Northeast India, most of the conflicts one experiences in the region centers on land. As land is an important source to draw people's identity, people feel threatened when they become aware of the limited size of their land and exhaustion of resources. This results in consciousness of the importance of land which leads to claim or own or expand the boundaries. This is aggravated by the notion that not even an inch of the ancestral land to be sacrificed for the cause of other.[65] Indeed, the Sumis experience land conflicts because of land encroachment, displacement of boundary stones which are mostly

---

[57] Lonkumar and Jamir, *Status of Adivasis/Indigenous Peoples Land Series-6: Nagaland,* 24-27.

[58] Achumi, *Sumi Lhoyezah: Sumi Customary Practices and Usages,* 98-102.

[59] Swu, *Sumi Xu Ghili,* 33.

[60] Achumi, *Sumi Lhoyezah: Sumi Customary Practices and Usages,* 83.

[61] Lonkumar and Jamir, *Status of Adivasis/Indigenous Peoples Land Series-6: Nagaland,* 24-27.

[62] Lonkumar and Jamir, *Status of Adivasis/Indigenous Peoples Land Series-6: Nagaland,* 24-27.

[63] Interview with Hojevi Kappo, 26th August, 2015.

[64] Lonkumar and Jamir, *Status of Adivasis/Indigenous Peoples Land Series-6: Nagaland,* 24-27.

[65] Shimreingam Shimrey, "Understanding Conflict Situation in North East India,"in *Peacemaking in North East India: Social and Theological Exploration* (eds. Yangkahao Vashum & Woba James; Jorhat: Tribal Study Centre, 2012), 33.

prompted by the need to protect one's ancestral land, one's greed to expand his/her boundary, misunderstanding, jealousy, etc.[66] An example of land conflicts between two individuals and between two villages will be discussed to give a picture of how issues regarding land take place among the Sumi Nagas:

(i) On May 2015, Mr. N. Sumi and Mr. A. Sumi, neighbors of a Sumi village had a conflict on the issue of land grab which Mr. N. Sumi accused Mr. A. Sumi of forcefully taking over a large part of his land by putting a fence over the land belonging to Mr. N. Sumi. The problem was aggravated when Mr. A. Sumi, being a relative of the village chief (*akukau*), made the rest of the villagers to overlook the issue even when injustice was clearly seen. Since Mr. N. Sumi did not have the power to fight for his land when it involved the chief, the matter was taken personally to the chairman of the village council to look into the matter. But the chairman and the rest of the council members remained calm on the matter to remain on the safe side. Only Mr. V. Sumi, a member of the council and a kin of the chief and the accused, took the courage to inspect the site and asked Mr. A. Sumi to remove the fence as the land truly belonged to Mr. N. Sumi. The matter was settled but it created animosity and personal conflicts between the council member and his relatives, and also between Mr. N. Sumi and Mr. A. Sumi.[67] This shows the prevalence of how the village chief and the elders of the village sometimes remain quiet and pervert justice even when injustice is visibly seen in land issue. It also shows the chain reaction of personal conflicts resulting from land issue even after the matter is settled.

(ii) Conflicts on land exist even between two Sumi villages. An example of conflict over land permit between two villages can be seen in a serious long term conflict between Mr. Thilixu who founded Thilixu village and Mr. Chekiye who founded Chekiye village. Mr. Thilixu received the permit to set up village but due to reason unknown, he was put to jail. While Mr. Thilixu was in jail, Mr. Chekiye took the permit and transferred it in his name. Later, Mr. Thilixu filed a case against Mr Chekiye, which was taken to a high court as serious conflict over land took place between the two villages.[68] The issue between Thilixu village and Chekiye village was finally settled by the court.

Usually, when a dispute arises while dividing the properties, the matter is examined on merits by the family members involved and the issue is settled amicably. According to the Sumi customary practice, if any dispute arises out of the gift property and the gift transaction is known to the people or is in written

[66] Interview with Hojevi Kappo, 26th August, 2015.

[67] Interview with Mr. V. Sumi, Council member of a Sumi village, 10th August, 2015. The names of the individuals and village are withheld as per the request of the interviewee.

[68] Interview with Mr. H. Sumi, 18th May 2015.

form then it cannot be reverted.[69] Longchar says that it was the custom of the tribals that the final settlement of land dispute between two individuals or parties is done by eating a lump of soil, saying "If I am wrong let the sacred power bring death upon me, even cruel death." The one who gets sick or dies prematurely is declared guilty.[70] This was a common practice among the Sumis. But, when problems between two villages are involved and unsolved at the personal level, it is taken to the village court according to customary law. Yet, in certain instances the conflict is left unsettled because of conflicting views. So, in serious land cases, it is taken to the government high court.[71]

In many cases of land conflicts, the conflicting parties bear ill will, anger and are hostile even after the matter is settled legally. In this regard, it becomes necessary for the conflicting parties and Sumis in general to learn how to oppose injustice, hatred, greed, jealousy, abuse of power and all forms of perversion that leads to and results from land conflict. Hence, an analysis of what Sumi Nagas can learn from 1 king 21 to participate in land conflict will be discussed below.

6. Implications of 1 Kings 21 to Sumi Nagas in Creating Change

In the Sumi society, it is unfortunate that the church which makes up the largest body in the Sumi society is almost silent and withdrawn from issues arising from land. The church should teach about the sacred value of land and its violation a crime and sin based on the scripture. As land is an important part of one's life and there is interconnectedness between God-land-people, Sumis as Christians should actively intervene in land issues, not to bring chaos but to bring peace, forgiveness, justice, etc., in the midst of conflict. Thus, some principles are brought out from the Naboth and Ahab-Jezebel land issue to guide the churches and individual Christians on how to engage in land conflicts to bring change in the midst of conflict situation.

(a) Opposing Boundary Tempering

Hamilton states that behind Naboth's refusal may be the teaching about the inviolability of boundary marker as in Deuteronomy, "*You must not move your neighbor's boundary marker set up by former generations*," (19:14) "*Cursed be anyone who moves a neighbor's boundary marker*" (27:17).[72] Usually, boundary tempering is a frequent issue for land conflicts among the Sumis which is caused by greed. Removing the boundary marker of someone's land and taking control over it is regarded as a great sin and a curse. One can learn from the attitude of Naboth on

---

[69] Achumi, *Sumi Lhoyezah: Sumi Customary Practices and Usages*, 95-98.

[70] Wati Longchar, "Eco-Theology: Resources from Primeval Traditions," in *A Living Legacy* (eds. Shimreingam L. Shimray & Yangkahao Vashum; Jorhat: Barkataki, 2014), 187.

[71] Interview with Dr. Hesheto, Director of indigenous cultural centre, 20th August, 2015.

[72] Victor P. Hamilton, *Handbook on the Historical Books* (Grand Rapids: Baker Academic, 2004), 438.

how to say 'no' to boundary tempering and also to be careful not to give in to such unethical practice as there is always a judgment that follows when one practice such act of greed, as it was in the case of Ahab and Jezebel. The Sumi churches can play an effective role by teaching of the seriousness of boundary violation from 1 king 21 and also from other incidents and passages of the scripture, as there is so much similarity between the Old Testament teachings and Sumi tribal laws on land.

(b) Challenging Power Abuses

In 1 king 21, we see that Ahab takes possession of the vineyard for himself by misusing his power. Today, in Sumi society, abuse of power including land grabs as obvious as Ahab's is present. In Ahab's time, abuse of power required the involvement of others who would rather tolerate injustice, even murder, than risk their own safety for the sake of their neighbors.[73] Victor P. Hamilton asserts, "Jezebel's philosophy is that if you have enough power, you can have whatever you want and use whatever means necessary to get it."[74] In the case of Ahab, his primary responsibility as a king was to maintain justice and righteousness, peace and wellbeing for his subjects, especially the weak and the defenseless. Instead, he abandons his duty for selfish fulfillment.[75] Only Elijah, the man of God, dared to oppose Ahab and Jezebel in 21:17-24. Although, his protests can do nothing to help Naboth, Elijah's opposition does curb Ahab's abuse of power, and no further abuses are recorded in Kings prior to Ahab's death.[76] If the Sumi churches are less hesitant in condemning the higher authority, are bold to pass on the message of judgment and be an agent of reconciliation instead of being indifferent, it can limit the abuse of power by the village chiefs or powerful individuals in land cases. More often than we might expect, opposition by a small group or even a single individual can restrain the abuse of power.[77]

(c) Voicing against Injustice

In 1 Kings 21, injustice is portrayed in 3 ways. Firstly, when Naboth understands his own land as a gift from God that cannot be sold, Ahab by contrast sees the land as a transferable commodity. Secondly, Israel saw monarchy as a gift of trust to help people but Ahab and Jezebel saw the throne as a means to acquire anything he wanted by force. Thirdly, the elders of Jezreel followed the command of Jezebel to do injustice while Elijah followed God to show justice.[78] In Sumi society, the elders in the village along with the village chief form the village council, to act

---

[73] http://www.theologyofwork.org/old-testament/samuel-kings-chronicles-and-work, 4th August.

[74] Hamilton, *Handbook on the Historical Books*, 438.

[75] Rice, *1 Kings: Nations under God*, 180.

[76] Samuel Wells, "Forgiving Ahab," in *The Christian Century* 4/17 (2013): 32–34.

[77] Wells, "Forgiving Ahab": 32–34.

[78] Wells, "Forgiving Ahab": 32-34

as law body for any matters related to the village and society. Unfortunately, as mentioned in the case study, many a times, the elders fail to raise strong voice against any faulty decision or stand for those who are wronged if the village chief is part of it or if he has made the decision. It is related to the issue of 1 king 21 where the elders participated in the crime of Ahab and Jezebel to carry out injustice against Naboth. Conflicts resulting from land can be curbed if the Sumi churches and society strongly voice against injustice even if it means standing against higher authority. Elijah gives a great example by speaking God's justice to Ahab by proclaiming the judgment.

(d) Freedom to Hold One's Land

Mordechai Cogan says that the story of Ahab's criminal possession of Naboth's "inheritance" (*nahala*) in 1 Kings 21 makes clear of a threat to land theology.[79] Ahab and Jezebel's unlawful and forceful possession of Naboth's inalienable family vineyard shows that the king was the first to violate the law of equal distribution of land.[80] Elijah confronted Ahab on Naboth's behalf in 1 Kings 21. Usually, among the Sumis, the village chief has control over the village land and so sometimes he takes control of someone's land if he wants to. In cases like this, the Sumis can learn from Elijah to voice out that every individual in the society has the right to hold one's land without threat from any authority.

(e) Human Rights Issues

In ancient Israel, it took a prophet to remind kings of their violation of God's law that protected the rights of weaker members of their society. One sees such example in Elijah's rebuke of king Ahab for violating the rights of Naboth (1 kings 21:17-22). Elijah's rebuke was taken seriously because Ahab was ruler of Israelite society that still recognized God's law and God's judgment. Elizabeth M. Bucar and Barbara Barnett say that, "The seriousness with which the moral rebuke of prophets was taken is not confined to Israel. It is not the only nation that considers itself answerable to God's law and God's judgment nor is the prophetic moral rebuke confined to Israel alone." The people listened because Elijah was an Israelite prophet reminding them to follow the God's law.[81] Elijah's rebuke of Ahab for violating Naboth's right must be taken as an example by the Christian leaders and individuals today, as most often the church and the society is silent

[79] Traditional law of Israel protected the rights of the individual against the alienation of family property through the law of jubilee (Lev. 25), that in the absence of a male heir, condition was made for female inheritance of ancestral land in order to guard against its transfer outside the tribe (Num. 36). In all these matters, the king had no right to take away the land (Rice, *1 Kings: Nations under God*, 176) (Cogan, Mordechai. "1 Kings."In *Anchor Bible.* New York: Doubleday, 2001), 10.

[80] Fachhai, *The Land must be Distributed Equally: The Promise and Covenant Aspects of Land in the Old Testament,* 135.

[81] Elizabeth M. Bucar, Barbara Barnett, *Does Human Rights need God?* (Michigan: Eerdmans, 2005), 55.

even when the fellow being is robbed of his/her rights in regards to land issue. Taking Elijah as a model, Christians must speak out that every human has the right to property, to exercise his/her will freely and to live in freedom without any threat to life and property.

Conclusion

In the Sumi society, the issue of land is a major issue which has greatly changed and continues to change the peace loving society into conflict ridden society. As the land is an important part of the Sumi life which forms an identity of a person and most often determines his/ her position in the society, there is constant struggle for the land among the Sumis. The problem is aggravated when the individuals and the church are mostly indifferent and silent on this issue. For a society to develop into peaceful society with less conflict situation, the role of individual Christians and churches is crucial in any society. How long can the Sumi churches be silent on this major conflict? How long can injustice by powerful authority against the weak be tolerated? For a change to take place in the Sumi society, equal rights and justice should replace "my place/my village" attitude which often leads to land grab and confiscation. So also, intervention in conflicts should replace the attitude of in difference. And forgiveness, humility and love must be shown to pacify the conflict situation. For this, 1 king 21 teaches a great lesson on how to intervene in land conflicts and more on how to end it. It warns against the use of authority to hide injustice and teaches that those who support the plots of wrongdoers whether by silent agreement or open involvement share in the crime. It is a loud affirmation that injustice touches God, that, "*as you did it to one of the least of these my brethren, you did to me*" (Matthew 25:40, 45). Rice remarks that, "the story shows that there is awesome power in the conscience and protest of the individual servant of God."[82] It also shows that even the weak and vulnerable have a right to inheritance because it is their palace, business or boundary. It shows of how forceful possession of other's land is a sin and that even a small confrontation with injustice can bring change in the conflict situation. 1 Kings 21 also teaches a beautiful lesson that forgiveness is effective in bringing an end to future conflicts. Indeed, it has a powerful implication which the Sumi churches and individuals can learn and relate to so as to bring change in the midst of constant land conflicts.

[82] Rice, 1 Kings: Nations under God, 181.

5

You are the Light of the World (Matthew 5:14-16) An Impetus for Christian Social Engagement

Z. Malsawmlien Gangte

Introduction

The question of responsibility and participation in the social sphere in Christianity is a very much needed area for discussion in today's theological studies and in other Christian arenas. As such, this essay is an attempt at addressing the issue of Christian social engagement by taking 'you are the light of the world' motif in Matthew 5:14-16. The passage taken from the Sermon on the Mount will be interpreted from different angles. The pericope will thus be studied and interpreted from the missiological, ethical, and postcolonial approaches. This paper will first of all exegete the passage, and based on this exegesis, bring out the various interpretive approaches, and then finally bring a synthesis of these interpretations from the social engagement perspective. The synthesis will try to draw out the overall sociological implications of the 'light of the world' theme. And these implications will provide the main arguments of the paper which attempts to demonstrate that the 'light metaphor' serves as an impetus for Christian social engagement.

1. Christians and Social Change

Change is a fact of life in human society. It is all around us, evident by the fact that things around us are constantly evolving. The impermanence of things attests to this truth. In fact, someone once said, 'change is the only permanent thing in the world'. And in this respect, 'social change' is a fundamental part of which, regardless of its agency, is an ongoing phenomenon that cannot be ignored. 'Social change' happens through a number of factors – various processes of governmental reforms and activities, technological advancements, media, natural calamities, climate change, new discoveries, religious and political goings-on, or simply by the natural process of development and human growth. 'Social change' thus takes place constantly all around us. And so the pertinent question is 'what should Christians do about it?' Do they have a role to play in it? Should they get involved, or ignore this phenomenon?

When it comes to the issue of Christian engagement in the social sphere, one major setback is 'indifference'. Other factors like exclusiveness, lack of concern, materialism and so on contribute to lack of involvement. And in reality, most Christians are detached from the social and political happenings around them. They are, more often than not, oblivious or indifferent towards the 'social changes' taking place in the society. In addition, a majority of Christians see involvements in these areas as wrong, and as such approaches, attitudes, and responses are mixed. However, the fact of the matter is that these changes affect everyone regardless of their religious or political inclinations including Christians in more ways than we know. And whether one is aware or not, they have the capacity to affect or shape the way we perceive things, our outlook, our relationship with others, our status, our identity, our faith, or simply put, 'our lives'. John Stott in regard to Christians' involvement in the social world says, "There are only two possible attitudes – one is escape and the other engagement."[1] And as is usually the case, escape tends to be the dominant one. However, a closer look at the Bible message reveals an inclination towards 'engagement'. And this is exactly what Stott advocates. He says, "engagement means turning our faces towards the world in compassion, getting our hands dirty, sore and worn in its service, and feeling deep with us the stirring of the love of God which cannot be contained."[2] This engagement aspect merits our urgent attention as this essay will try to highlight. Using one of Jesus' most famous metaphors of 'light' in regard to believer's responsibility to the world, the essay will argue for imperativeness of Christian social engagement.

2. Christian Social Engagement: A Paradigm from Matthew 5:14-16

(a) Context and Background of the Passage

Matthew 5:14-16 belongs to the first of the five great discourses of Matthew – the Sermon on the Mount. Brown calls this discourse segment (Mt 5:7) "Matthew's greatest composition."[3] The dominant theme of the Sermon on the Mount is the Kingdom of heaven motif. In fact, the whole discourse revolves around

---

[1] John Stott, *New Issues Facing Christians Today* (Mumbai: GLS, 2003), 17.

[2] Stott, *New Issues*, 18.

[3] Raymond E. Brown, *An Introduction to the New Testament* (Bangalore: Theological Publications of India, 2009), 178.

this theme. And hence the passage on light (Mt 5:14-16) should be read in the light of this. The passage for deliberation comes after the famous Beatitudes of Jesus (Mt 5:3-12). At the onset, a close inspection reveals that the discourse or in particular this pericope is primarily addressed to the disciples (5:1). But on the broader level, it also may be seen as addressing a larger audience ('crowds', 5:1). In a written format, Matthew extended his "audience beyond the previous oral setting."[4] Jesus' teaching in the Sermon on the Mount and particularly in this pericope reflects the experience of Matthew's group and its social situation.[5] And rather than specific communities, scholars commonly contend that Matthew "addresses a largely Jewish ideal audience who would understand his allusions, but also contains a recurring gentile mission theme while at the same time engaging in some sort of polemic against the Jewish authorities."[6] And having applied the Beatitude to his own community of disciples, "the evangelist takes the occasion to bring together several sayings (vv.13-16) to address his community concerning their role in the world, a role not unlike the 'prophets before you' (5:12)."[7] Jesus now explains that a 'disciple' who does not live this lifestyle of the kingdom is not worth about as much as an invisible light (Mt 5:15) – nothing.[8] The graphic description of the fate of a worthless disciple seen in the expression 'tasteless salt being thrown out and trampled underfoot' (Mt 5:13) continues for those not shining their light ('lamp under a basket). The same thought applies here.

(b) Exegetical Analysis of the Passage

2.2.1 MT 5:14 "You are the light of the world. A city built on a hill cannot be hid."

'You are' (ὑμεῖς) – The subject is clearly the same as that of the transitional Beatitude in 5:11-12 and also of v.13 ('you are the salt of the earth').[9] The declarative statement to φῶς τοῦ κόσμου ('the light of the world') is precisely parallel to ἅλας τῆς γῆς ('the salt of the earth') in Mt 5:13. It may be noted that "Matthew has just produced Jesus' public ministry in Galilee (4:15-16) as the fulfillment of Isa 9:1-2, the great light for those in the darkness."[10] This 'light of the world' image φῶς τοῦ κόσμου is now applied to the disciples.

---

[4] Craig S. Keener, *The Gospel of Matthew: A Socio-Rhetorical Commentary* (Michigan: Eerdmans, 2009), 45.

[5] Anthony J. Saldarini, *Matthew's Christian-Jewish Community* (Chicago: University of Chicago Press, 1994), 11.

[6] Keener, *The Gospel of Matthew*, 45.

[7] Robert Guelich, *The Sermon on the Mount: A Foundation for Understanding* (Dallas: Word, 1982), 120.

[8] Keener, *The Gospel of Matthew*, 172.

[9] Guelich, *The Sermon on the Mount,* 120.

[10] Guelich, *The Sermon on the Mount,* 122.

People as light is a very common metaphor in both the OT and NT (cf. Isa 42:6; 49:6; Dan 12:3; Lev 14:3-4; Job 31:5; Mt 4:16; 6:22-23; Acts 13:47; Rom 2:19; Eph 5:8-9; Phil 2:15).[11] In Isa 42:6, 49:6, Israel is 'a light to the nations', and Zion is also commanded in Isa 60:1 to 'Arise and shine, for your light has come and the glory of the Lord has risen upon you!'[12] In his gospel, Matthew portrays Jesus as the prophesied light who has come (Mt 4:16; 17:2; Isa 9:2). If this is so, "his representatives are also now light by Jesus' definition (Mt 10:40-42) because of their new destiny (13:43) rather than their past or environment."[13] Guelich says that the world (*κόσμος*) has three points of reference for Matthew:

> (1) In distinction to heaven, the spatial element where people live (Mt 4:8; 5:14; 13:38); (2) a personal element as the sphere where event, good (Mt 26:13) and bad (Mt 18:7), take place; and (3) a temporal element comparable to 'this age' whose beginning is the 'foundation' of this world (Mt 13:35; 24:21, 24:3).[14]

By 'city' most scholars see a reference to the city of Jerusalem on Mount Zion. Isa 2:2-4 and Mic 4:1-3 "speak of 'the mountain of the Lord', the city of Jerusalem towering above all others and depicting God's redemptive work for the nations in the day of salvation."[15] On the other hand, the 'city' may be "any elevated city at night, whose torch lights would make it visible to the surrounding countryside."[16] The lack of a definite article before 'city' adds to this point; and the parallel 5:15 also "belies the proposed interpretation because the lamp in that verse is no particular lamp: any lamp would fit the bill."[17] However, as a whole, "the force of 5:14b lies in 'hidden', not in 'city', as 5:15 (the lamp under a bushel) proves."[18] The interest is in the ridiculous image of trying to hide a city which is built for prominence, not in any particular city as such.[19] The city by virtue of its position can be seen for miles and certainly not meant to be hidden. And this is the gist of Jesus' statement to his disciples. The disciples are meant to be lights, and the nature of light is to shine, to be seen by the world.

---

[11] W. D. Davies and D. C. Allison, *Matthew 1-7,* The International Critical Commentary on the Holy Scriptures of the Old and New Testaments, Vol. 1 (Eds. J. A. Emerton, C. E. B Cranfield & G. N. Stanton, New York: T & T Clark, 2006), 475.

[12] Warren Carter, *Matthew and the Margins: A Sociopolitical and Religious Reading* (New York: Orbis, 2005), 138.

[13] Keener, *The Gospel of Matthew,* 175.

[14] Guelich, *The Sermon on the Mount,* 122.

[15] Guelich, *The Sermon on the Mount,* 122.

[16] Craig S. Keener, *The IVP Background Commentary: New Testament* (Illinois: InterVarsity, 1993), 57.

[17] Davies & Allison, *Matthew 1-7,* 475.

[18] Davies & Allison, *Matthew 1-7,* 475.

[19] John Nolland, *The Gospel of Matthew,* NIGTC (Michigan: Eerdmans, 2005), 214.

2.2.2. MT 5:15 "No one after lighting a lamp puts it under the bushel basket, but on the lampstand, and it gives light to all in the house."

'Nor does one' (οὐδὲ) is Matthew's "redactional bridge to this parable."[20] It signifies a continuation of the previous sentence. The two clauses (Mt 5:14b, 15a) linked by 'οὐδὲ' represent parallel 'impossibilities.'[21] The metaphor of lamp upon a lampstand is found in Mk 4:21 and Luke 8:16 (and 11:33). In Mark 4:21 and Luke 8:16, however, it occurs in reference to the mission of Jesus.[22] However, "despite the similarity of language, Matthew alone has the imperative about letting your light shine."[23] The verb καίουσιν ('to light') stresses the action of keeping something burning more than the act of lighting a lamp or fire.[24]

The λύχνια ('lamp') has been suggested to be the 'Hanukkah lamp' or the 'weekly Sabbath lamp.'[25] It is not a candlestick either but a lamp-stand (of pottery or metal), on which lamps were set (cf. Ex 25:31-40).[26] "A one-room house is envisioned in the parable here, since all who enter can see the light-stand."[27] The small wicker oil lamps of this period gave little light in the average home with hardly any windows; they would be most effective by being set on a lampstand.[28] μόδιον (grain basket), a Latin loanword referring originally to a quantity of grain (it became a standard for measurement of the quantity of grain), was an integral part of ordinary life those days and each home was likely equipped with one.[29]

'To give light to all in the house' (πᾶσιν τοῖς ἐν τῇ οἰκίᾳ) – "Matthew has the paratactic construction of 'and' (καὶ) rather than the purpose clause (ἵνα) of Mark 4:21, Luke 8:16, 11:33."[30] The phrase should not be understood in the restrictive sense but as parallel in meaning to the general τῶν ἀνθρώπων ('the people/men') or vv.13 and 16.[31] Jesus' point in this passage refers to the pointlessness, under normal conditions, of lighting a lamp one that obscures them from being visible.[32] It is possible, but unnatural to hide a light. 'No one after lighting a lamp puts in under the basket but on the lampstand and it gives light to

---

[20] Guelich, *The Sermon on the Mount,* 123.

[21] Nolland, *The Gospel of Matthew*, 214.

[22] Donald A. Hagner, *Matthew 1-13,* Word Biblical Commentary (ed. Ralph P. Martin, Dallas: Word, 1993), 98.

[23] Hagner, *Matthew 1-13*, 98.

[24] Guelich, *The Sermon on the Mount,* 123.

[25] Keener, *The Gospel of Matthew*, 174.

[26] Davies & Allison, *Matthew 1-7*, 477.

[27] Bruce J. Malina & Richard L. Rohrbaugh, *Social-Science Commentary on the Synoptic Gospels* (Minneapolis: Fortress, 1992), 51.

[28] Keener, *The IVP Background Commentary*, 57.

[29] Nolland, *The Gospel of Matthew*, 214.

[30] Guelich, *The Sermon on the Mount,* 123.

[31] Hagner, *Matthew 1-13*, 100.

[32] Keener, *The Gospel of Matthew*, 174.

all in the house. The purpose of a lamp is to give light, and thus it is placed upon a stand. Like v.14, the point here is one the ridiculousness of attempting to mask the light of a lamp. Trying to hide the lamp basically implies the attempt at hiding the 'purpose' of lamp which is 'to give light', and as such extremely preposterous.

2.2.3. MT 5:16 "In the same way, let your light shine before others, so that they may see your good works and give glory to your Father in heaven."

This verse serves a climax of the entire pericope. 'In such a manner' (*οὕτως*) – with this characteristic expression, "Matthew moves into the parenesis that summarizes and applies the previous metaphors."[33] The application of the metaphors lead the evangelist from the second person indicative of Mt 5:14 to the parenetic imperative 'let your light shine.'[34] The imperative use of *λαμπειν* ('to shine') gives the overall thrust needed to do their part as citizens of the kingdom. "The imperative, however, receives its force from the indicative, i.e., you are the light; let your light shine."[35] The integral relationship between the parenesis (5:16) and the metaphor (5:14-15) is apparent in the common vocabulary: 'light' (*φῶς*), 'your' (*ὑμῶν*), 'shine' (*λαμτω*).[36]

'Before men' is a "characteristic Mattheanism, and in the present text, 'men' refers to Jews and gentiles outside the church or anyone in general who are yet to be enlightened."[37] According to Davies and Allison, in this verse, "The universal mission (Mt 28:19) is presupposed."[38] 'To see' (*ἴδωσιν*) does not indicate spectators but those who discern (2:2; 4:16; 13:10-17; 28;1) and encounter (5:8) God's saving presence.[39]

The *οὕτως* ("in the same way") clause spells out the result of such a shining of the light. It thus "provides a most welcome aid to the interpretation of the metaphor."[40] Jesus now clarifies what it means to be 'light'. Light here designates good works, which in turn reveals the source of that light, i.e., the Father. 'Good works' (with *καλος* or *ἀγαθος*) is common in the NT occurring about thirty times.[41] The ultimate purpose is going out there to the world, to be involved, and to demonstrate the light through good works. "But disciples cannot be content to remain the world's light in a merely theoretical sense; they must 'be what they are', letting their light shine for their Father's honor (5:16)."[42] "The imagery shifts a

---

[33] Guelich, *The Sermon on the Mount,* 123-24.

[34] Guelich, *The Sermon on the Mount,* 124.

[35] Hagner, *Matthew 1-13*, 98.

[36] Guelich, *The Sermon on the Mount,* 124.

[37] Davies & Allison, *Matthew 1-7*, 478.

[38] Davies & Allison, *Matthew 1-7*, 478.

[39] Carter, *Matthew and the Margins*, 139.

[40] Hagner, *Matthew 1-13*, 100.

[41] Davies & Allison, *Matthew 1-7*, 478.

[42] Keener, *The Gospel of Matthew*, 175.

little: the light which you *are* becomes the light which you *have;* however, despite the movement in the imagery, this is the point of practical challenge to which vv. 14-15 have been leading."[43] The challenge is the call to be proactive, a shining of the light seen in terms of 'good works' that ultimately glorifies the Father. The disciples are exhorted to go out into the world and fulfill their purpose as those called to bring light to world shrouded in darkness. It is a call to engage, to be involved, to participate in the world, to let the light accomplish its purpose. And to enable others to 'give glory' to God is the very purpose of the community's existence (Mt 10; 28:18-20).[44] And to reiterate the point it means getting involved in the world around us. Such a calling conveys a high social, moral, and religious obligation for the disciples and believers in general.

3. Approaches to Interpreting the Passage

(a) Missional Approach

The 'light of the world' metaphor in Matthew 5:14-16 has often been interpreted from the missiological point of view. The WCC statement in 2005 affirms that the phrase 'you are the light of the world' is "the first mission proclamation and commission."[45] Carter says, "The image of salt and light emphasize the missional identity and lifestyle of the disciples."[46] The mission implication cannot be clearer. From the beginning, God has a mission to save the world which had fallen from his grace. It started with him and has always been his. Stott says in this regard, "The primal mission is God's, for it is he who sent his prophets, his Son, his Spirit; and of these missions the mission of his Son is central."[47] Jesus' mission is now passed on to his disciples. This aspect is explicitly seen in this passage. The use of ou{tw" ('in the same way') gives an impetus to this mission element. According to Guelich, the first evangelist by "introducing the saying in this context, has combined two symbols for Israel, the concept of light (Mt 5:14a) and the city on a hill (5:14b), and applied them to the disciple's mission in the world."[48] And this missional calling combines evangelism and social engagement. As such Stott says, "It seems legitimate to discern in it (light) the proper relation between evangelism and social action in the total mission of Christ in the world – a relation which perplexes many believers today."[49] Called to make an impression as 'lights' to the world means going where it is dark. They are also to make an impression

---

[43] Nolland, *The Gospel of Matthew*, 214.

[44] Carter, *Matthew and the Margins*, 139.

[45] *You are the Light of the World: Statements on Mission by the World Council of Churches, 1980-2005* (Geneva: WCC Publications, 2005), vii.

[46] Carter, *Matthew and the Margins*, 139.

[47] John Stott, *Christian Mission in the Modern World* (Illinois: InterVarsity, 1975), 22.

[48] Guelich, *The Sermon on the Mount,* 122.

[49] John Stott, *The Message of the Sermon on the Mount* (Nottingham: InterVarsity, 2009), 64.

upon humanity as doers of good works that will lead others to glorify the source, the Father.[50] The phrase 'cannot be hidden' expresses a note of assurance and confidence which rings through the commission of Mt 28:18, 'All authority is given to me…'.[51] The commissioning of the disciples echoes the same thought. It is no less than 'going' to the secular environment signified by darkness, and shining their lights through 'good works', a call to a missional identity. 'The same phrase, 'your good deeds' and "motif behind the context of 5:16 also underlies 1 Pet 2:12b."[52] Apart from the verbal similarity between 5:16b and 1 Pet 2:12b, 1 Pet 2:11-12 expresses a implication for the mission situation that sets the believers in contrast to the world (1 Pet 2:11-12a)), and contrast that leads to false accusations (1 Pet 2:12a, cf. Mt 5:11-12), and calls for conduct that not only counters the false accusations but also leads the one who 'observes' to 'glorify God (1 Pet 2:12, cf. 3;1-2).[53] The light that dawned in Galilee (4:16) will spread to the entire world that lives in darkness.[54] And the disciples have become the agents of this light, a light meant to be shone in the dark, an identity, a mission.

A very important aspect of the missional identity of the disciples is the call to 'make disciples'. The light aspect is based not on the identity of the disciples alone but on the imitation of the light who is Jesus. A disciple by definition is one who follows the teaching of a master or teacher. Thus, the discipleship approach is relevant in that, "In being lights, the disciples are imitating Jesus, who was light to those sitting in darkness (Mt 4:15-16)."[55] The disciples understood very well that the passage and the Sermon of the Mount as a whole was first and foremost a description of the life of Jesus, the Messiah, whom they were confessing and following.[56] The teachings were for those who had responded to Jesus' call to form a part of the community of disciples.[57] 'Let your light so shine before men, that they may see your good works and give glory to your father in heaven' (5:16). Here, good works seems to be synonymous with the 'righteousness' or 'righteous conduct', stressed so strongly in Matthew's Beatitudes.[58] Good works requires obedience to God, and this is what the disciples are instructed to do. And by imitating Jesus and being obedient to him, disciples express not only loyalty to

---

[50] David E. Garland, *Reading Matthew: A Literary and Theological Commentary on the First Gospel* (New York: Crossroad, 1993), 61.

[51] Guelich, *The Sermon on the Mount,* 122-23.

[52] Guelich, *The Sermon on the Mount,* 124.

[53] Guelich, *The Sermon on the Mount,* 124.

[54] Garland, *Reading Matthew*, 61.

[55] Davies & Allison, *Matthew 1-7,* 478.

[56] Driver, *Kingdom Citizens*, 49.

[57] Driver, *Kingdom Citizens*, 49.

[58] Stanton, *A Gospel for a New People*, 300.

God, but also care for others as well. Indeed, the primary meaning of 'works' must be practical, visible deeds of compassion.[59]

(b) Ethical Approach

The Sermon on the Mount is the best-known source of Christian Ethics.[60] The task given to the disciples in this passage is quite simply, 'to shine their lights' by way of 'good deeds'. This ethical conduct of the disciple is stressed in 5:16: τὰ καλὰ ἔργα ('good works/deeds') is almost synonymous with dikaiosunh ('righteousness') at 5:20.[61] Here, doing and speaking are implied and so ethical in nature since it amounts to doing what is right. The responsibility factor implied by being keepers of the light demands an appropriate behavior on the part of the disciples. Guelich therefore asserts, "With this Matthew intends to make a strong ethical statement in the passage, as indeed he does in 7:21-23."[62] "But he does so precisely in order to combat the dichotomy between one's words and one's actions, not to replace the one with the other."[63] Therefore, 'good deeds' imply essentially a life of discipleship that includes both spheres – words and works. In this passage there is an example (which is rarely noted) of a pattern found elsewhere in Matthew. The disciples follow after Jesus: his coming to "Galilee of the Gentiles' is a 'great light' (4:23); and they are now to be the 'light of the world' (5:14).[64] Christ's disciples are the light (Mt 5:14) of the world (and also salt (Mt 5:13), thus "responsible for the well-being of the entire created order and not only for their own religious community."[65] It, therefore, signifies the responsibility of having attitudes and behavior worthy of their calling.

(i) An Ethic of Witness

The passage also can be called an 'ethic of witness'. Nolland says, "To build a city on a hill is a piece of assertiveness; it expresses a certain confidence and a claim to importance, and flags a desire on the part of the inhabitants to play a wider role in human affairs."[66] The imagery of a city on a hill and the lamp conveys the aspect of disciples' calling to be witnesses. The norms of the kingdom, worked out in the lives of the heirs of the kingdom, constitute the witness of the kingdom.[67]

---

[59] Stott, *The Message of the Sermon on the Mount*, 63.

[60] Graham N. Stanton, *A Gospel for a New People: Studies in Matthew* (Louisville: Westminster John Knox Press, 1993), 328.

[61] Stanton, *A Gospel for a New People*, 328.

[62] Guelich, *The Sermon on the Mount,* 124.

[63] Guelich, *The Sermon on the Mount,* 125.

[64] Stanton, *A Gospel for a New People*, 328.

[65] George W. Forell, *Christian Social Teaching* (Minnesota: Augsburg, 1971), 15.

[66] Nolland, *The Gospel of Matthew*, 214.

[67] D. A. Carson, *The Sermon on the Mount: An Evangelical Exposition of Matthew 5-7* (Michigan: Baker, 1978), 31.

The disciples' new designation as 'light of the world' constitutes a commissioning to be testimonies of the source of their light. By their 'good works' they attest to origin of that light which is God, the Father. They have become witnesses of the kingdom of God. The challenge is to "live out in the public arena what one is intrinsically; that is neither private nor to be ghettoized in the Christian community."[68] The interest in public visibility here is of a very different kind from that which is criticized in Mt 6:1, 2, 5; 23:5). It is more akin to the visibility of the 'deeds of Christ' in 11:2 (also cf. v19) and of the great light of 4:16.[69] The disciples are called to be witnesses of God, the Father through their 'good works' in the socio-political realm.

(ii) A Communitarian Ethic

In regard to the witnessing aspect, the corporate dimension of the statement is also evident in the discourse. The teaching of Jesus in this pericope or the discourse segment as a whole "presupposes the existence of a new messianic community gathered around the person of the Messiah."[70] The teaching of the Sermon on the Mount reflects a common spirit, and this common life leads to testimony which is collective.[71] This communitarian lifestyle is not to be lived out in the confines of its own, but to the outside world also. "For the first time in the gospels, the Lord qualifies all his disciples as a community whose essence and mandate is not for itself, but for the world."[72] The emphatic ὑμεῖς ('you') is in the plural form denoting a corporate audience or address. It implies the "role of the church as a community, as an instrument for relationship to God, other people and the whole creation, as well as the concept of salvation in and through community."[73] The community is called to go out; beyond the borders that identifies them as Christians, to humanity in general.

(c) Postcolonial Approach

Postcolonialism mainly concerns principles or practices that seek liberation from the oppressive forces of the West; but here it is applied to those repressive structures present in the society in general. A postcolonial reading of this pericope is concerned with the "emancipation, and continuing attempt to dismantle these imperial institutions and dominating structures."[74] Therefore, in this approach, the aim is to search for change or liberation from these oppressive elements,

---

[68] Nolland, *The Gospel of Matthew*, 214.

[69] Nolland, *The Gospel of Matthew*, 215.

[70] John Driver, *Kingdom Citizens* (Pennsylvania: Herald, 1980), 50.

[71] Driver, *Kingdom Citizens*, 50.

[72] *You are the Light of the World,* vii.

[73] WCC, "You are the Light of the World," 74.

[74] R. S. Sugirtharaja, "Charting the Aftermath: A Review of Postcolonial Criticism," *The Postcolonial Biblical Reader,* ed. R. S. Sugirtharajah (Oxford: Blackwell, 2006), 17.

and a realignment of these structures using the 'light principle' to propagate "postmodern and postcolonial causes."[75] According to Young, "post colonialism is about a changing world, a world that has been changed by struggle and which its practitioners intend to change further."[76] The exclusive audience to whom the teaching of Jesus is directed to – 'the disciples' need to be discarded substituting it with an inclusive one referring to all those who participate in the ministry of Jesus. As such for those confessing solidarity with Jesus' cause, "while participation in God's empire is blessed, being 'light of the world' mandates an alternative way of life that challenges the status quo."[77] And this is exactly what the disciples are called to be – to be who they are in a world that is constantly changing in order to bring something better, that desperate need of liberation from world in darkness. "Darkness denotes political, social, economic, and religious acts and structures such as imperialism that are contrary to God's purposes."[78] This approach seeks to bring change/destroy the structures that represent this aspect. Darkness is death. To sit in darkness or death is to live in the midst of actions and structures contrary to God's will.[79] The disciples are instructed to bring down or institute a change in these oppressive structures of imprisonment under the dominion of worldly empire which is signified by darkness. This engagement is "simultaneously with and against colonialism."[80] It is an ongoing, constant participation in the world structures. Carter says, "Light is the image of Jesus' mission in the darkness and death of Galilee ruled by imperial power."[81] The image of God as Father who resists oppressive power structures now manifests mercy and life (cf. Mt 7:13-140.[82] Therefore, the disciples continue his mission of manifesting God's empire and saving presence of the Father by engaging in the socio-political affairs of the world. The disciples have become those responsible for bring this good news to those in darkness.

4. A Synthesis of the Approaches and an Application to Christians' Role in the Nation

The exegesis of the passage has brought out three approaches to interpreting the passage. These approaches have been discussed keeping the social dimensions in mind. Studying all these approaches together reveals vital clues and arguments

---

[75] R. S. Sujitharajah, *Exploring Postcolonial Biblical Criticism: History, Method, Practice* (West Sussex: Wiley-Blackwell, 2012), 172.

[76] Robert J. C. Young, *Postcolonialism: A Very Short Introduction* (New York: Oxford University Press, 2003), 7.

[77] Carter, *Matthew and the Margins*, 139.

[78] Carter, *Matthew and the Margins*, 115.

[79] Carter, *Matthew and the Margins*, 139.

[80] Sugirtharajah, *Exploring Postcolonial Biblical Criticism*, 123.

[81] Carter, *Matthew and the Margins*, 138.

[82] Carter, *Matthew and the Margins*, 139.

that serve as the impetus for Christian social engagement. They highlight the necessity of understanding our Christian social responsibility. The analysis of the pericope has revealed various social implications implicit as well as explicit. The nature of light as is understood is to transcend, to remove darkness. As such, a "disciple should be obvious as a city set on a hill (as most cities were), and a light in a home should be no easier to hide than a torch-lit city at night."[83] And this important aspect is what Jesus uses to teach his disciples about their identity and calling. They are to be shining examples of God's mission into the world of darkness. It is their vocation in the world which is pictured as dark and in need of illumination. A disciple who does not function as per his nature is likened to a 'lamp under a bushel'. This ridiculous act is unthinkable. Jesus' parable does not urge that one should not hide one's light under a basket but assumes that one does not do this.[84] "The point of comparison is that God does not do such things either. God does not provide a lamp to enlighten the world only to snuff it out with a basket."[85] It is unethical to be in possession of such treasure which is meant to be shared yet conceal it. Just as it is worthless and meaningless to attempt to hide a city on a hill, or to put a lamp under a bushel, a disciple who does not fulfill his purpose is worthless in the kingdom of God. A disciple whose life reveals none of the Father's works is like invisible light for vision: useless (5:14-16).[86]

The disciples' mission and ethical responsibility to the world as understood from the passage are what Christians worldwide are exhorted to emulate. The communitarian nature of Jesus' audience reveals the corporate character of believers everywhere regardless of where they are. Christians are called to be lights in the work-place, among their peers, neighbors, etc. It means they are encouraged to participate in the events and happenings around them. They are called to what is right and speak out against injustices when needed. The nature of light is all embracing as such; participation in social spheres is unavoidable. Indifference or apathy to social issues and changes would amount to being compared to the uselessness of a concealed lamp. Because a lamp is meant to give light, and so also the Christian is to be light to the world.

The world here is not simply to be understood in the metaphoric sense. It implies the social-political structures and systems around us. It includes the government, media, family and social institutions, environment, and anything that requires Christian participation. Take for instance the question of Christians' role in the government or in nation-building. What role do Christians have? To answer this important question requires that one looks to the Bible for clues or passages that deal with this particular issue. A very good example is Romans 13 where the Apostle Paul encourages the Roman believers to submit to governing

[83] Keener, *The Gospel of Matthew*, 173.

[84] Garland, *Reading Matthew*, 60.

[85] Garland, *Reading Matthew*, 60.

[86] Garland, *Reading Matthew*, 59.

authorities as these are instituted by God. Titus 3:1 also speaks of the importance subjecting oneself in obedience to the governing authorities. Basically, in these passages the submission or subjection to these authorities is seen as an act of obedience to God. And, it is not only this aspect, but also that since Christians possess eternal principles which if applied can contribute to the growth and development of the nation. Furthermore, being involved in these socio-political arenas means that Christians also need to take pro-active roles in upholding the basic fundamental rights of every citizen of our nation, to promote equality, growth, development, justice, freedom, and so on, as the so-called 'light of the world'. Ninan, advocating the importance of the church's role in nation building, hopes that "the Church universal will become a 'people's movement' to participate with all positive movements in India in furthering Justice, peace, and sustainable society."[87] Regardless of what role one plays, ignoring and opting "out of seeking to create better structures which guarantee justice in legislation and law enforcement, the freedom and dignity of the individual, civil rights for minorities and the abolition of social and racial discrimination."[88] It is important that Christians engage in promoting and protecting those institutions and structures that he has established. Stott says, "God has created both the state and the family as social structures to restrain evil and encourage goodness; and Christians have a responsibility to see that these structures are not only preserved but are also operated with justice."[89] As such, it is in taking active participation in the socio-political happenings of the nations that Christians shine as 'lights'. Passive engagement is not an option as the very nature of light suggests.

Therefore, Christian engagement in the world is not confined to the preaching the gospel alone, but also living out our Christianity all spheres of life. It is also very much a Christian duty to prevent social changes that are detrimental to both Christians and non-Christians alike. Christians as 'lights' mean we have something better to offer to the world around us. Our 'good works' should not be confined to helping the sick but also extending to the root cause of these sickness or problems. Social engagement includes all these spheres. Just as it is the nature of light to give light, it is also thus the same with those who profess Christ as their Lord. A Christian's nature and purpose is self-evident. Witnessing the 'light' in the social environment is the natural outcome; if not, they are like the lamp snuffed out as soon as it is lighted.

---

[87] A. George Ninan, *Church & Society: Challenges & Responses in the 21st Century* (Ed. Rajendra K. Sail & Akshay Sail; Mumbai: BUILD & RCDRC, 2001), 223.

[88] Stott, *The Message of the Sermon on the Mount*, 64.

[89] Stott, *The Message of the Sermon on the Mount*, 64.

Conclusion

In conclusion, the paper tries to argue that the metaphor 'you are the light of the world' has explicit social implications which merits Christian participation in social change. This passage and in particular, the 'light' metaphor, therefore, serves as an impetus for Christian social engagement. The disciples are called 'light of the world' by Jesus, and this aspect conveys missional and ethical implications with social connotations. The 'world' here includes all spheres of the secular world which is in darkness. And 'light' by virtue of its nature removes the darkness. It falls on everyone and everything within its reach. Likewise, Christians by virtue of their identity in Christ are obligated to do so through their good works. Just as a 'city on a hill cannot be hidden', Christians participation and involvement in the social dimensions is necessitated because they are called to go into the world to shine the light (Mt 5:16), and make disciples of all nations (Mt 28:19). Those who fail to understand this concept are 'lamp under a bushel', meaningless. Light gives and expends itself, and thus is the opposite of any and every kind of self-centered religiosity.[90] Therefore, being light goes against complacency, against selfish attitudes, greed; it transcends beyond the normal human capacity, it is out of this world. And that's exactly what the Christian identity entails. Being entrusted with this 'light' simply means going out into the world to shine, i.e., to engage, to participate, and to be involved in the world around us.

[90] Stott, *The Message of the Sermon on the Mount*, 64.

6

"The New Commandment" in the Farewell Discourse and Its Implications for Reaching out to the Marginalized Communities

Reji George

Churches must minister salve to the open sores while challenging and changing the factors that cause them.[1]

Introduction

What does God really expect of us? What is Christian life all about? Is it just going to Sunday service every week? Through his life and teaching, Jesus gives us a deep insight about God and his expectation of humanity. In fact, Christ calls us to be partners in challenging and changing the world. But members of the Christian community are usually trying to shrink from their social responsibility. There may be several reasons why Christians are showing some kind of hesitation in their engagement in the society. One of the reasons, of course, is the understanding of the exclusive nature of love and also the claims of Christians as a distinct community. John 13:34 says "A new commandment I give to you, that you love one another; even as I have loved you, that you also love one another."[2] John's[3] Gospel displays how God's love for Jesus was a demonstration of both God's

[1] Jack Dennison, *City Reaching: On the Road to Community Transformation* (Pasadena: William Carey Library, 1999), 168.

[2] Bible quotations are from NRSV unless otherwise mentioned.

[3] Researcher use the name John's Gospel without prejudgment to the identity of the author. The absence of any clear cut identification of the author of the Fourth Gospel, it is difficult to maintain the traditional identification with St. John, the son of Zebedee and one of the Twelve Disciples. (cf.

universal love for created humanity and Jesus' love for his followers. This love can be considered as missional love that flows out to reach entire humanity, which is a continuing theme in the Gospel. This unconditional love leads to social changes that envision to shape a world consistent with the message that Christ is the risen Lord and coming King to reign on earth. This love visualises a just society that bears witness to God's character over against values of the world that create inequality and oppression in every area of society. At the same time, in John, it raises questions like: What is the scope of this love commandment in John? Whether it is inclusive[4] or exclusive? In what ways can we love others as Jesus loved us? What is its implication in the contemporary ecclesiastical context, especially towards the marginalized people? This essay focuses on the exposition of the inclusive scope of "love one another" in John and its implication in creating social change focusing on the situation of the marginalized people.

1. An Exploration of the Locus of Christian Social Engagement

The world we are living in is in need of a change. The most important locus for this social action is the local Christian community established through the love relationships, formed by individual Christians. It is the set of relationships within which the love of God is manifested among themes as redeemed people (Jn 13:34-35, 17:23). This loving community is grounded with in the larger society that surrounds it. Even though it exists as a separate community, its social relations extends into the larger community through different activities. Church is actually implanted in the world without being conformed to the nature of it (Jn 17:14-16). Bradbury observes that since church "is always in a particular concrete historical context," it is "always in relationship with the world."[5] Since, the world encounters "the Word" through action and being, the quality of the relationships within the community and its outflow to the wider circle of their social relationships determines the success of the real transformation in the society.

(a) Scope of Christian Engagement

The New Testament use of the word "cosmos," to represent the "world" primarily point to "all the people" without any caste, colour, gender or age distinction. Jesus' teachings and practices have always had conflict with the religion of the Jewish people and also with values and practices of the pagan world. Jesus challenged the sectarian and exclusive nature of the Jewish community. God shows his

---

R. A. Culpepper, *John, The Son of Zebedee: The Life of a Legend* (Minneapolis: Fortress Press, 2000). Other claimants have been proposed but none of them received unanimous approval of scholars.

[4] By inclusivism is meant the position or approach that holds that, Christian believers are expected to share the love and blessings with outsiders. On the other hand exclusivism holds that love should be limited only to the members of the community.

[5] John P. Bradbury, *Perpetually Reforming: A Theology of Church Reform and Renewal* (Liverpool: T & T Clark, 2013), 15.

commitment to creation by the offer of love and mercy in the life and teaching of Jesus Christ. Christians should transmit that love and care to everyone, as God's agents of change. We hear alarming news about terrorism, ethnic and religious tensions, wars, poverty, corrupt governments, and even child trafficking in the world. And these problems seem too big and hard for us to solve or even help the victims. Therefore some Christians will think that, it is much easier to retreat than to take them on. But God has provided a model and deliverance through Jesus Christ. He showed "the way" (Jn 14: 6) that will produce social change and create equality and social justice.

(b) The Transformational Values of Christian Life and Teachings

The Christian who chooses to follow him must first love God and then his neighbour as himself. The transformation of values that Christian teachings proclaim include the conversion human heart through the unconditional love. Experience of Christ's unconditional love frees people to be the people of compassion because they have received and experienced the same compassion in their own life. Forell rightly says that "the experience of the love of God moves a person to render that same love real in the world, and to do so with limitless generosity."[6] The cause of the poor, the hungry and the oppressed and the marginalised are now the cause all those who follow Jesus. Churches cannot exist without having an outward movement towards the world through social engagement. but it exists to serve the society through the love of Christ. Church is the living community of people redeemed by the love of Christ to serve "one another." They are called to incarnate and continue Christ's mission in the world as his instruments. The people of God who form the community of God are empowered by God to engage the entire world in the name of God.

James Davidson Hunter says that "to be a Christian is to be obliged to engage the world, pursuing God's restorative purposes over all of life, individual and corporative, public and private."[7] The church has to live as a model within humanity through which God's will for justice, equality will be manifested to all people. The Spirit fills a person and also it overflows out to reach others. Joe Jones says that the members of the church "form a new community as an *alternative way of life* compared to how they used to live and how the communities of the world actually live."[8] James challenges others "I will show you my faith by what I do (2:18).

[6] George W. Forell, *Christian Social Teachings: A Reader in Christian Social Ethics from Bible to the Present* (Minneapolis: Fortress Press, 2013), 375.

[7] James Davidson Hunter, *To Change the World: The Irony, Tragedy, and Possibility of Christianity in the Late Modern World* (Oxford: Oxford University Press, 2010), 4.

[8] Joe R. Jones, *On Being the Church of Jesus Christ in Tumultuous Times* (Eugene: Wipf and Stock, 2005), 4.

The Bible is not silent about social and economic affairs.The scripture shows concern for the poor in the social structure of human life (Ex 22:25; 23:3; Lev 14:21, Deu 15:4; 15:11). The certainty of the Christian message as Christ's good news to the poor (Lk 4:18-19) should chiefly be sensed among the marginalized in the society.[9] God is concerned with the poor. Christians should be at the forefront of advocating for the downtrodden and should not overlook the injustice prevailing in the society. Now let us explore more on the "new commandment" in the Farewell discourse which itself became a source of intense debate and discussion.

2. What is "New" in the New Commandment in Farewell Discourse?[10]

The commandment is not new, in the sense that they have received it as part of the fundamental teaching from the beginning of their faith in Christ. The love commandment is the commandment which Christianity has had from the very beginning of the proclamation of the Gospel. In the OT, the Ten Commandments have a setting in the covenant between God and Israel at Sinai' and also they were the stipulations that Israel had to observe if it was to remain as God's chosen people. Thus, the command to love one's neighbour as oneself was not new (cf. Lev 19:18) and similarly the love within the community was highly regarded at Qumran community (1 QS 1:10).[11]

But most of the scholars consider a "newness" in this command which point to the expansive aspect of love. According to Raymond Collins "The commandment is new because it is the commandment for the new age."[12] In effect, the love commandment is new because it is the eschatological commandment, the commandment for the new age, ethics for the final times. Brown writes: "The newness of the commandment of love is really related to the theme of covenant at the Last Supper – the "new commandment" of Jn 3:34 is the basic stipulation of the "new Covenant" of Lk 22:20."[13]

Bultmann writes that, "Jesus' command of love is 'new' even when it has been long-known, because it is the law of the eschatological community, for which the attribute 'new' denotes not an historical characteristic but its essential

---

[9] Wonsuk Ma, "Discerning What God is Ding Among his People Today," in *Revisioning Christian Unity: The Global Christian Forum* (ed. Huibert Van Beek; Oxford: Regnum Books, 1988), 82.

[10] Most scholars consider that Jn 13: 31-16: 33 is written according to pattern of the farewell discourse.

[11] Paul N. Anderson, "John and Qumran: Discovery and Interpretation over Sixty Years," in *John, Qumran, and the Dead Sea Scrolls : Sixty Years of Discovery and Debate* (eds. Mary L. Coloe and Tom Thatcher; Atlanta: Society of Biblical Literature, 2011), 36.

[12] Raymond F. Collins, "A New Commandment I Give to You, that You Love One Another... "(Jn 13:34) in *These Things have been Written: Studies in the Fourth Gospel* (New York: Peeters Publishers, 1990), 244.

[13] R. E. Brown, *The Gospel According to John (xiii-xxi)* (The Anchor Bible; New York: Doubleday, 1970), 614.

nature."[14] Kanagaraj rightly pointed out that the newness "lies in Jesus and not in the commandment itself."[15] For the recipients, Collins considers that, "the verb *didonai* occurs some eight times in Jn 17, but it is relatively rarely used in the farewell discourses. However, it does serve to indicate that peace (Jn 14:27), the Spirit (Jn 14:16), and the 'new commandment' (Jn 13:34) are Jesus' gift to his disciples."[16] Now, let us look closely the phrase "love one another" which occur in this "new commandment."

3. "Love One Another" is Exclusive or Inclusive?

The most important instruction that Jesus left for the Eleven was the "new commandment" to love one another (Jn 13:34). The verse which encompasses "new commandment" appears within the Johannine farewell discourse (Jn 13:31-14:31).[17] In John, the disciples are commanded to love "one another" but Synoptic gospels typically speak of love for one's "neighbour" or love of one's "enemy" (Mat 5:44, Lk 6:27-28). The pericope 13:34-35 is related to the foot-washing scene (Jn 13:1-20) as well as to the relationship between the love commands of Jn 15:12, 17 and the parable of the true vine in Jn 15:1-11. All these point to the boundless phase of the unconditional love flowing out to reach others through fruit bearing. But Scholars are basically divided into two groups in their exposition of "love one another" especially in relation to the object of love. Let us look briefly the arguments of scholars who consider the limited scope of this love (exclusive) and also the wider scope (inclusive) in interpreting the phrase "love one another."

(a) Exclusive: Love Limited to a Fellow Believer

Some scholars give more focus to the exclusive interpretation of Johannine presentation of love. Brown and Kasemann are the leading proponents of this view, basing on the sectarian understanding of Johannine community. Brown says that the phrase "one another" means to love "those within the community."[18] According to Kasemann, "the object of Christian love for John is only what belongs to the community under the Word, or what is elected to belong to it,

---

[14] Rudolf Bultmann, *The Gospel of John: A Commentary* (Oxford: Blackwell, 1971), 527.

[15] Jey J. Kanagaraj, *The Gospel of John* (Secunderabad: OM Books, 2005), 453.

[16] Collins "A New Commandment...," 236.

[17] It is followed by other farewell discourse material (Jn 15-16) which also includes two more love commandments (Jn 15: 12 and Jn 15: 17). But this paper focus only on the "new commandment." Raymond Brown opines that Jn 15: 12 and Jn 15: 17 are "related to and perhaps a duplicate of" 13:34. See Brown, *The Gospel According to John*, 681.

[18] Brown, *The Gospel According to John*, 613. He also argues it by taking examples from Qumran community's attitude to outsiders. He says that "our brothers" in 1 Jn 3:14, Jn 21:23 point to community members only.

that is, the brotherhood of Jesus."[19] It is the love of Christ which constraints the brotherly love of Christians in the community. In agreement with them, Bultmann maintains that "it is no general love of mankind or love of one's neighbour or enemy that is demanded but love within the circle of disciples."[20] In support of the limited scope of Jesus' love, Stauffer argues that the Johannine corpus is not concerned with the "love for one's fellow man which Jesus proclaimed" but "it is the love of the Christian brother and fellow-believer."[21] Basing on the history of early church, Dodd noted that "probably ... the early church narrowed the concept of neighbour until it was equivalent to church member."[22] According to Collins, this exclusive view developed "because of interest in the possible Gnostic background of the Fourth Gospel as well as in the comparison of John and the Qumran writings."[23] But the arguments based on the Gnostic influence of the Fourth Gospel and sectarian understanding of Johannine community are increasingly questioned by scholars.[24]

(b) Inclusive: Includes Neighbour and/or Enemy too

Scholars like Borchert argue that "loving one another" is "not to be interpreted exclusively as my little in-group (as it was by many Jews…)" but it must be understood in relation to "the Sermon on the Mount (cf. Matt 5-7 and particularly 5:43-48; cf. also 1 Jn 4:7-21)."[25] The community showing forth their love of God (Deu 6:4-5) and love of neighbour (Lev 19:18) "just as Jesus spelled out his model in the Sermon on the Mount."[26] Schnackenburg also argues for the universality of Christian love in John in contrast to the particularism of Judaism.[27] Thus, love is more than a commandment for the disciple. It is the way of life and it must produce fruits. According to Collins "it is the ecclesial situation of the Johannine community which has prompted the seemingly restrictive formulation of the new commandment of love, but it is the Christological gift inherent in that commandment, which yields its richness,"[28] that points to the universality of mission. Keener contends that "like the Qumran community, John's outlook

---

[19] Ernst Kasemann, *The Testament of Jesus: A Study of John in the Light of Chapter 17* (Philadelphia: Fortress Press, 1968), 65.

[20] Bultmann, *The Gospel of John*, 528.

[21] Stauffer, cited by Collins, "A New Commandment…," 217-256.

[22] C. H. Dodd, *Gospel and Law* (Cambridge: Cambridge University Press, 1951), 42.

[23] Collins "A New Commandment…," 219.

[24] "…it is becoming increasingly evident that the Palestinian Jewish background and the Old Testament scriptures exerted the greatest influence on John." See. Elizabeth W. Mburu, *Qumran and the Origins of Johannine Language and Symbolism* (London: T & T Clark, 2010), 141-42.

[25] Gerald L. Borchert, *John 12-21* (NAC; vol. 25B; Nashville: Broadman & Holman, 2002), 100.

[26] Borchert, *John*, 100.

[27] Rudolf Schnackenburg, *The Moral Teaching of New Testament* (New York: Herder, 1969), 328-329.

[28] Collins "A New Commandment…," 255.

is sectarian and dualistic" but he proceeds to affirm that this does not negate "the love for those outside the community."[29] Beasley – Murray also agreeing with the above argument, says that "it is no denigration of OT command to love one's neighbour as one self" but showing a higher divine love to others.[30] Let us throw more light on this inclusive aspect of love by analysing it in relation to the phrase "as I have loved you" and also looking more closely at the foot-washing ceremony and also how the outside world experience this love and Johannine community understood and practiced it.

(i) "Love One Another" in Relation to "As I have Loved You"

The section Jn 13:1-35 begins and ends with love. According to Collins "the Christological reference which constitutes the essential novelty of the Johannine new commandment."[31] Christian message to the world centred around the ἀγάπη (*agape*) expressed through the mission of the Son of God. The love which sent Christ to Calvary in response to the Father's will and must bear fruit of the same nature in all who belong to him. It is the love manifested through Jesus' death and resurrection for the ungodly (cf. Rom 5:8). Pidgeon argues that[32] "chapter 15 is the exposition and application of Jn 13:34." Twice is this commandment repeated in Jn 15, and "the allegory of the vine and its branches brings out the truths contained or implied in it."[33] The disciples continual abiding with Jesus produces abundant fruit (Jn 15:4, 8).

(ii) "Love One Another" in the Context of Foot-washing

During the meal, Jesus had used the foot-washing incident to help the disciples recognize the meaning of his love and how they should exhibit that love to one another. The lesson of humility and mutual service was suggested by the example of the foot washing. The present scene offers Jesus' washing of his disciples feet as a ὑπόδειγμα (*hupodeigma*), an "example" (Jn 13:15), to be followed by his disciples. The "example" shows that the love which the disciples are to imitate is the example of loving service, directed to one another and beyond. This act foot-washing is more than a picture of Christ's love for us. It is a lesson in how to love as Christ loved. This act hits at the very heart of self-centeredness and desire to dominate. Tenney rightly notes that in foot-washing "the love of Christ transcended the barriers of social class."[34] The divine love crossed over all the boundaries set by human beings.

---

[29] C. S. Keener, *The Gospel of John* (Peabody: Hendrickson, 2003), 926.

[30] George R. Beasley-Murray, *John* (WBC; vol. 36; Texas: Word Books, 1987), 248.

[31] Collins "A New Commandment...," 234.

[32] George Campbell Pidgeon, "Root and fruit of Christian Love : Reflections on John 13:34-35; 15:1-14," *Theology Today* 9/ 2 (1952): 186.

[33] Pidgeon, "Root and fruit..," 186.

[34] Tenney, *John*, 198.

(iii) "Love One Another" and it's Experience by "the World"

In verse 35, Jesus says that through the mutual love of the disciples, the world will know that they are Jesus' disciples. This is the love which meets both the physical and spiritual needs of the people (1 Jn 3:17). In the Fourth Gospel, this love expressed through mutual service has its effect on the people who are outside of the community. Kanagaraj says that "agape love has both vertical and horizontal dimensions."[35] and summarizes services of Jesus to others as:[36]

> supplying wine to wedding guests, healing the sick, accepting both the learned and the marginalized in society, supplying food to a hungry crowd, delivering others from danger, restoring the sight to the blind, raising the dead, displaying servant hood, and dying on the cross to bear the sins of the world.

Jesus commanded his followers to practice the same kind of missional love that will flow to those who are outside of the community.

(iv) "Love One Another" in the Context of Johannine Community

The brotherly love is the mandatory force of the members of the sect which bound them together according to the views of the Qumran sectarians.[37] Some commentators suggest that John's exposition of the love commandment is similar to that of Qumran's.[38] At the same time, John's love commandment never explicitly challenges the disciples to hate those who do not belong to the brotherhood.[39] In fact John presents that many Samaritans and others believed in Jesus (Jn 4:39-42). His reflection simply calls for the relationships which ought to be maintained among the disciples themselves. Here to some extent, it presupposes a universality of love which includes those who are outside the circle of the chosen people.

4. "Love One Another" and Social Change

The "new commandment" of love has deep social dimension in the present world.[40] The reason for the "new commandment" is the love of Jesus for his disciples. The love enjoined on them has a purpose. In John, the love of the disciples to one another will be a sign and proof to all of their relation to Jesus (Jn 13:35). His

---

[35] Kanagaraj, *The Gospel of John*, 452.

[36] Kanagaraj, *The Gospel of John*, 452.

[37] "While the strict rules of joining and participating in this sectarian society probably did not apply in the same ways to the Johannine community in various phases of its development.." See, Anderson, "John and Qumran…," 36.

[38] Anderson, "John and Qumran…," 36.

[39] Anderson, "John and Qumran…," 36.

[40] Here, the researcher do not diminish other factors like culture, language, ethnic, religious practices and so on.

love for the disciples and their love for one another is expected to spread among all humankind. James Hastings therefore argues that "His love and theirs have alike have a universal intention; it is nor exclusive, but expansive."[41] Varghese John observes that the love commandment is situated within the frame of the departure of Jesus and has universal significance.[42] Mott considers that one of the greatest barriers to mission "is the failure of Christians to have significant relationship with non-Christians."[43] In this context, let us look at the social implications of this love in thc Indian society.

(a) Witnessing Inclusivism against Exclusivism in the Indian Context

Biblical teaching encourages individuals to engage in the society rather than nullify the personal responsibility in the society. Sharma observes that social inequalities is one of the causes "of crime and delinquency in India."[44] He defines social structure as a "nexus of relationships" and it is "sustained by those members who participate in social relationships."[45] Since, social change occurs in a society through internal and external factors, love one another and care for each other can play greater role in social change.

(b) Love Exercised through Service

Love is more than a commandment. It is a gift and "like other gifts of the Christian dispensation, it comes from the Father through Jesus to those who believe in him."[46] According to Collins "We must note the practicality of the love commandment's demand. Mutual love is a matter of exercise, practice, action."[47] The proclamation or sharing of the good news about the kingdom of God will be heard and accepted by people, whether they are literate or illiterate, rich or poor, young or old. But this happens only when they are attracted to the love shown by the Christians. Neuner says, "The Christian message must be communicated through the service of human promotion, in various activities of education, in many forms of healing ministry and in social service..."[48] The Bible is not silent about social and economic affairs. God is concerned with the poor and

---

[41] James Hastings, *The Gospel According to St. John* (The Speaker's Bible; vol.1; Grand Rapids: Baker Book House, 1987), 63.

[42] Varghese John, *The Imagery of Love in the Gospel of John* (Pilota: Gregorian & Biblical Press, 2009), 327.

[43] Stephen Charles Mott, *Biblical Ethics and Social Change* (New York: Oxford University Press, 1982), 124.

[44] K. L. Sharma, *Indian Social Change* (Jaipur: Rawat Publications, 2008), 273.

[45] Sharma, *Indian Social Change*, 308.

[46] Brown, *The Gospel According to John*, 612.

[47] Collins "A New Commandment...," 237.

[48] Josef Neuner, "A New Theology of Proclamation," in *The Future of the Asian Churches* (eds. James Kroeger and Peter Phan; Quezon City: Clareetian Publications, 2002), 100.

marginalised. Jesus' action of healing a blind person on the Sabbath (Jn 9:13-16) and liberating him from the suffering points to the compassion and love of Jesus. Thus Christians should be at the forefront of advocating for the downtrodden and should not ignore the injustice prevailing in the society.

Dodd[49] gives several reasons for the spectacular growth of Christianity in the early period. One reason is the witnessing and edifying life of Christians. Till the third century, a great majority of Christians belonged to middle and lower classes and many of them were poor and illiterate. But they were deeply united in faith and mutual love. They manifested the faith through their practice of love, equality and fraternity. He writes:[50]

> Christianity was open to all. It made no social distinctions; it accepted the manual worker, the slave, the outcast, the ex-criminals... Its members were bound together not by common rites but by common way of life.... Love one's neighbour is not an exclusively Christian virtue... but practiced more effectively than any other group.

The real influence of the good news can be achieved not so much through verbal proclamation but basically through the service out of love and compassion.[51]

(c) Love as Life Style of Christian Mission

There are diverse methods for continuing the work of social change in the context of Indian society. But the first and most important means of doing mission is the witness of an authentic Christian life through love. As Kavunkal rightly put it "the "new life in Jesus Christ" is the quality of the lives of the Christian and not a claim made over the followers of other religions. Christian mission in Asia must become a love affair and not a Truth affair."[52]

In this contemporary society, marked by critical thinking and reflection, people cannot be captivated merely by eloquence and flowery language. They will accept the message only when they are convinced that word have emanated, not just from lips, but from life. Christians should show "the love through active participation in the society."[53] Mother Teresa of Kolkata did not preach directly

---

[49] E. R. Dodd, *Pagan and Christian in an Age of Anxiety* (Cambridge: Cambridge University Press, 1965), 134.

[50] Dodd, *Pagan and Christian*, 134.

[51] M. M. Thomas, *The Acknowledged Christ of Indian Renaissance* (Madras: CLS, 1976).

[52] Jacob Kavinkal, "Church and Mission in Asia in the Light of Ecclesia in Asia: A Critical Study," *Jeevadhara* 30 (2000): 297.

[53] Bekeh Ukelina Utietiang, "New Evangelization in Africa: Learning from the Culture of Love in the Early Church," in *The Church as Salt and Light: The Path to an African Ecclesiology of Abundant Life in the Society* (eds., Stan Chu Ilo, Joseph Ogbonnya and Alex Ojacor; Cambridge: James Clark, 2012), 146.

about Jesus Christ. But she showed the mission of compassion for the poorest of the poor who had been neglected and marginalized for so many years. She exhibited the love of Christ in a very eloquent and tangible manner and made others experience it concretely.

5. Challenges and Opportunities in Reaching out the Marginalized

The present day India offers us with many challenges to live and proclaim the Gospel of liberation and wholeness that revealed through Jesus Christ. After evaluating the current political and economic situation in India, Parappally observes that "according to the signs and the indications given by the powers that govern our country today, it is clear that India is going through a transition from inclusivism to exclusivism, from cooperation to competition, from concordance to discordance and from tolerance to intolerance in all aspects of life."[54] In such a context, Christianity is a call to action. But Schnackenburg points out this problem in the life of modern day people: They "claim to find in loving God and in the commandment to love" but that love "consequently evaporates."[55] Most of them are not consistent in sharing the love with others. Even Bultmann[56] and Kasemann[57] underscore service as the content of the love commandment in John. Bultmann rightly says that "Jesus' love is not a personal emotion, but is the service that liberates."[58] Karickam rightly said that Christians should make their presence felt in the world.[59]

(a) Analysis of the Reasons of Marginalization in John's Gospel

Those who exercise religious authority are often concerned about how the person fulfils certain external religious requirements. People with different types of infirmities, such as the man born blind (9:1-41) and the paralytic at the Pool (5:1-15), were excluded from the mainstream by the Jewish religion. The Pharisees had a low regard for the crowd and looking at them as not knowing the law (7:49), but Jesus prays for their sake at Lazarus' tomb (11:42). The Jews considered the Samaritans as socially, religiously and politically excluded people. Women were excluded from the mainstream through different ways (Jn 4, 8:1-11, 12:1-8). The story of the Samaritan woman in Jn 4:4-42, tells of Jewish animosity towards the Samaritans. The reasons may be of ethnic and religious impurity and it also portrays the common cultural oppression of women.

---

[54] Jacob Parappally, "Witnessing to the Gospel: A Gift and a Task in the Present Day India," *VJTR* 79 (2015): 365.

[55] Schnackenburg, *The Moral Teaching of New Testament*, 107.

[56] Bultmann, *The Gospel of John*, 526.

[57] Kasemann, *The Testament of Jesus*, 65.

[58] Bultmann, *The Gospel of John*, 526.

[59] Abraham Karickam, "Mission from an Ecumenical Perspective," *Vision* 1/1 (1991): 43.

The Contemporary Church is similar in many ways. Mopas considers that "illness and diseases," "religious exclusion," "political and social exclusion" are some of the causes for the marginalization of people. Among these, illness and diseases are one of prominent causes of marginalisation. People who are affected with HIV/AIDS suffer deeper exclusion in the contemporary society also. Church closes the door to homosexuals and intravenous drug users.

(b) Situation of the Marginalized People in India

Sandra Kirby and Kate Mckenna define the margin as "the context" in which those who experience injustice, inequality and exploitation live their lives.[60] Both men and women suffer oppression, rejection and marginalization because of various reasons like poverty, illness, disability, gender and lack of social status. The caste, color, custom, culture and community background of the marginalized determine their position in the social life. The marginalized in our country are discriminated in the sectors of occupation, education, politics, and socio-economic development. According to Saksena "women belonging to lower classes, lower castes, illiterate, and the poorest region have different levels of marginalization than their better off counterparts" in the present day Indian context.[61] People who are suffering from various kinds of disabilities also undergo social and economic marginalization. The disabled population in India is about 26.8 million.[62] Children, especially girl child, "faces discrimination and differential access to nutritious food and gender based violence."[63] Different expressions of this violence are ranging from child trafficking, child labour and various kind of sexual exploitations.

(c) Johannine Jesus' Concern for the Marginalized

Some of the scholars opine that Fourth Gospel shows no interest to poor and marginalized people in the society. Rensberger argues that, rather than on social issues "John's focus... is on Christology itself."[64] He goes on to say that because of this, John's gospel "offers little light on the specific issues addressed by liberation theology."[65] But Motyer observes that one of the reasons for this interpretation was the proposed view of "the Fourth Gospel as a kind of doctrinal treatise in

---

[60] Sandra Kirby and Kate Mckenna, *Experience, Research, and Social Change: Methods from the Margins* (Toronto: Garaband Press, 1989), 33.

[61] Devesh Saksena, "The Problems of Marginalized Groups in India," n.p. http://www.lawctopus.com/academike/problems-marginalized-groups-india/ (Accessed on 17/8/2015).

[62] http://www.censusindia.gov.in/Census_And_You/disabled_population.aspx (Accessed on 17/8/2015).

[63] Saksena, "The Problems of Marginalized Groups in India," n.p.

[64] David Rensberger, *Overcommg the* World: *Politics and Community in the Gospel of John* (London: SPCK, 1989), 110.

[65] Rensberger, *Overcommg the* World: *Politics and Community*, 110.

gospel form" by the older scholarship.[66] In John 5, Jesus heals a sick man by the pool of Bethesda. Stibbe points out that this sick man is a poor man, because a κράβαττόν (*krabaton*) is a poor person's mat.[67] This makes this man and also the blind man of chapter 9, as the only two characters in John's Gospel who are "socially marginalised."[68] But Karris[69] and other scholars include Samaritan woman in chapter 4 also into that group. The Samaritan narrative is followed by that of the healing of the royal official's son (4:43-54) and the pericope of the Greeks who seek Jesus appears in Jn 12:20-36. When non-Jews ask Jesus for his help, he does not refuse them. In John's gospel, Jesus interacts with people who came from different walks of life like Samaritans, woman caught in adultery, paralysed man and a blind man and also with Greeks. John's Gospel clearly shows that Jesus associates not only with the upper classes who were wealthy, educated, and powerful but also fellowshipped with the disabled: "the blind, the lame, the paralyzed," (Jn 5:3) and often helped them in Jerusalem. Schnackenburg notes that the love that is rooted in God "even without natural affinity, meets others with goodwill, readiness to help, understanding and forgiveness for the sake of God and Christ."[70] Kopas rightly summarizes Jesus actions and attitude towards the marginalized:[71]

> Jesus invites into his circle of friends are marginalized because of illness, poverty, occupation or social status, he helps them discover personal and social values that transcend the standards of worth set in the larger society. He integrates them into a community that is prophetic and that functions as a continuing challenge to the larger community when that populace fails to recognize and do something to include the marginalized.

It is the responsibility of the Christian community to continue the task by opening the doors of the church to the marginalized people.

6. Developing a Counter Culture: Involvement of Local Churches

- Local churches must become vibrant communities of love, replicating Christ's love in their day to day affairs. The Christian families are called to set an example by bearing witness to God's love in their neighbourhood and

[66] Stephen Motyer, "Jesus and the Marginalized in the Fourth Gospel," in *Mission and Meaning: Essays Presented to Peter Cotterel* (eds. Antony Billington, Tony Lane and Max Turner; Carlisle: Paternoster, 1995), 72.

[67] Mark W. G. Stibbe, *John: A Readings Commentary* (Sheffield: JSOT Press, 1993), 75.

[68] Stibbe, *John: A Readings Commentary*, 75.

[69] R. J. Karris, *Jesus and the Marginalized in John's Gospel* (Collegeville, 1990), 67-70.

[70] Schnackenburg, *The Moral Teaching of New Testament*, 107.

[71] Kopas. "Outsiders in the Gospels, 118.

becoming the agents of cooperation, service and emphatic understanding of another.

- Love for the neighbor necessitates aims to change the structures which oppress men, women and children especially those denying the privileges God means them to have. Preach and teach in a way that help members to develop a passion for justice and form a biblical framework for political and social engagement that create equality to everyone irrespective of caste, colour and gender.
- Apart from the Sunday worship gathering, the members of the church can come together and participate in the joys and sufferings of others, share with the poor and the needy and also fight for the rights of the oppressed and the dehumanized people in the Indian society.
- In schools, colleges and other institutions, Christian students must be motivated to take every step to fight against corrupt and dishonest practices that devalue the privileges of the marginalized people. They are challenged to create a new culture of honesty out of love towards one another.
- Churches should integrate evangelism and social ministry because the physical, spiritual, moral and relational dimensions of human nature are intertwined. Bring social issues in the attention of the members particularly those bearing on the Church's community of ministry.

Conclusion

The mark of Christian love is expressed in the "new commandment" and that love is spontaneous and directed to all who are sinners and unworthy of love. Such a love challenges the world even as Jesus challenged the world and also which inspires the Christian community to practice new morality and thus produce social change. The teachings of Jesus in John reveal that the kingdom community must endorse freedom, justice and equality in all levels though mutual love. There is no individualism or triumphalism or arrogance that hinders and contradicts the right relationship with the fellow human beings. It is a call to all those who are committed to serve Christ. Thus, as long as Christian love is in the world, the world will meet Jesus and a new morality can be precipitated by those who come to Christ.

7

Paul's Moral and Social Ethics in 1 Corinthians 5:1-8

Holika

Introduction

In today's world, there are many changes taking place both in positive and negative way. The changes are taking place in all spheres of life, i.e., politically, socially, economically, culturally, religiously, morally and so on.. In this changing world, how should Christians engage or involve? Is it necessary for Christians to involve? And what will be the consequences or outcome of the Christian engaging in social change? These are some of the questions that are to be considered and be part of theological learning.

According to Ram Ahuja,[1] "Social change is a change in established patterns of social relations, or change in social values, or change in structures and subsystems operating in society." Social change can be partial or total, most probably partial. From the aforementioned changes that are taking place, one of the main changes are in Science and Technological development. The world has become a computerized world and many people, irrespective of their age and background, are engaged in technology in urban and rural places.

The Political system is changing in many ways, the economy is down because of corrupt leaders and there are many people who live in slums and some do not even have a meal in a day and die due to starvation. And also the moral life of a person in this generation is degrading.

---

[1] Ram Ahuja, *Society in India* (Jaipur: Rawat, 2011), 436.

There are many religions in Indian society and religious conflict is taking place due to envy, jealousy or due to the feeling of superiority over the other. As many religions in our society are exclusive and not inclusive, they do not want to respect other's faith. In this context of religious conflicts and the social changes, what is the work of Christians? If we, Christians, think carefully, one of our responses to this social change is to engage or involve in it and not to be isolated from the society in which we are living. Christians should be responsible in every aspect of changes and should make a change for good.

Many a times, we Christians think that it is not important for us to be involved or engaged in the political process as we think this is not an integral part of the missional call to demonstrate love in action, to fight for civil liberties and social justice. Christians should be engaging with the challenge to bring the distinctive flavour and light of Christ through public service and leadership in most public and visible parts of society. Perhaps, Christian engagement in the public life can bring integrity and service back to the heart of society.

Geoff Schirmer, as cited by Sue Leppert and Francis Sullivan, reminds that Christian engagement with society is essentially an encounter with Christ and is therefore shaped by the Christ of compassion. In a world where turbulent social change is now treated as 'natural,' only those faith communities that explore faithful and novel ways of engaging our social context will bear fruit, and perhaps, exist in the future.[2]

Schirmer further raises a question about how can the churches, and their agencies of care and education, not engage, both theologically and practically, in all aspects of society? How can they not recognise that political and social change has deep relevance for spirituality, for mission and for worship, and more importantly, that the reverse is true – that the church's theology and practice, and spiritual expression, are critical to an authentic engagement of faith with this ever-changing world?[3]

Hence, the Church today should never be isolated from the things that are taking place and should not think to withdraw from the changes that are faced but should be courageous to face the world and engage in this social change like Jesus and his disciples did during their time.

Of the changes that are taking place, change in morality is one of the biggest challenges that is very much prevalent in the society and the role of the Church to bring change in one's moral life is crucial. Sexual immorality is very rampant these days and there are many sexual activities that are going on in the society which degrade the moral life of a person. In 1 Corinthians 5:1-8, Paul brought Moral and Social Ethics to the Corinthian Church because of the sexual immoral person who was a member of the Corinth Church. This essay, by using a socio-

---

[2] Sue Leppert and Francis Sullivan, *Church and Civil Society: A Theology of Engagement* (Hindmarsh: ATF, 2004), xiii.

[3] Sue Leppert and Francis Sullivan, *Church and Civil Society: A Theology of Engagement,* xiv.

rhetorical method, focuses on how Paul engaged in the issue of sexual immorality of a person and the Church to bring change. It then proceeds to discuss what the Church can learn from the text to bring change first among the individuals, then the church and the society at large.

1. Social Context of the Roman-Corinth

The following are the two aspects of the social context of the Roman-Corinth for the background of understanding the text.

(a) Patronage and Power in the Roman-Corinth

In the Roman world, patronage and power was prevailing and there was a patron-client relationship. Thus, "a patron-client tie is basically an asymmetrical exchange relationship. The parties on both ends of such a tie are unequal in the control of resources, and so differ in terms of power and status. They are bound together mainly because their tie can serve their mutual interests through the exchange of resources."[4]

In the text, the immoral man was found to be one of the powerful patrons in the church.[5] The case of immorality concerned a man with material possessions. So the problem in 1 Cor. 5:1 was not a problem of the have-nots or of the slaves, but of the rich men who have concerns about preserving or increasing wealth. The church's boasting of the immoral man's action also can be seen against this background of patronage and power.[6]

(b) Honor and Shame in the Roman-Corinth

In the New Testament usage, the rhetoric of shame refers to both 'shameful deeds and shameful status imposed by others.' The Pauline letters offer a remedy to shameful status by conveying that in Christ's ministry of grace, those held in contempt by society were raised to a position of righteousness and honor.[7]

According to David A. deSilva, honor is a dynamic and relational concept while the meaning of shame is somewhat more complicated. "If honor signifies respect for being the kind of person and doing the kinds of things the group values, shame signifies, in the first instance, being seen as less than valuable because one has behaved in ways that run contrary to the values of the group."[8]

---

[4] John K. Chow, *Patronage and Power: A Study of Social Networks in Corinth* (Sheffield: Sheffield Academic, 1992), 41.

[5] Chow, *Patronage and Power: A Study of Social Networks in Corinth,* 139.

[6] Chow, *Patronage and Power: A Study of Social Networks in Corinth,* 139-140.

[7] Robert Jewett, "Paul, Shame, and Honor," in *Paul in the Greco-Roman World: A Handbook,* edited by J. Paul Sampley (Harrisburg: Trinity Press International, 2003), 551.

[8] David A. deSilva, *Honor, Patronage, Kinship & Purity: Unlocking New Testament Culture* (Downers Grove: InterVarsity Press, 2000), 25.

According to Ben Witherington, "In the Roman world, honor was bound up with male ideology and was a male value. It was only educated males who could aspire to most public offices (except some specifically religious roles such as that of priestess) or lawyers, rhetors, or masters of the games."[9] Mainly honor was bound up with the public order and it was a matter of establishing one's public reputation by public works. It is also said that honor was very closely linked to *exousia* (power), and also to authority. Thus, "the common quest for honour and praise was one of the main forces that bound society together."[10]

In the Roman world, it was difficult to shame a person who had a high status or considerable power or authority because shaming was normally what superior do to inferiors. Since, honor in a Roman city like Corinth had a public and male face, it had only little to do with a man's sexual involvements. But "apparently it is within the area of 'lifestyle' that Paul wants to establish the distinctive characterizations of a specific Christian identity."[11] Thus, "Paul was redefining the whole zone of honor and shame for his converts."[12]

2. Exegesis of the Text

In 1 Corinthians 5:1, Paul turns to a new problem in Corinth, i.e., 'a case of sexual immorality' that was within the church. This new issue was reported to Paul. There is a tie between this section (5:1-8) and 4:14-21, especially, "(1) the 'arrogance' of 'some' in 4:18-19 and the 'arrogance' of the church in 5:2 and 6, and (2) the lack of 'power' among the arrogant in 4:19-20 with the 'power of our Lord Jesus' in 5:4."[13]

Charles H. Talbert suggests that, "In 1 Corinthians, there is a shift from the body of the letter (1:10-4:21) to the exhortations (5:1-16:12). Chapter 5 is linked by several key terms; boasting (1:29, 31; 3:21; 4:7-5:6); power (4:19-20-5:4); being puffed up or arrogant (4:6, 18, 19 -5:2)."[14] Thus, chapter 5 and 6 are closely related and Paul begins with the case of sexual immorality, and encouraged the church to 'exercise its own judicial discipline' (5:1–13). In chapter 6, Paul is unhappy that the members have been resorting to secular courts (6:1–11) and then he returns to the question of sexual immorality in 6:12–21.[15]

---

[9] Ben Witherington, *Conflict & Community in Corinth, A Socio-Rhetorical Commentary on 1and 2 Corinthians* (Michigan: Eerdmans Press, 1995), 154.

[10] Witherington, *Conflict and Community in Corinth*, 154.

[11] Witherington, *Conflict and Community in Corinth*, 154.

[12] Witherington, *Conflict and Community in Corinth*, 154.

[13] Gordon D. Fee, *The First Epistle to the Corinthians* (NICNT; ed. by Ned B. Stonehouse, F. F. Bruce, Gordon D. Fee, Michigan: Eerdmans, 1987), 194.

[14] Charles H. Talbert, *Reading Corinthians, A Literary and Theological Commentary on 1 and 2 Corinthians* (New York: Crossroad, 1989), 12.

[15] Craig S. Kenner, *1-2* Corinthians (Cambridge: Cambridge University Press, 2005), 48.

(a) Accusation (5:1-2)

V. 1 It is actually being reported of sexual immorality among you and such sexual immorality that is not even in Pagans, that a man has his father's wife.

V. 2 And you are arrogant, you not rather have mourned, so that who have done this work would have been removed away from your midst?

In this section the first word "Ὅλως (actually) has a local meaning, 'everywhere.' It can be seen that when Paul moves to a new topic generally, his style calls for a transitional word and so after the admonition about overbearing conceit in 4:18-21, he specifies in this section an extreme instance of their error.[16] David E. Garland suggests that "Paul's indignation is prompted by an oral report from unnamed sources that the Corinthians have not made inquiries about the problem of sexual immorality of the man that involved incest.[17] Regarding Πορνεία (sexual immorality), Orr and Walther states that, "in classical Greek the word πορνεία usually refers to the practice of selling sexual favors."[18] This word is related to the frequenting of prostitutes and in Paul's era it was a term for all sorts of sexual aberrations, i.e., including incest.[19] According to Garland,[20] πορνεία is a "flexible term that covers all prohibited sexual intercourse and here applies to a case of unnatural sexual vice 'incest.'"

Paul says that this sin is not tolerated "even among Pagans" which serves rhetorically to heighten the Corinthians' guilt and it has similarities with Amos 1-2, where the prophet condemns Israel's sins as worse than those of the surrounding nations. Garland states that "the Pagan world is awash in πορνεία, but this kind of πορνεία is not even heard of among them. Incest – sexual relations with primary or adoptive kin – was regarded as a serious infraction in this culture."[21] Thus, Talbert states that the morality of the Christians in the Roman period had fallen below that of the outside world.[22]

Verse 1 states, "...that a man has his father's wife." Archibald Robertson and Alfred Plummer assert that the woman was not the real mother of the offender

---

[16] William F. Orr and James Arthur Walther, *I Corinthians,* (AB; New York: Doubleday, 1979), 185.

[17] Anthony C. Thiselton, *The First Epistle to the Corinthians,* (NIGTC; eds. by I Howard Marshall and Donald A. Hagner, Michigan: Eerdmans, 2000), 385.

[18] Orr and Walther, *I Corinthians,*185.

[19] Witherington, *Conflict & Community in Corinth,* 156.

[20] Garland, *1 Corinthians,* 163.

[21] Garland, *1 Corinthians,*157.

[22] Talbert, *Reading Corinthians,* 14.

but his step mother.[23] The expression "father's wife" refers to one's stepmother in Lev 18:8.[24]

It has been assumed that the woman was not a Christian because Paul makes no mention of what the church should do with her. He says in 5:12-13, "he is not responsible for judging outsiders, but God will judge them, we might note, society will judge them as well in the case of such flagrant sin. For whatever reason, he does not address what is to be done with her."[25]

Paul never addresses or explains the man directly but only the community because the entire community is caught up by sin. He regarded the community guilty for failing to correct the person who has committed incest. Thus, the community is responsible for the moral behavior of its members. "When sinful excesses go unchecked, the church is exposed to God's vengeance."[26]

In verse 2, the rhetorical question καὶ ὑμεῖς πεφυσιωμένοι "And you are arrogant," by Paul is directed to the members of the community leaders whom he had previously addressed in 4:18,19, as they were arrogant with their pride of their own knowledge.[27] Paul was not concerned for that immoral person and his status.[28] Paul use the verb evpenqh, sate "to mourn" in 1 Cor. 5:2,[29] as he reprimanded the church that they should have mourned in shame rather than with pride, and removed the person involved in sexual immorality.[30] In the following passages, Paul shares the fear that when he visits the community he will have to mourn because many have failed to repent their sexual immorality.[31] Hence, "Paul says that the Corinthians ought to have been in mourning, as though there had been a death in the family."[32] Paul tells the Corinthians to enter a period of grieving and thus exhibit repentance with godly sorrow. He desires that they humble themselves repentantly before God and then experience God's forgiveness and love.[33]

Paul continues the rhetorical question to rebuke with a clause by implicitly commanding that "so that who have done this work would have been removed

---

[23] Archibald Robertson and Alfred Plummer, *A Critical and Exegetical Commentary on the First Epistle of St Paul to the Corinthians* (ICC; Edinburgh: T & T Clark, 1958), 95.

[24] Talbert, *Reading Corinthians,* 12.

[25] Garland, *1 Corinthians,* 158.

[26] Garland, *1 Corinthians,* 159.

[27] Raymond F. Collins, *First Corinthians.* (SP, Vol. 7; ed. by Daniel J. Harrington, Collegeville, Minnesota: The Liturgical, 1999), 210.

[28] Garland, *1 Corinthians,* 163.

[29] Collins, *First Corinthians,* 210.

[30] Garland, *1 Corinthians,* 163.

[31] Collins, *First Corinthians,* 210.

[32] Witherington, *Conflict & Community in Corinth,* 157.

[33] Simon J. Kistemaker, "Deliver This Man to Satan" (1 Cor 5:5): A Case study in Church Discipline," in *The Master's Seminary Journal,* 3/1 (Spring, 1992): 36-37.

away from your midst" (5:2).[34] The ἵνα (so that) clause is explicative and it explains the nature of the mourning. The decision includes the man be removed from membership in the community. In some sense it involves excommunication.[35] Πράξας (done this) specify a moral point of view. Thus, the attitude of Christians in Corinth towards such conduct is probably to be accounted by traditional Corinthian laxity.[36]

(b) Adjudication (5:3-5)

V. 3 For I am absent in body, I am present in Spirit and as if present I have already pronounced judgment.

V. 4 In the name of the Lord Jesus, when you are assembled, my spirit is present in the power of our Lord Jesus.

V. 5 You are to hand this man over to Satan for the destruction of his flesh, so that his spirit may be saved in the day of the Lord.

Anthony C. Thiselton says that the personal pronoun ἐγώ (I) denotes an emphatic expression of Paul's attitude in contrast to the ὑμεῖς (you) (v. 2) of those who refuse to mourn.[37] Here, the contrast present participles ἀπών, being 'absent,' and παρών, being 'present,' are qualified by two datives which are either modal (in effect adverbial) or locative, i.e., τῷσώματι, *in body*, i.e., physically, and τῷπνεύματι, Spirit.[38] While Thiselton suggests that Paul does not express a mind-body contrast, but he used τῷπνεύματι (the Spirit) and refers to the Holy Spirit, even if there is a secondary allusion to πνεῦμα (spirit) the human. Paul is present because of the power of the Holy Spirit who indwells the corporate body.[39] The intention of Paul's words is that the members of the Corinthian church must take immediate action to eliminate the evil in their midst. He instructs them to meet in assembly and to do so as if he himself were present. "While they are gathered, they should call on Jesus' name, who Himself had promised that where two or three people gather in His name, He will be present" (Matt 18:20).[40] The perfect indicative active κέκρικα 'I pronounce judgment,' implies that Paul has already reached a settled public verdict as part of the community upon the man who has

---

[34] John Paul Heil, *The Rhetorical Role of Scripture in 1 Corinthians* (Atlanta: Society of Biblical Literature, 2005), 93.

[35] Orr and Walther, *I Corinthians,* 185.

[36] Robertson and Plummer, *A Critical and Exegetical Commentary,* 96.

[37] Thiselton, *The First Epistle to the Corinthians,* 390.

[38] Thiselton, *The First Epistle to the Corinthians,* 390.

[39] Thiselton, *The First Epistle to the Corinthians,* 390.

[40] Kistemaker, "Deliver This Man to Satan" (1 Cor 5:5): A Case study in Church Discipline," 39.

perpetrated such an act.[41] Thus, "the hope for Paul and his audience then is that the man will come to his senses, repent, and be restored to the community."[42]

In verse 4, the delivery of the man to Satan was not random nor was it Paul's decision alone. There is an allusion to the teaching of Jesus in Matthew 18. The decision to hand the man over to Satan is to be made "when you are assembled" (1 Cor 5:4). Jesus spoke of being "gathered together in My name" (Matt 18:20). Paul uses virtually the same expression, for the word "assembled" in 1 Cor 5:4 is the same word as the word "gathered" in Matt 18:20. And both the texts speak of being gathered in Jesus' name. As in Matthew 18, Paul did not call upon the leaders of the church to expel the incestuous man. While Paul's intention was that the discipline is to take place when the congregation is gathered formally in Jesus' name, indicating that the decision to excommunicate is the task of the entire congregation. Thus, Paul emphasizes that the power of the Lord Jesus is present with them and perhaps he called attention to Jesus' power to assure them that the action they take is effective.[43]

The term "power" is referred to the Spirit that is strongly present among them when they assembled together. Hence, Paul's word of 'prophetic judgment' is to be heard and acted upon. Paul tried to say that the whole community should take an action because the "leaven" referring to the man who committed incest has affected them as a community. So, as a community of the Spirit (3:16), they must act in accordance with the Spirit's direction that has now been given them through Paul.[44] Here, Raymond F. Collins suggests that "Power is better than all of divine attributes. Thus, the power is an attribute of Jesus who was raised from the dead and was given the title Lord. Paul's reference to Jesus' power implies that the invocation of the name is a way of appealing to the power of the Lord."[45]

Verse 5 says: παραδοῦναι τὸν τοιοῦτον τῷ σατανᾷ (You are to hand this man over to Satan). In the Greek literature "to hand over" is a legal term that suggests of either handing over a person for trial or handing over someone for punishment.[46] This phrase means "solemn expulsion from the Church and relegation of the culprit to the region outside the commonwealth and covenant (Eph. 2:11, 12), where Satan holds away."[47] The 'flesh' to be destroyed is thus not his physical body,[48] but his fleshly lusts. By putting the fleshly lusts to death (Rom

---

[41] Garland, *1 Corinthians,* 177.

[42] Heil, *The Rhetorical Role of Scripture in 1 Corinthians,* 94.

[43] Thomas R. Schreiner, "The Biblical Basis for Church Discipline," in *Those Who must give an Account: A Study of Church Membership and Church Discipline*, edited by John S. Hammett and Benjamin L. Merkle (Nashville: B&H, 2012), 116.

[44] Fee, *The First Epistle to the Corinthians,* 206.

[45] Collins, *First Corinthians,* 212.

[46] Collins, *First Corinthians,* 212.

[47] Robertson and Plummer, *A Critical and Exegetical Commentary,* 99.

[48] Thiselton, *The First Epistle to the Corinthians,* 397.

8:13; Gal 5:24; Col 3:5), the offender's spirit would be saved 'in the day of the Lord.'[49] And also, "the interpretation of the phrase 'day of the Lord' is broader than a reference to the end of time when the judgment will take place. It can also mean a unique period during which God's people rejoice in the Lord."[50]

(c) **Ethical Exhortation (5:6-8)**

V. 6 Your boasting is not a good thing. Do you not know that a little yeast leavens the whole batch of leaven?

V. 7 Clean out the old yeast so that you may be a new batch, as you really are unleavened, for your Paschal Lamb has been sacrificed, Jesus.

V. 8 Therefore, Let us celebrate the festival, not with the old yeast, the yeast of malice and evil, but with the unleavened bread of sincerity and truth.

In verse 6, καύχημα 'boast,' probably means 'active self-glorification.'[51] Paul continues to deal with the problems of their arrogance (5:2) and says that their boasting is not good.[52] Paul says that they have to give up their boasting and set their house in order.[53] Thus, Gordon Fee states that "the present concern centres not on their boasting in general; rather, it focuses on their boasting as it relates to the sin in their midst (cf. v. 2)."[54]

Here, through the rhetorical device "Do you not know that?" (cf. 3:16), Paul tries to show the 'absurdity of their headiness when they are in such imminent danger of being spoiled by fermentation.' And what the Church should know in this case comes in the form of a proverb: "A little leaven leavens the whole batch of dough" (cf. Gal. 5:9).[55] The phrase 'do you not know that' occurs ten times in 1 Corinthians and only once in Paul's established letters (1 Cor 3:16; 5:6; 6:2, 3, 9, 15, 17; 9:13, 24; and Rom 6:16).[56] The "little leaven," emphasing upon the "little," that characterizes the sexually immoral man as one, though only one member ("a little") of the community, can damagingly influence the entire community if his sexually immoral relationship with his father's wife is tolerated.[57]

---

[49] James T. South, "A Critique of the 'Curse/Death' Interpretation of 1 Corinthians 5:1-8," in *New Testament Studies,* Vol. 39/4 (October, 1993): 544-545.

[50] Kistemaker, "Deliver This Man to Satan" (1 Cor 5:5): A Case study in Church Discipline," 45.

[51] Conzelmann, *1 Corinthians,* 98.

[52] Garland, *1 Corinthians,* 178.

[53] Garland, *1 Corinthians,* 178.

[54] Fee, *The First Epistle to the Corinthians,* 215.

[55] Fee, *The First Epistle to the Corinthians,* 215-216.

[56] Thiselton, *The First Epistle to the Corinthians,* 400.

[57] John Paul Heil, *The Rhetorical Role of Scripture in 1 Corinthians* (Atlanta: Society of Biblical Literature, 2005), 95.

Paul then illustrates the principle with a leaven metaphor.[58] Paul's first metaphor refers to the 'corrupting power of leaven.' Leaven is also associated with sexual sin in Hos.7:4: "They are all adulterers; they are like a heated oven, whose baker does not need to stir the fire, from the kneading of the dough until it is leavened." However, the main point of comparison is the remarkable ability of a small amount of leaven to go through and transform dough. Likewise, if a little leaven can contaminate a whole batch of dough, so also this man's one sin can infect a whole church.[59]

In verse 7, Paul's ethical exhortation is characterized often by language of the daily life of Christians. Paul affirms that Christians are unleavened dough and urges them to become a new batch.[60] 'That you may be a new batch,' i.e., make a new start in sanctification free from old and evil influence.[61] Thus, a new batch of dough implies that they were previously contaminated. The singular "batch" "denotes the oneness of the church" and reveals Paul's "corporate understanding of the church." But the word "unleavened" is plural and it suggests that the character of each individual makes up the character of the whole.[62] This verse introduces the Jewish association of leaven and Passover, the leaven becomes the symbol of what is unclean and indeed actively polluting ἐκκαθάρατε "cleanse out." Hence, the important thing is to remove the "old" leaven from the house.[63] Thus, Paul uses 'Christ' "to evoke the memory of the death of Christ, but it is only here that he interprets Christ's death in an explicitly sacrificial fashion."[64] "Paul apparently knows the tradition that Jesus died at the afternoon hour when the Passover lambs were being sacrificed."[65] The "paschal lamb" metaphor confirms that Paul fears a spiritual corruption of the church community. Paul used the imagery from the Jewish rite of Passover where a family would rid the house of leaven and eat only unleavened bread with the Passover lamb. Just as the Israelites ate the Passover lamb only with pure, unleavened bread, so should the church celebrate Christ's death in a likewise pure state (1 Cor. 5:7-8). Paul indicates that the church as a whole should give concrete expression by maintaining moral purity in the church's daily life.[66]

In verse 8, Paul's use of the first plural for 'let us celebrate the Passover festival' implies that Paul was writing this epistle from Ephesus at the time of

---

[58] Witherington, *Conflict & Community in Corinth*, 159.

[59] Garland, *1 Corinthians*, 178.

[60] Collins, *First Corinthians*, 214.

[61] Robertson and Plummer, *A Critical and Exegetical Commentary*, 101.

[62] Garland, *1 Corinthians*, 179.

[63] Conzelmann, *1 Corinthians*, 98-99.

[64] Collins, *First Corinthians*, 214.

[65] Orr and Walther, *I Corinthians*, 185.

[66] Stacy R. Obenhaus, "Sanctified Entirety: The Theological Focus of Paul's Instructions for Church Discipline," in *Restoration Quarterly*, vol. 43/1 (2001): 4.

the Passover.[67] There is a twofold point to the linear exhortation: "a) as the rest of the sentence shows, Paul emphasizes the ethical dimension of Christian life, which is here marked by sacrament observance; b) he anticipates his discussion in chapter 11 dealing with a Corinthian problem related to sacrament observance."[68] Conzelmann says that "this verse begins with the metaphor of the Passover. When the lamb has been slain, the festival is celebrated."[69] The word εἰλικρινείας (sincerity) occurs in 2 Cor. 2:17 to denote 'purity' or 'transparency.' And these join together well with the meaning of ἀληθεία (truth). "Paul uses 'truth' not only in contrast to falsehood, illusion, and deception but also in the sense of an honesty or integrity in which word and deed correspond." Thus, what Paul seems to be implying in these verses is that in baptism the Christian has become a new 'lump,' and has to live the calling in ειλικρίνειας and ἀληθείας. Paul summed up all of Christian morality with this two terms with a life of fidelity and rectitude according to the Paschal Mystery.[70]

3. Motifs from the Interpretation for Social Change

(a) The Corporate Responsibility Motif

The text is not only directed to the sinner himself but also to the believers in Corinth as a group. The church is addressed by Paul as a body. Paul wants the discipline to be upheld when they are assembled and rebukes them in 5:2, 6 as a group. The metaphor used by Paul for cleansing by the removal of leaven is applied in a corporate fashion; the Corinthian Christians are to be "a new yeast" (5:7). In addressing himself to the whole community, Paul makes it clear that there can be no boasting in the exercise of freedom to do evil (1 Cor 5, 6). And, the whole community was exhorted to renounce evil (5, 8), and to resist its presence and take appropriate disciplinary steps when necessary to ensure the community's integrity. The Christian community cannot be a partner to moral relativism nor can it adopt a posture of non-interference. Paul told the community to arouse and to assume its responsibility.[71] The church as a whole is responsible for the moral life of each individual; they should take the responsibility to change the individuals in the church and the society at large. The corporate responsibility motif is an important motif for Christians engaging and bringing change.

---

[67] Thiselton, *The First Epistle to the Corinthians,* 403.

[68] Orr and Walther, *I Corinthians,* 186-187.

[69] Conzelmann, *1 Corinthians,* 99.

[70] George Ossom-Batsa, "Responsible Community Behaviour or Exclusion: Interpreting 1 Cor 5:1-13 From a Communicative Perspective," in *Neotestamentica,* vol.45/2 (2011): 302-303.

[71] Pascuzzi, *Ethics, Ecclesiology and Church Discipline, A Rhetorical Analysis of 1 Corinthians 5,* 196.

(b) The Holiness/Purity Motif

One of Paul's concerns is the purity of the community and it is reflected in the language about the holiness of the church as God's temple, sanctified by the Holy Spirit (3:16-17).[72] Here, "the Christian faith is to have ethical consequences and to bring about moral transformation. They are to become what they are: unleavened bread a symbol of purity."[73] According to J.W. McMillan, Christians must maintain its purity because if they do not maintain the purity, they cannot fulfil the purpose as the temple of God.[74] Paul insists on the expulsion of the sinner in 1 Corinthians 5 in order to restore the holiness of God's temple, the church. Thus in the holiness motif, a person or thing must be removed because of the holiness of God who has sanctified the community. A holiness motif is most clearly perceived in 1 Corinthians 5 in light of this development in the use of Deuteronomy 23:2-9.[75]

(c) The Discipline Motif

The interpretation of the text points in understanding the early Christian discipline in particular and Christian communal life in general.[76] In spite of having a gross immorality in the church of Corinth, the Corinthians had done nothing about it and so Paul rebukes them for the neglect of church discipline.[77] Here, the exclusionary form of Church discipline by Paul has a goal for the restoration of the sinner, i.e., the removal of the offender from the assembly was probably to stimulate him/her to an in-depth reflection, a realization of the gravity of his sin and the need for reconciliation.[78] "It was a discipline with a view to spiritual restoration. For this reason, it must be done by the church in humility and with love."[79] In the present context of the churches, there is a lack of discipline about the moral.

(d) The Judgment Motif

Maria Pascuzzi states that "the judgment pronouncement constitutes *prima facie* text evidence that Paul's intention was to champion his authority and

---

[72] Thiselton, *The First Epistle to the Corinthians,* 390.

[73] Garland, *1 Corinthians,* 154.

[74] J. W. McMillan, *Answers to Church problems: A Book Study of 1 Corinthians* (Mussorie: Hyratt, NY), 58-59.

[75] Brian S. Rosner, "Temple and Holiness in 1 Corinthians 5," in *Tyndale Bulletin*, Vol. 42/1 (May 1991): 137-138.

[76] South, "A Critique of the 'Curse/Death' Interpretation of 1 Corinthians 5:1-8," 561.

[77] M. M. Thomas, *Spiritual Body: 1 Corinthians* (CTBC; Tiruvalla: CSS Books, 2005), 79.

[78] Ossom-Batsa, "Responsible Community Behaviour or Exclusion: Interpreting 1 Cor 5:1-13 From a Communicative Perspective," 307.

[79] McMillan, *Answers to Church Problems: A Book Study of 1 Corinthians*, 57.

resolve the case in a unilateral manner needs to be reconsidered."[80] According to Witherington, the expulsion should be made not by the Corinthian leaders but by the believers as a body. The offender is to be cast out into the realm where Satan is still the ruler "for the destruction of the flesh." Thus, "the ultimate aim of the expulsion is not punitive but rather that the spirit may be saved on the eschatological Day of Judgment."[81] Paul passed judgment on the man who has committed sexual immorality but here the judgment motif is not of the physical death but to let the offender realize his/her sin by passing a judgment by expelling or excommunication from the church.

(e) The Repentance Motif

In God's infinite wisdom, he brings a sinner to repentance through various means and methods (cf. 11:32; 1 Pet 4:6). He is interested in the salvation of man's soul and earnestly desires that all people come to repentance (2 Pet 3:9). With respect to the man who committed incest, Paul hopes that even though Satan may destroy the physical body, the man's spirit may be saved "in the day of the Lord" (v. 5).[82] From the interpretation of the text, it is seen that, "Paul tells the Corinthians to enter a period of grieving and thus exhibit repentance and godly sorrow. He desires that they humble themselves repentantly before God and then experience God's forgiveness and love."[83] The immoral man should learn to repent so that there will be change in his life and will also change the whole church and then the wider society.

(f) The Salvation Motif

According to Paul, the judgment for the immoral man was to lead him to repentance so that his spirit will be saved in the day of the Lord. Collins asserts that ἡμέρᾳ τοῦ κυρίου 'Day of the Lord', should be a day of ultimate salvation for those who belong to the Lord (3:15)."[84] Salvation motif is an important message for the church and also for the society at large. In verse 5, Paul does not guarantee that the man will be saved on the last day. The purpose of the discipline is for the man's salvation. Nevertheless, the ultimate aim and goal of discipline is salvific. And recognizing the goal of discipline should not be underestimated. The purpose of discipline is not ultimately punishment but salvation. Thus, the church practices discipline to rebuild what has been torn down in someone's life.[85]

---

[80] Maria Pascuzzi, *Ethics, Ecclesiology and Church Discipline: A Rhetorical Analysis of 1 Corinthians 5* (Rome: Gregorian University Press, 1997), 180.

[81] Witherington, *Conflict & Community in Corinth,* 158.

[82] Kistemaker, "Deliver This Man to Satan" (1 Cor 5:5): A Case study in Church Discipline," 46.

[83] Kistemaker, "Deliver This Man to Satan" (1 Cor 5:5): A Case study in Church Discipline," 37.

[84] Collins, *First Corinthians,* 213.

[85] Schreiner, "The Biblical Basis for Church Discipline," 117.

(g) The Sincerity and Truth Motif

In verse 8, Paul exhorts, "...let us celebrate the festival not with the old yeast, the yeast of malice and evil but the unleavened bread of sincerity and truth." Here, Paul was saying that Christians must make a practice of celebrating the festival not in a literal sense, but spiritually by living continuously without evil and in an atmosphere of sincerity and truth. Thiselton says, "Sincerity and truth means the living out a Christian life in actions which reflect the identity and reality of the new creation, as against that which is tainted by the self-interest and moral degeneracy, which must be cleaned out."[86]

4. Implications for Christian Social Engagement Today

In 1 Corinthians 5:1-8, Paul addressed a case of scandalous immorality and broadened its resolution into a theological lesson for the church.[87] In this section, the key issue is not that Paul was to reassert his 'authority over the community with a show of force.' But the root problem is their spiritual arrogance combined with moral laxity. Paul is seen to be more vexed with the congregation than with the culprit, because the man committed sin but the congregation permitted the person guilty of such sin to continue as a member in good standing without taking any disciplinary action. Thus, Garland suggests that "Paul wanted to shake them out of their blasé attitude toward this sinful conduct, to purify the community of the contagion, and to create a situation that drives home the seriousness of the man's sin and his need for repentance."[88]

Paul's advice to the Christian church at Corinth is relevant for the church in India. The responsibility of the Indian church is to promote the renewal and discipline of good moral life within its fold and relate to its commitment for participating in socio-political changes in wider society.[89]

The church today should help the missionary or existing church leadership recognize that the members of the church should be taught from the very beginning to handle the matter of discipline of moral failure within itself as a whole. It can also be a call to community discipline. The "Moral teaching has to be a fundamental of foundation lying, and a constant feature in the building up of an effective and safe community."[90] High standards of morality should be promoted by the church.

Thus, 1 Corinthian 5 challenges the Church today both to awaken from the politically correct passivity which sometimes can characterize the responses

---

[86] Thiselton, *The First Epistle to the Corinthians,* 403.

[87] Orr and Walther, *I Corinthians,* 189.

[88] Garland, *1 Corinthians,* 153.

[89] Thomas, *Spiritual Body: 1 Corinthians*, 80-81.

[90] Collin P. Warner, *The Issues Facing the Emerging Churches in the Light of First Corinthians* (Chennai: Mission Educational Books, 2005), 59-60.

to immoral behaviour and to cease to champion immoral choices and acts as testimonies to freedom. One can assume that freedom is a good thing which the whole Church acknowledges. However, it can be cherished improperly and open the way to evil snares. This is to be acknowledged by the Church today. The ignorance and widespread confusion can lead some Christians to ignore or even champion immoral behaviour. On the other hand, other Christians can be too easily co-opted by the talk of non-interference which goes hand in hand with the freedom ethic of radical individualism. The diverse paths where Christians travel must always be respected but they must always be directed to sanctification and bring a social change. Hence, the Church today should enjoin on each the responsibility to aid one another to greater holiness of life. However, Christian today have a responsibility to engage themselves in the process of the renewal, purification and sanctification of the Church so that the Church may fulfil its vocation of witnessing to the world and contributing to its sanctification.[91]

Conclusion

The primary reason for discipline is the purity of the church and the glory of God. If the church tolerates sin in its midst, then the sin will spread like an infection and the church will lose its witness to the world. Therefore, they must judge those who are in sin and such judgment does not violate what Jesus said about judging (Matt 7:1-5). True discipline comes from a humble heart, and the motive of discipline is the salvation of the one who has been strayed. Therefore, one of the main goals and aims of discipline is not punishment or criticism but the health and salvation of the one who has strayed from the truth and sincerity.[92]

Sexual Immorality is seen as one of the prevailing issues in our present scenario, and through the exegesis of this text we see how Paul engaged with the immoral person through his moral and social ethics. Paul was concerned for the sin committed by an individual because the sin of one person could infect the whole church. Through the motifs from the interpretation of the text, the church today should be conscious of one's moral and social life because when he/she is put in discipline then there will be change not only in him/her but also in the church as a whole and in the wider society.

[91] Pascuzzi, *Ethics, Ecclesiology and Church Discipline: A Rhetorical Analysis of 1 Corinthians 5,* 199.

[92] Schreiner, "The Biblical Basis for Church Discipline," 126-127.

8

Paul's Appeal for Onesimus as a Model for Christian Participation in the Eradication of Female Foeticide in India
A Socio-Rhetorical Approach

Mary Grace

Introduction

Heraclitus of Ephesus, a pre-Socratic Greek philosopher, said, "Change is the only constant in the world."[1] The world is subject to change and is always changing, even in ways we do not fully understand. Political regimes rise and fall, economies grow and crash and, society and culture change colours with the onslaught of technological and scientific development. "Social change is the transformation of culture and social organization/ structure over time."[2] Change happens everywhere though its pace may vary from place to place. It is sometimes intentional and often unplanned. It is beneficial for some and a curse to others, and often results in controversies and human made boundaries between different sections of the society.

Changes are brought about by invention, discovery and their diffusion.[3] New inventions and discoveries bring about and effect change in the lives of people as they are accessed by the public. Conflict that arises between people because of their class, caste, region and land also effect change as each strives

[1] www.ancient.eu/Heraclitus_of_Ephesos (accessed on 09/09/15).

[2] worldanimal.net/documents/2_Social_Change_Introduction.pdf (accessed on 04/08/15).

[3] worldanimal.net/documents/2_Social_Change_Introduction.pdf (accessed on 04/08/15).

to define their distinct identity and boundary from the other. Circulating ideas, beliefs and values that reach a vast majority of the masses also stimulate change from traditional belief and thought systems to that of a global modern pattern. Globalization is also responsible for social change worldwide. It has made access possible to the mode of life and development occurring in different nations across the world, enabling exposure and integration.

The world at present is beset with issues generated by change at the scientific, political, economic, social, and cultural and religious level; each level affecting the other. There is a cry for recognition of the gay/lesbian/transgender identity; political propaganda is suffused with religiosity; economy nurtures materialism giving way to selfishness and the survival of the fittest. The less fit, women, children at risk and the elderly thus find themselves at the bottom of the social grid. Perhaps the most sensitive issue that pervades the whole scenario of social change is the value of life over another life.

We need to be engaged in social change so that human life may be preserved and improved, and not be overcome by all the issues pertaining to social change. We need to recognize the concept of social change and recognize that critical societal issues exist and need to be acknowledged and addressed. The critical need of the hour is exploring the paradigm of human interaction and relationship, human identity and the value of human life.[4] Engaging in social change concerns not just the benefit of human beings but also that of the living and non-living inhabitants of our world.

We can be engaged by acknowledging the issues and striving for a dialogue. Actions can be taken where need be. Those who feel they cannot act can be generous with their time and money. Social media and technology can be used in creating awareness of the issues and getting the mass to participate and be involved. Engaging however not only demands creating awareness, or volunteering or financial support. It also requires personal involvement outside of technology and money.[5]

Christian engagement in social change is mandatory in these days. Gone are the days when Christian engagement was limited to mission works in the form of education and medical institutions. Social change asks that the engagement transforms from a soul-saving approach to going out to the streets and active involvement. The ecumenical movement has embraced inclusivity of evangelism, fieldwork and involvement in social change. Women issues are being dealt with in Feminist theology, environmental issues in Eco-Theology, LGBT issues in Transgender readings, issues of caste in Dalit Theology. Issues are being addressed and theologized in the context itself. Liberation and Contextual readings have been major Christian engagements with the issues of social change.

---

[4] Myles Collier, "Why Engage in Social Change? New Report Gives Surprising Answers from Around the World" www.christianpost.com (accessed on 04/08/15).

[5] Collier, "Why Engage in Social Change?

The reasons for Christian engagement vary. As humans, engagement may be because of personal reasons arising out of personal experiences or the desire to be an agent of improving the conditions of humankind through one's actions. There may be economic reasons, moral reasons, political reasons and religious reasons. For Christians, the guiding reason, I assume, is the concept of stewardship that is found in the book of Genesis of the Christian Bible. Stewardship requires us of accountability and responsibility over the order of the world and the changes it goes through. Christians are required to engage and participate in all means possible – through dialogue and theologizing, as volunteers and active participants, supporters, and taking initiatives to seek answers to social solutions and compromises, to create awareness of the value of human life and the importance of protecting nature and animals.

One of the most important reasons for Christian engagement in Social Change ought to be the humanization of those who have been dismissed and degraded in society. Human beings make up society and a society is what it is made up of. Human beings are the heart of society and they are valuable and important. Every human life is as significant as the other, the dignity of a human life is not determined by one's social status, financial standing, or religious and political affiliations; dignity is the very essence of each human being. Christians need to reclaim this dignity of human life for those at the periphery whose lives are often compromised and often overlooked. For Christians, humans are created in the image of God and it is obligatory that every Christian participate in creating this awareness to a world that is either ignorant of it or has forgotten it.

This essay is an attempt to look at how society has degraded human life in the lowest form through the act of Female Foeticide (FF). It proposes that Paul's appeal for Onesimus in the Letter to Philemon is an appropriate biblical model that could be adopted by Christians/Churches in addressing the issue of FF in India. The implications from the Letter to Philemon for FF in India are given towards the end of the paper. The paper has adopted the Socio-Rhetoric Approach in studying the Letter to Philemon. In his letter, Paul's style of writing and the words he uses are persuasive in nature. To get Philemon to do what he thinks is the right thing, Paul appeals emotionally and uses words to generate his concern and compassion and evoke an emotional yet voluntary response.[6] The paper does not in any way attempt to compare and contrast the two different contexts of Philemon and FF. The concern of the paper is how Paul, by using rhetoric, is able to persuade Philemon to do his rightful Christian duty towards Onesimus, his slave.

---

[6] Ben Witherington III, *The Letters to Philemon, the Colossians, and the Ephesians. A Socio-Rhetorical Commentary on the Captivity Epistles* (Grand Rapids/Cambridge: Eerdmans, 2007), 51.

1. Female Foeticide

In the Indian society, the lowest form of human degradation is the prevalent hushed-up affair of Female Infanticide (FF). FF is "the selective abortion/elimination of the female child, done deliberately by the mother, after the detection of the child's gender through medical tests."[7] It is a common social evil propagated by a fanatic preference for male child and is specially confined to South Asian countries like China, India, Vietnam, and Korea, but has mushroomed to western nations like the US and Canada.[8] Female foeticide is a two-step practice. First, the sex of the unborn baby is determined. Second, the decision is made to have or not have the child. FF is a gross violation of human rights. The right to life of the unborn child and woman's right over her body are violated.[9]

(a) Methods of Abortion of Female Foeticide

The methods used in the abortion of female foetuses can be divided into three[10] main categories:

(i) invade the uterus and kill the child by instruments which enter the uterus through the cervix (Suction Aspiration, Dilation and Curettage) in the first three weeks of pregnancy
(ii) kill the preborn child by administration of drugs and then induce labour and the delivery of a dead baby (Dilation and Evacuation, Salt Poisoning [Saline injection]) at 12-18 weeks
(iii) invade the uterus by abdominal surgery (Prostglandin Chemical Abortion, Hysterotomy or Caesarean Section) at six months to 40 weeks.

(b) The Emotional and Physical Post-Abortion Trauma in FF:[11]

Emotionally and psychologically, there is regret, anger, guilt, shame, a sense of loneliness or isolation, loss of self-confidence, insomnia or nightmares, relationship issues, suicidal thoughts and feelings, eating disorders, depression and anxiety. Physically, there is abdominal pain and cramping, nausea, vomiting, diarrhoea and bleeding. Despite the emotional and physical trauma attached to abortion,

---

[7] Female Feticide: Causes & Effects of Sex-Selective Abortion, September 1, 2015. http://silverstararrow.hubpages.com/hub/Female-Feticide-Causes-Effects-and-Solutions (accessed on 09/09/15).

[8] Female Feticide: Causes & Effects of Sex-Selective Abortion, September 1, 2015. http://silverstararrow.hubpages.com/hub/Female-Feticide-Causes-Effects-and-Solutions (accessed on 09/09/15).

[9] http://www.edudel.nic.in/yuvacontent/Let_Everyone_Live.pdf (accessed on 09/09/15).

[10] J. C. Willke, *Abortion: Questions and Answers.* (Cincinnati: Hayes, 1985).

[11] http://americanpregnancy.org/unplanned-pregnancy/abortion-emotional-effects/ (accessed on 09/09/15).

some Indian mothers will keep doing it for their fanatic preference of male child. Such is the scenario of FF in India.

(c) Reasons behind FF

The reasons behind FF range from religious, social and cultural to the legal and industrial.

Religiously, the cremation ceremonial procedure in the Indian Hindu society is an auspicious event with the privilege of the last rites bestowed on the son. "It is considered that cremation through a son guarantees that parents are blessed with direct passage to heaven."[12] So, the parents want a son who will free them from all their sins after their death.

Socially and culturally,[13] the common notion is that male children are a better investment. They will take care of the parents when they are old. They are bread earners of the family. For the agricultural society, male strength is an asset. For the warrior society, male courage wins battles. Daughters, on the other hand, will be married off to another family at the expense of a heavy dowry. In a society like India which is defined by institutional and cultural sexism, women tend to have less power, status, rights, and money in the society. They are also often victims of rape and assault which spoils their life and dishonours the family. Thus, an abortion of a female foetus appears less expensive in view of the greater anticipated expense in the later life of girls.

Legally, the illegalization of abortion in India has resulted in illegal sex determination and termination of pregnancies. It would not be wrong to say illegalization has resulted in the profitable business of illegal abortions across the country.[14] Also, the Medical Termination of Pregnancy Act passed in 1971, Prenatal Diagnostic Techniques Act (PDNT) in 1994, and Pre-conception and Pre-natal Diagnostic Techniques (Regulation and Prevention of Misuse) (PCPNDT) Act in 2004 have proved to be "insufficient and inefficient to curb the brutal custom of female foeticide."[15] FF is still prevalent and still poses a danger to female foetuses.

Industrially, sex determination of the foetus has become much easier with the advent of CVS, amniocentesis, and ultrasound. The manufacturers of these equipment and gadgets benefit from the preference for male children. "Many hospitals are known to sign long-term contracts with the firms involved in the

---

[12] Nisha Jitendra Singh Kushwaha and Kiran Arun Sharma, "Factors Responsible for Female Foeticide," in *Research Journal of Language, Literature and* Humanities 1/7 1-4 (Nov 2014), 1.

[13] Kushwaha and Sharma, "Factors Responsible for Female Foeticide," 2.

[14] Female Feticide: Causes & Effects of Sex-Selective Abortion, September 1, 2015. http://silverstararrow.hubpages.com/hub/Female-Feticide-Causes-Effects-and-Solutions (accessed on 09/09/15).

[15] Kushwaha and Sharma, "Factors Responsible for Female Foeticide," 2.

production of these types of machines."[16] FF has built a booming industry made profitable by the demand for equipment that will help in the detection of female foetus and has also resulted in the easy availability of such equipment. This contributes towards the disregard for the dignity of female life as long as money is made off of it.

Last but not the least, mothers are themselves the perpetrator of such a crime. This could be accounted for their mentality steeped in the tradition of patriarchy that attaches pride and glory to male children. They are often more concerned for their standing in the society as a mother of sons. The mothers could also be pressured by her in-laws or her husband to abort the foetuses once they know it's a girl. And they do so to please them and affirm their preference for male children, too.

(d) Consequences of FF[17]

Aborting a female foetus is not the end of the story; the act results in a couple of events that are detrimental to the life and future of the Indian population:

(i) Skewed sex ratio (Panipat, Hariyana has among the lowest child sex ratio in the country, 837 girls to 1000 boys)[18] which will result in the need to import brides.
(ii) Scarcity of women will lead to female/women trafficking.
(iii) Availability of few women will result in increase in rape and assault in a society driven by a testosterone high.
(iv) Abortion of female foetus is not a remedy for the boom in population. It will only lead to decline in population when there will only be few women to give birth.

(e) The Indian Christian Church and the Issue of FF

In India, FF comes under the umbrella of women's issues. It is listed as one of the many problems faced by women and is often dealt with in the context of other women's issues. For the Christian community, it is taken for granted that human life is precious and therefore, FF might as well be considered a mockery of Christian faith. However, two official documents of the Catholic Church of

[16] Female Feticide: Causes & Effects of Sex-Selective Abortion, September 1, 2015. http://silverstararrow.hubpages.com/hub/Female-Feticide-Causes-Effects-and-Solutions (accessed on 09/09/15).

[17] Female Feticide: Causes & Effects of Sex-Selective Abortion, September 1, 2015. http://silverstararrow.hubpages.com/hub/Female-Feticide-Causes-Effects-and-Solutions (accessed on 09/09/15).

[18] Himanshi Dhawan, "PM Modi launches 'Beti Bachoa, Beti Padhao' Campaign, says female foeticide is a sign of 'mental illness,'" *Times New Network*, Jan 23, 2015 (accessed on 04/08/15).

India, have listed FF as a grave concern which the Church needs to address. Below are the statements for provision:

> Strictly enforce laws against prenatal sex selection, female foeticide, female infanticide, child marriage, child abuse, child prostitution, child trafficking and child labour.[19]
>
> The entire church should be involved in providing needed personnel; budget and infrastructure for the campaigns for women empowerment. These campaigns which should cover both clergy and the laity, should aim at changing the mind-sets, by creating a deeper awareness of women's issues and presenting a relevant vision of the role of women in the Church and society. It should also address concrete issues such as female foeticide, neglect of girl child, Domestic Violence, female trafficking, Child sexual abuse, Rights of daughters to care for parents, Duty of men to care for parents-in-law, Right of women to participate in decision making bodies at all levels and Duties of men to facilitate women's participation in public sphere, should become the subjects of the campaign. Special attention must be given to target at bringing about mindset changes in the adolescent boys and youth.[20]

FF is a national concern and that makes it a concern of the Indian Christians too. The provision for the Church's involvement in the issue of FF is considerate and praiseworthy but this essay would like to suggest what could be a more effective way of dealing with the issue. It would like to draw from the Letter to Philemon a few pointers especially from Paul's manner of appeal and how they could be used to address a grave issue such as FF. It proposes Paul's appeal for a slave as a biblical model for addressing the issue of FF in India.

2. The Letter to Philemon

Philemon is the shortest Pauline letter in the New Testament understood to be from Paul to Philemon. It contains the usual Pauline greeting, a praise for Philemon's seemingly good work in terms of his love and faith in Christ and an appeal on behalf of Onesimus, Philemon's slave, which takes up almost two thirds of the letter. The letter ends on Paul's request to prepare him a room for his supposed visit followed by his final greetings and benediction.

The main concern of the letter to Philemon is Paul's plea for Onesimus, the slave of Philemon. The appeal takes the form of a letter. Letters contain stories from which the narrative worlds of both the letters and stories are constructed,

---

[19] Empowerment of Women in the Church and Society. Gender Policy of the Catholic Church of India (New Delhi: CBCI Centre, 2010), 26.

[20] Kerala Catholic Bishops' Council Gender Policy (Kerala), 5.

in this case the context of Paul's letter to Philemon.[21] Letters accomplish what the sender cannot accomplish in person. According to Petersen, there are three aspects of social relationship implied in the sending of letters. They are: a letter presupposes the existence or non-existence of a previous relationship; a letter received marks a new moment or event in the relationship between the sender and receiver and, a letter implies the expectation of the receiver's response.[22] A letter also encompasses the rhetoric of the sender, Paul in the context of the letter to Philemon. Witherington calls Philemon, and Colossians "rhetorically-shaped letters, being basically oral in character."[23] In the light of this understanding of letters and their social function and the rhetoric used, the context and aspects of Paul's appeal will be looked at.

(a) The Context

The narrative world that can be constructed from the story in the letter is Onesimus, the slave of Philemon whom Paul addresses as a "dear friend and co-worker," is with Paul at Ephesus. Paul writes to Philemon on behalf of Onesimus asking him to welcome back the slave as a beloved brother and to charge it to his (Paul) account any wrong he (Onesimus) may have committed. From what can be gathered from the letter, Philemon was wealthy enough to host the church in his home at Colossae, if he is the Philemon mentioned in Col 4:9. He had been converted through Paul's ministry and is involved in the ministry of the church. Paul's address of others in his seemingly private letter indicates that it ought to be read to the church as a whole, what Dunn calls "a factor which influences the character of the whole appeal."[24]

(b) The Appeal

Paul's appeal to Philemon has often been compared to an ancient letter that Pliny the Younger wrote to a slave owner, Sabinianus, on behalf of a freedman who had incurred his master's wrath.[25] In the letter, he speaks of the master's justifiable anger with the freedman at the same time that he acknowledges the freedman's penitence and appeal for forgiveness, and who has been rightly warned of future punishments in case of repeated offence. Paul, on the other hand, speaks on behalf of a slave which made it a little more complicated than the case of Pliny's freedman. He does not speak of anger or penitence or threats of punishment.[26]

---

[21] Norman R. Petersen, *Rediscovering Paul. Philemon and the Sociology of Paul's Narrative World* (Philadelphia: Fortress Press, 1985), 43.

[22] Petersen, *Rediscovering Paul*, 63.

[23] Witherington, *The Letters to Philemon, the Colossians, and the* Ephesians, 3.

[24] James D. G. Dunn, *The Epistles to the Colossians and to Philemon: A Commentary on the Greek Text* (Michigan: Eerdmans, 1996), 301.

[25] David E. Garland, *Colossians and Philemon* (Michigan: Zondervan, 1998), 312.

[26] Garland, *Colossians and Philemon,* 312.

Instead, he asks Philemon to welcome him back as a brother and even more so as if he were welcoming Paul himself. The aspects of Paul's appeal are being dealt with in three sections: Paul as a Friend (1-7), Paul as an Intercessor (8-16) and Paul as a Partner (17-25).

(i) Paul as a Friend (1-7)

Paul identifies himself as a prisoner of Jesus Christ (vv1) on which Witherington comments, "[r]hetorically this is an effective tactic in that it already generates sympathy for Paul."[27] Dunn says that Paul's style of beginning the letter "immediately generates emotion and concern for him."[28] He also further identifies himself as the fellow co-worker and friend (vv 1) to Philemon, gives an introductory address (vv 2-3) and then gives the introduction of his plea for Onesimus (vv 4-5). He begins his letter by praising Philemon for possessing ἀγάπῃ 'love' in vvs[29] 5 and 7. The phrase, 'love for all the saints,' was used by Paul to indicate Philemon's willingness to share his valuable contribution, both material and spiritual, to the welfare of the little church community. Paul points out that this same genuine character of Philemon's faith and attitude of liberality should be extended with any given opportunity (vv 6).[30] Praising him is a rhetoric tactic that Paul is using to appeal to Philemon's inner emotions and thereby put him in a receptive frame of mind and make him oblige to the request he was going to make.[31] The obligation that Paul expects from Philemon is that his faith and love should be exercised by responding positively to Paul's appeal.[32] Paul does not jump to his appeal immediately. He first of all generates concern for his imprisoned state and appeals to Philemon's emotions. He then builds a rapport with Philemon by praising him for the reports of his good works, so prepares him for another opportunity to exercise his love in such manner. Then he notes the resultant effect of such exercise of love which is ἀναπαύω 'refreshment' of the hearts of the saints and for Paul καιπαράκλησιν ἐπὶ τῇ ἀγάπῃ σου 'even much joy and encouragement' (vv 7).

(ii) Paul as an Intercessor (8-16)

In this section, Paul once again resorts to rhetoric. He uses ἐπιτάσσειν which is a term used to strongly suggest a superior's authority over an inferior (vv 8). This term indicates "how potentially grave Paul views the situation"[33] yet he deliberately chooses not to exercise his legitimate right to command him. And

[27] Witherington, *The Letters to Philemon, the Colossians, and the Ephesians*, 53.

[28] Dunn, *The Epistles to the Colossians and Philemon*, 311.

[29] vv. for verses from here on.

[30] William Hendriksen, *Exposition of Colossians and Philemon* (Michigan: Baker Books, 1964), 212.

[31] Witherington, *The Letters to Philemon, the Colossians, and the* Ephesians, 58-59.

[32] Ralph P. Martin, *Ephesians, Colossians, and Philemon* (Atlanta: John Knox, 1991), 142.

[33] Witherington, *The Letters to Philemon, the Colossians, and the Ephesians*, 66.

also as Dunn says, Paul is not referring to the civic duty of Philemon because that would get Onesimus into legal trouble for running away from his master; instead he talks about Philemon's Christian duty and responsibility (vv 9).[34] Then, Paul again refers to himself πρεσβύτης νυνι 'as an old man,' and δέσμιος Χριστοῦ 'Ιησοῦ 'prisoner of Christ' to make his appeal more convincing (vv 9). "This is yet another rhetorical attempt to excite as much sympathetic feeling as he can before he mentions Onesimus and then makes his request."[35] Paul finally broaches the subject of Onesimus in vv 10 by laying a personal claim on Onesimus. He is a father to Onesimus whom he calls ἐμοῦ τέκνου 'my son' (vv 10). His choice of personal relationship calls to mind "one of the most precious and intimate of human relationships."[36] Paul is bound to Onesimus as a father to his son.

To Paul, Onesimus is ἄχρηστον 'useful' though he may have been εὔχρηστον 'useless' for Philemon (vv 11). It is not clear if Paul is making a general assessment here or he is referring to Onesimus' former conduct in his master's household. But the use of the two words is "meant to indicate Onesimus' change of status in his conversion so that his change of social status will be easier to effect."[37] Onesimus is now spiritually a brother and therefore there is no need to hold on to his former social status of a slave. And Paul is sending him back at a great cost as is evidenced by the emotionally-packed phrase ἐμὰ σπλάγχνα 'my own heart' (vv 12) to describe Onesimus. For Paul, Onesimus has become a "profound part of himself, taken into his heart, life, and ministry."[38] He speaks as if he is parting with a part of himself.

Paul wished to keep Onesimus with him so διακονῇ 'he may serve' Paul (vv 13). Here, he seems to equate Philemon's service to Onesimus' service ὑπὲρ σοῦ which indicates how much he has come to consider the usefulness of Onesimus. But he has to send him back not because Onesimus was anxious to go home but because "Roman law demanded that a deserting slave be returned to his legal owner."[39] Paul could not risk straining his relationship with Philemon by keeping Philemon's slave with him without any information whatsoever. In vv 14, a favor is implied but is not specified. But from Paul's emotive rhetorical appeal, his statements of intimate relationship with Onesimus and his stress on Onesimus' usefulness like Philemon himself to Paul, it can be assumed that Paul

---

[34] Dunn, *The Epistles to the Colossians and Philemon*, 288.

[35] Witherington, *The Letters to Philemon, the Colossians, and the Ephesians*, 67.

[36] R. Kent Hughes, *Colossians and Philemon. The Supremacy of Christ* (Westchester: Crossway Books, 1989), 164.

[37] Witherington, *The Letters to Philemon, the Colossians, and the Ephesians*, 74.

[38] Witherington, *The Letters to Philemon, the Colossians, and the Ephesians*, 74.

[39] Bruce B. Barton and Philip Wesley Comfort, *Philippians, Colossians, Philemon* (Wheaton: Tyndale, 1995), 260.

wanted Philemon to welcome back Onesimus cordially and then send him back for service to Paul.[40]

Paul does not talk about what Onesimus has done to his master, instead he affirms that Onesimus had indeed run away but ascribes this to be the work of God (vv 15-16). This is rhetoric to motivate Philemon so that he may discern a "larger divine design beyond the surface reality"[41] of what had happened. Onesimus is no longer to be a slave for Philemon but ἀδελφὸν ἀγαπητόν 'a beloved brother,' like he is to Paul. But Paul stresses more on the implications for Philemon, δὲ μᾶ λλον σοὶ καὶ ἐν σαρκὶ καὶ ἐν κυρίῳ and much more to you, both in flesh and in the Lord.'This could be a reference to the changed relation of Onesimus and Philemon in two circles – the household and the church,"[42] a result of the spiritual transformation that has taken place in Onesimus.

(iii) Paul as a Partner (17-25)

Paul makes the appeal to Philemon by indirectly stating that he considers him to be a fellow worker who shares his priorities of the work and ministry of the Gospel (vv 17). Paul offers Philemon "an appeal that elicits a partnership to be freely accepted."[43] For Witherington, "the request that follows is built on the fact of this existing partnership in ministry."[44] Therefore, Paul is confident "that Philemon would know how to put the righting of Onesimus' wrong in its proper perspective"[45] by welcoming Onesimus as if he was welcoming Paul himself. His failure to do so would mean a violation of the relationship and partnership that Paul believes they both share.

Paul offers to pay for whatever Onesimus owes to Philemon (vv 18). However, this offer is made in the light of Paul being Philemon's spiritual patron. Philemon is as much obliged to Paul even as Onesimus is and Onesimus' debt is canceled by Philemon's own debt which is expressed by Paul as καὶ σεαυτόν μοι προσοφείλεις 'even your own self' (vv 19). "The force of Paul's words is neither coercive nor paternalistic but firmly persuasive."[46] Witherington also says in vv 19, Paul mentions the very thing that he says he will not mention.[47] It indicates the employment of rhetoric to imply that as "Philemon was saved by grace, though undeserving, so let him be gracious to the repentant Onesimus."[48] Showing such grace would be for Paul a ὀναίμην 'benefit' (vv 20). Paul here

[40] Witherington, *The Letters to Philemon, the Colossians, and the Ephesians*, 76.

[41] Witherington, *The Letters to Philemon, the Colossians, and the Ephesians*, 79.

[42] Anthony Lee Ash, *Philippians, Colossians & Philemon* (Joplin: College Press, 1994), 17.

[43] John A. Zeisler, *Pauline Christianity* (New York and Oxford: Oxford University Press, 1983), 120.

[44] Witherington, *The Letters to Philemon, the Colossians, and the Ephesians*, 79.

[45] Dunn, *The Epistles to the Colossians and to Philemon*, 337.

[46] Robert W. Wall, *Colossians & Philemon* (Downers Grove: InterVarsity, 1993), 18.

[47] Witherington, *The Letters to Philemon, the Colossians, and the Ephesians*, 85.

[48] Ash, *Philippians, Colossians & Philemon*, 19.

uses ὀναίμην which most closely approximates the verb from which the name Onesimus is derived implying a word play-let your benefit be 'Beneficial.'[49] Again he refers to ἀναπαύωas in vv 7. Paul is confident that his rhetoric will have the likely result of persuading Philemon whom he is sure will do even more than he has asked; welcoming Onesimus not as a slave but as a brother and even sending him back to Paul (vv 21). ἅμα δὲ καὶ (vv 22) is "Paul's attempt to link the plea for Onesimus with his request for hospitality for himself."[50] The rest of the letter (vv 23-25) deals with the final greetings and the closing benediction.

(c) Paul and the Situation of Onesimus

Paul is making a plea for a person who was a slave in a time when slavery was an important institution of the society's economy. The Greco-Roman society in I Century CE was a slave dependent economy.[51] Like the slaves of the OT, the slaves were prisoners of war, foreigners and those kidnapped or separated from their families. Slavery was not defined by race or creed but was solely a matter of revenue.[52] Slaves were goods that were sold off and bought and over whom the owners had exclusive rights, "which meant that the owners who were responsible for protecting their slaves also had the legal right to inflict punishment and even death."[53] The life and conditions of the slaves therefore depended on the owners who could choose to do with them what they wished to. Those who owned slaves could own from few hundreds to even thousands of them.[54] The works of slaves range from hard labor in the fields or mines to domestic works in and out of the house, a position which Onesimus is believed to have held.[55] Another kind of work was management of their owners' estates especially if the owners were wealthy and prominent in the society because of their expertise in law, medicine and teaching.[56]

The slaves belonged to their owners exclusively and freedom, if they want it, was only attained by running away. However, laws came to be enacted which made a runaway slave a fugitive and if found, the owner could even punish him

[49] Ash, *Philippians, Colossians & Philemon*, 20.

[50] Witherington, *The Letters to Philemon, the Colossians, and the Ephesians*, 86.

[51] Bonnie B. Thurston and Judith Ryan, *Philippians and Philemon*, Sacra Pagina, vol. 10 (ed. Daniel J. Harrington; Minnesota: Liturgical, 2005), 174.

[52] Tacitus, *Ann.* 13.21 cited in Moses I. Finley, *Ancient Economy* (Berkley: University of California Press, 1985), 72.

[53] Keith R. Bradley, *Slaves and Masters in the Roman Empire: A Study in Social Control* (New York: Oxford University Press, 1987), 15-16.

[54] Tacitus, *Ann.* 14.43.4, cited in Bradley, *Slaves and Masters*, 15-16.

[55] Raymond E. Brown, *An Introduction to the New Testament* (New York: Doubleday, 1997), 503-505.

[56] Dale Martin, *Slavery as Salvation: The Metaphor of Slavery in Pauline Christianity* (New Haven: Yale University Press, 1990), 11-22.

with death and anyone who helped such a runaway slave was guilty before the law.[57] However, slaves could approach or find refuge with the friend of their owner who could mediate "benefit to both the parties involved."[58] The friend (*amicus domini*) could "legally provide temporary refuge but might still be responsible for any financial loss to the slaveowner."[59]

The closest to freedom that the slaves could get was being manumitted. This happens when the slaves bought off their freedom. Manumission was not liberation in the modern sense of the term, it was limited freedom and they still remained obligated to their previous owners. Tacitus wrote that the manumitted slave who failed to show grateful reverence to his former owner should be punished.[60] The manumitted slave was still considered a slave and there was little change in his status in the society. The only change perhaps was s/he had a voice in the society which a slave did not have.[61]

Slavery in the Greco-Roman society, therefore, was a commercial business where the slaves had little or no access to justice. They had no voice in the society and their owners had exclusive rights over them, even their very lives. Not all slaves could buy their freedom but those who could do so were manumitted to enjoy limited freedom in the society though they could not completely break themselves off from their previous owners. And for such a slave caught in the situation of slavery, Paul exercises his rhetoric of persuasion so it could result in the establishment of a Christian love between slaves and masters. Paul is seeking for a master-slave relationship that is counter to what the society establishes.

(d) Paul's Rhetoric of Persuasion

From the exegesis of the letter, what can be gathered is Paul's prominent use of rhetoric in the plea for Onesimus with the aim to persuade Philemon in his performance of his obligatory Christian duty. In the first century world where rhetoric was "relished and applauded," Paul needed a "very strident and bold rhetoric" to deal with a situation like slavery which is a by-product of "power inequities in relationships and social inequities."[62] He employed the normal rhetorical conventions by combining references to persuasion and command and repeated appeal to the emotions to make his discourse achieve the goal of its intention.[63] By using familial words like 'brother,' 'son,' 'father' in his plea, Paul is hinting, at a larger level, his vision of a Christian family where all the members are

[57] Thurston and Ryan, *Philippians and Philemon*, 171.

[58] Thurston and Ryan, *Philippians and Philemon*, 174.

[59] Alan Watson, *Roman Slave Law* (Baltimore: John Hopkins University Press, 1987), 171.

[60] Tacitus, *Ann.* 13:26 cited in Andrew Wallace-Hadrill, ed., *Patronage in Ancient Society* (London: Routledge, 1989), 33.

[61] Thurston and Ryan, *Philippians and Philemon*, 172.

[62] Witherington, *The Letters to Philemon, the Colossians, and the Ephesians*, 87.

[63] Witherington, *The Letters to Philemon, the Colossians, and the Ephesians*, 87.

equal before God. There are reasons to believe his appeal was met with a positive response since the letter was preserved, copied and circulated in the early church. Thurston and Ryan do not claim that Onesimus was freed as a slave but they believe enough freedom[64] is given to him to accompany Paul in God's ministry (Col 4:7-9). Bruce suggests that Onesimus preserved the letter as a charter of his freedom.[65]

Paul's rhetorical plea in dealing with a difficult situation is a good example for Christians in this age and time. He dealt with the grave issue of slavery which dehumanizes and distorts the God-given dignity of human beings by the use of persuasion in evoking a sense of Christian responsibility from Philemon. Brute force is not an answer to problems, instead Paul shows that persuasion could enable others to embrace our vision as their own. God also, who Himself is the Lord of lords "prefers to operate as Lover, wooing his people to do the right thing and be their best selves."[66] The situation that Paul addressed was grave and urgent, a human life was at stake and he used his eloquent rhetoric prowess to thwart the situation for the benefit of the one for whom the plea was made and for himself and Philemon in working out παντὸς ἀγαθοῦ τοῦ 'all the good' which signifies the blessings of redemption in Christ and which should prompt the receivers to respond to God and to all fellow human beings in love.[67]

3. Paul's Rhetoric of Persuasion as a Biblical Model for Approaching FF

In the Indian context, the issue of female foeticide dehumanizes just as slavery in the Philemon context did. They indeed present two very different contexts (slavery and FF) but the focus here is on the similar element of dehumanization that constitutes the graveness of both the issues. And this essay is an attempt to prove the hypothesis that what the Christians need when dealing with the issue of FF is the rhetoric of persuasion after the example of Paul. This rhetoric is not to the perpetrators of the crime because their identity is unknown; it is to the Christians individually and corporately. The rhetoric of persuasion will evoke in others the same passion and responsibility that is in us. The appeal or the persuasion is to be based on love, just like Paul's rhetoric was based on love in Christ.

Love in Christ is a love which is genuine and self-giving, a love which transcends all human-made barriers of caste, race, gender, color and status. It is a love which transforms relationships, imparts importance to the 'social liabilities,' and sets a social equilibrium. It reclaims and restores the human dignity that has been corrupted. It clothes an individual with all the splendid worth it was originally created with. It does not identify someone as rich, poor, female, male, slave or free. Instead it considers the human aspects of each individual and ascribes their

---

[64] Thurston and Ryan, *Philippians and Philemon*, 192.

[65] F. F. Bruce, *Paul, Apostle of the Heart Set Free* (Grand Rapids: Eerdmans, 1977), 406.

[66] Witherington, *The Letters to Philemon, the Colossians, and the Ephesians*, 94.

[67] Hendriksen, *Exposition of Colossians and Philemon*, 213.

value as a human accordingly. It sees each individual as human and therefore, each individual matters because of his/her possession of the worth ascribed to humans by this love that is in Christ. With this same love, Paul raises his voice so that his fellow believers may also see in Onesimus all the goodness and worth he carries as a human being created by God. Paul asks them to remove the biased shades put on their eyes by the society. He calls for them to see him with the love in Christ so they may see and regard him for the human he is, and not his identity as slave.

It is with this love in Christ that an appeal for the unborn lives should be made. Like Paul, let us appeal to our church, our neighbors and our community because a life is at stake. By the choice of our words, our tone and our gestures, let us tug at the strings of their emotions so that their hearts may stir in compassion and evoke in them a sense of Christian duty and love for neighbors which can result in a fight for the eradication of this evil in our society. The Christian church is a redeemed church and our blessings should overflow in the service towards our neighbors even if it may be an experience we have not personally undergone throguh. Wright says "Living Christianity makes people more human, not less. No Christian should grumble at the extra demands of love, and in so doing become more fully oneself in Christ, more completely in the image of God, more authentically human."[68] Only when we show empathy, respect and love to others do we connect with them as humans and in the process, we realize how human we are as well.[69]

The same rhetoric of persuasion can also be used for the non-Christian community. India is a pluralistic society and the non-Christian community may not be familiar with the love of Christ as much as the Christians do. Therefore, the love of Christ in our hearts may not stir their heart in compassion and they may not be moved to action. But if we were to speak to them in a way that evokes their innate love for their fellow beings, their inherent sense of respect for others, their distinct emotion of solidarity with other humans and their awe of the mystery of life at the deepest level of their conscience, they too will make our passion their own, our vision their own and they will definitely work for the eradication of FF in India.

4. Implications of Paul's Rhetoric of Persuasion for Indian Christians/ Churches' Approach to FF

For Christians, each person is created in the image of God stated very clearly in the creation story and David's psalm (139:13-14), which acknowledges God to be the One who formed his inward parts and knit him together in his mother's womb. Based on Paul's Rhetoric of Persuasion, the Indian Christians/Churches could involve themselves in the difficult situation of FF through the following ways. Since, Paul made his appeal in a different context to a different issue, the

[68] N. T. Wright, *Colossians and Philemon* (Grand Rapids: Eerdmans, 1980), 180.

[69] Witherington, *The Letters to Philemon, the Colossians, and the Ephesians*, 94.

following principles are mere derivatives and not an exact reproduction of the appeal.

(a) Be a Voice for the Voiceless

Proverbs 31:8-9 says "speak out for those who cannot speak, for the rights of all the destitute...speakout...." Isaiah 1:17 says "learn to do good; seek justice, rescue the oppressed, defend the orphan; plead for widow." Like Paul did for Onesimus (though a different context), speak for every unborn baby, not over them or for them, but on behalf of them. Plead for their right to be born, to be alive and to take their first breath. Evoke the emotion of love for these tiny lives growing in the womb. Use your words to ascribe due regard for the dignity and sanctity of life. Be a reminder of the precious worth of each human life. Appeal to the tender side of the conscience which considers life as a miracle and a wonder. Call out to imagine the joys and laughter which baby girls can bring aplenty. Be the voice of the baby girl inside the womb of her mother.

(b) Make One Life Count

A life created in the image of God cannot be useless or worthless or without purpose. Each life is precious and sacred and carries the worth and dignity with which it was created in the first place. Each life bears within it the possibilities and the right to be someone, to be heard, to be respected, to be afforded equal chances, to make one's experiences and perspectives matter. Let this message get across to everyone and let them remember, if they have forgotten, that they should not deny a baby girl the chance to be in the world like they are. The female foetus is a life that is going to take shape soon and she is a personality unlike no other and she is important in the divine scheme of things. Propagate that who she is, who she will be, what she can achieve and what she can be matters, more than anyone can imagine. She does not deserve to be killed as much as anyone who is alive. She does not deserve to be denied the opportunity to live. Make her life count.

(c) Instigate the Community (of Faith) to Act

Speak up, make others understand the graveness of the situation and get the community (of faith) to act. Christians are beings of free will and free choice which they must learn to exercise towards the eradication of FF as a social evil in India. Spread awareness of the extant prevalence of FF, explain the disastrous impact that is beginning to show in the sex ratio, describe the horrendous methods used to abort the female foetuses, ascribe significance to the human life that is within the female foetus, awaken the sense of responsibility for another human life, derive compassion for the tiny innocent female babies condemned to mass female genocide, denounce the people involved in the business of illegal abortions and the industry that produces the CVS, amniocentesis, and ultrasound, and make plans with the community to combat this evil practice in the Indian society.

Conclusion

Humans are all subject to change. Change is a universal phenomenon that shapes the relations and interactions of and within social systems. It also gives rise to different societal ills that affect the lives of those who make up the society. As members of the society, Christians have an important role to play in the eradication and alleviation of certain social ills. The social ills that dehumanize and degrade life, even to the point of termination, are of the utmost concern. Such one social evil is FF in India. FF is the cruellest act that humans could ever commit because it involves destroying a person even before she has taken the first breath. It is an inhumane act propelled by traditional and technological absurd reasons and carried out in a brutal manner. It leaves its marks on the psychology and body of the mother. It threatens the life and future of the Indian population. Christians are aware of it and the Church has made a provision in its official documents to ensure strict laws against it. This essay is an attempt to propose a biblical model of approaching FF in India. In a different time and different context, Paul addressed a social issue, slavery, and without an exercise of authority or brute force, he beautifully makes an appeal for the case of a person devalued and dehumanized by the social system of slavery. He employs the rhetoric of persuasion to evoke a voluntary humane attitude, Christian responsibility and duty through love in Christ, in the owner of the slave. The same rhetoric of persuasion has been suggested in the approach to FF in India. With this rhetoric of persuasion, let us raise a voice for these unborn girls, make their life count and instigate the community, both Christian and non-Christian, to respond voluntarily and compassionately through love in Christ and love for humanity so that FF in India can be eradicated.

Part 3

Philosophical, Theological & Religious Perspectives

9

Moving beyond the Rhetoric
Plato, Paul and Substantial Social Change

John Jebaseelan

Introduction

"Social change is primarily the restructuring of human social institutions and social conditions" explains the concept paper of this book. In the past, pulpits had been powerful instruments in bringing out this social change. Edwin Charles Dargan in his book 'A History of Preaching' says, "The life and progress of nations, the rise and fall of governments have often been closely connected with preaching... Preaching has profoundly and for the most part wholesomely influenced the morals and customs of mankind."[1] One could think of John Wesley and the complete transformation he brought out in the society of eighteenth century England and the Puritan preachers in bringing a social order into the new world of America. One can never forget the role of preachers in aiding the political activism to bring apartheid in South Africa to an end and claiming equality for blacks in America. These brave people preached the Word of God, undiluted from the pulpits and brought significant change in the souls of the hearers. These examples show that Pulpits, if used properly, could bring out a complete transformation in the society.

But sadly, we do not see these kinds of tectonic change happening in our Christian community, let alone society, through the correct use of pulpits. One of the reasons is that today's preacher is not aware of the power to change offered by

[1] Edwin Charles Dargan, "A History of Preaching" (Grand Rapids: Baker Book House, 1974), 8-9.

the pulpit and sticks instead to mere rhetoric which entertains people and keep them happy by saying what they want to hear.

This paper will try to understand the role of preaching in the process of bringing out substantial social change. This will be done by studying the attitude of Plato and Paul towards rhetoric in their works *Gorgias* and *1 Corinthians* respectively. Plato offers a secular perspective and Paul provides a biblical perspective. The final observations from these two works will be used to find the role rhetoric plays in the pulpits towards bringing a substantial social change.

1. Plato

Plato lived during a time when rhetoric was a way of public life. For the Greeks of Classical Athens, in which Plato lived and worked, public speaking is a pivotal thing which defined and measured the success of a person. In Greek city-states the role of citizens took three forms, "holding office, attending Assembly, and participating in the courts, whether as a litigant or judge."[2] The important decisions for the city were taken by deliberation in the Assembly and the disputes between people were settled in the courts. The officials were selected by lot, among the citizens, for one year. In this set up, the art of persuasion which is called Rhetoric emerged and became the way of Greek life.

Thus, due to these needs, there arose a class of men named Sophists, who taught people how to argue and speak. They collected fees for imparting skills of rhetoric. The dialogue of Plato – *Gorgias*, which is referred to in this paper, consists of three such Sophists arguing with Socrates. They claimed to make anyone appear intelligent, taught their students to argue in favour or against any proposition irrespective of the truth in it, and claimed to enable anyone to persuade the masses on any given subject irrespective of the level of knowledge they have about it.

(a) Plato's *Gorgias*

Plato's dialogue *Gorgias* is the account of the conversation, Socrates, the protagonist of the dialogue, has with Gorgias and his two friends: Polus and Callicles. This dialogue at length deals with how Gorgias and his friends Polus and Callicles use rhetoric for their personal and professional gain. Through dialectic arguments, Socrates asks them about the nature of persuasion that rhetoric produces and the end result of such persuasion, etc. Before the end of the dialogue, we learn each one's position clearly through systematic questioning of Socrates. Polus claims that by rhetoric one can achieve supreme power to do whatever they want – even anything evil. Callicles assert that by the law of nature only a strong person ought

[2] David Cohen, "The Politics of Deliberation: Oratory and Democracy in Classical Athens" in *A Companion to Rhetoric and Rhetorical Criticism*, edited by Walter Jost and Wendy Olmsted (Malden: Blackwell Publishing, 2004), 24.

to rule over the weak and this strength could be gained by a person through rhetoric alone.

Socrates ends the dialogue by explaining how the rhetoric should be used for the upliftment of the soul of fellow human being. How this act of persuasion could be used to live a life of virtue and improve the society at large. He especially talks to the politicians of his days about the ethical use of rhetoric. Because, Politicians use rhetoric to advance their own career and forget the uplifting the lives of people.

(b) Plato's Critique of Rhetoric in Gorgias

In his dialogue *Gorgias,* Plato critiques his contemporary society's obsession with rhetoric. It is not rhetoric per se that he is in loggerheads with, but the way rhetoric, the art of persuasion, is used by the Athenians. He raises several ethical issues in their use of rhetoric. In the beginning of the dialogue itself, Socrates – the protagonist of the dialogue, distinguishes his method of simple conversation against the 'display-speech' (*epideixis*) which Gorgias is doing. In his opinion, a pompous speech will not teach the truth to anyone, only a conversation where issues are discussed elaborately would bring out the truth.

Socrates also points out that the conviction which is produced by rhetorical persuasion is based on belief and not knowledge, thus loses the permanency, depth and reason. He also accuses them of using rhetoric to gain power over others through gratifying the desires than helping or improving the life of Athenians. The politicians of his day spoke things which pleased Athenians to retain their power and never uttered anything which would be hard and bitter at the time of hearing, but good for them in the long run. The Classical Athenians associated the ability to speak well and defeat others in arguments in Assembly or Court as success. But Socrates says that investigating truth through these speeches and striving to find the truth is more important than being victorious in debate. Thus, when he has conversation with anyone on any issue, he says that he is just a fellow-seeker of truth and not a person who knows everything already.

Another defect in the Classical Athenians' use of rhetoric is playing with the emotions of the masses in assembly or court instead of making them think logically. At one point in the dialogue, when Polus was trying to emotionally work up things against Socrates, Socrates remarks "While I thought you admirably well trained in oratory, you seemed to me to have neglected the art of reasoning."[3] By this, Socrates is pointing out to the lack of logic in what Polus is saying. To the politicians of his days, Plato is telling through Socrates that they should use the rhetoric to do justice and they ought to stop manipulating truth. Socrates says to Callicles, "in the event of any wrongdoing, a man should be ready to accuse himself or his son or his friend, and that this was the end for which oratory should

[3] Plato, *Gorgias*, translated by Walter Hamilton and Chris Emlyn-Jones (London: Penguin Books, 2004), 44.

be employed."[4] He also says that a person should readily suffer wrong than to increase his pleasure through manipulation.

Plato, though seems to condemn the practice of rhetoric in *Gorgias*, is actually trying to redeem it from the clutches of the selfish politicians who persuade masses for their gain. Instead, he tries to make the art of persuasion a tool to improve the lives of people and make their Souls better. At the end of the dialogue, Socrates says, "Then our orator, the good man of expert knowledge, will have these ends in view in any speech or action by which he seeks to influence the souls of men."[5] In midst of people who used the knack of persuasion to gain power, Plato acted as conscience keeper by sounding the alarm bell and sought a clear change of course from his contemporaries. He believed that if the art of rhetoric was practised in a proper way, it would bring change, not only in the lives of individuals, but also in the society at large.

2. Paul

Paul also lived in a time when rhetoric was much in use both in the society and within the Christian community. Preaching, or Public proclamation of the Gospel to the gentiles is the central activity of the Christian Church from its birth. Early Church flourished and expanded due to the preaching of the apostles. The very genesis of the Church itself rests on the 'first and possibly most fruitful sermon ever preached' by Simon Peter on the day of Pentecost after the ascension of Jesus Christ which brought three thousand people into the messianic fold[6] (Acts 2). Then, when the Church grew in number, the apostles determined that they would spend time only in the 'ministry of the word of God' and delegated the administrative responsibilities to other capable men (Acts 6:2). The Book of Acts is full of accounts of several preaching and public discourses of teaching and defending the Christian faith. The content of the preaching (*kerygma*) was described in the New Testament as 'Christ Jesus' or 'the Crucified Christ' or 'word of faith' or 'the Messiah' or 'the Kingdom of God.'[7] Thus, the preaching or the public oratory, whose content is 'Jesus,' was and is one of the ways, through which God chose to touch and turn the hearts of people to Him.

(a) Paul's Preaching in Corinth

Paul was a zealous apostle. He claims that he is 'set apart for the gospel of God' (Rom 1:1). In Acts 9:20, the Bible says that he did not wait for long after his conversion experience, but he 'began to preach in the synagogues that Jesus is the Son of God'. This task of preaching the gospel entailed "hard work (1 Cor

---

[4] Ibid, 107.

[5] Ibid, 100.

[6] Earle E. Cairns, *Christianity through the Centuries* (Thiruvalla: SuVartha Bhavan, 2004), 60.

[7] J. B. Polhill, "Kerygma and Didache," *Dictionary of the Later New Testament and its Developments*, edited by Ralph P. Martin and Peter H. Davids (Leicester: InterVarsity Press, 1997), 626.

15:10; 2 Cor 11: 24-28), facing strong opposition (1 Thess 2:2), suffering (2 Tim 1:8) and even imprisonment (Phil 1:16; Eph 6:19-20; Philem 13)."[8] Paul, who is superior in his lineage, educational training and suffering for the gospel than other apostles, considers all these things as loss for Christ. Thus for Christ he adapts and adopts so that through his preaching and life, Christ would be glorified.

Paul, who is well educated and who has written unparalleled eloquent portions of the Bible with masterful rhetorical devises like Philippians 4, Romans 8 and 1 Corinthians 13, says in 1 Corinthians 1: 17 that Christ sent him to preach the gospel 'not with words of human wisdom' and in 2 Corinthians 11: 6 that he was 'not a trained speaker'. In Corinth, a cosmopolitan city of ancient Greece, where rhetoric and speaking well can guarantee good following, Paul was avoiding it.

In 1 Corinthians 1: 17 he confesses that he does not preach with 'wisdom and eloquence', but does this necessarily follow that Paul was naive in rhetorical training? When we see his writings, his language and style surpasses any other New Testament author. His use of rhetorical devises to persuade his readers in his writings betray his claim to ignorance. Though, scholars like Pogoloff[9] argues that Paul, like the ancient rhetor Isocrates, must be good in producing written rhetorical pieces and not well versed with presenting it himself, we could dismiss this by pointing out that it is not through his epistles that many were converted but through his preaching and teaching activity. Book of Acts testifies to his extensive preaching tours which paved way for many Christian communities in the Roman world. Then the only possibility is that Paul is using the phrase 'untrained speaker' in a sarcastic way to counter the allegation of Corinthians, which itself is clever use of rhetoric.

He may not have had formal and advance training in rhetoric but he definitely had a superior knowledge in the use of rhetoric. Supporting this view, Paul Barnett says, "Few places he visited did not appear to lack a messianic assembly as a result of his ministry. His verbal skills must have been, at the very least, adequate, and, quite possibly, considerable, even though he lacked the high professionalism of the trained rhetorician."[10] Murray J. Harris also says the same thing regarding Paul's training in rhetoric. He says, "There is no unambiguous evidence that Paul had mastered the arts of rhetoric through tertiary-level training under a recognized Sophist, but even if he was not formally trained in rhetoric,

---

[8] R. H. Mounce, "Preaching, Kerygma," *Dictionary of Paul and His Letters,* editors Gerald F. Hawthorne and Ralph P. Martin (Leicester: InterVarsity Press, 1993), 735.

[9] S. M. Pogoloff, *Logos and Sophia: The Rhetorical Situation of 1 Corinthians* (Atlanta: Scholars Press, 1992), 149.

[10] Paul Barnett, *The Second Epistle to the Corinthians* (Grand Rapids, Michigan: William B. Eerdmans Publishing Company, 1997), 510.

he must have been familiar with the rhetorical fashions of his time and area."[11] It is therefore clear that Paul was not naive to the rhetorical traditions of his times and his writings and other speeches in the bible are witnesses to this fact. Just like Plato who 'derided the art of sophists' by deploying 'great eloquence in the very process of refuting them', Paul is also using lots of rhetoric to deny the claims of the accusers.[12]

Corinth, in which Paul was avoiding the use of rhetoric, was a Greek cosmopolitan city because of its harbour and flourishing trade through the principal sea routes. It was steeped in the culture of Ancient Greece. Paul ministered to Corinthians for a year and a half (Acts 18: 11). He had written the two letters, which we have in the New Testament, to the Corinthians. In both the letters he defends his ministry from the accusation that he did not speak like an orator. The 'rhetorical milieu' of Corinth was just like any other Greek city of his time, as we saw in the Athens of Plato – even though they were five centuries apart. People expected good rhetorical speeches in the Church, just like other secular places and religious gatherings. The same expectations in the secular realm – appreciation for a good speech laden with rhetorical style and not the truth – crept into the church.

Dean Anderson writes about T. H. Tim who talked about this scenario. "He (Tim) tries to understand the text (in which Paul talks about his disdain for rhetoric) against the background of the kind of preachers active in Corinth to whom Paul was opposed. These preachers he characterises as men who took pay for their teaching, as was common among the Sophist of the Second Sophistic, and who also emphasises eloquence for its own sake."[13] So these preachers, whom Paul calls 'super-apostles' (2 Cor 11: 5), were using all rhetorical skills of the culture and appeared superior to Paul who was weak in his body and does not speak like other orators do.

Paul is doing the same thing to Corinth which Plato tried to do in Athens – pointing out the defects in using rhetoric which is not serving the intended purpose. The very rhetoric, which could persuade masses into doing and believing things, became a hindrance in preaching the gospel in Corinth.[14] Paul had to abandon rhetoric in Corinth because of the mind-set of people to listen to good argument with rhetoric than hard truth about the life, which the gospel brings. In 1 Cor 1: 22 & 23 Paul talks about the Greeks who 'look for wisdom' and

[11] Murray J. Harris, *The Second Epistle to the Corinthians* (Grand Rapids, Michigan: William B. Eerdmans Publishing Company, 2005), 749.

[12] Timothy A. Brookins, "Rhetoric and Philosophy in the first century: their relation with respect to 1 Corinthians 1 – 4," *Neotestamentica* 44/2 (2010), 242.

[13] R. Dean Anderson Jr, *Ancient Rhetorical Theory and Paul* (Leuven: Peeters, 1999), 267.

[14] I don't think he is shunning rhetoric in any other city. Even in Athens Paul's speech is eloquent (Acts 17:16-34). But in Corinth because it has become a stumbling block for the people in appropriating the gospel in their lives, Paul is not using it deliberately.

to whom the cross and the Christ crucified is 'foolishness'. Greeks try to see wisdom, not the divine revelation, which all the Greek orators try to display by clever argument, impeccable structure and superior presentation, which is not present in the message of the crucified Christ. This agrees with the position of Ben Witherington III who says, "Paul's opposition is not to rhetoric per se but to any form of speaking that emptied the gospel of its content and power."[15]

(b) Problematic Issues in Rhetoric

For Paul, using rhetoric in Corinth brings several problems. The first we can say is the expectation of 'rhetorical ornamentation' which obscures the message of Cross and its power. Victor Paul says that, "Apparently he [Paul] believes that unadorned speech is more appropriate for conveying the "folly" of the cross, in the very weakness of which God's power is disclosed."[16] It is the conflict between the 'form' and 'content', in which Paul is giving highlight to the content but the Corinthians are looking for the form. In order to emphasise the content and the message, Paul had to abandon the form with which Corinthians are fond of. Paul, in the words of Dean Anderson, is 'contrasting the persuasive power of words with the real tangible proof of the presence of the Holy Spirit.'[17] As Gordon Fee says, "The cross is not something to which one may add human wisdom and thereby make it superior; rather, the cross stands in absolute, uncompromising contradiction to human wisdom."[18]

Secondly the impact of rhetoric would be temporary, as Plato says that it can only produce conviction based on belief and not knowledge. A good rhetorical preaching may win applause from the audience but leave their souls untouched. Anthony Thiselton says, "Rhetoric alone may win the emotions and even the mind and perhaps the will, but the human self is more than all of these modes of being... "psychological" conversion... may result causally from manipulative factors without touching the self's spiritual depths in an authentic turning not simply toward a new set of belief and lifestyle, but to God."[19] Change in the heart and the lifestyle of people will be affected only when it touches the soul of the people. Paul wanted the gospel to show forth the power of God to change people on its own. Just as how Plato wanted rhetoric to touch and improve the soul of the hearers, Paul wanted his preaching of the Cross to be a pathway for them to

[15] Ben Witherington III, *Conflict & Community in Corinth* (Grand Rapids, Michigan: William B. Eerdmans Publishing Company, 1995), 110.

[16] Victor Paul Furnish, *II Corinthians* (New York: Doubleday & Company Inc, 1984), 505.

[17] R. Dean Anderson Jr, *Ancient Rhetorical Theory and Paul* (Leuven: Peeters, 1999), 266.

[18] Gordon D. Fee, *The First Epistle to the Corinthians* (Grand Rapids, Michigan: William B. Eerdmans Publishing Company, 1987), 66.

[19] Anthony C. Thiselton, *The First epistle to the Corinthians* (Grand Rapids, Michigan: William B. Eerdmans Publishing Company, 2000), 146.

experience the power of God to transform their lives and not just to touch their curious minds.

3. Contemporary Preaching

Contemporary preaching in the Indian churches has become mere rhetoric. Contemporary preachers, like politicians of Plato's time and preachers of Paul's time, strive to please the men at the pews and say what the audience wants to hear. It is rare to hear sermons on social evils which prevail in the society. The social evils like discriminations based on caste and status, dowry, female infanticide, etc., are never heard in the pulpits of the Indian churches. Pulpit is not used to guide the congregation to deal and engage with hate-rhetoric of the pseudo-nationalists against the minorities and other political issues which directly affect the Christian community. If more sermons are heard from the pulpits, interpreting the contemporary scenario through the radical words of the Bible, it would definitely bring out change in the individuals and the society.

Daniel Baumann says, "...a sermon has the explicit purpose of eliciting behavioural change...Explicit preaching is directed toward life-style changes."[20] He specifically calls for social-prophetic preaching in the church to effect a social transformation through explicit and implicit preaching about social issues with the support of biblical truth. In the same line, Vima Dasan says, "We need to preach in order to discern for the people the meaning of everyday occurrence in the light of God's kingdom to come; to interpret the signs of the times in the light of the gospel; to spur men on to service in the light of the great commandment to love God and neighbour."[21]

In the same way, Indian Church bodies like National Council of Churches in India and Catholic Bishops' Conference of India urges that 'the laity must bear witness to Christian principles and values and contribute to the creation of a better society through their professional work.'[22] This would become reality only if the pulpits are used effectively to teach, to admonish and to confront the evils of the individuals and the society through the word of God.

Conclusion

What Plato and Paul learned about rhetoric is true for our Pulpits today. Mere rhetoric cannot transform the individuals and the society. It will entertain people for a short period of time and make them forget about it. But thoughtful sermons which interpret the events of the world in the light of the word of God would bring about a great change in the life of the individual and ultimately transform

[20] J. Daniel Baumann, "An Introduction to contemporary preaching" (Grand Rapids, Michigan: Baker Book House, 1981), 205.

[21] Vima Dasan, *Preaching Sharp* (Bangalore: Asia Trading Corporation, 2007), 10.

[22] John Desrochers, *The Social Teaching of the Church in India* (Bangalore: NBCLC/CSA, 2006), 184.

the society. Each preacher should use the pulpit to effect transformation. Plato shunned rhetoric which was used by sophists for individual gain and Paul longed for the power of God to be revealed through the simple, unadorned message of the cross. In the same way the Indian pulpits should be used, not to entertain but, to transform the individual soul and the society.

10

Towards a Dialogue of Subjectiveness in the Upsurge of Homosexual Culture

Nicky Sangma

Introduction

Christianity is an institution deeply involved in social change and therefore has never been a stranger to controversy. Yet, one of the current controversies that plague the Church is people claiming to be Christian in spite of being of alternate sexuality. "Christian homosexuals" maintain that there is no conflict between their religious beliefs, and their sexual orientation – in the West, there are many Christian books, Bibles, Christian support groups, and churches that help propagate this belief. Although such support groups and literature are less common in the Indian Christian community, it is imperative the Indian Church address the issue of homosexuality within and outside the Christian community even before a situation such as in the West arises. Homosexuals will not disappear simply because the Church is not paying them any heed. Rather, homosexuals garner much sympathy and attention from the world at large, and with skilled apologists validating their views; they are likely to gain supporters from the Christian community too. Hegel's dialectical method of thesis, antithesis and synthesis would be a valuable tool to utilize in the formation of a model for dialogue between homosexuals and the Church, especially given the extreme views and tenacious attitudes of both sides.

1. Fundamentals of Social Change

Social change is the change that takes place in social relations as a result of modifications in lifestyles and life patterns of people as a result of all societies being in perpetual flux.[1] Change is one of the inherent characteristics of nature. There is a constant flux in time, civilization, culture, and humankind. Society has been created by change – evolving trends, beliefs, discoveries can be seen to being instrumental in the social metamorphosis, which is evident if examined and compared across time. History itself is the unerring proof of change being the law of life – society has changed from an age of stone tablets filled with commandments, to the age of digital tablets filled with anything and everything. Human beings are social animal and have many relationships with other human beings – society is thus an intricate web of relationships, and hence a change, even in one person, denotes a social change. With any change in a person's usual or traditional behavior comes the beginning of social change, be it in attitudes or in activities, knowledge or personal beliefs.

2. Homosexuality: A Factor in Social Change

Human knowledge is constantly changing, as is human belief; therefore with each change, society itself changes. There is no society that is immune to change. A society may accept an idea in one age, then reject it in the next. One such example of change is homosexuality; once accepted in older civilizations, then widely condemned, there is now an escalating acceptance and consequently, a growing impact of homosexual culture the world over. In the recent past, homosexual adherents have not only become increasingly vociferous, but also have found sympathizers, even among public figures. The renowned and widely respected Tim Cook, CEO of Apple Computers, for instance, revealed his sexual orientation towards the same sex last year after many years of speculation.[2] Taking a cue from numerous liberal European nations, America, the world's most powerful nation, also joined the fore in June 2015 by legalizing gay marriage.[3] Although, there is celebration amongst homosexual groups throughout the world, including in India, fear has started to grip others regarding the change in societal pattern spun by unnatural same gender relationship. Furthermore, tensions are brewing within conservative groups, especially Christians as many mainline churches have accepted same sex relationships and marriages. The present situation is such that even conservative Christians are giving much thought about accepting homosexuality rather than dismissing it, as was the trend about a decade ago. Head of the Vatican, Pope Francis also seemed to condone acceptance of homosexual

---

[1] Puja Mondal, "Essay on Social Change: Meaning, Characteristics and Other Details," accessed November 15, 2015, http://www.yourarticlelibrary.com/sociology/essay-on-social-change-meaning-characteristics-and-other-details/8590/.

[2] Brian X. Chen and Vindu Goel, "Apple's Tim Cook Says That He Is 'Proud to Be Gay' - The New York Times," October 30, 2014, http://www.nytimes.com/2014/10/31/technology/timothy-cook-apples-chief-executive-says-he-is-proud-to-be-gay.html?_r=0, accessed November 2, 2015.

[3] "US Supreme Court Rules Gay Marriage Is Legal Nationwide - BBC News," June 27, 2015, http://www.bbc.com/news/world-us-canada-33290341, accessed November 2, 2015.

behavior by openly encouraging Christians to accept homosexuals as a part of God's creation. In one interview he was quoted as saying:

> A person once asked me, in a provocative manner, if I approved of homosexuality. I replied with another question: 'Tell me: when God looks at a gay person, does he endorse the existence of this person with love, or reject and condemn this person?' We must always consider the person.[4]

Hence, it becomes a matter of grave importance for Christians to engage the rising trend of homosexuality with utmost care and caution.

3. Terminology of Homosexuality

Encarta Dictionaries defines homosexuality as "sexual attraction to or sexual relations with somebody of the same sex," in contrast to heterosexuality, which is defined as "sexual desire or sexual relations between people of opposite sexes."[5] The term homosexual, literally meaning "of the same sex," was first seen in print in 1869.[6] The term gay is synonymous to homosexual – though it is more frequently used for homosexual men, it can be used interchangeably for either gender (e.g. gay men, or gay women). The term lesbian, or lesbianism, used earliest in 1732,[7] is also used for homosexual women. Bisexuality is defined as being "sexually attracted to both men and women, or engaging in both heterosexual and homosexual activity."[8] A transsexual or a transgender is defined as one who does not identify with their anatomical gender with or without undergoing a sex change surgery.[9] This not to be confused with transvestism, which is defined as the "practice of wearing the clothing of the opposite sex for emotional or sexual expression."[10] The acronym LGBT (lesbian, gay, bisexual and transgender) is often used to refer to all the alternate types of sexuality. Another phrase used to describe the group is "person/s of different sexual orientation" or PDSO. For the sake of simplicity and ease of language, the term 'homosexual' will be used to indicate all the above types of alternate sexuality.

---

[4] "Pope Francis Named 'Person of the Year' by Leading Gay Rights Magazine | News | The Independent," accessed November 17, 2015, http://www.independent.co.uk/news/people/news/pope-francis-named-person-of-the-year-by-leading-gay-rights-magazine-9009729.html.

[5] "Feminist Theology," *Microsoft® Encarta® 2009*, DVD (Redmond, WA: Microsoft Corporation, 2008).

[6] "Terminology of Homosexuality," *Wikipedia, the Free Encyclopedia*, July 2, 2015, https://en.wikipedia.org/w/index.php?title=Terminology_of_homosexuality&oldid=669605865.

[7] "Terminology of Homosexuality."

[8] "Feminist Theology."

[9] "Feminist Theology."

[10] "Feminist Theology."

It is not the aim of this discussion to decisively conclude the controversies concerning homosexuality in the Christian context, but it is the author's intention, rather, to understand the dire need for the initiation of meaningful dialogue between the Indian Church and the homosexual community. "The Church" will hereafter refer to the Indian Church, unless otherwise specified.

4. History of Homosexuality

(a) Medical History of Homosexuality

Religious and cultural beliefs aside, from the medical perspective homosexuality was once considered a psychiatric illness. There were many explanations and theories regarding the cause of homosexuality, and thus many treatments to cure it as well. The 19th-century psychologist Richard von Krafft-Ebing considered homosexuality to be entirely hereditary in nature. Sigmund Freud, on the other hand, suggested that it occurred due to faulty psychosocial development and identification with the opposite gender parent during childhood.[11] Alfred Kinsey, a sex researcher, suggested in his 1948 report that people cannot be classified exclusively as having one type of sexuality, as people can have a spectrum of different types of sexual behavior. Although, numerous attempts have been made to prove the genetic cause of homosexuality, no such theory has thus far been either proved or disproved.

Until 1973, the American Psychiatric Association included homosexuality as a psychiatric illness in its manual, Diagnostic and Statistical Manual of Mental Disorders (DSM), listing it among sexual disorders such as pedophilia, necrophilia and sadism. However, in 1973, it was decided (although not unanimously) that since the definition of a psychiatric condition entails either subjective distress, or some generalized impairment in social effectiveness or functioning, homosexuality cannot be included in the same as a significant proportion of homosexuals were generally content with their sexual orientation and were able to function effectively in society. However, a section was added in DSM titled Sexual Orientation Disturbance, which described people interested in others of the same sex and were "either disturbed by, in conflict with, or wish to change their sexual orientation."[12] Homosexuality in itself is no longer considered a psychiatric illness but simply a form of sexual behaviour and the current edition of DSM (DSM5) no longer includes homosexuality as a psychiatric disorder.[13]

---

[11] "Homosexuality | Britannica.com," accessed October 31, 2015, http://www.britannica.com/topic/homosexuality.

[12] "DSM-II Homosexuality Revision - Dsm-Ii_homosexuality_revision.pdf," accessed October 31, 2015, http://www.torahdec.org/downloads/dsm-ii_homosexuality_revision.pdf.

[13] "DSM-II Homosexuality Revision - Dsm-Ii_homosexuality_revision.pdf."

(b) International Scenario

Homosexuality is far from a new problem, or even a temporary social trend. Rampant in ancient times, homosexuality is documented in the infamous (or for the homophile, famous) Sodom and Gomorrah, in ancient Greece, which encouraged homosexuality and bisexuality,[14] and closer to home, the Kama Sutra texts and Khajuraho temples[15] portray homosexual acts. The prevalence of homosexuality in ancient civilizations, however, is a moot point, since if the age of a practice were to endow moral status, murder and adultery would be considered morally acceptable. However, the issue that is new, is the proverbial skeleton walking out of hitherto locked closets to demand a plethora of civil rights such as decriminalization, employment rights, same-sex marriage, even adoption. More worrying is the number of homosexuals who claim to be Christian. The international Church's relationship with homosexuals, if any, was traditionally tense. It is argued that the prevailing orthodox Judeo-Christian homophobic opinions strongly affected the entire world's views on homosexuals, leading to homosexuality being considered evil and unnatural, culminating in cruel and horrifying acts such as medical experimentation during the Second World War.[16] Although, to a lesser degree, homosexuals from Christian backgrounds also reported unjust treatment. They spoke of being subjected to hypocritical judgment and rejection- some were compelled into heterosexual marriages, others forced to remain celibate, and still others "cured" of their homosexuality. The Church conventionally declared homosexuals damned to hell's eternal fires – modern times saw the Church sitting in uncomfortable silence in the midst of bitter debates. It is only recently that some churches, especially in the United States, have welcomed the homosexual flock, performed same-sex marriages and even gone so far as to condone and encourage homosexual behavior. The Indian scenario however, is vastly different from that in the West.

(c) Indian Scenario

In India, homosexuality is not just frowned upon by most religions, it is also illegal and punishable for up to ten years imprisonment under section 377 of the Indian Penal Code (IPC). The homosexual population in India is estimated to be 2.5 million – this entails, of course, only the homosexuals who have declared themselves.[17] The true number is difficult to estimate given the sensitive nature of

[14] "Feminist Theology."

[15] R. Raj Rao, "Bleak Chance," *Pune Times Mirror*, July 7, 2015.

[16] Peter Tatchell, "The Nazi Doctor Who Experimented on Gay People – and Britain Helped to Escape Justice | Peter Tatchell | Comment Is Free | The Guardian," accessed October 31, 2015, http://www.theguardian.com/commentisfree/2015/may/05/nazi-doctor-gay-people-carl-vaernet-escaped-justice-danish.

[17] "Homosexuality in India," *Wikipedia, the Free Encyclopedia*, July 28, 2015, https://en.wikipedia.org/w/index.php?title=Homosexuality_in_India&oldid=673434772.

such a census especially since homosexuals in India are less vociferous than their western counterparts. Recent times have however, seen a steadily more vocal and openly defiant homosexual community, especially after the Delhi High Court repealed 377 IPC in July 2009 (the Supreme Court, however, overruled this decision in December 2013).[18] The workings of the Indian Church itself has thus far remained relatively unaffected by the ongoing demonstrations and debates between different factions, or at the very least, it has garnered only temporary attention from the public and the media. However, there will come a time when not just the legislative authorities, but the Christian authorities too, are forced to make a stand about homosexuality. Homosexuals from Christian families in India usually remain safely ensconced within their closets, or if they did venture out, it would be in a metropolitan, a safe distance from their own hometown. After revealing their sexual preferences, these individuals often find themselves preached at, avoided, rejected, humiliated and judged. The Church may, in the not so distant future, find members of their congregation openly declaring themselves "homosexual Christians" or even more disheartening, homosexual ex-Christians, members who left the church feeling confused and questioning the love of God, then losing their faith entirely. The presenter interviewed a young homosexual man in Pune, who said, "Maybe the Bible is wrong if it says homosexuality is a sin. After all, God made me this way. I'm not sure if I'm reading the wrong Bible or going to the wrong church."[19] A more damaging reaction would be for these individuals to establish their own Christian homosexual support groups, Bibles and even churches, as in the West. Such groups claim that the Bible's teachings regarding homosexuality are either irrelevant or have been misinterpreted.

Various denominations and churches in India have had differing responses to the growing gay culture in India. Although, the bishops of the Church of North India (CNI) collectively opposed the installation of a homosexual individual as bishop in the Episcopal Church, USA, in 2003,[20] a consultation hosted at CNI Bhavan in New Delhi in 2004 decided that homosexual orientation alone was not sinful, as opposed to homosexual behavior. The group, consisting of all manners of eminent church and community leaders, agreed that gay people too deserve to be treated with respect and compassion, and apart from advising a reanalysis of scriptures regarding homosexuality, also recommended a sensitization program for church and lay leaders.[21]

---

[18] "Homosexuality in India."

[19] KM, Interview on Homosexuality, English, July 7, 2015.

[20] A. J. Philip, "The Tribune, Chandigarh, India - Editorial," accessed October 31, 2015, http://www.tribuneindia.com/2003/20030822/edit.htm#5.

[21] Pratap Chandra Gine, "Homosexuality: An Indian Issue in Church and State," *Continuing Indaba*, accessed October 31, 2015, http://continuingindaba.org/2013/09/18/homosexuality-an-indian-issue-in-church-and-state/.

The Delhi high court ruling in July 2009 forced various churches to state their views on homosexuality to the media – the Catholic Church, for one, did not have such liberal opinion as the CNI on the matter. Father Dominic Emanuel of the Indian Catholic Bishop Council said unambiguously, "Our stand has always been very clear. The church has no serious objection to decriminalising homosexuality between consenting adults, the church has never considered homosexuals as criminals. But the church does not approve of this behavior. It doesn't consider it natural, ethical, or moral."[22] The Telegraph reported in August 2009 on statements made by representatives of the National Council of Churches in India (NCCI), such as Reverend Christopher Rajkumar, the secretary of the Justice, Peace and Creation Commission of the NCCI, who said, "Homosexuality traits in a person could be genetical, hence natural. It is unscientific to throw stones at some people because of their natural instincts over which they have no control."[23] He also added that a "rethink" is need on the stand Christians have traditionally taken on homosexuality, and that it is the Church's "duty" to educate people that "homosexuality is a natural process."[24] NCCI released a statement and document stating that its member churches need to "accompany the People with Different Sexual Orientation (PDSO) in their journey" in order to protect their civil rights; it also suggested "re-reading and re-interpreting scriptures from the PDSO perspective."[25] There was no conclusive decision made regarding gay marriage. NCCI represents various organisations such as the YMCA and YWCA, and 31 denominations including the Church of North India (CNI), the Church of South India (CSI), the Mar Thoma Syrian Church and the Malankara Orthodox Syrian Church, which accounts for approximately 1.3 crore Christians in India.[26] Five months after the Delhi ruling, the NCCI, the Presbyterian Church of India, the Student Christian Movement of India and the Senate Centre for Extension for Pastoral Theological Research (SCEPTRE) met in Kolkatta to formulate "Theological Roundtable on Churches' Response to Human Sexuality" directed at Indian Christian communities. This message called for understanding of and outreach to the homosexual group since the Church as a "Just and Inclusive community" should not avoid any group or withhold its "ministries of love, compassionate care, and justice" from any peoples.[27]

---

[22] "BBC NEWS | South Asia | Gay Sex Decriminalised in India," accessed October 31, 2015, http://news.bbc.co.uk/2/hi/south_asia/8129836.stm.

[23] Cithara Paul, "The Telegraph - Calcutta (Kolkata) | Frontpage | Protestants Support Gay Rights," accessed October 31, 2015, http://www.telegraphindia.com/1090805/jsp/frontpage/story_11322140.jsp.

[24] Paul, "The Telegraph - Calcutta (Kolkata) | Frontpage | Protestants Support Gay Rights."

[25] Paul, "The Telegraph - Calcutta (Kolkata) | Frontpage | Protestants Support Gay Rights."

[26] Paul, "The Telegraph - Calcutta (Kolkata) | Frontpage | Protestants Support Gay Rights."

[27] John Malhotra, "Church Urged Not to Eschew Sexual Minorities | Christian News on Christian Today," accessed October 31, 2015, http://www.christiantoday.co.in/article/church.deliberates.

Churches in India are now facing a barrage of change, and not in mere words but in deeds too. Take for instance, the case of a church in Madras affiliated to Evangelical Church of India (ECI), which in February 2012 hit headlines for having a transgender pastor.[28] Pastor Bharati, now known only by her first name, was the son of a poor fisherman who brought her up as a boy and always reprimanded her for her distinctly feminine behavior. Bharati converted to Christianity at the age of 12 and was baptized in 2000.[29] She went on to complete a Bachelor's degree in Theology (B.Th) from Idhayam College, Chennai and Bachelor of Divinity (BD) in the Tamil Nadu Theological Seminary. She is now pastoring to an ECI church in Chengalpattu, Chennai. Bishop Ezra Sargunam, head of the Evangelical Church of India, said that although the church constitution does not comment on the ordination of transgenders, Bharati's case was unique as she demonstrated exceptional devotion and fervency. The Hindu reported Reverend V. Devasahayam, Bishop of the Diocese of Madras, as saying that Bharati's ordination was "certainly on the cards. Theologically, we are not against a transgender becoming a priest. We see every human being as one created in the image of God and deem any discrimination as against the will of God. Any person who has been baptised has the right to receive the sacrament of ordination."[30]

5. The Homosexual Perspective

Prominent homosexual apologists argue that the Bibles currently in use by conservative anti-homosexual churches[31] incorrectly call homosexuality a sin, that Christians who do so have based their belief on an erroneous translation. Allegedly, the Bible does not have any significant comment on homosexuality – newly edited "gay-friendly" Bibles and study guides omit any homophobia inducing verses. Ann Nyland, a classic Greek lexicographer, authored a Bible study guide for the homosexual community – *Study New Testament for Lesbians, Gays, Bi and Transgenders*. Nyland's contention is that the Greek word *arsenokoites*

on.human.sexuality/4924.htm.

[28] B. Kolappan, "CSI to Ordain Transgender a Priest - OTHERS - The Hindu," accessed October 31, 2015, http://www.thehindu.com/todays-paper/tp-miscellaneous/tp-others/csi-to-ordain-transgender-a-priest/article2864240.ece.

[29] Pratiksha Ramkumar, "Meet India's First Transgender Pastor - The Times of India," accessed October 31, 2015, http://timesofindia.indiatimes.com/india/Meet-Indias-first-transgender-pastor/articleshow/11772802.cms.

[30] Kolappan, "CSI to Ordain Transgender a Priest - OTHERS - The Hindu."

[31] Matthew Vines, *The Gay Debate: The Bible and Homosexuality*, 2012, https://www.youtube.com/watch?v=ezQjNJUSraY.

(which appears in 1Timothy 1:10[32] and 1 Corinthians 6:9[33]) has traditionally been translated as "abusers of themselves with mankind" or "homosexual", but actually the term has several possible uses "including one who anally penetrates another (male or female), a rapist, a murderer, or an extortionist."[34] The Center for Gay and Lesbian Studies in Religion and Ministry teaches that the Greek term used for effeminate (*malakoi*) could also mean 'soft' or 'all things feminine.'[35] However, over the years and as social perceptions of homosexuality changed, what Paul wrote in AD 55 was translated in various Bibles as weaklings, effeminate, catamite, sodomite, male prostitutes then finally, homosexuals.[36] Thus, what could have originally just meant 'weak' was apparently wrongly translated as 'homosexual'. The widely popular *Queen James Bible* (QJB), or the Gay Bible, was published anonymously in 2012, and is based on the *King James Bible*.[37] The QJB editors claim that before the publication of the Revised Standard Version in 1946, no Bible in circulation contained references to homosexuality – the eight mistranslated verses[38] have been edited in the QJB for a non-homophobic impression. For example, the passage in Leviticus[39] apparently condemns "pagan" homosexual sex in the temple of Molech as an "abomination", not a "committed" homosexual relationship.[40]

Pratap C. Gine, professor of New Testament department in Serampore College, explains that according to the creation account in Genesis 2:4-25, man was created first and then a helper made for him because God said it was not good for man to be alone, showing that humans are interdependent. Gine argues that God thought man would suffer from loneliness without a helper, therefore

---

[32] *"Knowing this, that the law is not made for a righteous man, but for... whoremongers, for them that defile themselves with mankind..."* (1 Timothy 1: 9-10, KJV).

[33] *"Know ye not that the unrighteous shall not inherit the kingdom of God? Be not deceived: neither fornicators, nor idolaters, nor adulterers, nor effeminate, nor abusers of themselves with mankind."* (1 Corinthians 6:9, KJV).

[34] "Christian Stores Boycott Gay Bible Guide - National - Smh.com.au," accessed August 4, 2015, http://www.smh.com.au/news/national/christian-stores-boycott-gay-bible-guide/2007/11/25/1195975870483.html.

[35] "Arsenokoités and Malakos: Meanings and Consequences | CLGS," accessed August 4, 2015, http://www.clgs.org/arsenokoit%C3%A9s-and-malakos-meanings-and-consequences.

[36] "Malakoi Is NEVER Used in the Bible to Mean Gay, Lesbian, Bisexual or Trans.," accessed August 4, 2015, http://www.gaychristian101.com/Malakoi.html.

[37] "Queen James Bible Claims To Be First-Ever 'Gay Bible,' But Some Say It Rewrites Scripture," accessed August 4, 2015, http://www.huffingtonpost.com/2012/12/18/queen-james-bible-claims-first-ever-gay-bible_n_2324962.html?ir=India&adsSiteOverride=in.

[38] Genesis 19:5, Leviticus 18:22, Romans 1:26–27, 1 Corinthians 6:9, 1 Timothy 1:10, Jude 1:7.

[39] *"Thou shalt not lie with mankind, as with womankind: it is abomination."* (Leviticus 18:22, KJV) *"If a man also lie with mankind, as he lieth with a woman, both of them shall have committed an abomination..."* (Leviticus 20:13, KJV).

[40] Matthew Vines, *The Gay Debate*.

a helper was made for him – this does not mean that only woman can be man's helper, nor is woman the only solution to his loneliness. Man too, can be man's helper and company.[41]

Matthew Vines, a popular proponent of the homosexual Christian movement, has taught extensively why a homosexual can be a Christian without being at odds with the Bible.[42] His book, *God and the Gay Christian: The Biblical Case in Support of Same-Sex Relationships,* has become a driving force for the Christian homosexual movement. Well acquainted with the Bible and the Church, Vines has several convincing arguments about why homosexuality was never considered a sin by God. He used Matthew 7:16 ("Ye shall know them by their fruits." KJV) to argue that since the Church's traditional teachings on homosexuality has not borne good fruit, but only depression and rejection, the Church's stand on homosexuality must be incorrect.[43] Vines also said that God decided to destroy Sodom and Gomorrah because of their immorality,[44] not specifically because they practiced homosexuality. The men in Sodom who wanted to have sex with the angels in Lot's house were punished because of the proposed act of gang rape, violence and humiliation; not because they were homosexuals.[45] Vines argues that Romans 1:24-27[46] was not directed at same sex relationships, but against excessive, lustful relations, whether heterosexual or homosexual. Since, a Christian is bound by the Bible to have a loving, committed relationship, this does not forbid a committed homosexual relationship like same sex marriage. Many homosexuals dismiss Leviticus as irrelevant since the same passage forbids eating of pork and shellfish amongst other meats, which was later recanted in the New Testament.[47]

6. A Christian Perspective

The arguments presented by homosexuals may persuade many that the Christian teachings are bigoted and incorrect, especially swaying those with a poor grasp of the Bible or theology, which would be a majority of non-clerical Christians, perhaps some cleric as well. However, there are many fundamental problems with

---

[41] "Homosexuality: An Indian Issue in Church and State | Continuing Indaba," accessed October 31, 2015, http://continuingindaba.org/2013/09/18/homosexuality-an-indian-issue-in-church-and-state/.

[42] "Transcript," *Matthew Vines*, accessed August 4, 2015, http://www.matthewvines.com/transcript/.

[43] "Transcript."

[44] *"Because the cry of Sodom and Gomorrah is great, and because their sin is very grievous…"* (Genesis 18:20, KJV).

[45] "Transcript."

[46] "*For this cause, God gave them up unto vile affections: for even their women did change the natural use into that which is against nature. And likewise also the men, leaving the natural use of the woman, burned in their lust one toward another; men with men working that which is unseemly, and receiving in themselves that recompense of their error which was meet.*" (Romans 1:26-27, KJV).

[47] "*Rise, Peter; kill, and eat… What God hath cleansed, that call not thou common.*" (Acts 10: 13-15).

the homosexual re-translation of the Bible. Douglas J. Moo, a professional Bible translator, said of the Gay Bible, "Few, if any English translations use the actual words 'homosexuality' or 'homosexual.' But the history of English translation shows that versions have consistently used other language to refer to what we would call homosexual relationships."[48-49] Bible translation is no frivolous endeavor, as there are warnings in the Bible against alteration of its contents.[50] Christopher Yuan, a teacher in Moody Bible Institute, but more interestingly, someone who has "come out of homosexuality," comments that supporters of homosexuality, including Vines, start "… with the conclusion that God blesses same-sex relationships and then moves backwards to find evidence. This is not *exegesis*, but a classic example of *eisegesis*."[51] (eisegesis is defined as "the process of interpreting a text or portion of text in such a way that the process introduces one's own presuppositions, agendas, or biases into and onto the text.")[52] The Old Testament does indeed lay out many laws which are absent in the "new law", such as consumption of certain foods; but many laws in the OT are reiterated in the New Testament, among these, laws forbidding homosexuality. Denny Burk, in *God and the Gay Christian: A Response to Matthew Vines,*[53] says that paradoxically, Vines based his arguments on a verse preceded by a warning about false teachers- "Beware of false prophets, which will come to you in sheep's clothing, but inwardly ravening wolves."[54] Burk says the reason *arsenokoites* (*arsen-* male, *koite-* bed) does not appear prior to Paul's usage, is because Paul himself coined it from the Greek translation of Leviticus 18:22 and 20:13, two very unambiguous verses that leave no room for debate on etymology or incorrect translations. Paul used *arsenokoites* and *malakos* to indicate the active and passive partners in a male homosexual act. Another popular argument used by homosexuals is that Jesus never said anything about homosexuality.[55] This is correct – Jesus never commented directly, but He did quote Genesis 2:24 while discussing divorce, saying, "…Have ye not read,

---

[48] "Queen James Bible Claims To Be First-Ever 'Gay Bible,' But Some Say It Rewrites Scripture."

[49] "Recently Released 'Queen James' Purports to Be First-Ever 'Gay Bible,'" accessed August 4, 2015, http://www.christianpost.com/news/recently-released-queen-james-purports-to-be-first-ever-gay-bible-86627/.

[50] Deuteronomy 4:2, Proverbs 30:5-6, Revelations 22:18-19.

[51] "Why 'God and the Gay Christian' Is Wrong About the Bible and Same-Sex Relationships | Christianity Today," accessed August 4, 2015, http://www.christianitytoday.com/ct/2014/june-web-only/why-matthew-vines-is-wrong-about-bible-same-sex-relationshi.html?start=2.

[52] "Eisegesis," *Wikipedia, the Free Encyclopedia*, July 21, 2015, https://en.wikipedia.org/w/index.php?title=Eisegesis&oldid=672396024.

[53] R. Albert Mohler Jr, ed., *God and the Gay Christian?: A Response to Matthew Vines* (Louisville, KY: SBTS Press, 2014).

[54] Matthew 7:15 KJV.

[55] "If Homosexuality Is a Sin, Why Didn't Jesus Ever Mention It?," accessed August 4, 2015, http://www.gotquestions.org/Jesus-homosexuality.html.

that he who made them in the beginning made them male and female, And said, For this cause shall a man leave father and mother, and shall cleave to his wife..."[56] Jesus explained in this passage that one could either be in a faithful heterosexual marriage, or be a celibate single. He did not give an option of other sexuality.[57] As Yuan explained about his personal struggle with homosexuality, "My years of biblical language study in Bible college and seminary, and doctoral research in sexuality, only strengthened this conclusion. No matter how hard I tried to find biblical justification and no matter whether my same-sex temptations went away or not, God's word did not change."[58]

7. The Need for Dialogue

The Christian LGBT community in India was quick to quote Cardinal Oswald Gracias, Archbishop of Mumbai, who said, "The Catholic Church has never been opposed to the decriminalization of homosexuality, because we have never considered gay people criminals."[59] However, although it may not be a necessity to pronounce homosexuality a crime, criminality and morality are two very distinct issues. Homosexuality may not be a crime in a secular country, but according to the Bible, it is a sin. The church must, however, accept homosexual individuals into the community and church, because God is a God of love, and "...while we were yet sinners, Christ died for us."[60] Christ died for people of the LGBT community too. But the Church must do so without any compromise on its stand on homosexuality. Jesus protected and forgave the adulterous woman who was about to be stoned, but also told her, "...go, and sin no more."[61] In the same manner, the Church must not only forgive homosexuals and welcome them into the church, but also teach them right and wrong without a judgmental attitude. There is an ocean of bitterness and mistrust dividing the Church from the LGBT community. Condoning alternate sexuality is not only a superficial remedy, it is simply not correct. New translations, churches or legislation are not the methods to bridge this divide. It is discussion and reconciliation. Hegel's dialectical method would be a useful tool in bringing together the Church and homosexuals to discuss their views.

---

[56] Matthew 19:4-5, KJV.

[57] "If Homosexuality Is a Sin, Why Didn't Jesus Ever Mention It?"

[58] "Why 'God and the Gay Christian' Is Wrong About the Bible and Same-Sex Relationships | Christianity Today."

[59] "INDIA Supreme Court Rules Homosexuality Is a Crime. Archbishop of Mumbai: Gays Are Not Criminals - Asia News," accessed August 4, 2015, http://www.asianews.it/news-en/Supreme-Court-rules-homosexuality-is-a-crime.-Archbishop-of-Mumbai:-Gays-are-not-criminals-29778.html.

[60] Romans 5:8, KJV.

[61] John 8:11, KJV.

8. Meaning of Dialectics

The Oxford Dictionaries defines dialectics as "the art of investigating or discussing the truth of opinions."[62] Greek philosophy considered dialectics the art of discovering truth by exposing contradictions in an opponent's reasoning. Until the 19th century, most usage of 'dialectics' conveyed a rational engagement of contradictions. The development of German idealism added a new facet of contradictions not just in discussion, but also in reality.

(a) Dialectic is not a Dialogue

Dialogue is defined in Oxford Dictionary as "a discussion between two or more people or groups, especially one directed towards exploration of a particular subject or resolution of a problem."[63] Dialectics is distinct from argument or conversation, though it can be considered a special type of dialogue. David Bohm's *On Dialogue* explains:

> The objective of dialogue is not to analyze things, or to win an argument, or to exchange opinions, rather it is to suspend your opinions and to look at the opinions—to listen to everybody's opinions, to suspend them, and to see what all that means.... We can just simply share the appreciation of the meanings, and out of this whole thing, truth emerges unannounced—not that we have chosen it.[64]

(b) Dialectic is not a Debate

Dialectics is not synonymous with debate. Edward P. J. Corbett and Robert J. Connors contend that though debaters, theoretically, should not necessarily be emotionally involved in their arguments, practically, there is frequent display of emotional commitment that may cloud rational judgment. A combination of proving an argument, disproving an opponent and persuading an opponent, wins a debate.[65] A prompt identification of a winner is not mandatory at the end of a debate; however, winners are frequently determined by a judge, jury, or by group consensus. Dialectics is also not synonymous with 'rhetoric', a method or art of discourse that seeks to persuade, inform, or motivate an audience.[66]

---

[62] "Dialectic - Definition of Dialectic in English from the Oxford Dictionary," accessed July 29, 2015, http://www.oxforddictionaries.com/definition/english/dialectic.

[63] "Dialogue - Definition of Dialogue in English from the Oxford Dictionary," accessed August 4, 2015, http://www.oxforddictionaries.com/definition/english/dialogue.

[64] David Bohm, *On Dialogue*, ed. Lee Nichol, Routlege classics ed. (London; New York: Routledge, 2004), 30.

[65] Edward P. J. Corbett and Robert J. Connors, *Classical Rhetoric for the Modern Student*, 4th ed (New York: Oxford University Press, 1999), 1.

[66] Corbett and Connors, *Classical Rhetoric for the Modern Student*, 1.

9. Hegelian Dialectics

Georg Wilhelm F. Hegel, a German philosopher renowned for his work in dialectics, described it as a method wherein "an interpretive method in which the contradiction between a proposition (thesis) and its antithesis is resolved at a higher level of truth (synthesis):"[67] this came to be known as Hegel's dialectics. However, this method began in 1808, when Hegel was developing some sort of link between traditional logic set out in classical form by Aristotle and his own. Aristotlean logic had been the standard for 2,000 years and the reason Hegel was working on a different logic, which he described in his Phenomenology as his "psychology", was because it was a work that dealt with the existential issues and of the world, not those dealing with Absolute Mind (or Spirit) but to quite ordinary minds like our own. It traced a path from our everyday commonsense states of mind to the vantage point of "Systematic Science."

(a) Hegel's Dialectical Thinking

Hegel's different way of thinking has become known as dialectical thinking. What makes dialectical thinking so difficult to explain is that it can only be seen in practice, in fact it is not a "method" or a set of doctrines, like Aristotle's, which can be simply stated and then applied to whatever subject matter one chooses.[68] In Hegel's treatment of logic, thinking dwells on itself, rather than trying to comprehend the world. The Science of Logic engages with logical categories, "not the accidents of history or various modes of relating to the world. It is rather absent or distant from the world as such."[69] Hegel tackles with a structure of "logical categories: being, becoming, one, many, essence, existence, cause, effect, universal, mechanism, and "life." Each is examined in turn and made to reveal its own inadequacies and internal tensions. Each category is made to generate another more promising one, which in its turn will be subject to the same kind of scrutiny."[70]

(b) The Dynamics of Dialectical Thinking

Hegel calls the dynamic aspect of his thinking as the power of 'negation'. "It is by means of this 'negativity' of thought that the static (or habitual) becomes discarded or dissolved, made fluid and adaptable, and recovers its eagerness to push on towards 'the whole'."[71] In fact, the dialectical thinking from its ability

---

[67] "Hegelian Dialectic | Define Hegelian Dialectic at Dictionary.com," accessed August 2, 2015, http://dictionary.reference.com/browse/hegelian+dialectic.

[68] Lloyd Spencer and Andrzej Krauze, *Hegel for Beginners*, ed. Richard Appignanesi (Trumpington: Icon, 1996), cited in "Hegel FOR BEGINNERS," accessed October 21, 2015, https://www.marxists.org/reference/archive/hegel/help/easy.htm.

[69] Spencer and Krauze, *Hegel for Beginners* cited in "Hegel FOR BEGINNERS."

[70] Spencer and Krauze, *Hegel for Beginners* cited in "Hegel FOR BEGINNERS."

[71] Spencer and Krauze, *Hegel for Beginners* cited in "Hegel FOR BEGINNERS."

to reveal "contradictions" within almost any category or identity derives the dynamics of negation. In his elaboration of Science of logic, Hegel observed that this involved three different modes of contradictions, viz. **Being**, **Nothing** and **Becoming**, which is further explained below.

(i) Being

George di Giovanni explained that for Hegel 'Being', which is 'Pure Being' is that which is 'without further determination.'[72] It is identical just to itself and concurrently not unequal with regard to another in, what he termed as, 'its indeterminate immediacy.' Moreover, both within and outside, it posits no difference. "If any determination or content were speculated in it as distinct, or if it were posited by this determination or content as distinct from an other, it would thereby fail to hold fast to its purity."[73] For Hegel, being is a pure abstraction which has no concrete meaning and which is prior to any specific. Unlike Aristotle, who said that nothing can be taken out of being, Hegel believes that everything is related to everything and since Being is undefined, it passes into non-Being and thereby there occurs a movement of dialectical process.

(ii) Nothing

'Nothing', or in specific 'Pure nothingness' is "simple equality with itself, complete emptiness, complete absence of determination and content; lack of all distinction within."[74] While 'intuiting and thinking', it distinguishes whether something or nothing is being intuited or thought. Hegel considers that "to intuit or to think nothing has therefore a meaning; the two are distinguished and so nothing is (concretely exists) in our intuiting or thinking; or rather it is the empty intuiting and thinking itself, like pure being. Nothing is therefore the same determination or rather absence of determination, and thus altogether the same as what pure being is."[75]

It is therefore identical with Being, except that it is thought of as its very opposite. This distinction is therefore meaningful as posited by thought.

(iii) Becoming

Pure Being and Pure Nothing, although are similar in feature yet absolutely distinct from each other. Now the contradiction between the two is resolved by their engagement, i.e., one into the other. The result becomes what is called 'Becoming', that takes the form of reciprocal 'Coming-to-Be' and 'Ceasing-to-Be.' In other words, Giovanni asserts that for Hegel "the truth is neither being

---

[72] George di Giovanni, trans., *Georg Wilhelm Friedrich Hegel: The Science of Logic* (New York: Cambridge University Press, 2010), 59.

[73] Giovanni, *Georg Wilhelm Friedrich Hegel: The Science of Logic*, 59.

[74] Giovanni, *Georg Wilhelm Friedrich Hegel: The Science of Logic*, 59.

[75] Giovanni, *Georg Wilhelm Friedrich Hegel: The Science of Logic*, 59.

nor nothing, but rather that being has passed over into nothing andnothing into being – 'has passed over,' not passes over. But the truth is just as much that they are not without distinction; it is rather that they are not the same, that they are absolutely distinct yet equally unseparated and inseparable, and that each immediately vanishes in its opposite."[76] This movement of 'being' to 'nothing' and vice versa is what Hegel opined as the truth and a movement where the immediate vanishing of the one into the other occasions 'becoming', "a movement in which the two are distinguished, but by a distinction which has just as immediately dissolved itself."[77]

(iv) Objective of Hegel's Dialectics

Hegel used the dialectic for a purpose different than arriving at first principles. To understand what the dialectic meant for Hegel, it must first be understood that Hegel was an idealist.[78] Like his predecessor Immanuel Kant, Hegel believed that one does not have a direct perception of the world or anything in it, but any access one's mind might have are mere ideas of the world, i.e., images, perceptions, and concepts.[79] Each individual has unique ideas depending on their background and context, resulting in tension. Instead of dismissing such tensions, Hegel's dialectics contrives to bring together dissimilarities to initiate argument such that there is resolution. Thus, the objective of Hegel's dialectic is to arrive at the truth through the exchange of logical arguments, which is a system of thought process. Recognizing the limitations of the mind, Hegelianism stipulates "that the human mind cannot understand anything unless it can be split into two polar opposites. Good / Evil, Right / Wrong, Left / Right."[80]

Furthermore, Glenn Alexander Magee asserts that Hegel recognized that "dialectic sets concepts in opposition to each other and reveals their problematic nature; speculation overcomes these dichotomies through a third term that reconciles or transcends their opposition."[81] His dialectical method defined the framework for guiding thoughts and actions into conflicts that lead one to a predetermined solution. Hegel used the proven dialectical process used in Aristotle's time, which implies that this was not an impractical theory, but had applications and repercussions in the real world. Hegel also took the concept of

---

[76] Giovanni, *Georg Wilhelm Friedrich Hegel: The Science of Logic*, 60.

[77] Giovanni, *Georg Wilhelm Friedrich Hegel: The Science of Logic*, 60.

[78] Idealism is the group of philosophies, which assert that reality, or reality, as we can know it, is fundamentally mental, mentally constructed, or otherwise immaterial.

[79] Robert B. Pippin, *Hegel's Idealism: The Satisfactions of Self-Consciousness* (Cambridge: Cambridge University Press, 1989), 21.

[80] "The Hegelian Dialectic and Its Use in Controlling Modern Society Alex Jones' Infowars: There's a War on for Your Mind!," accessed July 30, 2015, http://www.infowars.com/the-hegelian-dialectic-and-its-use-in-controlling-modern-society/.

[81] Glenn Alexander Magee, *The Hegel Dictionary* (London ; New York: Continuum, 2010), 72.

the dialectic a step further by proposing that a newly formed synthesis was not the ultimate truth, but rather became the new thesis with its corresponding antithesis and synthesis. This process would continue effectively and incrementally, until it reaches the final synthesis, which Hegel termed "the absolute idea."[82]

(v) Functioning of Hegelian Dialectics

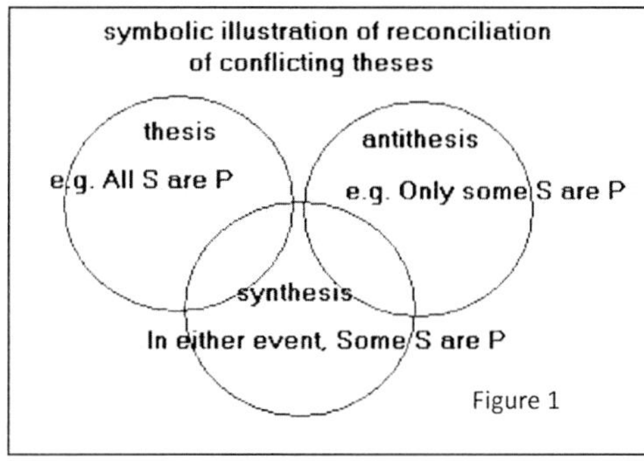

Figure 1

Hegelian dialectics does not involve a dialogue between two thinkers or between a thinker and his subject matter. Rather, it functions in a progressive manner involving three dialectical stages of development: a *thesis*, which gives rise to its reaction, the *antithesis*, which contradicts or negates the *thesis*, and the tension between the two is in turn resolved by a *synthesis*. Although, this model is often referred to as Hegel's, he himself never used this specific formulation.[83] The Hegelian Formulais represented by figure 1.[84]

An interesting feature of the Hegelian dialectic is that even after engagement between the thesis and antithesis has reached synthesis, one never arrives at a final outcome. Instead, a new thesis with its corresponding antithesis is created, initiating a kind of "dialectic helix"[85] (figure 2) that progressively spirals towards the next predetermined outcome.[86]

(vi) The Consciousness of Self-Alienation over Self-Affirmation in Subjectivity

Chronologically, Hegel was not the first to suggest that the development of subjectivity is dialectical rather than temporal, pursuing its course from self-affirmation to self-alienation. It was St. Augustine who first employed the term and explored its moral significance.[87] But Hegel was certainly the first thinker to articulate a reinterpretation of self-consciousness in reference to self-realization.

---

[82] "Georg Wilhelm Friedrich Hegel > By Individual Philosopher > Philosophy," accessed August 2, 2015, http://www.philosophybasics.com/philosophers_hegel.html.

[83] Michael Allen Fox, *The Accessible Hegel* (Amherst, N.Y: Humanity Books, 2005), 29–30.

[84] "Hegelian Dialectics for Dummies | Therightplanet.com," accessed August 2, 2015, http://www.therightplanet.com/2014/01/hegelian-dialectics-for-dummies/.

[85] "Hegelian Dialectics for Dummies | Therightplanet.com."

[86] Peter Crafts Hodgson, *Hegel and Christian Theology a Reading of the Lectures on the Philosophy of Religion* (New York: Oxford University Press, 2005), 8.

[87] Joseph L. Navickas, *Consciousness and Reality: Hegel's Philosophy of Subjectivity* (The Hague: Martinus Nijhoff, 1976), 115.

According to this view, self-alienation alone can bring self-consciousness to fruition and one should look for its possibility in a subject able to negate and perform the act of self-mediation. This does not mean, however, that Hegel considered "… alienation was the driving force of the dialectical development."[88] As mentioned in the earlier section, the driving force of the dialectical process lied in the subject's negativity, whereas self-alienation arises from the process that causes an inner schism within the self-conscious ego.[89]

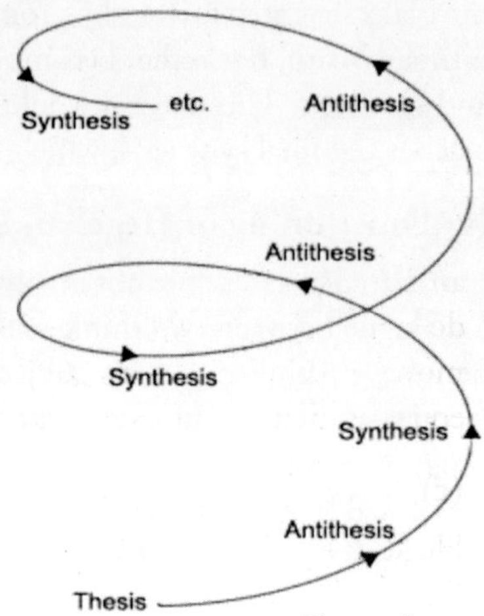

Figure 2

10. Criteria for Hegel's Dialectics

(a) Subject's Subjectivity

Subjectivity denotes "interpretation based on personal opinions or feelings rather than on external facts or evidence."[90] In critical theory and psychology, "subjectivity is also the actions or discourses that produce individuals or 'I'—the 'I' is the subject."[91]Hegel defines subject from Aristotle's perspective: "the unmoved which is also self-moving". That is, the outside force does not cause the motion but the self moves on its own.[92] This is crucial in the Hegelian dialectic process, as each polarity has to have their subjectivity, barring any external influences, in order for the outcome of the multi-tiered engagement between thesis and antithesis to be an optimistic resolution.

(b) The Abstract Symmetry of "Left" & "Right"

In order to explain the importance of two conflicting polarities, Hegel draws an analogy to succinctly explain the abstract symmetry of the Left & Right:

> When we think of Left as something immediate (as Hegel uses the term), it marks for instance half of the space (or line which is in front of us, etc.), and Right as something immediate marks the other half of the space (or line, or whatever). But if we take now those half-spaces, or half-lines by themselves, or *if we limit our thinking just to those*

---

[88] Louis Dupre, *The Philosophical Foundations of Marxism* (New York: Harcourt, Brace & World, 1966), 122.

[89] Quoted by Hans Wenke, *HegelsTheorie des Objektiven Geistes* (Halle: Max Niemeyer, 1927), p. 96.inNavickas, *Consciousness and Reality*, 116.

[90] Microsoft® Encarta® 2009.© 1993-2008 Microsoft Corporation.

[91] "Subject (philosophy)," *Wikipedia, the Free Encyclopedia*, May 18, 2015, https://en.wikipedia.org/w/index.php?title=Subject_(philosophy)&oldid=662872590.

[92] G. W. F. Hegel, *Phenomenology of Spirit*, trans. A. V. Miller (Delhi: Motilal Banarsidass, 1998), 12.

> *abstractions*, we can figure out that there is ideal symmetry between them. There is nothing that distinguishes them internally. The half-space that we named Left can be Right, and the half-space that we named Right can be also Left.[93]

Many opposing ideas can be equated once viewed as Hegel suggests, in an abstract symmetry. One has to agree that Left and Right are different and do not mean the same, yet are equal, likewise the eureka moment in dialectical movement, when two abstract ideas are found to be poles apart, nevertheless are equal in their abstract symmetry.[94]

(c) Negativity of Consciousness

Hegel considered consciousness to be negativity of the mind never taking a simple fact at face value but worrying it into many opposing fragments. Negativity will simultaneously deny the differences and disagreements it just created.[95] Consciousness, thus, is a continuous and creative process, which is able to rise above everything, tangible, or not. Negativity enables the consciousness to extend even beyond itself.[96] The multi-tiered dialogue should create a self-consciousness, which according to Hegel is a negativity of mind, leading to the realization of the negativity of one's own mind. In other words the uncompromising mentality of two opposing groups should decline the moment the self attains the consciousness.

11. Applying Hegel's Dialectics Towards a Dialogue Between the Church and Homosexuals

(a) Accommodating dialogue even for uncompromising factions

Usually, for any meaningful dialogue to occur, a certain level of commonality is required between two factions. If there is no common ground to initiate discussion and no undebatable agenda, dialogue cannot take place, much less be effective. Very contrary to the norm, any dialogue arising from Hegelian dialectics is both effectual and worthy if opposing views seem irreconcilable. Hegel's dialectics thrives on impossible and defeated dialogues. Conservative Christians and LGBT groups have never and can never come to a dialogue due to the uncompromising and diverging nature of their views. The mudslinging from both banks over centuries of mistrust only serve to create an ever-widening gap. Since, neither group will entertain the other, this Mexican standoff is the perfect situation to utilize Hegel's dialectical methods.

---

93 "Simple Explanation Of Hegelian Dialectic Method « A Brood Comb," accessed August 4, 2015, https://broodsphilosophy.wordpress.com/2006/10/29/simple-explanation-of-hegelian-dialectic-method/.

94 "Simple Explanation Of Hegelian Dialectic Method « A Brood Comb."

95 Navickas, *Consciousness and Reality*, 19.

96 Navickas, *Consciousness and Reality*, 19.

(b) Negativity of Consciousness as a Starting Point Towards Agreement

If the consciousness has an inherent negativity, it will create questions about every subject, then create questions on those questions. In a similar fashion, the multi-tiered dialogue generated by negativity should create a self-consciousness, which will bring two warring factions to naturally and eventually come to a consensus. Correspondingly, the dialogue between the church and LGBT can reach agreement, provided the dialogue is directing towards the self-consciousness of the negativity of mind.

(c) The Consciousness of Self-Alienation as a foundation for dialogue

If as Hegel proposed, self-alienation alone can bring self-consciousness to fruition, one should seek it in a subject with the ability to negate and self-mediate. Consequently, the church and the LGBT groups through their conflict in dialogue should create consciousness of self-alienation that, as the dialogue progresses, will gradually reduce the tension and creates common ground of understanding. The end of tension then between the two can be second to impossible, yet such self-alienation inculcated through the engagement of subjectivity keeps the tension strategically at bay, creating room for a common ground.

(d) Optimistic outcome through dialectic helix

A dialogue that ended in a conclusion of irreconcilable differences would not, usually, be considered an optimistic outcome. However, if Hegel's dialectic helix were to be applied to the deadlock between the Church and LGBT community, there would be no cause for despair, as this would simply be the newly created thesis and antithesis, which was progressing towards a new solution or synthesis. Thus, even if at present there seems to be no possibility of further dialogue, the Church can indeed still attempt discussion with hope of a resolution. Even if this discussion were not brought to fruition, there would be the optimistic confidence of a newly generated thesis in the future.

Conclusion

Decades of suspicion between the Church and homosexuals seem only to confirm that dialogue, much less reconciliation, between the two are impossible. The homosexual camp accuse the Church of bigotry, hypocrisy and vindictive mistranslation of the Bible, whereas the Church is outraged by the sacrilegious re-translations of two millennia of Scripture, and fumble with homosexuals who still desire to follow Christ. Homosexuals point out that it is Christians who teach, "Judge not, that ye be not judged. For with what judgment ye judge, ye shall be judged: and with what measure ye mete, it shall be measured to you again."[97] However, the Bible also says that homosexuality is a sin and teaches that we should

[97] Matthew 7:1-2, KJV.

lovingly point out each other's faults – "Brothers and sisters, if someone is caught in a sin, you who live by the Spirit should restore that person gently. But watch yourselves, or you also may be tempted."[98] Some churches are wary of talking about homosexuality; others only emphasize the sinfulness of homosexuality and yet fail to preach Jesus's love and salvation. It is such unwillingness to engage homosexuals that led to the formation of churches and literature that are muddying the Scripture's clear waters. Hegel's dialectic methods give a new option for both groups, showing that dialogue is possible even without common ground. Even the thought of a failed talk seems buoyant if viewed in the light of the helical model – to know that every new argument is actually just a new thesis leading on to the ideal solution. The Church can now establish contact with homosexuals, forgiving them without compromising their stand against homosexual behavior, condemning the sin without condemning the sinner.

[98] Galatians 6:1-2, NIV.

11

Viable Social Philosophy for Religious Commitment towards Social Change

Wilson Paluri

Introduction

Human life is a means for socio-ethical interaction; it can be a setting for collective action in advancing social welfare of humanity as well as an individual's emancipation. From this perspective, the social process becomes a way of seeking social values by practical activity aimed at the welfare of humankind as a whole. The question is: how do we understand the contribution of the ongoing social process and the ways in which they interact with the collective social mentality and religious institutions in promoting the best interest of the whole of society?

Society and the different problems of social life constitute an interesting subject matter of some of the branches of knowledge like political science, social psychology, ethics and economics. Besides these, there is another branch of knowledge called sociology, which studies social facts and laws not from any definite viewpoint, but in general. It views social life as a whole.

While studying the different aspects of social life, there are some questions generally asked – what is the ideal of the society? What are the ultimate values of social life and what are the means of attaining them? Is there any norm of social unity with reference to which different social relations are to be interpreted? Is religion an important force for bringing about social solidarity? What are the methods of combating social evils on moral and religious ground?

All these and various other questions relating to ends, ideals and values of social life fall into the domain of a separate branch of knowledge called social philosophy. It is a normative discipline which is concerned not only with the study of social facts but also social values.

Hence, the task of social philosophy is to find an answer to the deepest questions regarding the meaning and purpose of human life as a way of achieving humanization. This paper will reflect on the nature and scope of Indian social philosophy, with its emphasis on religious engagement for social change.

1. Nature and Function of Social Philosophy

Social Philosophy has a number of functions: firstly, it has an explanatory function, as it analyzes and defines the social phenomena. Secondly, it constructs methodological criteria by formulating principles and delineating the ways and means of investigating the social conditions. Social philosophy as a methodological tool can be applied to the sciences that deals not only with the laws of the historical development of society, but also with the specific forms and ways of the material and spiritual activities of human being in ethics, sociology, social and general psychology, theoretical medicine, ecology, and so on.[1] This makes it an important tool to verify religious engagement in social change.

The objective of contemporary social philosophy is to fulfil following requirements:

(a) It is to formulate the principles that later could serve as criteria for the evaluation of social progress. E. Maziarz stresses that a humanist who wishes to exert an effect on the conditions of humanism needs first of all strict standards for their evaluation. These principles ensure that while studying social phenomena the scientific criteria will not be replaced by emotional, moral or "common sense" evaluations.[2]

(b) Social philosophy can play a methodological role, not only as a cognitive tool marking further ways of studying the conditions and premises of a good society, but also as the criteria revealing the level of goodness of the material and spiritual phenomena in a society.[3]

(c) It seeks to find out the philosophical implications of social phenomena. P. B. Sengupta states that a social philosopher should not be exclusively critical, but must have a constructive outlook in addition. He/she has to carefully study the different principles of social cohesion.[4]

(d) It attempts at a critical enquiry into all the intellectual enterprises concerning human being in relation to his/her society by making an

[1] Jurate Morkuniene, *Social Philosophy: Paradigm of Contemporary Thinking* (Washington D.C.: The Council for Research in Values and Philosophy, 2004), 7.

[2] E. A. Maziarz, "Authentic humanism and the scientists", in *Philosophy of the Humanistic Society*, ed. by A. E. Koenig (Washington D.C.: University Press of America, 1981), 121.

[3] Morkuniene, *Social Philosophy*, 7.

[4] P. B. Sengupta, *Handbook of Social Philosophy*, (Calcutta: Banerjee Publishers, 1965), 5-8.

analysis of the fundamental social ideas of any particular place at a particular time. Any social or moral theory has to be grounded on a metaphysical or a philosophical conception of the relation between human being and the ultimate nature of things. Social and moral consciousness must include a conviction of the reality of ideals. When a person realizes his/her essential unity with the whole of being, he/she expresses this unity in his/her life and conduct.[5]

(e) Social philosophy, in Indian context, is more specifically a normative or evaluative inquiry of social and moral values, and the ways in which these shape individuals and establish a good social order helping human beings to live and act together. Stephen is of the opinion that the task of social philosophy is to provide a coherent and definite uniting value from which individuals form a common pattern of social life, and which enables them to accomplish social unity.[6]

(f) It tries to determine the different factors that account for the stability of a society. For this purpose it examines the nature of mass sentiment, common interest, language, ethos of the people, and also the social role of religion for bringing about social solidarity. It also studies whether religion is a cohesive force or a disintegrating force. It discusses the naturalistic theories of religion to find out the exact meaning of religion in a society.[7]

2. Role of Religion in Social Development

Religion is undoubtedly an individual as well as social phenomenon. Certain sociologists, however, maintain that religion is an entirely social phenomenon. J.S. MacKenzie, S. Radhakrishnan, W. Trotter, Emile Durkheim and some others view religion as a social requirement. MacKenzie suggests that when religion is viewed from the standpoint of society there is hardly any distinction between religion and morality. Religion incorporates the values of truth, beauty and goodness within it.[8] S. Radhakrishnan says, "The search of the mind for beauty, goodness and truth is the search for God."[9] Looking at religion from the same standpoint, Miall Edwards mentions that the question of the truth of the religious worldview is largely the question of the objectivity of our higher values.[10]

---

[5] Prativa Verma, *Social Philosophy of the Mahabharata and the Manu Smrti* (New Delhi: Classical Publishing Company, 1988), 23.

[6] Abraham Stephen, *The Social Philosophy of Swami Vivekananda: Its Relevance to Modern India* (Delhi: ISPCK, 2005), xiii.

[7] Sengupta, *Handbook of Social Philosophy*, 8.

[8] J. S. Mackenzie, *Outlines of Social Philosophy* (London: George Allen & Unwin, 1956), 212.

[9] S. Radhakrishnan, *Religion and Society* (London: George Allen & Unwin Ltd., 1947), 47.

[10] Miall Edwards, *The Philosophy of Religion* (New York: George Doran Company, 1929), 255.

W. Trotter states that religion was manifestation of collective feelings. Individuals, living in isolation, form religious groups because of the feeling of incompleteness. Individuals behave in accordance with the traditional norms of the group and in return religious feeling satisfies certain deeply rooted needs of individuals.[11]

According to Emile Durkheim, the main function of religion consists in strengthening social solidarity. Religious ideas are actualized in society. In primitive type of societies religious worship takes the form of totem worship. Totem is the rallying-symbol of a clan, which helps in unifying the system of beliefs of the members of a community.[12] Hence, for Durkheim, religious outlook is the concentrated expression of corporate living and the idea of society constitutes the very spirit of religion.[13]

William McDougall believes that religion is not only a social requirement but also has profound influence on social development. Fear was the most dominant emotion in the earliest forms of religious experience and people usually did not violate religious customs owing to the fear of punishment. However, the emotion of fear got transformed into reverence when religion was raised to a higher plane.[14]

R. H. Thouless maintains that the laws of social cohesion operate in religious groups. The members of a religious community are swayed by the same kind of emotions under the same conditions. The similarity of thought and belief of the members of a religious group is determined to a large extent by the group suggestion.[15] Religion is a cohesive force which helps the stabilization of the society. The establishment of well-ordered society depends to a great extent upon religious sentiments.[16]

Hence, religion could be considered as an important force for bringing about social solidarity in the early stages of social development. In the initial stages it could hardly be distinguished from morality. Religion is a force of social cohesion and so is integrally related to the social philosophy.

3. Religious Humanism and Social Philosophy

P. T. Raju states that "humanism has been so closely identified with the temper and mode of thought of a contemporary person that our age may be regarded as an age of humanism."[17] Humanism is of 'materialistic', 'pragmatic',

---

[11] W. Trotter, *Instincts of the Herd in Peace and War* (London: Ernest Benn Ltd., 1947), 113.

[12] Emile Durkheim, *The Elementary Forms of Religious Life* (New York: Macmillan Co., 1915), 167.

[13] Durkheim, *The Elementary Forms of Religious Life,* 419.

[14] William McDougall, *An Introduction to Social Psychology* (London: Methuen & Co., 1908), 267.

[15] R. H. Thouless, *An Introduction to Psychology of Religion,* 3rd edition (Cambridge: Cambridge University Press, 1971), 16.

[16] Thouless, *An Introduction to Psychology of Religion*, 40.

[17] P. T. Raju, *The Concept of Man* (London: George Allen & Unwin Ltd., 1960), 15.

'naturalistic', 'realistic' and 'spiritualistic' form. The term 'humanism' is associated with the **materialistic** form of socialism propounded by Karl Marx and other materialistic philosophers. They maintain that every human being should have economic equality, and there should be no exploitation of anyone in society. They adopt class-war, violence and struggle as means and methods for its realization.[18]

F. C. S. Schiller popularized his version of **pragmatism** as humanism. He accepts that human experience is essentially dynamic and is the sole criterion of truth. Trans-empirical or non-human truth is meaningless.[19] Corliss Lamout, the chief exponent of **naturalistic** humanism, summarizes his viewpoint: "Humanism is the view-point that man (sic) has but one life to lead and should make the most of it in terms of creative work and happiness...and that human beings, using their own intelligence and co-operating liberally with one another, can build an enduring citadel of peace and beauty upon this earth."[20]

Bertrand Russell, representative of **realistic** humanism, on the one hand, pleads for the preservation of human respect for truth, beauty and perfection in life, and on the other hand, he wants people to be united with the tie of common good and work for the reconstruction of our social institutions with a view to removing human suffering and inequality.[21] According to Robert Redfield, 'humanity' is the central subject matter of social science and humanism, as it is the vital interest of humankind.[22]

Modern India has also produced several humanists who emphasize **spiritual** humanism, a bit different than the western scholars. Raja Ram Mohan Roy, Mahatma Gandhi, Rabindranath Tagore, Swami Vivekananda are such thinkers, to name a few. The humanism of Raja Ram Mohan Roy, who brought many social reforms in India, was essentially a part of his fight against the evil aspects of Hinduism. He contemplated a universal religion which would be embraced by all humanity in upholding humanism. Mahatma Gandhi and Rabindranath Tagore were humanists, too. Their humanism had a mystical and religious basis.[23] V. S. Naravane explains "Gandhi's humanism had a moral-social bias while Tagore's was coloured by his aesthetic-mystical experience; but both were firm believers in the

---

[18] R. S. Srivastava, "Spiritual Humanism" in *Facets of Recent Indian Philosophy; The Philosophy of Life*, vol. 4, ed. by S. P. Dubey (New Delhi: Indian Council of Philosophical Research, 1998), 181.

[19] G. B. Gupta, "Humanism: An Over-View" in *Humanisation of the World Religions*, ed. by G. B. Gupta and S. K. Banerji (Delhi: Global Vision Publishing House, 2001), 8.

[20] Corliss Lamont, *Humanism as a Philosophy* (New York: Philosophical Library, 1950), 21f.

[21] Gupta, "Humanism: An Over-View", 9.

[22] Robert Redfield, *Human Nature and the Study of Society: The Papers of Robert Redfield*, vol. 1, ed. by Margaret Park Redfield (Chicago: University of Chicago Press, 1966), 10.

[23] Gupta, "Humanism: An Over-View", 19.

worth and dignity of the human individual."[24] Our engagement in social change, no doubt, needs moral and social basis, and should centre around upholding the dignity of human individual.

The analysis and arguments of *Advaita* philosophy by Swami Vivekananda is based on his new interpretation of *Karma Yoga*. This interpretation is given in just one sentence: 'Work is worship'. This principle of 'work is worship' has been used as a principle of bringing social change. Sibajiban Bhattacharyya is of the view that Vivekananda's Advaitism affects human life in all spheres, individual as well as social. Hence, Vivekananda's philosophy is not dry humanism, but a dynamic one.[25] Engaging in social change as a *karma yogi* provides a creative social and spiritual ideal with a practical emphasis.

Spiritual humanism looks upon humankind as a family and maintains human relations on the basis of love, sympathy, co-operation and fellowship. It takes morality as a *yoga* – the path of action which unites the individual with humankind and Divine. Spiritual humanism lays down principles for the growth of the spiritual society, wherein each one lives in moral and spiritual perfection.[26] It is a "culture that conceives of life as a movement of the Eternal in time, of the Universal in the individual, of the Infinite in the finite, and of the Divine in man (sic)."[27] The divinization of humanity through the realization of the divinity of each individual is the basis of Indian social philosophy.

4. Socio-Ethical Philosophy of *Sarvodaya*

The socio-ethical and political philosophy of *sarvodaya*[28] was first propounded by Mahatma Gandhi and later on translated into action by Vinoba Bhave. Another prominent leader of this order, Jayaprakash Narayan, joined *sarvodaya* movement as a *jivandani* from 1954.[29] The *bhoodan*, *gramdan*, and *jeevandan* are some of the expressions of the *sarvodaya* philosophy. Some of the major problems facing India during that period were economic and land exploitation. Mahatma Gandhi tried to tackle this problem by reviving village industries and land distribution schemes as a part of his *sarvodaya* philosophy.[30]

---

[24] V. S. Naravane, *Modern Indian Thought* (Bombay: Indian Council for Cultural Relations, 1964), 113.

[25] Sibajiban Bhattacharyya, "Swamiji's Advaita Vedanta is not Dry Humanism" in *Bulletin of the Ramakrishna Mission Institute of Culture*, vol. LXII, no. 11 (November 2011), 511.

[26] Srivastava, "Spiritual Humanism", 183-186.

[27] Sri Aurobindo, *The Foundations of Indian Culture*, vol. 14 (Pondicherry: Sri Aurobindo Birth Centenary Library, 1972), 172.

[28] The term *sarvodaya* is derived from two Sanskrit words *Sarva* meaning 'all' and *Udaya* meaning 'awakening or development'. Thus *sarvodaya* means "welfare of all".

[29] Shriman Narayan, *Vinoba: His Life and Work* (Bombay: Popular Prakashan, 1970), 4-11.

[30] K. S. Bharathi, *The Philosophy of Sarvodaya* (New Delhi: Indus Publishing Company, 1990), 15-16.

Sarvodaya literally means "the awakening, upliftment or emancipation of all." Vinoba Bhave says, "The term *Sarvodaya* means arising of all but not the arising of some and decline of other....The concept of welfare of all creatures is contained in the term."[31] *Sarvodaya* does not subscribe to the utilitarian formula of the greatest good of the greatest number. Mahatma Gandhi said, "The greatest good of all inevitably includes the good of the greatest number, and therefore a *sarvodayi* and the utilitarian will converge in many points in their career, but there does come a time when they must part company, and even work in opposite direction. The utilitarian to be logical will never sacrifice himself. The *sarvodayi* will even sacrifice himself (sic)."[32] Thus, the objective of Gandhi's teaching is not for a particular group, but the good of each and everyone. Christian engagement in social change needs to be strengthened by such *sarvodayi* concept.

Sarvodaya as a scheme of social product holds as its ideal the upliftment of all, that embraces spiritual regeneration of morally depraved and the material redemption of the poor. Jayaprakash Narayan states that *sarvodaya* stands for a society which would strive for the good of all and where everybody would be happy. In such a society there would be no distinction of high and low.[33]

The important feature of the socio-ethical philosophy of *sarvodaya* is the primacy of the spiritual values. Gandhi's political, economic and social endeavours and programmes were mainly directed towards upliftment of human consciousness through the service of the poor and the down-trodden, and intrinsically integrated into the realization of the divine spirit. This spiritual orientation and belief in ultimate eternal values like truth, non-violence, love and compassion have made an impact on the leaders and workers of *sarvodaya* movement.[34] For Vinoba, *sarvodaya* activities are the fulfillment of *Brahmajijñāsa*; the realization of the Absolute through selfless service to all living beings.[35]

For Gandhi, the spirit of *sarva-mukti* must be inculcated prior to joining the battle for establishing a *sarvodaya-samaj*. *Sarva-mukti* means both – the release of all and the release from all bondages. To achieve this goal, one must be fixed in truth, which is another name for God, should apply only non-violent means, and must care for the purity of means above the achievement of desired ends. Gandhi insisted on building up of character. A discipline of body and soul is pre-requisite to the establishment of an egalitarian society.[36]

---

[31] Vinoba Bhave, *Sarvodaya Vichar Aur Swarajya Sastra* (Tanjore: Sarvodaya Pracharalayam, 1957), 48.

[32] M. K. Gandhi, *Sarvodaya* (Ahmedabad: Navjeevan, 1954), 4.

[33] Jayaprakash Narayan, *A Picture of Sarvodaya Social Order* (Tanjore: Sarvodaya Pracharalayam, 1956), 6.

[34] K. S. Bharathi, *The Philosophy of Sarvodaya*, 43-44.

[35] Shriman Narayan, *Vinoba: His Life and Work*, 4-5.

[36] Archana Sinha, *The Social and Political Philosophy of Sarvodaya* (Patna: Janaki Prakashan, 1978), 165-66.

The social philosophy developed by the modern Indian thinkers provides directive to arrive at the authentic Indian Christian social philosophy for our engagement in social change.

5. Seeing through a Mirror Dimly

We are making an attempt to see the ideal social philosophy with the mirror of the viewpoint of modern Indian thinkers for Christian engagement in social change.

At the present historical juncture, religion and professional social work are in several important respects moving in opposite directions. As religion is losing its authority and broad moral influence, social action is gaining in economic affluence and institutional power. Religion faces the constant challenge in its position of social inclusiveness. In relation to the society, it is becoming increasingly voluntary and personal in orientation and more and more sensitive to the need for freedom of expression and practice. Social service, however, is moving in the opposite direction. It started at the point religion is now reaching, with emphasis upon individual charity, voluntary philanthropy, and a personalized approach to the service of the needy. It is the social agencies that are now becoming inclusive, often impersonal, and collective in orientation. In Indian social philosophy, religion and social welfare blends beautifully; it emphasizes the social need of religious quest as well as the necessity of spiritual inclusiveness in social services. Hence, in the formation of social theory of values and the ministry of the church, it remains profitable, even imperative, for social change or reform to maintain its alliance with religion. It is important to recognize that spirituality and social welfare are consistent and complementary.

Troeltsch observes that it is the discontented minorities that produce the creative and critical social protests.[37] Perhaps it is incredible to imagine Christians as the discontented and creative social prophets. John Bennett states that the special contribution Christianity can make to social change arises "from the very fact that churches are under no local or national authority. They exist in response to a divine revelation which local or national public opinion cannot control."[38] The statement obviously requires critical observation but it does point to the religious stance of a significant section of Indian society, which can make a considerable difference in the society by considering the welfare of all as divine ordinance.

We cannot create a social philosophy in the isolation of our academic studies. It is better known by social reformers than by sociologists and theologians. However, without underestimating the contribution that the academic theorists can make, the new philosophical model must emerge out of the flux of the

[37] Ernst Troeltsch, *The Social Teachings of the Christian Churches* (Louisville: Westminster John Knox Press, 1992), 991.

[38] John Bennett, *When Christians Make Political Decisions* (New York: Association Press, 1964), 107.

changing social environment. The minimum requisites of Indian Christian model of social philosophy appear to be as follows:

(a) A social philosophy must be based on principles that are subject to empirical and pragmatic verification. We must know that the cherished truths of the most powerful secular and religious groups are subject to the tests of historical, social and scientific experience. We should give more serious consideration to *sarvodaya* as a theory of ethics that is grounded in the assumption that all humankind has the same basic needs which must be fulfilled. The universal striving for equity and justice between human beings is a reflection of our common needs and inclinations. Reinhold Niebuhr points out that there are some general principles of justice that define the right order of life in any community, which needs to be explored and further affirmed.[39] The task of the Christian *sarvodayi* is to critically engage with these values embedded in the Indian religions and society, and work towards the good of each and everyone.

(b) A Christian model of social philosophy must be based on a morality that synthesizes the knowledge of revelation theology, rational philosophy and the empirical social sciences, which Swami Vivekananda calls 'practical Vedanta'. The corresponding conceptions in theology, philosophy and social sciences may enrich the implicit hope for an integral society in Indian context.

(c) The content of the liberative social theory must be discovered in the continuing dialogue between diverse interests and powers, with no religious or secular group claiming a monopoly over truth. Consensus with respect to fundamental principles, values, and goals must be maintained and affirmed. An agreement must exist with respect to our basic beliefs about the nature and destiny of human being and society. John C. Murray states that "we hold certain truths; therefore, we can argue about them. There can be no argument except...within a context of agreement."[40] A constructive dialogue between Christians and other religious and secular groups may help us to work together towards required social change in our Indian society.

(d) Social philosophy must reflect the view that human problems are both spiritual and social. Along with the material achievements of justice, the visible concern of the community to achieve that justice is also important. The spiritualism and materialism are polar opposites only

---

[39] Reinhold Niebuhr, *The Children of Light and the Children of Darkness* (Chicago: University of Chicago Press, 2011), 67f.

[40] John Courtney Murray, *We Hold These Truths* (Maryland: Rowman & Littlefield Publishers, 2005), 25.

in the sense that each pursue excessive measures in opposite directions with the one-sided conception or misconception of the nature of human being. S. Radhakrishnan is of the view that spiritual awareness and social efficiency are not only consistent but also complementary. Such religious humanism is the prerequisite of Christian engagement in social change.

(e) The Christian social theory must speak of the welfare that is universal in nature. It is at this point that the contribution of religious thinkers should be most clearly enunciated. Religious belief of Neo-Vedantins as well as Christians present the understanding of the universal God. We have learned through the experience of pluralism that no group possesses the universal truth in all of its grandeur. We must learn that the welfare of all communities require the consensus between all of them and a concern for the social welfare of all human beings.

This model affirms the basic truth of the cultural and religious life of India, that is, the realization of Supreme Reality in the human heart. There can be no realization of this highest principle in us without the formation of an elevated personality permeated with all social and moral values in life. Human activities in the practical sphere of life should be so disciplined, ordered and value-oriented to reach the apex of life after realizing the oneness with all other beings and things of the world through social and moral practice. The social philosophy based on religious humanism encourages Christians to recognize the metaphysical conception of oneness of life and equality of all living beings and to consciously uphold human dignity in bringing social change.

Conclusion

Social philosophy studies the most fundamental laws which influence social cohesion, social progress and social disintegration. It reflects upon the basic nature of human relationships in society. The scope of social philosophy includes everything which has human and social significance. It is not concerned with the discovery of social facts but with the interpretation of social values. The important feature of contemporary social philosophy is that the human problem is being solved in new conditions, in which a person acquires a new form of identification, recognizing himself/herself in both his/her spiritual rational constructions and his/her material production.

Social philosophy in general is seen as to reveal the basic features in the society in which the holistic development of each individual becomes the goal of whole society. It studies the most fundamental laws which influence social coherence, social progress and social disintegration. Social philosophy, in Indian context, is a normative inquiry of social and moral values, and the ways in which these shape individuals and establish a good social order helping human beings to live and act together. The Christian social philosophy in India needs to seek a blend of metaphysics, religion, ethics and politics, which is highly synthetic and comprehensive in character. The belief that religion has an intimate contact with the entire human life gives a religious touch to the social and political ideas. The destiny provided to an individual by such religious humanism is to realize oneness with other social beings and through it with the Universal Being, in their efforts of bringing social change.

12

Towards an Active Christian Public Engagement in the Context of Hindu(tva) Fundamentalism

Muthuraj Swamy

1. Introduction

Religious fundamentalism is now a global phenomenon, and it affects human life at various levels.[1] It may have a long history within each religion, but in the 21st century it has become a dominant reality, posing dangers to collective and community life of human beings as well as to their personal identities and individuality. While religious fundamentalism is a global phenomenon, and can be found in different societies all over the world, for those living in India today, Hindu fundamentalism, which is also variedly called Hindutva, Hindu Nationalism or Sangh ideology, has become a serious threat. Especially, for the lives of religious and other minorities, the situation has worsened since 2014, when Bharatiya Janata Party (BJP), the major political party supporting the ideology of Hindu fundamentalism, won the Indian elections and came to power. Since then, Hindu fundamentalism has come to affect Christians in India more seriously than ever though we are not the only group to be affected. There are other religious minorities such as Muslims and groups based on caste, ethnicity and gender: like Dalits, Tribals, Women, LGBT groups who are also at the receiving end of Hindu fundamentalism. Hence the urgent task for us, Christians in India today, is to understand, interpret and address the various consequences that have come as a

[1] An earlier version of this essay has been published in Clark Theological College Journal VI/2 (January 2017): 21-37.

result of Hindu fundamentalism, and to continue to struggle with finding ways and means to resist it.

In responding to Hindu fundamentalism, one of the crucial challenges remain for Christians in India today, which needs to be seriously reflected on, is how we Christians, who also have fundamentalist wings and tendencies within our own religion, both in India and outside, both in the present and in the past, can make our responses effective to challenge this dangerous phenomenon. This invites us to address the problem of religious fundamentalism in general, and Hindu fundamentalism in particular, and at the same time by being self-critical of our own excesses wherever necessary. Also, one of the important steps in responding to Hindu fundamentalism is to understand it in terms of its complex historical developments, manifestations and consequences. Further, in the context of the necessity to challenge it, Christians in India also need to think about and assess their level of public engagement in society in responding to the issues affecting Indian society.

Hence, in this essay, I discuss Christian responses to Hindu fundamentalism in a three-fold approach: first by highlighting some of the important aspects and factors connected with it both historically and in the current situation; second by surveying some of the common ways by which Christians in India have been and are responding to Hindu fundamentalism and the advantages and limitations in such responses and finally by discussing how Christians in India need to strengthen and expand their efforts in understanding Hindu fundamentalism and challenge it by becoming self-critical, open and engaged in society.

2. The Growing Menace of Hindutva Fundamentalism in Contemporary India

Like every fundamentalism,[2] Hindu fundamentalism is also a complex phenomenon and evades an easy definition. However, it does not mean that it cannot be defined or a framework cannot be developed to understand and interpret it, if one is mindful of the whole lot of complex aspects and developments

[2] There are a number of studies on the phenomenon of religious fundamentalism all over the world, and almost every researcher has expressed the difficulty of defining fundamentalism easily. For instance see, Lawrence Kaplan, *Fundamentalism in Comparative Perspective* (University of Massachusetts Press, 1992); Malise Ruthven, *Fundamentalism: A Very Short Introduction* (Oxford: Oxford University Press, 2004). The Fundamentalism Project which researched fundamentalism all over the world and has published the works in a series by the Chicago University Press in six volumes between 1994 and 2004 (*Fundamentalisms Observed*, ed. Martin E. Marty, 1994; *Fundamentalisms and the State: Remaking Polities, Economies, and Militancy*, ed. Martin E. Marty, 1996; *Fundamentalisms and Society: Reclaiming the Sciences, the Family, and Education*, ed. Martin E. Marty, 1997; *Strong Religion: The Rise of Fundamentalisms around the World*, ed. Gabriel A. Almond, 2003; *Accounting for Fundamentalisms: The Dynamic Character of Movements*, ed. Martin E. Marty, 2004 and *Fundamentalisms Comprehended*, ed. Martin E. Marty, 2004) also uses different conceptual tools and frameworks to define, study and interpret religious fundamentalism.

involved in it and the factors which sustain it. Hence, instead of attempting to merely define it, what would be helpful is tracing its historical developments in the last two centuries and its current manifestations especially in the political and cultural realms, its consequences in terms of its attitudes of hate and violence towards minorities and its effects on every walk of life in Indian society.[3] In this essay, in a broad way I am concerned with Hindu fundamentalism in terms of its attitudes towards the other: the process of othering which sustains fundamentalism.[4]

Hindu fundamentalism by no means is a recent phenomenon that abruptly entered into the modern Indian society. For centuries, it has been shaped and nurtured by various social cultural, political and economic conditions and factors. The word "Hindu" is a colonially constructed term to appear in the middle of the 19th century to refer to the people living in the Indian peninsula, and this collective word would be used later to unite Hindus and unify Hinduism against colonialism. However, narrow and rigid mindsets associated with different dominant Hindu traditions leading to conflict and violence have a long history.[5] The long time conflicts and violence that took place between those following Saivite and Vaishnavite traditions in the early medieval India is a case in point,[6] even though Hindu fundamentalist wings always oppose any move today to talk

---

[3] Among the numerous studies tracing the development of Hindu fundamentalism historically, the following are some of the significant works: Andrew J. Nicholson, *Unifying Hinduism: Philosophy and Identity in Indian Intellectual History* (New York: Columbia University Press, 2010); D. Anand, *Hindu Nationalism in India and the Politics of Fear* (New York: Palgrave Macmillan, 2011); Dwijendra Narayan Jha, *Rethinking Hindu Identity* (London & New York: Routledge, 2009); Prabhu Bapu, *Hindu Mahasabha in Colonial North India, 1915-1930: Constructing Nation and History* (London & New York: Routledge, 2013); Sylvie Guichard, *The Construction of History and Nationalism in India: Textbooks, Controversies and Politics* (London & New York: Routledge, 2010); Walter K. Andersen, Shridhar D. Damle, *The Brotherhood in Saffron: The Rashtriya Swayamsevak Sangh and Hindu revivalism* (Westview Press, 1987); and William Gould, *Hindu Nationalism and the Language of Politics in Late Colonial India* (Cambridge University Press, 2004). See also Dwijendra Narayan Jha, *The Myth of the Holy Cow* (London & New York: Verso, 2002).

[4] The connection between religious fundamentalism and 'othering' is dealt with well in a recent work: Ragini Sen, Wolfgang Wagner and Caroline Howarth, "Transcending Boundaries: Fundamentalism, Secularism and Social Capital in Multi-faith Societies" in *Perspectives on Violence and Othering in India,* edited by R. C. Tripathi and Purnima Singh (New Delhi: Springer India 2016), 215-234.

[5] There are recent works focusing on how, contrary to the notion that Hinduism is a peace-loving religion from the ancient times, there were many instances of conflicts and violence between different Hindu traditions. William Pinch in his work *Warrior Ascetics and Indian Empires* (Cambridge: Cambridge University Press, 2006) have traced these developments well.

[6] For detailed accounts of Saivite-Vasihnavite conflicts in the pre-colonial India see N. Jagadeesan, *History of Sri Vaishnavism in Tamil Country (Post-Ramanuja)* (Madurai: Koodal, 1997); S. Subrahmanyam, "Before the Leviathan: Sectarian Violence and the State in Pre-colonial India," in K. Basu and S. Subrahmanyam, eds., *Unravelling the Nation: Secular Conflict and India's Secular Identity* (New Delhi: Penguin Books, 1996), 44-80; and V. Dalmia and H. von Stietencron, eds.

about the internal divisions within Hindu traditions in the past because it directly goes against their project of one unified Hinduism that they claim existed in India from the beginning.[7] However, the modern Hindu fundamentalism has strong roots in the Hindu revivalism that began in the 19th century India especially in Bengal and Gujarat.[8] In the context of the Western Christian criticisms of Hindu traditions, as well as the atrocities committed by European imperialists on various aspects of life and culture in India, Hindu reformers and revivalists such as Raja Rammohun Roy and Dayananda Saraswati attempted for serious reforms in Hinduism as well as made attempts to unite Indians to fight Western imperialism. The struggle for Indian independence also offered a platform for this development. The extremist strides of these reforms and revivalism were used by the Hindu fundamentalists in the early 20th century who began to unite Hindus against Muslims, Christians and other minorities. Hindu extremist organizations such as Hindu Mahasabha and Rastriya Swayamsevak Sangh (RSS) are some of the results of these developments which strongly put forth and shaped Hindu fundamentalist ideologies. A demand for Hindu rashtra (nation), comprised only of Hindus where minorities can have an existence solely at the mercy of the former, became stronger, and is now identified as the ideology of Hindu nationalism.

In the post Independent India Hindu fundamentalism started to take political shape, and with the formation of Bharatiya Jan Sangh in the early 1950s, it started to assert itself in the political sphere. Especially since 1980, when Bharatiya Jan Sangh was re-founded as BJP, the Hindutva ideologues have intensified their demand for making India as a 'Hindu rashtra' which has posed threats to religious minorities. With the demolition of Babri Masjid in 1992 and attacks against Muslims in Godhra in 2002 and Christians in Kandhamal in 2008, Hindu fundamentalism has become more extremist and fanatic and threatening to the lives of minorities. As BJP and its ideology have started to gain political support by winning in state and national elections, Hindu fundamentalism has been becoming more assertive and attempting to design new ways to expand its influence in the country and abroad. Now, after BJP forming a government at the centre with a majority, rarely a day goes without some atrocities by the Hindu fundamentalist groups against religious minorities.

In the contemporary context, Hindu fundamentalism has also intensified attacks on those who do not correspond to or support its ideologies. Secularism is one of the major victims here. But also lately there is a systematic attack on

---

Representing Hinduism: The Constructions of Religious Traditions and National Identity (New Delhi: Sage Publications, 1995).

[7] The Hindu fundamentalist groups' threat to the Indian film 'Dasavatharam' for portraying Saivaite-Vasinavite conflicts in the movie is an example. See http://www.behindwoods.com/tamil-movie-news-1/may-08-01/dasavatharam-02-05-08.html, accessed on 25 November 2016.

[8] See Partha Sarathy Ghosh, *BJP and the Evolution of Hindu Nationalism: From Periphery to Centre* (New Delhi: Manohar Publishers & Distributors, 1999).

intellectuals, rationalists and artists who pose critical perspectives, reactions, oppositions and challenges to the Hindutva ideology. There are many efforts by the Hindu fundamentalists to undermine and undo the Nehruvian secular legacy[9] that has protected and sustained the idea of unity in diversity in India since Independence. The bureaucracy is influenced and modified to suit the Hindu fundamentalist agenda, as those sympathetic to such ideologies are appointed to lead many of the government and public institutions. Another major area of life that is under attack by Hindu fundamentalism is civil society. NGOs, especially that struggle for human rights and minority rights and those who do not support the Hindutva ideology, are villanised, demonized and termed as anti-national.[10] This makes the wider Hindutva ideologues to mount severe attacks on these NGOs.

Today anti-nationalism has become a powerful weapon in the hands of Hindu fundamentalists who try to settle score with those who do not toe their line. It has now become a habit of the BJP government to appeal to nationalism and national interest for every single issue, and those who are critical of its policies are straight away termed as anti-nationals, and the conflation of Hindu fundamentalist interests with national interest is done at every possible level,[11] and the notion of development has been carefully and strategically used by those at the top to keep common citizens away from understanding this conflation. Moreover, common people's food choices and cultural practices are increasingly controlled and influenced by the ideologies of Hindu fundamentalism. In the name of saving cows ('cow politics' as it is called) minorities such as Muslims, Dalits and Tribals are targeted. Ghar Wapsi (literally meaning 'home coming')

---

[9] The attacks on Nehuruvian legacy are increasing especially after the BJP came to power in 2014. For instance see Tarun Vijay, "Failed Ideas" in *Frontline*, December 12, 2014 where he ends his article saying "Nehru needed to be undone, to let India find its soul and speed." http://www.frontline.in/cover-story/failed-ideas/article6629932.ece, accessed on 25 November 2016. Of course, there are good responses from secular minded thinkers and activists for this destructive act of Hindu fundamentalists. For instance see Ram Puniyani "India: Reversing Nehruvian Legacy" in *South Asian Citizens Web*, 10 November 2014, http://sacw.net/article9968.html, accessed on 25 November 2016; and Anil Nauriya, "Sectarian Politics and the Partition of India: The Targeting of Nehru and the Congress" in *The Hindu Centre for Politics and Public Policy*, September 26, 2016, http://www.thehinducentre.com/multimedia/archive/03024/127_Sectarian_Poli_3024950a.pdf, accessed on 25 November 2016.

[10] Recent attacks on eco-welfare NGOs like Greenpeace, human rights organizations such as Amnesty International, and human rights activists like Teesta Setalvad and their NGOs, who played a major role in exposing the role of political Hindutva forces in violence against minorities, show how Hindu fundamentalists are opposed to civil society movements that dare to challenge them and their chauvinistic worldview.

[11] A wonderful essay has been recently written by G. Sambath, a columnist in the news daily *The Hindu,* on this. "Morality of Binaries" *The Hindu*, November 18, 2016. http://www.thehindu.com/opinion/lead/demonetisation-the-morality-of-binaries/article9357888.ece, accessed on 18 November 2016.

which is a reconversion of people to Hinduism has returned as a useful tool to attack Christians and Muslims,[12] and is intensely exercised and promoted by the followers of Hindu fundamentalism.

Thus, the development of Hindu fundamentalism and the various factors associated with it and the consequences it has brought have posed many challenges to minorities like Christians in India. These developments have invited strong reactions from some quarters such as those committed to secular values and ideals and Hindu moderates and other religious minorities, and it is my observation that concrete and constructive responses from Christians to these developments are still due even though there have been and are some Christians who have taken attempts to challenge Hindu fundamentalism. Their limitations are discussed in the following section.

3. Limitations in the Current Christian Responses to Hindu Fundamentalism

In the 19th century context of Hindu revivalism, there was comparatively a good engagement between sections of Hindu reformers and Christians – both foreign missionaries and Indian Christians.[13] Some of these engagements were in dialogue form and contributed to mutual learning and appreciation and some of them were critical of each other. Today among some sections, Christianity is believed to have caused reformation in Hinduism – Bengal renaissance is often cited as an example.[14] Even though there were supremacist tendencies among Christian missionaries, nevertheless the interactions and engagement of Christians with the others for the development and welfare of the Indian society could be found. Similarly, against the accusation that Christianity was a foreign religion, many Indian Christian theologians such as Keshub Chunder Sen, P. Chenchiah, V. Chakkarai and others argued for the Asianess of Christianity or Christianity's Indian connections and encouraged Christians in India to join movements that were involved in struggling for the independence of India. Further, the role of Christians in nation building was also strongly encouraged at the eve of the Indian independence and immediately after that by many Christian theologians and leaders.[15]

---

[12] Of course, reconversion to Hinduism is not a new phenomenon, and it has its history from the time of Hindu revivalism in Gujarat since the early 19th century, though after 2014 it has become stronger. Dayananda Saraswati, the founder of Arya Samaj is considered to be its earliest proponent.

[13] For instance, the interactions between Serampore missionaries and Raja Rammohun Roy in the early nineteenth century is often referred to and are appreciated in the history of Indian Christianity. These dialogues are believed to have led to a number of changes in the Indian society.

[14] Sisir Kumar Das, *The Shadow of the Cross: Christianity and Hinduism in a Colonial Situation* (Delhi: Munshiram Manoharlal Publishers, 1974).

[15] Several essays, books and collections have appeared on this theme based on conceptual analysis and empirical research. Among them the works by P. D. Devanandan and M. M. Thomas in

However, in the post-Independent India, especially when Hindu extremism started to grow and make wider influence, the Christian responses to it have somewhat slipped into an ambiguous, if not a decline, mode. Some Indian Christian theologians and church leaders have indeed taken attempts to engage with these issues predominantly within the framework of interreligious dialogue, to point out how a dialogue with these extremist and fundamentalist groups is important that they may offer a solution for co-existence.[16] But generally an active and constructive response in terms of challenging and resisting Hindu fundamentalism has not emerged within the broad Christian community in India. This, as noted earlier, is not to undermine the serious engagement that some theologians and Christian leaders in some circles have undertaken in the past, but my opinion is that an effective response to Hindu fundamentalism from Christianity is yet to emerge. Sometimes, the fact that Christians being minority in India may be cited as a reason for this, i.e., they really cannot do much with these chauvinists who are not open for diverse communities co-existing. However, challenging and resisting structures of oppression is a call for being Christian and this applies to Christians in India as well.

First, Christian efforts in understanding Hindu fundamentalism and Hindutva agenda are generally limited. True, many Christians do live with the Hindus in ordinary living contexts – some in good relationships and some in tensions due to various factors that go beyond religious identity or a religious divide. But, the poisoning of ordinary people by Hindu fundamentalists has not received the attention it deserves and not taken the central stage in the Indian Christian circles for contemplation and action, except when Christians are the direct target. Therefore, to what extent Christians in India take serious efforts to understand and comprehend the many complex factors associated with Hindu fundamentalism, and not simply in terms of its effects on Christian community alone, is a genuine question. In my opinion, among Christian community in India in general, the predominant response so far has been to point out how Hindu fundamentalism works against Christian missionary activities and how it leads to persecutions of Christians, and sometimes its attacks on the secular fabric of the Indian constitution. Other perspectives and approaches to assess and analyse Hindu fundamentalism's wider impacts and make the responses accordingly are relatively less. What then is necessary is to understand Hindu fundamentalism within a wider framework to see how it affects people's overall life in India.

---

the 1950s and 1960s are significant. See their work, *Christian Participation in Nation Building* (Bangalore: CISRS, 1960).

[16] P. D. Devanandan's reflection in short works such as *Resurgent Hinduism: A Review of Modern Movements* (Bangalore: CISRS, 1958) and *The Gospel and Renascent Hinduism* (London: SCM Press, 1959); S. J. Samartha's *The Courage for Dialogue: Ecumenical Issues in Inter-religious Relationships* (Geneva: WCC, 1997); and many articles appeared in the journal *Religion and Society* of CISRS, Bangalore have this perspective.

What I mean here is that Hindu fundamentalism should not be seen simply as anti-Christian and obscurantist to Christian activities or interests, or only in terms of a cause for persecution of Christians, but in terms of how it affects and can lead to destroy the entire Indian society if it is left unchecked. Let me narrate here a personal encounter with a church pastor from a semi-urban part of India. Sometime back, I had a conversation with him regarding the violence meted out towards religious minorities by the Hindutva forces. While appreciating the responses from some Christian circles in terms of organizing processions and protests and raising their voices against the Hindutva violence when Christian communities were targeted, nevertheless, I also pointed out how Christians remained silent when other minorities including minorities from other religious are targeted and attacked by Hindutva forces.[17] The pastor was vehemently arguing that why he should be concerned at all when other religious minorities are targeted and attacked. 'They [the Hindu fundamentalists] now attack only Christianity so I have to have a concern for my religion; let others take care of themselves when they are attacked' was his response. My primary problem here is not with a selective response he indicated, though it has its own problems, but the very perception of the challenge of Hindu fundamentalism only as anti-Christian. The pity is that many of us Christians prefer to respond to Hindu fundamentalism in part especially when and where we are affected but not as a whole. That how Hindu fundamentalism poses a serious threat to the overall life in India, and which only eventually affects Christians is not appreciated often.

Second, when Hindu fundamentalism is causing a concern for Christians, we appeal to the secular constitution of India which we believe can protect us. However, we miss the point about how Hindu fundamentalism also has grown in spite of the presence of a powerful Indian secular constitution.[18] Of course, various social and political factors have shaped the growth of Hindu fundamentalism in spite of secular worldviews and values being active in India. However, a more serious issue is to do with the fact that Christians in India have been and are exercising an ambiguous relationship with secularism – to appreciate when they think it can protect them and to reject it when they believe it is not

[17] In a visit to Gujarat a few years back I had a conversation with a bishop of a mainline church there about the reactions of Christians in Gujarat during the violence against Muslims in 2002, and he mentioned that Christians couldn't and didn't do much to show their solidarity with the Muslims, with a few exceptions.

[18] This has led many intellectuals like Asish Nandy and others to get disillusioned with secularism. See his essay "An Anti-secularist Manifesto" in *Seminar* 314 (October, 1985), 14-24. Also see his chapter "Closing the Debate on Secularism: A Personal Statement" in Anuradha Dingwaney Needham and Rajeswari Sunder Rajan, *The Crisis of Secularism in India* (Ranikhet: Permanent Black, 2007), 107-117; and Anuradha Dingwaney Needham and Rajeswari Sunder Rajan, *The Crisis of Secularism in India* (Durham and London: Duke University Press, 2007).

helpful for them.[19] Our common idea is that the secular framework of the Indian constitution is just a protection for minorities. We rarely go beyond that in terms of how a secular worldview in the context of many religions can help and set right democracy, human rights and the welfare of the common people especially the minorities of different kinds and we often fail to protect that worldview. In spite of its limitations, secular framework works against chauvinistic forces on one hand and totalitarian and autocratic rulers on the other, and hence it is the responsibility of Christians to support movements and perspectives that struggle against these destructive forces. Abandoning the values associated with secularism or ambiguously relating with it has severe problems.[20] This is important especially when secularism itself now is undergoing serious transformation to reform itself after it has been critiqued for its inability to check fanaticism in Indian society.

Third, threatened by Hindu fundamentalism, there have also been attempts to strengthen religious identities among the minorities in India. In the context of diverse communities in India, affirming our identity and rights is necessary for us as Indian citizens, but attempts to ghettoise communities based on religious identities will only aggravate the problems for the religious minority groups particularly if they attempt to create and maintain narrow and fixed religious identities. Because, religious identity is not the sole identity with which people function or are identified and hence making it as a separate and concrete identity has its limitations. The communities that concretise religious identities become less open to others and promote a sense of isolationism which can become an acute problem.[21] Our religious identity is important, but it has to be exercised in co-existence with others and in the light of many other identities we share with our fellow human beings.[22]

Fourth, pointing out the Indian Christian contribution to the building of the Indian nation may be a good way of responding to Hindu fundamentalism

---

[19] I have dealt with this ambiguity briefly in my recent book. Muthuraj Swamy, *The Problem with Interreligious Dialogue: Plurality, Conflict and Elitism in Hindu-Christian-Muslim Relations* (London: Bloomsbury, 2016), 78, 95-99.

[20] This is not to say that secularism perfectly works in India, but what is important is the framework and mindset offered by secularism for an inclusive and democratic society is important. Hence, my proposal is that instead of antagonizing those promoting secular values we can relate with secular framework to transform it as it also is now undergoing through the process of reformation not just in India but also in many multicultural societies all over the globe. See Muthuraj Swamy, "Imagining Christian Identity in Relation to Reformed Secularism," in NCC Review CXXXVI/9 (October 2016): 525-543.

[21] In a recent work brilliantly done, Robert F. Shedinger studies the process of isolating and narrowing religious identities in the American Context and the consequences it brings. *Radically Open: Transcending Religious Identity in an Age of Anxiety* (Eugene, Origen: Cascade Books, 2012).

[22] Amartya Sen presents a strong case for an affirmation of multiple identities which can be a solution to the many conflicts India is facing today: *Identity and Violence: The Illusion of Destiny* (London: Penguin Books, 2006).

which dubs Christianity as a foreign religion promoting alien culture and practices that are not helpful to the Indian culture.[23] However, first of all, one should note that the appeal of some of the Christian theologians and leaders to common Christians in India to contribute to the nation building has not always impacted Christian community as a whole in India. For instance, though we know and live our lives as Indian citizens, many Christians in India have not come beyond the stereotypes involving religious and non-religious divides. Christian participation in politics is still a contested issue for many Christians in India as Christian leaders who take a religion-in-politics approach are normally criticised. While common Christians' response towards national-building is limited, at least in terms of their worldview, the most important problem is that even the sincere and genuine contributions made towards nation-building by some sections of Christians have not really softened the tone of Hindu fundamentalists who are keen on insisting Indian Christianity's foreign status and exploiting it to further their political divisive agenda. I think, in the context of nationalism being used to exclude, stigmatize and ostracize religious minorities, Christian response in terms of nation building has to be rethought. In my opinion, Christianity in India has failed to bring alternative definitions of nationalism that is inclusive and is built on the care for the neighbour rather than simply an emotional appeal to unity of the nation and to maintain its divisive boundaries.

Thus, mostly Christian responses to Hindu fundamentalism are conditioned by the binaries and stereotypes in terms of Christianity versus Hindu fundamentalism, religious versus non-religious, religion versus politics, minority religious identities versus others and similar divides which lead to a kind of isolationism or a separationist tendency prevalent among many Christians in India. This is very much evident in the light of a question we can ask ourselves: in responding to Hindu fundamentalism, to what extent we cooperate with Hindu moderates and secularists? In fact in the Indian context, the challenge to Hindu fundamentalism and its attacks on minorities come strongly from Hindu moderates and those working within secular framework. Apart from some theological or institutional dialogues with these people, Christians in India hardly go beyond and critically appropriate in their responses the perspectives from the moderates and those supporting a secular approach to resist Hindu fundamentalism.

Overall, Christian responses to Hindu fundamentalism in India for the last few decades have been limited. In them, one can see a failure in understanding Hindu fundamentalism in a wider context affecting Indian citizens, not merely Christians, lack of engagement and isolationist tendencies, failure to be critical of the narrow interpretation of Indian nationalism and also the failure to coordinate

[23] M. S. S. Pandian shows how the Indian Christian attempts to challenge the notion that Christianity was a foreign religion did not really make success with Hindu fundamentalists. See his essay "Nation as Nostalgia: Ambiguous Spiritual Journeys of Vengal Chakkarai" in *Economic and Political Weekly* XXXVIII/51-52 (December 27, 2003), 5357-5365.

with secularists and Hindu moderates and other open minded thinkers and activists in responding to Hindu fundamentalism.

4. Possible Ways for Strengthening the Christian Responses to Hindu Fundamentalism

(a) Towards Understanding Religious Fundamentalism Better

First of all, there has to be a holistic understanding of the phenomenon of religious fundamentalism in general and Hindu fundamentalism in particular, and Christians in India need to take serious efforts in unpacking this complex issue. Rather than simply considering and interpreting Hindu fundamentalism as merely anti-Christian, that is, working against the Christian missionary activities and Christian interests, how its basic worldview is dangerous to human beings in general and particular for India should be explored.

Hindu fundamentalism is first of all a narrow mindset and attitude to others filled with hate and violence and conditioned by chauvinistic, totalitarian and authoritarian worldviews. The othering process is crucial to its existence and it attempts to exclude the other but at the same time impose a totalitarian mindset that homogenises everyone. But its exclusionary practices are detrimental not only to religious and other minorities but also to the lives of many ordinary Hindus as well. It has strong connections with and sympathies for caste system in spite of the modern advancements in community living. Even though, it always denies the existence of caste today Hindu fundamentalism itself actually endorses and practises caste. In fact many who follow Hindu fundamentalist ideology are casteist and work for the maintenance of this ancient menace in one or other way. This means that along with the growth of Hindu fundamentalism there is a resurgence of caste system which is mainly powered by those dominant castes who think they have lost their privileges and power over marginalised communities like Dalits and Tribals. Hindu fundamentalism in this context is an attempt to regain their lost privileges.[24] The analysis of Ram Puniyani who points out how those who thought they were losing power in the wake of modernisation resorted to religious fundamentalism to capture political power by founding organisations with totalitarian and hierarchical mindset, like 'Hindu' 'Mahasabha' and 'Muslim' 'League, and the progressives who had inclusive vision and founded organisations such as Indian National Congress and Republic Party of India is

[24] The current word affairs show that religious fundamentalism is making a resurgence and mostly in the form of those privileged communities seeking to regain the privileges once they had on vulnerable communities. In fact the election of Donald Trump as US president, supported by a huge percentage of white Christian evangelical and conservative votes is interpreted as the revenge of white race which claims to regain the privileges it lost *to* (over) others like Blacks, immigrants, etc. Of course, there is a very good example from the Bible for appealing to religious fundamentalism when one perceives that he/she loses the privileges: the story of Demetrius found in Acts 19 illustrates this.

helpful here and should be taken seriously.[25] Further, Hindu fundamentalism has many characteristics that are found in other fundamentalisms – patriarchy, age discrimination, authoritarianism and totalitarian tendencies, anti-democracy and violation of human rights. Hindu fundamentalism should be understood against all these developments if Christians are to respond effectively.

(b) Overcoming Isolationism and Moving towards Engagement and Openness

As mentioned earlier, if Hindu fundamentalism is to be challenged effectively by Christians, we need to be aware and self-critical of how Christian fundamentalism works in India. Though, Christian fundamentalism is also a global phenomenon with centuries of history, its central location of influence has been the Europe and America. Positively, it may have been associated with various Christian revivalist events and movements in the 18th and 19th centuries. But since the mid 19th century, it has also been promoting extremist perspectives with racist tendencies. The connection between Christian fundamentalism and slavery, its resurgence in the early 20th century in the wake of abolition of slavery and freeing black people in the late 19th century, and the role of extremist Christians in electing Donald Trump as the US president even after, on many occasions, he openly expressed support for racism and exhibited a totalitarian mindset. In India, Christian fundamentalism may not exhibit all the extremist tendencies of its counterpart in the West. But its existence is undeniable. For me, there are basically two manifestations of Christian fundamentalism in India: first, the exclusivist attitudes towards people of other faiths and secular ideologies; and second, the lack of engagement in society which is built on the faith-world binary and expressed through indifference and isolationism.

The first aspect is often the subject of interreligious dialogue which attempts to overcome fundamentalist attitudes that affect good relations between religions. Outside the dialogue circles, Christian fundamentalism is also questioned for various practices that are followed by Christians toward others. Of course, the major one is conversion to Christianity. Even though, in spite of the very meagre percentage of Christian population, there are political strategies and calculations for projecting conversion to Christianity as a serious issue, some scholars studying Christian fundamentalism do find problems with it. For instance, Pradip Thomas who has studied Christian fundamentalism and has highlighted various issues connected with it, especially in terms of using media for Christian missionary ends, says that the Christian groups in India "may not use real physical violence, though they are well-versed in using the media and non-media means to propagate 'symbolic violence' that is often backed up by economic enticements to persuade or

---

[25] See Ram Puniyani, *Contours of Hindu Rashtra: Hindutva, Sangh Parivar, and Contemporary Politics* (Delhi: Kalpaz Publications, 2006).

coerce individuals and communities to become Christian."[26] While acknowledging that the spiritual yearnings of many Christians are being fulfilled by the growth on new Christian movements that may have fundamentalist tendencies, Thomas says that "before Christians point their fingers at other fundamentalisms and fundamentalists, they have a responsibility to 'clean their own stables', and nodal and apex church bodies need to rein in Christian fundamentalists who are doing their utmost best to wreck inter-faith relationships in India."[27]

While Christians need to be self-critical of their fundamentalist attitudes, what makes their responses to Hindu fundamentalism more limited, in my opinion, is the lack of Christian engagement with the society and developing a kind of isolationism. This doesn't mean that the Christians in India live in ghettos – though the missionary compound idea was prevalent during the missionary times – but in attitudes and discourses. This also does not mean that Christians don't engage at all – as Christians in India, whether they like it or not they have to participate in political and civil institutions – but the general mindset and worldview is a kind of anti-engagement. This is because Christianity's ultimate goal is presented generally as something not to do with this world. This aspect of the lack of engagement has been integrated within a religious fundamentalist mindset. Thus, if Hindu fundamentalism can be defined as an attempt for Hindu rashtra that keeps religious minorities out, Christian fundamentalism can be associated with isolationist or separationist tendencies of Christians in India. There is generally a kind of indifference, if not aversion, many Christians in India have towards other religions, politics, social concerns and the public sphere.

In order to make an effective response to Hindu fundamentalism, Christians have to first of all come out of the belief that religion, let alone Christianity, is distinct from the other aspects of life such as politics, culture, economics, science and so on. This is the blunder in the conceptual development of the idea of religion and religion as a distinct entity: this cannot be useful at all to understand the way people live their religious life in everyday context. Because, religious life is always integrated with other forms of life – whether one likes it or not – and we need to consciously go forward with this idea, which will enable to view ourselves not as distinct from society but as part of the wider society. Today in India, many religions are concerned with this aspect of participation and engagement in society and thus liberation theologies and public theology have significance for Christians in their responses to Hindu fundamentalism.

(c) Critical Scholarship from Christian Communities in India

Earlier while pointing out the limitations in the Indian Christian responses to Hindu fundamentalism I discussed how Christians in India have to start with

[26] Pradip N. Thomas, *Strong Religion, Zealous Media: Christian Fundamentalism and Communication in India* (New Delhi: Sage Publications Pvt. Ltd., 2008), xv.

[27] Thomas, *Strong Religion, Zealous Media*, xvi.

understanding it better. True, whenever Christians or churches are attacked by Hindu fundamentalists, we do respond through declarations, statements, processions, appeals to the President, Prime Minister and so on. But one area where Christians in India have to concentrate is undertaking in-depth research on the development, manifestations and impacts of Hindu fundamentalism. Of course, many historians, secularists and Hindu moderates have done crucial research on these, and it is very important for us Christians to join them in such research. Recently a well-known Indian scholar from Hindu religious tradition who has done works on various aspects of Hindu fundamentalism was pointing out to me in a personal conversation that the amount of research activities Christian community spends on this area is very minimal. This observation is true as research on Hindu fundamentalism really does not get enough attention among Christians. There are a whole lot of works from historians such as Romila Thapar and others, and other public intellectuals like Amartya Sen, Ramachandra Guha and Ram Puniyani that are critical of Hindu fundamentalism, but Christians in India hardly are willing to undertake serious research in it, with some exceptions, let alone critically utilise the resources already developed.[28] At the outset it should be clear that the Christian responses to Hindu fundamentalism cannot be simply from a biblical point of view or from a Christian worldview – though they are important and may help in a society with diverse religious experiences – but we need to go beyond that. Christians in India need to develop in-depth research on the various aspects of Hindu fundamentalism. Especially when there is a push by Hindutva fundamentalists for a united Hinduism which is built on dubious historical facts and a mythological and pseudo-historical reading of the ancient times, one has to continue to explore it and expose it through research. A Christian scholarly community committed to do serious research on the emergence, functioning and development of Hindu fundamentalism, not simply in terms of its effects on Christians, has to emerge.

(d) Working with Hindu Moderates

Another area an effective Christian response should make use of is the presence of Hindu moderates, who are committed to Hindu religious values and worldview but are critical of the vendetta of the Hindu fundamentalists and take genuine efforts to challenge them even at the point of giving their lives. In fact, extremist

---

[28] The works recently done by Indian Christians theologians such as M. T. Cherian, *Hindutva Agenda and Minority Rights* (Bangalore: Centre for Contemporary Christianity, 2007); and Rodinmawia Ralte, *Hindu and Hindutva: Hindu Tolerance, Hindu Exclusivism, Emergence of Assertive Hinduism* (Tainan: Programme for Theology and Cultures in Asia, 2014) are important here. Also the following works contains some collective voices that offer a response to Hindutva: J. Mattam, SJ & P. Arockiadoss, eds. *Hindutva: An Indian Christian Response* (Bangalore: Dharmaram Publications, 2001); and Mark T. B. Laing, ed., *Nationalism and Hindutva: A Christian Response*, Papers from the 10th CMS Consultation (Pune: CMS/UBS/New Delhi, 2005). But we need more works like this with more research on the complex development and consequences of Hindu fundamentalism.

ideologies throughout the world and throughout the history always first target the moderates within them,[29] because their self-critical values become a serious challenge to them. It is essential for Christians to engage with these moderates to critically learn from them to make our responses to Hindu fundamentalism effective.[30] Of course, Christians may sometimes feel that Hindu moderates can be critical of Christianity's extremism. As I have already pointed out, a religion committed to constant self-criticism should not be worried about it, and rather it should work with the Hindu moderates. This is especially important in the Indian context, to challenge Hindu fundamentalism.

Conclusion

This essay has attempted to throw some lights on the current practices in the Christian responses to Hindu fundamentalism which is becoming a growing concern for many in India, as it poses a huge threat especially to the minorities and all those who are critical of it. While pointing out the limitations in the existing Christians responses, I have focussed on the importance of understanding Hindu fundamentalism better in its entirety and complexity, the need to overcome isolationist tendencies and engage with issues affecting the wider society, which also involves self-critical attitudes for Christians, the necessity to develop serious and in-depth research on the various dimensions of Hindu fundamentalism and finally the significance of joining hands with Hindu moderates to resist the damaging impacts of Hindu fundamentalism. While Christians in India need to assess and strengthen our existing approaches in responding to Hindu fundamentalism, we also need to continue to explore new possibilities that will make our responses more dynamic and fruitful.

[29] There are numerous examples from all over the world regarding how before the eruption of major ethnic, religious and ideological conflicts, moderates in the powerful group have been systematically eliminated. The Rwandan genocide is one example where just before the genocide against the Tutsis started how the Hutu moderates were killed. Similar pattern is emerging in India where Hindu fundamentalists have started to systematically target the Hindu moderates and secular minded people and intellectuals within Hinduism. These moderates are targeted at many levels and some of them have been murdered as well.

[30] Recently a research was undertaken in Pune to study this. Themreichon Kasar, *Hindu Moderate Criticisms of Hindutva: Implications for Indian Christians*. Unpublished Thesis (Pune: Union Biblical Seminary, 2016).

Part 4

Missiological
&
Ministry Perspectives

13

Ecological Crisis and Christian Engagement

James Wesly

Introduction

"The earth is crying out and the poor are crying out, both victims of both social and environmental injustice,"[1] are the words of Sally McFague, one of the contemporary eco-theologians in the world. Today the modern idea of development has severely affected the lives of the poor and the creation primarily because of the ways the natural resources are consumed. The consumption of natural resources in the name of development is based on two ethical viewpoints. Frontier Ethics, believes that humans are separate from nature and the resources of the earth are for human consumption and development. Sustainable development ethics believes that humans are part of nature and resources are limited and have to be judiciously and carefully used.[2] Frontier Ethics reflects the modern development paradigm envisioned in spreading the dominant unsustainable development life style. George Zachariah states "Clean Development Mechanism *(CDM,)* a project to assist the global South to achieve sustainable development is yet another attempt to find solutions for climate change within the neo-liberal paradigm."[3] Through this essay, we shall critically examine the cleaner, greener development technology

---

[1] Sallie McFague, "The Loving Eye and Arrogant Eye," *The Ecumenical Review,* 49/2 (April, 1997):185.

[2] K. P. Joy, *Greening of Minds* (Thiruvalla: Christava Sahitya Samithi, 2001), 92-93.

[3] George Zachariah, "Musings on Climate Justice: A Subaltern Perspective," *Journal of Lutheran Ethics,* 9/4 (April, 2009): 2.

namely Bio-fuel and critique the sustainability of development paradigm, from an Ethical perspective.

1. The Development Saga

The modern development paradigm grew from post Second World War noble endeavour to achieve economic progress for the whole human family. President Harry Truman stated, "Greater production is the key to prosperity and peace."[4] "Many hopes for such "development" in those early years were genuine, idealistic, and often motivated by concerns of global justice."[5] It was believed that the optimum use of natural, labour and capital resources in the long run would result in the trickle down of fruits of growth to a widening circle of people.[6] But the increasing fight against communism brushed aside the fight against poverty and the goal of development. The mega development projects like "building dams, highways, power stations and factories" that were undertaken in order to facilitate development instead of eradicating poverty, infant mortality, malnourishment among children and farmers suicide has in manifold ways furthered and increased the problems faced by marginalised communities. The benefits of the modern economic projects has only resulted in creating and adding people to an elite minority in the developing countries "whose life style, aspirations and careers" are modelled in line with the high energy consuming unsustainable life style of the rich in the developed countries.[7] This very lifestyle based on "continued economic growth and expansion of affluent economies, spreading its economic life to the 'developing' societies, as the means for human liberation, was questioned at its core" by the present ecological crisis. For "the planet simply could not sustain this; three or four extra planets with their resources might be required."[8]

2. Rush for Growth:[9] The Present Scenario

In the midst of economic down turn and the visible consequences of global warming;[10] the need for economic growth and the need to control environmental

[4] Wesley Granberg-Michaelson, *Redeeming the Creation* (Geneva: Risk Book Series, 1992), 1.

[5] Ibid., 2.

[6] P. T. Kuriakose, "Development: Synthesising Conflicting Goals," in *Ecology: A Theological Response,* edited by Andreas Nehring (Madras: Gurukul, 1994), 123.

[7] Wesley Granberg-Michaelson, op cit., 2-3.

[8] Ibid., 4.

[9] The dominant and competing economic models of our time fail to value the creation itself, and to insure its survival. Instead, versions of "growth" and "progress" to which are given various ideological labels result in the steady destruction of the ecological foundations of life itself. (P. T. Kuriakose, op cit., 128).

[10] Human made polluting agents usually in gaseous form (particularly carbon dioxide: C02 ; methane: CH4; chlorofluorocarbons: CFCs; nitrous oxides; low-level ozone), leads to Global warming through the warming of atmosphere. Although, the "natural greenhouse effect has always existed, as part of the natural hydrological cycle and of the breathing cycle of plants, in the last

pollution are in the forefront of much discussions, deliberations, and debates. But these two issues (Stopping environmental degradation and economic growth) seem to be of two opposite poles. "The priorities for ecological health do not find immediate expressions within the market. Moreover, capitalist economies based on meeting consumer demands through continual growth have been the chief cause of resource depletion and ecological destruction."[111] "By applying economic parameters the west classified the countries of the Third World spread around the continents of Asia, Africa, and South America as 'poor,' 'backward.' and 'primitive.' The solution to overcome this backwardness is 'Modernization' or 'Economic Growth.'"[12] Development is measured in terms of infrastructural advancement and economic growth is measured in terms of high productivity and higher consumption life style.[13] The issue of sustainability and the conservation of rich natural diversity is sidelined and forgotten in this rush for growth.

(a) Development: the Indian Scenario from the Perspective Poor[14]

"Aruna Gnanadason says that ecological history is closely linked with global economic processes. After India's independence in 1947, the government set in place the process of planned development built on the back of Western science and technology... prime minister Nehru the 'architect of *modern* India;'...his efforts were on combining of Western science and technology with 'development' but under the socialist frame... The neo-liberal market economy that came several decades later within the new phase of globalization has merely continued on this way, even more aggressively."[15] In India, in conformity to the philosophy of 'modernization', there is a blind rush for economic growth and development. But the flip side of government policies of development reflects the global trend "of environmental degradation, callous use of natural resources and the western

century and a half human activity has introduced into the atmosphere enormous amounts of gaseous substances that have significantly increased global warming and the greenhouse effect." (Elias Crisostomo Abramides, "Ethical aspects of climate changes," in *Ecumenical Review*, 44/3 (July, 1992): 333.

[11] P. T. Kuriakose, op cit., 123.

[12] I. John Mohan Razu, "An Ethical Evaluation of the Influence of TNC's in the Socio-Economic, Political-Cultural and Environmental Sphere of India and the Philippines from the Christian understanding of Development" (Doctoral Dissertation, UTC Archives, 1996), 168.

[13] Development/Growth is measured in terms of number of transnational companies, multistory building, big shopping malls, possession of latest goods, eating continental high calorie fast food, etc.

[14] Here, the word poor is used to mean the poor nature (all non-human creation, both animate and inanimate beings) and the poor Dalits and Adivasis (*Indigenous People*) who live close to nature and depend on the land for their livelihood.

[15] Aruna Gnanadason, *Listen to the Women, Listen to the Earth* (Geneva: WCC Publications, 2005), 21.

concept of lifestyle, etc."[16] "The Mega 'development' projects like huge dam projects (for example; the Sardar Sarovar project), Nuclear projects (like Kaiga power plant)... the impact of commercial agriculture (Green Revolution) on the fertility of the indigenous soil is also a matter of great concern."[17] The SEZ (Special Economic Zone) policy and the boom in automobile industry, rapid decrease of forest cover are just a part of the development saga of the Indian government. The outcome of these development projects are global warming and climate change and this has resulted in very severe and disastrous weather patterns. News of flash flood, unseasonal rain and drought has now become a common annual event in India. Such unpredictable and volatile weather pattern has severely affected the agricultural sector of our country. The agricultural yields have also considerably reduced in the recent years. Many farmers migrate to cities in search of jobs in order to sustain their family and some are forced to commit suicide. The number of vehicles added each day is growing at an alarming rate but it does not match with the infrastructural development in terms of developing roads or even efforts to control pollution level. "India – unlike China, Europe and America – does not set any fuel economy standards."[18] This results in increase in air pollution severely affecting the health of common people especially the health of poor people living in the cities.[19]

(b) The truth[20] has not set us free

The *truth* about global warming, climate change and the threat to the very survival of the planet Earth is well acknowledged *truth*. The need to have sustainable eco-friendly development is also well accepted and acknowledged universal *truth* including in India. But the development programmes and policies clearly show that we neglect the *truth*. For "the ecological battles presently being fought in India have as their epicenter in the conflict over nature between the subsistence and largely rural sector and the vastly more powerful commercial-industrial sector. Perhaps the most celebrated of these battles concerns the Chipko *(Hug the Tree)* movement."[21] The marginalized poor and the poor nature, both are the victims

---

[16] Pravin Sheth, *Environmentalism; Politics, Ecology and Development* (Jaipur: Rawat Publications, 1997), 297.

[17] George Mathew Nalunnakkal, *Green Liberation; Towards an Integral Ecotheology* (Delhi: ISPCK/NCCI, 1999), 50.

[18] http://www.guardian.co.uk/environment/2007/mar/26/globalwarming.china/print. (18th August, 2009).

[19] http://everylifecounts.ndtv.com/delhis-polluted-air-is-turning-dangerous-doctors-explain-how-6832 (22nd February, 2017).

[20] John 8: 32: "You shall know the *Truth* and the *Truth* shall set you free." In this essay, the word truth (small 't') is used not to signify Christ, but to signify the truth about the Imminence of ecological crisis.

[21] Chipko movement is a peasant movement against deforestation in Himalayan foothills. Ramachandra Guha, "Radical American Environmentalism and Wilderness Preservation: A Third

of our blind rush for growth and development. Another good example of blind rush for lopsided development is the Narmada valley dam[22] projects. Two things were clearly neglected in the planning for the Dam project. Arundhati Roy states, "The People whose lives were going to be devastated were neither informed nor consulted nor heard."[23] And the environmental devastation and the ecological destruction of this Dam project were never considered. India under the present model of development has diluted laws that protect environment and those who fight against development projects that are ecologically unsustainable and those which affect the livelihood of the poor communities are seen as people who work against the interest of the nation and are branded as anti-nationals.[24] In the midst of such destructive development projects the arrival of Bio-fuel and other clean technologies is seen as herald of good news for an 'eco-friendly' development. Now, we shall try to explore and examine, what the arrival of Bio-fuel has promised to offer.

3. Biofuel: How Green and Clean is It?

The atmospheric pollution caused by the burning of fossil fuels has caused enormous damage to the environment and it is the major contributor in damaging the ozone layer and the subsequent global warming. In this context the arrival of Bio-fuels like Bio-ethanol and Bio-diesel derived from plants seem to be an elegant solution to this dilemma because they decrease dependency on fossil fuels and only return sequester carbon dioxide to the atmosphere. The governments of many industrialized and developing countries are therefore creating and expanding policies and research programmes to increase the production and use of bio-fuels.[25] These days, bio-diesel is mostly derived from oils or fats of plants like Jatropa, Sunflower, Canola, Rapeseed, Soybean, etc.[26] Fans of Bio-fuels give the impression we could soon be running cars on maize, producing electricity

---

World Critique," in *Applied Ethics: A Multicultural Approach,* edited by Larry May and Shari Collins Sharratt (New Jersey: Prentice Hall, 1994), 130.

[22] The Narmada Valley Development Project is the single largest river development scheme in India. It is one of the largest hydroelectric projects in the world and will displace approximately 1.5 million people from their land in three states (Gujarat, Maharashtra, and Madhya Pradesh). The environmental costs of such a project, which involves the construction of more than 3,000 large and small dams, are immense. The project will devastate human lives and biodiversity by inundating thousands of acres of forests and agricultural land. The State (India) wants to build these dams on the Narmada River in the name of National Development. But how can you measure progress if you don't know what it costs and who has paid for it? (http://www.umich.edu/~snre492/Jones/narmada.html#Problem. (3rd September, 2009).

[23] Arundhati Roy, *The Greater Common Good* (Bombay: IndiaBook Distributors, 1999), 17.

[24] http://america.aljazeera.com/multimedia/2015/4/narendra-modis-war-on-the-indian-environment.html (11th January, 2017).

[25] http://www.nature.com/embor/journal/v9/n2/full/embor20086.html. (3rd September, 2009)

[26] http://www.merinews.com/catFull.jsp?articleID=130389. (1st September, 2009).

with sugar, and getting power from palm oil.[27] The reason for switching over to Biofuel is: it is biodegradable, nontoxic, easy to use and free of Sulphur. It acts as a substitute for the fast depleting fossil fuels, as it is renewable. Thousands of wasteland can be exploited for economic development and unemployment can be reduced.[28]

But, there are many unanswered questions with regard to bio-fuel production and usage. First we shall explore the production mechanism in view of ever growing demand for fuel. Day by day the amount of vehicles that is added to the roads is increasing. With the growth in the number of middle class and upper middle class people the number of vehicles owned by individuals has increased. On the one side there is an increase in the production and sales of small *(Nano)* and affordable cars as well as large and powerful vehicles. Similarly, new job opportunities and fat income has resulted in "the expansion of high energy consumption western life style" among growing pockets of elites and urban middle class. In this context, fuel consumption is increasing in an alarming rate."[29] With the ever increasing demand for fuel, there will be the ever increasing need to expand the production of bio-fuel plantation. However, the question is how wise or how feasible would it be to replace agricultural food grains for bio-fuel plantation. Especially, "in the context of food crisis, the conversion of agricultural land into bio-fuel plantations shows a shift in the government policy from feeding the communities to feeding the cars,"[30] and feeding the mammoth consumption life style of the affluent living in the cities. There is growing scientific evidence that the conversion of land to grow feedstock — such as corn and soybeans — for bio-fuels could release more CO2 into the atmosphere than these alternative fuels save when compared to petroleum. The issue comes down to converting native habitats and other carbon-rich lands into croplands. "These natural areas store[31] a lot of carbon, so converting them to croplands results in tons of carbon emitted into the atmosphere."[32]

"On September 12, 2008, the Government of India introduced a new national bio-fuel policy which aims to meet 20% of India's diesel demand with

---

[27] http://thestar.com.my/lifestyle/story.asp?file=/2007/3/13/lifefocus/17074530&sec=lifefocus. (1st September, 2009).

[28] http://www.merinews.com/catFull.jsp?articleID=130389. (1st September, 2009).

[29] George Zachariah, op cit., 1.

[30] Ibid., 2.

[31] "Through the light of the sun, green plants absorb carbon dioxide in a process called photosynthesis, by which the plants produce carbohydrates from carbon dioxide and water, chlorophyll being the organic molecule on which carbon dioxide is transported. In the absence of light plants give off carbon dioxide while they absorb oxygen: this is their "breathing" process. Thus, plants through breathing, and rivers, lakes and oceans through evaporation, contribute to the natural "greenhouse" phenomenon, which always had a natural equilibrium as the atmosphere regenerates itself in a perfect self-purification process." (Elias Crisostomo Abramides, op cit., 333).

[32] http://www.mnn.com/technology/research-innovations/stories/does-biofuel-harm-the-environment. (1st September, 2009).

fuel derived from plants rather than fossils by 2017 by setting aside 14 million hectares of land for producing bio-fuel... (and the continual conversion of) agricultural land into bio-fuel plantation in the name of 'ecologically sustainable rapid economic growth'... according to The Guardian report up to 10.7 million people in India alone would be pushed over the poverty line as a result of projected price increases."[33]

4. Clean Development Mechanism (CDM): A Critique

When it come to eco-friendly, sustainable development, often it is seen from colonial top down perspective. One of the very good examples of colonial idea of sustainable development in view of global warming is replacing fossil fuel with Biofuel. As George Zachariah states it is a clear example of finding solution "born out of logic of capitalism."[34] It is also a clear example of seeing things through the eyes of the powerful and the elite. Even if there is zero (the fact is, replacing diverse natural habitat by mono-cropsfor Biofuel production will contribute more to global warming) pollution, the outcome of damage done to environment, destruction of natural habitat and destroying the food security, in the midst of every increasing demand for fuel, etc. would be far worse than the present crisis faced by the poor and the poor nature.

Today growth and development is measured in terms of commodities and possession of latest gadgets. But, the "Climate change shows with particular clarity that there are limits to the exploitation of the earth's resources. Consequently, it forces us to rethink our way of life radically."[35] But within the present idea of development, the "high consumption" and unsustainable energy consuming lifestyle is seen as something good and such lifestyle is seen as an important mark of development. Such high energy consumption lifestyle has already caused lots of damage to environment but a rapid spread of such lifestyle to rest of the world would only worsen and further increase the damage to environment. Our planet earth cannot support such lifestyle and it would destroy "earth's ability to support much of human and non-human life. Suffering and death would be multiplied many times over."[36] The Clean Development Mechanism as George Zachariah calls it, "a neo-liberal capitalistic"[37] solution to the present ecological crisis. But, today "the economic ordering of society must be built upon and seek to enhance participation. It must maximize the responsible utilization of resources for the common benefit and promote human wellbeing"[38] and wellbeing of all creation.

---

[33] George Zachariah, op cit., 2.

[34] Ibid., 2.

[35] Lukas Vischer, "Climate Change, Sustainability and Christian Witness," *Ecumenical Review*, 49/2 (April, 1997): 144.

[36] Elias Crisostomo Abramides, op cit., 336.

[37] George Zachariah, op cit., 2.

[38] Wesley Granberg-Michaelson, op cit., 3.

5. An Ethics for Sustainable Living

Life "at home in the Earth"[39] is essentially a complex web of relationship. An ethics for sustainable living depends on the quality and nature of such relationship. Holmes Rolston is right when he said, "Ecology is about relations to nature."[40] Relationship is very important for ethics, for, sustainable living should be based on two important spheres of relationships. The first sphere is the triangular, three dimensional God, human and creation relationship. The second is the horizontal dimension of human-to-human relationship.

(a) God, Human and Creation Relationship

The current debate of ecological crisis has revolved around reviewing and reinterpreting the question of this triangular God, Human and Creation relationship. It will not be wrong to say that the perspective that one holds about this relationship (between God, human and Creation) matters the most in our current ecological debate. Many of the Biblical, and non-biblical imageries of this relationship has proved detrimental by pushing God to the transcendent realm and putting humans at the centre of creation. Martin Buber's famous distinction I-Thou and I-It emphasises the need to emphasise the interconnectedness and mutual interdependence with respect. Pannikkar by stating, "Creation, humanity and God are one,"[41] furthered the aspect of interconnectedness. Sallie McFague uses the metaphor of world as God's body and Leonardo Boff states,

> Ecology has to do with the relations, interaction, and dialogue of all living creatures (whether alive or not) among themselves and with all that exists. This includes not only nature (natural ecology) but culture and society (human ecology, social ecology and so on). From an ecological viewpoint everything that exists, co-exists. Everything that co-exists pre-exists. And everything that co-exists and pre-exists subsistsby means of an infinite web of all-inclusive relations. Nothing exists outside relationships. Ecology reaffirms the interdependence of beings, interprets all hierarchies as a matter of function, and repudiates the so-called right of the strongest. All creatures manifest and possess their own relative autonomy; nothing is superfluous or marginal. All beings constitute a link in the vast cosmic chain. As Christians, we say that it comes from God and returns to God.[42]

---

[39] "At Home in the Earth" is the title of the book, written by Neil Darragh.

[40] Holmes Rolston, "The Bible and Ecology," *Interpretation,* 50/01 (January, 1996): 18.

[41] K. C. Abraham, "A Theological Response to Ecological Crisis." *Bangalore Theological Forum,* XXV/1 (March, 1993): 7.

[42] Leonardo Boff, *Ecology and Liberation, a New Paradigm,* (Maryknoll, New York: Orbis Books, 1995), 7.

An Ethics for sustainable living has to be based on two basic principles as Leonardo Boffstates above. Firstly, a principle that upholds interdependence, mutual co-existence and secondly a principle that sees life as a gift from God. Paulose Mar Gregorios saw life as "God's gift – a gift of grace, an offering of love, the creative love of the Creator."[43] Boff saw the distinctiveness of creation not in hierarchical terms but in terms of intrinsic value of all creation and the difference is only on functional ground. In the context of relationship, Neil Darragh speaks about Participation. "We are participants in the Earth – we are not its creators, not its sustainers, nor its custodians, nor its independent arbitrators, nor its observers. We participate in its processes, including its caring... and we are not the only ones who care for it. Our function is just a small one within a much larger caring entity."[44]

From the above discussion, it is evident that an Ethics of sustainable living should be based on relationship. Firstly, it is a sacred relationship, a relationship with God sustained through the fellowship with co-creations, for as Boff states everything "comes from God and returns to God." Therefore, we are ethically and spiritually responsible for all our activities for everything that we have is not of us but of God. We are neither owners nor custodian for everything belongs to God including ourselves. Secondly, the relationship between the creation and human is not hierarchical; rather it is one of mutual *interdependence* and mutual *participation*. For humans and non-human creation depend on each other in a web of relationships for the existence of one another. The "feminists have often suggested a 'quilt' metaphor as an appropriate methodology: for each of us can contribute only a small 'square' to the whole."[45] George Zachariah saw the present ecological crisis as a crisis of meaning, purpose and vocation of life, he calls it a deep spiritual problem integrally related to human relation with the Diving, other humans and rest of creation.[46] Therefore, the essence of this relationship is responsible participation and not irresponsible, self-centred domination. For, creation, like the humans, plays an important role in this web of relationship and humans can only contribute to a very small part of it.

(b) Human-to-Human Relationship

However, even though it is not wise to dichotomise the human-to-human relationship as distinct from the relationship with creation and the creator God, it is important to do so to understand how the unjust and unequal division

---

[43] Robin Gill ed., *A Text Book of Christian Ethics: A New and Revised Edition* (Edinburgh: T & T Clark, 2006), 314.

[44] Neil Darragh, *At Home in the Earth; Seeking and Earth-centred Spirituality* (Palmerston North: K & M Print, 2000), 67-68.

[45] Sallie McFague, "An Earthly Theological Agenda," *The Christian Century*, 108/9 (January 2-9, 1991).

[46] George Zachariah, op cit., 3.

found within the human-to-human relationship contributes to ecological crisis. According to K. C. Abraham, a closer look at "global warming brings into sharp focus the injustice of economic relationship between the North and South."[47] He further states, "The uneven distribution, control and use of natural resources are serious justice issue. It is estimated that one-fifth of the world's population that inhabits the Northern hemisphere consume, burn or waste at least 40-50% of the world's non-renewable resources."[48] The World Council of Churches views the issue of a global warming not only as a serious threat to the well-being of God's whole creation but also as an equity and justice issue, since the problem is caused largely by the polluting *life-style* of industrialized countries while many of the most severe consequences will be experienced by the poorer developing nations.[49]

The present ecological crisis makes a prophetic call for fighting the unjust relationship between the affluent and the impoverished. "It is often the poor, often people of colour ... often the developing nations who pay a greater price for environmental waste ... than others do."[50] All our theological and ideological jargons will be only a noisy gong if it does not address the unethical life style that contributes to ecological crisis. This is not to undermine the importance of all the theological and ideological formulation. For Rolston, Bible is more about how to live justly. He sees ecological crisis more in terms of a justice issue in the relation between humans and humans, humans and nature. This is human ecology with a focus on ethics... [51] In view of the un-sustainable life style of the affluent, German Greens states that there is the need to "advocate the creation of a 'nogrowth' economy, to be achieved by scaling down current (and clearly unsustainable) consumption level. This radical shift in consumption and production patterns requires the creation of alternate economic and political structures...the expansionist character of modern Western man *(sic)* will have to give way to an ethic of renunciation and self-limitation in which *spiritual* and *communal* values play an increasing role in sustaining social life."[52] There is no easy answer to how we could move away from this unjust, un-sustainable life style to a simpler living. We should be wise enough to change our life style before it is too late, because there will be a time when we will be forced to do so due to lack of resources and we will be left with no other choice.

---

[47] K. C. Abraham, et al., *Global Warming: Implication for South Asia and the Role of Churches* (Bangalore: SATHRI, 1994), 14.

[48] K. C. Abraham, "A Theological Response to Ecological Crisis," op cit., 5.

[49] Elias Crisostomo Abramides, op cit., 336.

[50] NCC fights global warming, *Christian Century,* 115/24 (September 9-16, 1998): 813.

[51] "Holmes Rolston, op cit., 21.

[52] German Greens cited in Ramachandra Guha, op cit., 129-130.

Conclusion

An Ethics for sustainable living depends in the humble acknowledgement that we are not the rulers or authors of life on Earth. The life that we have is a gift from God and we are just one among the many participants in the larger plan of God. Being created in the Image of God, our dominion is God's commission to be responsible participants; we have this responsibility to act responsibly, reflecting the self-giving and self-emptying love of Christ Jesus towards all Creation including humans. As George Zachariah states, our present ecological crisis is a crisis of meaning and purpose of life. It is also a spiritual problem; it is a problem of what we value the most in our lives. The present ecological crisis cannot be addressed effectively by just planting more trees, creating more national parks or even by bringing to stop all the development projects. Even alternative Clean Development Mechanism, no matter how clean and green it will be; will be inadequate unless and until our unethical, un-spiritual, unjust, selfish lifestyle is transformed by a more simple, sustainable and just living that reflects the call and purpose of life, as we see it in our Lord and Saviour Jesus Christ.

14

The Role of the Church in Addressing HIV/AIDS in Mizoram

H. Lalnunmawia

1. What does Social Change Mean?

The term "social" would mean very vast and wide. Paul Abretchs defines "Rapid social change means for all the countries of Africa, Asia, and Latin America the revolutionary transformation of their life, politically, economically, socially, and culturally."[1] This indicates that every society has experienced change in every sphere with good and bad consequences.

2. Christian Involvement in the Transformation of Society

Churches have often opposed involvement in politics out of a sincere desire to maintain the purity of the Gospel, to avoid identifying it with a particular political party, and to keep the Church safe from the political tensions and passions which have often divided the community.[2] The other reasons for Christians having no obligations in the political life is that they want the church not to engage in politics but only to preach the gospel. But the development of thoughts in this regard within the Indian Christianity shows that the political developments are also criticized from the churches.

Everything in human culture is subject to change whether the change may be slow or fast. M. M. Thomas declares that Christianity is one of the most

[1] Paul Abrecht, *The Church and Rapid Social Change* (New York: Doubledry & Company, Inc., 1961), 13.

[2] Abrecht, *The Church and Rapid Social Change,* 86.

potent dynamic factor which has brought about wholesome change in the culture and structure of tribal society everywhere in the world. [3] The churches have also contributed so significantly to the awakening to the possibilities of economic development. One of the mission agencies like Basel mission has started several industries and training for the economic development of the people in different parts of the world. Especially in the north-eastern part of India, Christianity improved their economic condition by entering civil service or by being engaged in the different trades.[4] The churches in India sometimes had to expand its economic activities to provide work for new members who were often deprived of their old employment when becoming Christians.[5]

The work of Christian missions in India is definitely regarded as an important factor responsible for social reform and change. Missionaries to India were involved in the transformation of Indian society. The mission stations and compounds were refuge for escaped slaves, for orphan and children as well. 'Serampore trio' are regarded as reformers of Indian society. William Carey was one of the prominent people who worked very hard for the abolition of sati, child marriage, etc. William Ward was very much involved in educating Indians. Tranquebar mission was also well known for their zealous works not only in evangelism but also for the development of education in the society. From the above, what we come to know is that Christians in the past have had participated actively in the social changes except in politics.

3. Why should Christians Engage in Social Change?

The church must be concerned about social change because the Gospel is for the world, including the world of changing human affairs.[6] The reason why Christians should engage in the social life and politics of the people is that we see several passages recorded in the Bible where people of God involved in social life'. God is sovereign over political life. One example is Pharaoh who was in effect the deified ruler of the Egyptians, and who set his face against God and against just treatment of the Israelites. But the great victory song of Moses and the Israelites ends with the words "The Lord will reign forever and ever" (Ex. 15:18). The prophets were also very much involved in the political life of the society. Jesus Christ engaged with the society. He taught us to love our neighbours. His mission was not merely confined in the spiritual life of the people, but reached the lowest, downtrodden and physically marginalized in the society. He came to announce the good news to the poor, to proclaim freedom for the prisoners and to release the oppressed. Where the government is not doing much in the direction to the poor and needy,

[3] M. M. Thomas, ed., *Tribal Awakening* (Bangalore: Christian Institute for the Study of Religion and Society, 1965), 51.

[4] Thomas, ed., *Tribal Awakening,* 86.

[5] Abrecht, *The Church and Rapid Social Change,* 134.

[6] Abrecht, *The Church and Rapid Social Change,* 49.

and where in fact the oppression or injustice is coming from the government itself, Christians must exercise their prophetic voice and speak out against abuse and misuse of power.[7]

As the government itself is in fact the source of oppression and injustice, it seems like more and more problems are to be faced in the days to come. So, Christian citizens are demanded of an active involvement in the political life of the country. Hence, Christians have to be involved in politics in order to fulfill their responsibilities for the emancipation and progress of all sections of people suffering from social disabilities. The churches of India should be concerned with the life of the nation much more than they have done so far.. The National Christian Council and other regional Christian councils also have a great role to play in the formulation of Christian opinion on current political issues. Moreover, we Christians are part of society in which we live, that's why we cannot ignore to deal with the changes happened in the society.

Nevertheless, the engagements which have been done by Christians in social life are very few. How much have we done as Christians to solve unemployment problems? Do we preach enough on the theme of climatic change? Do we work hard to fulfill the Nazareth Manifesto? Are we going to keep silence while the crime rate has been increasing in India? Our mission should focus on these issues rather than only converting people of other faith. Our mission should widen its view to our neighbours. To tackle the different kinds of changes we are facing in the society, there is none other than Christians.

The obvious loss of moral authority by the "Christian" West after the two World Wars, the rise of nationalism among the formerly colonized states, and the resurgence of non-Christian religions, the rise of secularism and materialism, and the ecological crisis have contributed to the realization that humanity needed mutual understanding and cooperation to sustain the world.[8] So, the paradigm had been shifted in the understanding of Christian mission that Christian mission was not to confined only to "saving souls" or "making converts", it should include body, spirit, world and cosmos. The idea of liberation, although present in the concept of mission as salvation from sin, is interpreted mostly in terms of spiritual liberation among the evangelicals. Liberationists in general interpret liberation in terms of socio-economic liberation although spiritual liberation is not altogether absent.[9] So, involvement in social change is to be seen as the responsibility of Christianity and its missions.

---

[7] Afe Adogame, Janice McLean and Anderson Jeremiah, eds., *Engaging the World* (Oxford: Regnum Books International, 2014), 5.

[8] Lalsangkima Pachuau, "Ecumenical Missiology: Three Decades of Historical and Theological Development (1952-1982)," in *Ecumenical Missiology: Contemporary Trends, Issues and Themes*, edited by Lalsangkima Pachuau (Bangalore: The United Theological College, 2002), 32.

[9] F. Hrangkhuma, "Missiological Methodologies," in *Missiological Approaches in India: Retrospect and Prospect*, edited by Joseph Mattam & Krickwin C. Marak (Mumbai: The Bombay Saint Paul

In light of that, this paper is an attempt to bring to light the work of the Church in the state of Mizoram. One of the so-called Christian states, Mizoram is being ruined by the HIV/AIDS since more than a decade ago. It has a population of around only 10 lakhs, in which 9637 are infected with HIV/AIDS. 587 people have died in the state since 1990 when the first HIV case was detected, a study by the Aizawl-based NGO, the Mizoram AIDS International Network has said.[10] The Church[11] also has done great works to tackle the problem. This paper is therefore, an attempt to find out the further role of the Church to tackle the problem and to suggest the Church to extend its mission field inside the state while she (the Church) has been focusing abroad. This paper employs J. C. Hoekendijk's "*world-centric*" and M. M. Thomas' "*Humanization*" paradigms as its methodology to analyze the mission works of Mizoram Presbyterian Church.

4. Defining HIV/AIDS

AIDS (Acquired Immune Deficiency Syndrome or Acquired Immuno Deficiency Syndrome) is a syndrome caused by a virus called **HIV** (Human Immunodeficiency Virus). The illness alters the immune system, making people much more vulnerable to infections and diseases. This weakness worsens as the syndrome progresses.[12]

Both the virus and the syndrome are often referred to together as **HIV/AIDS**. People with HIV are called HIV infection. The virus destroys the human immune system and causes AIDS. Technically AIDS is not a single disease since AIDS patients usually have many diseases, with their own signs and symptoms. When the body cannot produce a sufficient number of immune-specific cells, it becomes very weak to infection, which leads to terminal illness.[13] In common language, we say that HIV causes AIDS and that people die from AIDS.

HIV is found in the body fluids of an infected person (semen, vaginal fluids and blood). The virus is passed from one person to another through blood-to-blood, sexual contact and contaminated needles.[14]

According to research, the origins of HIV date back to the late nineteenth or early twentieth century in west-central Africa. AIDS and its cause, HIV, were first identified and recognized in the early 1980s.[15]

Society, 1999), 276-277.

[10] http://www.dnaindia.com/india/report-mizoram-has-second-largest-number-of-those-with-aidshiv-in north- east-1375791 (4.7.2015).

[11] The "Church" (capital C) in this paper would mean the Presbyterian Church of Mizoram which comprises of majority of Mizo Christians.

[12] www.medicalnewstoday.com/articles/17131.php (8.7.2015).

[13] Donald E. Messer, *Breaking the Conspiracy of Silence* (Delhi: Indian ISPCK, 2007), xxv.

[14] Philip Kuruvilla, ed., *HIV/AIDS: A Handbook for the Church in India* (Delhi: ISPCK, WCC & NCCI, 2004), 4.

[15] www.medicalnewstoday.com/articles/17131.php (8.7.2015).

5. HIV/AIDS Cases in Mizoram

The following Table shows HIV/AIDS cases in Mizoram in between 1990-2014:

Age Sex Proportion of HIV Positive Cases (1990-2014):[16]

AGE GROUP	MALE	FEMALE	TOTAL
Less than 14	183	197	380
15 - 24	1218	913	2131
25 - 34	2668	1388	4056
35 - 49	1668	975	2643
50 above	290	136	426
Not Specified	0	1	1
TOTAL	6027	3610	9637

From the above table, we came to know that majority of the HIV+ cases are among the youths. It would mean that the situation of Mizoram society is very bad. The reason is that this period is formative socially and psychologically as well as from a religious view. Unfortunately, Mizo youths are trapped in this pathetic condition.

Case: A prominent Psychiatrist Dr. C. Lalhrekima tells the "Vanglaini" (Mizo Daily News paper) that within two days after 2nd July 2015, when he opened a time to contact him through telephone by those who are in despair, 69 youths who gave up hope contacted him. HIV/AIDS problem is one of the biggest problems which these people have been facing. He said, "When these people are in a pathetic situation, they dare not to tell their families and church leaders because of shame and guilt."[17]

Thus, the above data shows the bad situation of Mizoram which would definitely affect the social and spiritual life of Mizos.

6. Impacts of HIV/AIDS

HIV/AIDS affects the physical and spiritual life of individual, family, society and the church as well. Here are some of the impacts:

(a) Psychological Impact

(i) Shame

The guilt and shame suffered by HIV/AIDS patients are sometimes imposed on them by the society; not necessarily because patients deserve the guilt or shame by virtue of their behaviour, but because of the judgmental attitude of the society

[16] http://mizoramsacs.nic.in/newsite/hiv_status/latest_status.html (5.7.2014).

[17] Vanglaini News Paper (7.7.2015).

– linking HIV/AIDS with 'immoral living.'[18] This shame would control the patients from mixing with others and to spend their daily lives with despair in the society.

(ii) Fear

The most common ones may be fear of death, fear of condemnation, fear of abandonment, rejection or ostracism, fear of losing career, of alienation and of disfigurement.[19] Excepting fear of death and other physiological symptoms, all the fears that haunt the patient are primarily caused by the intolerance and judgmental attitude of the society on the moral life of the HIV/AIDS patients.

(iii) Hatred

A strong desire to take revenge on someone or on the society as a whole is to be found in some patients. The hatred may be particularly on someone who infected the person through sex, or negligence in medical treatment, etc. This would make the society unpleasant and uncomfortable to live in.

Case:[20] A man met a woman in Mumbai and took her to his apartment. He spent the whole night with her. When he got up in the morning the woman had already gone. When he entered the bathroom, he was in for a shock. On the mirror in the bathroom was written with a red lipstick, "Welcome to the world of AIDS!" That boy would surely hate that girl, and surely would attempt to take revenge.

(b) Economic Poverty

The relationship between AIDS and poverty is a powerful one. AIDS tends to affect the poor more heavily than other population groups. "Research in New Delhi, India, found that average monthly expenditures exceeded income among families of people living with HIV, partly because of a doubling in purchases of medicines. While these families spent less on entertainment and on children's education to cope with rising care, support and treatment costs due to HIV, most were also forced to sell assets and borrow from friends and relatives."[21] Most people have to sell their properties and use up their savings for protection and treatment of an earning member. Their bad situation forced them to borrow money and to be in debt. Some families are also migrating usually from the rural areas to the cities for treatment which causes to settling in crowded cities leading the family to a worse situation.

---

[18] Charles Waldegrave, "Just Therapy," *Dulwich Centre Newsletter*, No. 1 (1990), 15.

[19] Klaus Wendler, "Ministry to Patients with Acquired Immunodeficiency Syndrome: A Spiritual Challenge," *The Journal of Pastoral Care* XLI/1 (March, 1987), 6-7.

[20] I used to hear this true story from my friends. I could not mention the source properly.

[21] "The Impact of AIDS on People and Society" http://data.unaids.org/pub/GlobalReport/2006/2006_gr_ch04_en.pdf (11.8.2015).

(c) Orphans and Widows

Normally, there are more deaths in people aged over 30 years. Many deaths in this age group lead to an increase in orphans, widows, helpless or dependent elderly people. Many grandparents are forced to find work to support themselves and their grandchildren.[22]

(d) Stigmatization and Discrimination

Donald E. Messer clearly tells how stigma has been faced by HIV/AIDS infected people."If I am diagnosed with cancer tomorrow, I have no doubt that people wouldn't care how I got it, but people would care for me unconditionally. But if I'm diagnosed as HIV-positive, I know many people would care how I got it, and people would care for me conditionally."[23] Parents have rejected their children. Life partners have been excluded and treatments denied. "When the famous tennis player, Arthur Ashe, learned he was infected due to a blood transfusion, he feared discrimination against himself and his family that he lived with the knowledge for three and one-half years before revealing he had the disease."[24] Social forces such as discrimination and stigmatization affect who gets HIV and what kind of treatment they get when they become ill. People and governments need to accept that HIV is everyone's problem and work together to stop the spread of the disease.[25]

As HIV/AIDS has great impacts on the society in several ways, the church also is affected very much. This means HIV/AIDS affects the economic, politics, society as well as the Church. In reality, however, problems faced by individuals and families are not always the problems of their own. Many a times, these problems are rooted in the structure of the society, which in turn affects the society resulting in poverty, orphans and widows, hatred, etc. It is to note that these problems would affect the spiritual lives as they are not in a normal situation to nourish their spiritual life. Church is responsible to save the patients in the society from such a pathetic situation.

7. The Church and HIV/AIDS Combat

Some years back, the church has become conscious of the fact that HIV/AIDS is affecting not just people outside the church but alse the individuals and families within the fold of the church. So, the Mizoram Presbyterian Church has three places/departments through which it concerns on the issue: Synod Rescue Home, Family Guidance and Counseling Centre, and Grace Home. Of these, only Grace

---

[22] The writer of this paper is aware of this kind of problem in Mizoram.

[23] Messer, *Breaking the Conspiracy of Silence*, 28.

[24] Messer, *Breaking the Conspiracy of Silence*, 29.

[25] Reuben Granich & Jonathan Mermin, *HIV, Health, and Your Community* (California: Stanford University Press, 1999), 98.

Home is dedicated to HIV/AIDS whereas other two concern different kinds of problems of the society.

(a) Why the Church?

The uniqueness of Jesus' healing ministry is his astonishing availability and openness to give time to everyone, especially the diseased. These people were despised and isolated and made to suffer doubly because society considered them morally responsible for the present trouble. Jesus did not treat them as such. Jesus instead defended them against prevailing attitude that suffering is due to sin.[26] As Christ identifies with human suffering and enters into it, the church is called to enter into the suffering of those infected and affected people, to stand with them against all rejection, despair, discrimination and stigmatization. Those challenges are not the option which the church has to take, but it is the church's vocation.[27] Now let me discuss how the church has been involving in combating HIV/AIDS in Mizoram:

(b) Synod Rescue Home

The major project of the Social Front[28] of Mizoram Presbyterian Church is the rehabilitation center for substance abusers. It was established on 21st September 1987.[29] It is situated in a quiet and peaceful surrounding at Durtlang, about 10 kms from the heart of Aizawl. Functioning under a Director it accommodates 30 seats for men and 10 seats for women. This is the only Rehabilitation Centre that furnishes three separate units for the patients, i.e., Detoxification Unit, Rehabilitation Unit and After Care Unit. The main purpose of this Home is providing rehabilitation and help to victims of alcoholism, substance abusers which are causes for concern both in the family and society. The former Director of Synod Rescue Home Rev. H. Lalrinmawia told me that it is estimated that around 15-20% of the patients have completed the course (6 months course + 3 months After Care).[30]

(c) Family Guidance and Counseling Centre

A Counseling Centre called Family Guidance & Counseling Centre (under Mizoram Presbyterian Church) was established in 1997. Many couples as well as individuals have received proper guidance from this Centre. Since then, four centres have been opened inside and outside Aizawl city. The Centre is always

---

[26] Philip Kuruvilla & Wati Longchar, eds., *HIV & AIDS Towards Inclusive Communities* (Nagpur: NCCI, 2013), 101.

[27] Kuruvilla & Wati Longchar, eds., *HIV & AIDS Towards Inclusive Communities*, 122.

[28] Social Front is one of the departments of Mizoram Presbyterian Church.

[29] http://mizoramsynod.org/index.php?phek=bawm&bid=9 (15.7.2015).

[30] Interview with Rev. H. Lalrinmawia, Director, Synod Rescue Home - 2008-2010 (20.5.2015).

open for those who may require its services; for families with conflict between couples, regarding children, or economic problems; for individuals seeking help with regard to alcohol or drug abuse, sex-related, choice of life partners, health - related including HIV and AIDS, studies, questions on faith or work. The Centre offers aid in finding solutions through confidential guidance and prayer support. Each centre contains counselors and office workers.[31]

The present Director Rev. Lalhmingthanga of Family Guidance and Counselling Centre told me that most of the clients who came to the centre have returned successfully.[32] HIV/AIDS infected people are referred to Grace Home.

(d) Grace Home

Synod Social Front department provides care and support through its Hospital in Durtlang, Aizawl. Grace Home is established for HIV/AIDS patients in the year 2004 and is attached to Synod Hospital, Durtlang. It contains 30 seats but only 20 patients could be accommodated due to lack of facilities and workers.[33] The budget estimated for this Home (2015-2016) is 30 lakhs only.[34] Here, counseling and medication are employed in order to provide physical and spiritual healing. The followings are the statistics of the workers in this Home:[35]

1)	Doctor	- 2
2)	Coordinator/Social worker	- 1
3)	Counselor	- 1
4)	Staff Nurse	- 5
5)	Outreach worker	- 4
6)	Cook	- 1

"Many patients who could not be admitted due to limited seats wait even for long time", Doctor In-charge of Grace Home Dr. Sanghluna said. He suggested enlarging this Home as the need is great.[36]

(e) Non-Denominational Involvements

There are several Para-Church Organisations and Christian NGOs that are also actively participating in the prevention and intervention activities. There are also outstanding Christian individuals who spend their efforts in caring and supporting the HIV/AIDS infected people. In regard to preventive measures, literature, audio visual campaigns and awareness campaigns through seminars, etc. are directed

---

[31] http://mizoramsynod.org/index.php?phek=bawm&bid=13 (18.7.2015).

[32] Interview on 25th May, 2015.

[33] Telephonic conversation with Dr. Sanghluna, Doctor in-charge, Grace Home (10.7.2015).

[34] Report received through email from Dr. Sanghluna (20.7.2015).

[35] Report received through email from Dr. Sanghluna (20.7.2015).

[36] Telephonic conversation with Dr. Sanghluna, Doctor in-charge, Grace Home (10.7.2015).

towards school children, the youth and the general public in attempts to educate people to keep away from infection through different ways and means including the use of disposable syringes and condoms. From my experiences, the mode of transmission of the virus is one of the prominent topics in these campaigns.[37]

8. The Reasons of Weaknesses of the Church in Combating HIV/AIDS

A reason for church resistance to involve in HIV/AIDS issue is the belief **that it's not Christian to talk about sex and condoms.**[38] This is obviously true in Mizoram church context. The church leaders rarely chose these topics in preaching due to the negative notion in the mindset of Mizo Christians. "Christians have no problem talking about blood transfusions, organ transplants, cancer or even war, but typically are tongue-tied and hesitant to talk about condoms, 'safer sex' or oral or anal sex."[39] People have become infected and suffered enormously with HIV/AIDS because of the silence in the church and the lack of campaign and proper sex education.

The traditional interpretation of the salvation of Jesus by the churches in Mizoram is salvation in terms of souls only. One of the Mizo theologians, Rev. Dr. Tlanghmingthanga has also pointed out that even today, the primary goal of Mizo mission is **'only for the salvation of souls.'**[40] The Mizoram Presbyterian Church's budget reveals the reality. The Church's mission budget for one year (2015-2016) is 78,60,35,000[41] whereas it spend very less to combat HIV/AIDS in Mizoram (only Rs 30,00,000 for Grace Home[42]). I don't claim these figures should be in balance, but it seems the Church overlooks her internal mission works. If the biggest church in Mizoram (MPC) could maintain only twenty seats for HIV/AIDS infected people, where will the other people 10000 infected patients be treated? Although, few groups like MSACS (Mizoram State AIDS Control Society) and World Vision have been involving to tackle this issue, the Church is to be the most influential and responsible.

Another reason of less involving in such social issues is grounded in the belief that **it's somebody else's responsibility.** Of course, getting involved in HIV/AIDS education is to invite conflict and controversy, to risk misunderstandings and misinterpretations, and to stretch the church's mission and ministry beyond

---

[37] I have attended more than ten times in the seminars on HIV/AIDS.

[38] Messer, *Breaking the Conspiracy of Silence*, 34.

[39] Messer, *Breaking the Conspiracy of Silence*, 34-35.

[40] Tlanghmingthanga, "Mizo Christian View of Eschatology," *Didakhe* XXIV/ 9 (May-June, 1996), 10, cited by Lawmsanga, "Church and Mission: The Mizo Perspective," in *The 31st Annual Magazine: Aizawl Theological College* (Aizawl: The Students' Body, Aizawl Theological College, 2010-2011), 90.

[41] *Synod Budget Bu 2015-2016* (Aizawl: Synod Publication Board, 2014), 79.

[42] Report received through email from Dr. Sanghluna (20.7.2015).

previous expectations.[43] Very often the church leaders would give the task to the governmental agencies or charities. The church is sometimes too busy in its own administration.

9. Missiological Perspectives from Hoekendijk's and M. M. Thomas' Mission Concepts

(a) Hoekendijk's World Centric Paradigm

The "World-centric" paradigm of mission advocated by Johannes Christian Hoekendijk (1912-1975), a Dutch missiologist is employed in this study. Already in 1950, he argued that church planting is not a legitimate goal of mission. This fostered Conservative Evangelical Protestants mission to change of emphases – from the church as goal of mission to the church as instrument, and from the church to the reign of God as the basis for missionary witness.[44] At the International Missionary Conference (IMC) at Willingen, Germany (1952), he vigorously criticized the church-centered orientation of the missionary enterprise.[45] He strongly protested against the church-centric view of missions of the Willingen Conference 1952.[46]

He claimed that the church can be no more than a function of God's work for worldly *shalom* (peace) and criticized all tendencies toward *ecclessio-centrism.*[47] For him to say that "the church is the starting point and the goal of the mission" is only to make a phenomenological statement. Rather "the gospel of the Kingdom will be proclaimed throughout the *oikoumene.*"[48] He said that our God is not a temple dweller. However, he argues that to maintain the right order in thinking and speaking about the church, the order is **God-World-Church**, not God-Church-World.[49]

This God-World-Church order has connection with the concept of *missio Dei.*[50] God is indeed revealed in the missions of the church but not only in and

---

[43] Messer, *Breaking the Conspiracy of Silence*, 35.

[44] Wilbert R. Shenk, "Church Growth," in *Dictionary of the Ecumenical Movement*, edited by Nicholas Lossky (Geneva: WCC Publications, 2002), 202.

[45] Tom Stransky, "Missio Dei," in *Dictionary of the Ecumenical Movement*, edited by Nicholas Lossky (Geneva: WCC Publications, 2002), 780-781.

[46] T. V. Philip, *Edinburgh to Salvador: Twentieth Century Ecumenical Missiology, A Historical Study of the Ecumenical Discussions* on *Mission* (Delhi: CSS / ISPCK, 1999), p.46. (Hereinafter cited as T. V. Philip).

[47] Libertus A. Hoedemaker, "Hoekendijk, J.C.," in *Biographical Dictionary of Christian Missions*, edited by Gerald H. Anderson (Grand Rapids, Michigan: William B. Eerdmans Publishing Company, 1998), 297.

[48] J. C. Hoekendijk, *The Church Inside Out* (Philadelphia: The Westminster Press, 1966), 40.

[49] Hoekendijk, *The Church Inside Out*, 70-71.

[50] According to D. J. Bosch, the author, originator and sustainer of mission is God and mission is not primarily an activity of the church, but an attribute of God. God is a missionary God and

through the church.[51] The church as the instrument of God's mission has to participate in the social issues to bring the Kingdom of God into the world.

As Hoekendijk states that the church in this contemporary world needs to recognize that *our God is not a temple dweller*,[52] He is the God of the outcaste, poor, helpless, victims of violence, and the victims of the HIV/AIDS as well.

(i) God-World-Church

Hoekendijk's paradigm of mission takes the root to *missio Dei* concept of mission; that is mission is not the church's but God's. God sends his Son to the world because of his love for the world. The church needs to realize that 'church' is not the focus of God rather the 'world' God is the source of mission and fountain of love. [53] The church must go out to do God's mission in order to reach those who are marginalized that they may live with freedom as their Creator has made.

The church has nothing to do other than accomplishing God's mission. The church cannot and should not have different mission which is divergent to God's mission. Bosch argues that the *missio Dei* is God's activity, which embraces both the church and the world, and in which the church may be privileged to participate.[54] For Hoekendijk, the church has no proper fixed place in God's mission, her role is to bring the Reign of God to this world.

(ii) The Kingdom of God and the World

Hoekendijk maintains that when the Bible speaks of Messianic fulfillment, the key issue is the Kingdom for the world[55] - *Oikoumene*, "the whole inhabited earth, the world"[56] and *oikoumenikos*, "open to or participating in the whole world." Like many biblical words, these were invested with Christian meaning. The *oikoumene* describes the place of God's reconciling mission (Matthew 24:14); and of the kingdoms of the earth (Luke 4:5); and the world destined to be redeemed by Christ (Hebrews 2:5).[57]

---

mission is what God is doing ***to*** and ***through*** the servant, not what the servant (church) does. (David J. Bosch, "Reflections on Biblical Models of Mission" in James M. Phillips & Robert T. Coote, *Toward the 21st Century in Christian Mission* (Grand Rapids, Michigan: William B. Eerdmans Publishing Company, 1993), 175-192.

[51] Tom Stransky, "Missio Dei," in *Dictionary of the Ecumenical Movement*, 781.

[52] Hoekendijk, *The Church Inside Out*, 70.

[53] David J. Bosch, *Transforming Mission: Paradigm Shifts in Theology of Mission* (New York: Orbis Books, 1996), 490.

[54] Bosch, *Transforming Mission: Paradigm Shifts in Theology of Mission*, 491.

[55] J. C. Hoekendijk, *The Church Inside Out*, 32.

[56] "The New Testament Greek Lexicon" in http://www.studylight.org/lex/grk/view.cgi?number=3625 (11.7.2015). It also mean "All people living on the inhabited globe" in http://biblehub.com/greek/3625.htm (17.7.2015).

[57] "Christianity, Ecumenism," in *http :/ / www. britannica. Com / EBchecked / topic / 115240 / Christianity / 67623/Ecumenism?anchor=ref927590* (11.7.2015).

For this *oikoumene,* the Kingdom is destined; world (*kosmos/oikoumene*) and kingdom are correlated to each other; it is the *world* which has been reconciled (II Cor. 5:19), the *world* which God loves (Jn. 3:16), the *world* is the field in which the seeds of the Kingdom are sown (Mat. 13:38) – the *world* is consequently the scene for the proclamation of the Kingdom.[58] He advocated that instead of thinking of apostolate as a function of the church, we should think of the church as a function of the apostolate.[59]

The whole concept of mission theology was to embrace the secular world as the arena of God's action. From this point of view, the church today should break through or infiltrate every corner of the social life. Mission work of the church ought to permeate the freedom, liberty, and dignity of human beings to protect them from elements which can ruin them.

(b) M. M. Thomas' Mission of Humanisation

Another tool employed for constructing the model would be the mission of Humanization proposed by M. M. Thomas who was born in 1916 in Kerala. For Thomas, the nature and form of the Church are necessarily derived from the mission of the Church. He says, "*By 'mission' we mean the mission of the Church to witness to Christ the Lord and Redeemer of the whole man.*"[60] The church is addressed as the body of Christ. The church is the divine instrument to continue Christ's work of humanization and as a continuing incarnation. This body of Christ is initiated by the sacrificial death and the resurrection of Jesus Christ. As Church is the body of Christ, it has to participate in the struggles of the marginalized for humanization as an authentic imitation of Christ.[61]

According to Thomas "The mission of the Church is to participate in the revolutions of our time. The Church's mission is primarily one of humanization and not of salvation."[62] To him Salvation or redemption is only one aspect of humanization, catering to the inward or to the spiritual aspects of mankind.[63] The recipients of Christian mission are not individuals anymore but structures such as cultures, religions and ideologies. The method is no more proclamation, but now

---

[58] Hoekendijk, *The Church Inside Out,* 40-41.

[59] T. V. Philip, *Edinburgh to Salvador – Twentieth Century Ecumenical Missiology* (Delhi: CSS & ISPCK, 1999), 82.

[60] Sunand Sumithra, *Revolution as Revelation* (New Delhi: International Christian Network, 1984), 200.

[61] Jesudas M. Athyal, *M.M.Thomas The Man and His Legacy* (Thiruvalla: The Thiruvalla Ecumenical and Charitable Trust, 1997), 53.

[62] Maong Lemtur, *Christ in the Changing Context,* (Dimapur: Tribal Development and Communication Centre, 2008), 115.

[63] Bernard J. F. Lonergan, *Method in Theology* (London: Darton, Longman & Todd Limited, 1972), 363.

it is participation or as he calls it the confession of participation.[64] The bearers are no more the called and sent missionaries, but rather organizations or the churches that do the work. He comes to the conclusion that "E*vangelism in our time equals service.* Unless the church exercises its prophetic ministry of constructive criticism, the priestly ministry of the suffering servant has lost its salt."[65]

The implication of the revolution for mission and the missionary structure of the congregation have perhaps been spelt out, and this seems very important for the future of mission and church in the modern world. It is significant that the study on the Missionary Structure of the Congregation reported in the "*The Church for Others*" lifted up *shalom* or 'humanization as a goal of mission, because, in a world where men are struggling for their true humanity and well-being, it best communicates the meaning of the messianic goal.[66] He said, "*Christian participation in mission therefore involves participation in the struggle for a just society.*"[67] Again Thomas said, "*The Church had to have a concern with the active participation in the struggle for secular fellowship on a Christ-centered basis.*"[68] He further said that, in the area of humanization, the Church must be able to meet, outside the Church, not only "*fighters*" for freedom but also "*bearers*" of it and the grace behind it.[69]

M. M. Thomas's humanization concept stands on the church as the divine instrument to continue Christ's work of humanization and as a continuing incarnation. The church has the responsibility to participate in the struggles of the marginalized for humanization as an authentic imitation of Christ. To him, the secular involvement is a must from his Christ-centred concept. When we see the ministry of Jesus, we boldly could claim it as humanization. The Church should re-examine her mission whether it is biased or not. Only soul saving activity would never accomplish the expectation from Christ, rather our neighborhood is to be given importance as well.

10. Towards a Better Society

(a) Importance of Home Mission towards HIV/AIDS Infected Persons

As David Bosch has pointed out, the missionary activity of the church cannot simply be the planting of the churches; rather, it has to be service to the *missio*

---

[64] Lonergan, *Method in Theology*, 363.

[65] M. M. Thomas, "Indian Christian Theology: The Church and the People", in *Religion and Society,* vol. XXX, nos. 3 & 4, September-December, 1983, 74-75.

[66] Thomas, *Towards the Theology of Contemporary Ecumenism* (Madras: Diocesan Press, 1978). 160-161.

[67] Thomas, *Towards the Theology of Contemporary Ecumenism*, 161.

[68] M. M. Thomas, *Salvation and Humanization: A Discussion*, eds., Gerald H. Anderson, et.al., *Mission Trends No.1* (Michigan: Paulist Press, 1974), 218.

[69] Thomas, *Salvation and Humanization: A Discussion*, 218.

Dei, representing God in and over against the world.[70] In line with this, Hans Kung has also stated that the church cannot shut itself off from the world and live a life of its own in splendid isolation, but rather must exist for the world by being linked to the world.[71] That is to say, the mission of church should not be limited within the four walls of the church. The Church needs to be aware that mission is the mission of God, it is *missio Dei.* It is God's mission and God's activity, which embraces both the church and the world, and in which the church may be privileged to participate.

In a context where social problems ruin the church as well as the society, salvation should be reinterpreted not in terms of souls alone but should include the whole being of human in such a way that the dignity and rights of human being will be taken into consideration. The Church should turn its mission towards saving the marginalized from their bad situation of poor and stigmatized in the society instead of focusing only to souls.

The mission is not just an activity of those who might be interested but the ministry in which all people should be involved.[72] Therefore, I do suggest the Church to focus more on the internal mission works. It is definitely right to move on in sending missionaries and planting churches and soul hunting. But the Church should examine itself whether it neglects the 'world' nearby. Let the Church extend its mission field inside Mizoram while focusing planting churches in its mission fields. Does the Church open her ears to hear the cry of the infants and children affected by the HIV/AIDS pandemic?[73] Let the Church examine itself whether it spends too much money for its own administration? How much must the local churches spend for the church buildings while the helpless people fall beside them?

(b) Awareness Campaign to Eliminate Negativity

"Stigma kills more than HIV itself."[74] In all the laudable attempts and services however, education of the general public to develop positive attitude towards the patients seems to be lacking. We have seen that guilt, shame and fear are mostly caused by social attitude. The church is called to be the salt and the light of the earth, identifying, preventing and breaking down all forms of stigmatizing and discriminating barriers. As some patients dare not to come out for counseling, home based care by home visits will be helpful.

---

[70] Bosch, *Transforming Mission: Paradigm Shifts in Theology of Mission,* 491.

[71] Hans Kung, *The Church* (London: Burns & Oates Limited, 1969), 486.

[72] Patrick Johnstone, *The Church is Bigger than you Think* (Great Britain: Christian Focus Publications, 1998 & 2000 reprint), 194.

[73] WCC, *Facing AIDS: The Challenge, the Church's Response* (Geneva: WCC Publications, 1997), 94.

[74] Kuruvilla & Wati Longchar, ed., *HIV & AIDS Towards Inclusive Communities* (Delhi: ISPCK & NCCI, 2013), 6.

(c) Sex Education

As I have said, Mizoram church is too conservative in educating the people. Some people would consider that discussing about sex and condoms by church leaders in not approproiate. But, the church leaders as well as the members also should change their mind in order to save the spiritual and physical body of its members. The Church can play a positive and active role in promoting the use of condoms to save lives in the context of wider health messages that include abstinence and faithfulness. For Christians, there should be no reservations whatsoever about the use of condom or sex education where the aim is to save the life.[75]

(d) Equipping the Counseling Centres

The Mizoram Presbyterian Church has only four centres over Mizoram, which is very less to combat the problem. Especially to treat the psychological problems like fear, guilt and shame, the church should be generous in order to increase and equip the counseling centres in different parts of Mizoram. Besides this, I would like to suggest three phase counseling which has been employed by Church of North India[76]- *Pre-test counseling* (convincing a person indulged in unsafe activities to go for HIV testing), *Post-test counseling* (by testing positive, lots of questions, fear, doubts and other unpleasant emotions come up) and *Family, neighbours and friend's counseling* (the attitude and behavior of the those who are nearby the infected people).

Besides the above suggestions for the Church's role, there could be some other roles to be played which this paper does not accommodate. Anyway, in order to have a successful mission work for HIV/AIDS patients, the Church need to spend much more strength and vigor in financial as well as spiritual matters.

HIV/AIDS is possibly the most serious current health (spiritual and social) problem in Mizoram. The Church has been involving in helping the infected people and to tackle the issue by different means. But this paper found out that the mission concept of Mizos should be turned to the local area as some people neglected. This short study reveals the need of giving priority to give a better and just society to the people instead of too much earnestness in planting churches and conversion.

[75] Dr. Patrick Dixon, *AIDS Action* (Brentford, UK: Acet International Alliance, 2010 rep.), 41.

[76] Philip Kuruvilla, ed., *HIV/AIDS: A Handbook for the Church in India* (Delhi: ISPCK, WCC & NCCI, 2004), 100.

15

Missional Engagement of the Dimapur Ao Baptist Arogo among Differently Abled Children

Watirenla Jamir

Introduction

This paper is an attempt to understand the ways in which the DABA is working towards the upliftment of Differently Abled Children as the society is ignorant of the needs of the Differently Abled Children. The issue of Disabled people has shifted from medical or welfare approach towards social and right-based approach. It is obvious that the society, especially the church mostly fails to communicate to the society that Differently Abled Children are also created in the image of God and thus need special attention and care. Today the unacceptable attitude of the Church and Society towards the DAC has generated serious concerns in theological discussions and ministry of the church. So, Christians should engage in social change for the benefit of the Differently Abled Children by meeting their needs and regarding them as capable individuals. There are many words that are used to describe Differently Abled Children such as children with special needs, disabled to name a few. Most often one finds people stumbling over trying to say the current politically correct word. In this paper, the researcher will use "Differently Abled children" (DAC) and "Disabled" interchangeably in discussing how the DABA is bringing out the change in the society by uplifting the children, to see the areas of progress and neglect, the challenges faced by and suggest areas of change in DABA ministry towards DAC.

1. Christian Engagement in Social Change

The past few decades have witnessed rapid and consistent change in the state of affairs around the world, be it in politics, economy, demography, science and technology, social media, etc., to name a few. This influence is seen on an even greater level in the developing nations of the world. The involvement of the leading nations in pursuing the development of the underdeveloped ones also encourages change.[1]

The world is also witnessing a great turn of vicissitudes as American President Barack Obama is leading in an untested "(S)ocial change is in the wind"[2] perception in the United States of America, empowering the Gay marriage agenda. Closer home, in India, we can see our Prime Minister Narendra Modi's campaign for a *Swachh Bharat Abhiyan* (clean India). Locally, the Church (DABA) manifests a social concern, stepped out with the theme "touch Dimapur" for the welfare and good of the people. Change, wrought by social issues or government mandate can be a force for good, or for evil. It appears that almost every nation in their own way is being affected by the devastation due to conflict, war and civil unrest. Another example is that of the growing issue of the migrant crisis in West Asia, making world news headlines, as day after day more people are fleeing their homes and country and the persistent increase in death toll. It is true that growing "environmental degradation, financial crisis, civil and international conflict, and a growing sense of lost spirituality"[3] are constantly feeding the news channels. "Social change in modern times has become the symbol of a continued movement towards modernization."[4] With upheavals in societal and governmental structures happening across the globe, an observation that human activities in our own world have changed more in the past few decades than ever before seems undeniable. The momentum of social change is felt in almost every corner of the earth, and of course, in each individual life.[5]

India has a long history of oppression and suffering through western colonization, martial law, militarism, dictatorship, communalism and capitalism. As a third world country, India is going through several socio-economic problems, such as the enormous change in demographic structures, prostitution and sex tourism due to poverty, migration, corruption and injustices, etc. The gap between the rich and the poor is widening, corrupt practices are posing a great threat to financial and economic stability, farmers in India are taking their own lives at an

---

[1] Ran Singh Mann, *Social Change and Social Research: An Indian Perspective* (New Delhi: Concept Publishing Company, 1988), 11.

[2] Jay Weinsten, *Social Change* (United Kingdom: Rowman & Littlefield Publishers, Inc, 2010), xxiii.

[3] Weinsten, *Social Change*, xxiii.

[4] Raghuvir Sinha, *Social Changein Indian Society* (New Delhi: Naurang Rai, 1978), 149.

[5] Sinha, *Social Change in Indian Society*, 149.

alarming rate and "social inequality is increasing within both the more and the less industrialized societies."[6]

There is a different picture when we look at North East India. The people of North East India were living in isolation from the Western world for many centuries, in fact from the rest of the world. However, with the oncoming of the British rule and the coming of Christianity in the mid-nineteenth century, the face of the region has undergone radical changes. "Social and cultural changes are, of course, inevitable for any community."[7] But up until this day, many states are overshadowed and indoctrinated by the British rule, still holding onto British customs, although their presence has long been diminished. Before the advent of the different Christian missions, the British administration was the primary agency of change among the people in the North East.[8] The British represented a symbol of authority and oppression for those in the Northeast, who did not have equal access to education, and one can still see the faint mindset of captivity in their lifestyles from that societal and cultural change.

These kinds of social issues makes it pertinent for Christians and churches to be responsible stewards of God's creation by "delighting in creation as God's gift, and enjoying it as God's provision, in ways which sustains and heal the damaged fabric of the creation which God has entrusted…"[9] "The passion to engage the world, to shape it and finally change it for the better, would seem to be an enduring mark of Christians on the world in which they live. To be a Christian is to be obliged to engage the world, perusing God's restorative purposes over all of life, individual and corporate, public and private. This is the mandate of creation."[10] We see a powerful example in the New Testament when Jesus sent out the twelve disciples, and because of the pure, selfless teachings of their Messiah, the world was changed forever through their message of forgiveness. God enables Christians to walk in the same power through the Holy Spirit, the Word of God, intimate communion with Him, and the gifts of the Holy Spirit, through which the church is edified. When the church is walking in these four foundational

---

[6] Jay Weinsten, *Social Change*, XX.

[7] Angeline Lotsuro, "Contribution of Catholic Women Missionaries to the Socio-Cultural Change among the Tribes of Northeast India," in *Christianity and Change in Northeast India*, edited by Tanka Bahadur Subba, Joseph Uthenpurakal and Shaji Joseph Puykunnel (New Delhi: Concept Publishing Company, 2009), 321.

[8] O.L. Snaitang, "Christianity and Change Among the Hill Tribes of Northeast India," in *Christianity and Change in Northeast India*, edited by Tanka BahadurSubba, Joseph Uthenpurakal and Shaji Joseph Puykunnel, (New Delhi: Concept Publishing Company, 2009), 147.

[9] John Schmalzbauer, "Whose Social Justice? Which Evangelism?: Social Engagement in a Campus Ministry," in *The New Evangelical Social Engagement*, edited by Brian Steensland and Philip Goff (New York: Oxford University Press, 2014), 56.

[10] James Davison Hunter, *To Change the World: The Irony, Tragedy, and Possibility of Christianity in the Late Modern World* (New York: Oxford University Press, Inc, 2010), 4.

principles, then will the world experience social change, no matter how big or small.

The kind of world that we leave for the future generations will be largely determined by the way "we use new capacity to work together as individuals, groups and nations."[11]

The Church is hand picked by God, and mandated to be a powerful agent of love, that can effect social change, and have its own voice. As a body of believers, Christians have a purpose and a call to play an active role in God's plan for their own society. Part of our responsibility as Christians is to exercise our compassion and love for others in tangible ways. Christians should feed the hungry, comfort the sorrowing, and visit the sick, as part of the Kingdom service. These biblical principles, practically executed, are some of God's people's greatest tools to show Jesus to those who have never tasted the truth. What India needs today is a mission that gives hope and brings social change. Mission has to be liberating praxis for human promotion, a prophetic proclamation of the Kingdom and its values of justice and peace for all. Particularly in India, mission deals with human beings wrestling with concrete religious, cultural and socio-economic issues. The Church of Christ has a unique opportunity in India, a nation with a culture obsessed with the concept of gods and goddesses, to bring the concrete reality of a Savior to a hopeless and clueless generation, thereby quenching the ripples of negative world change.

One of the emerging visions of the Church leaders should be the social transformation in the light of the Kingdom values. As Christians, we are faced with a daily decision to give into the temptation to fit in, and to keep quiet, but it is the love of Christ, and His powerful message of liberation that should utterly compel us. Christians are commanded to follow the example of Christ by caring for each other (John 15:12; Gal 6:2). This Scripture is fulfilled not only in helping the needy, and taking care of the parentless, but speaking out in truth in the face of forces that push Christians to compromise every day. The mandate to care comes in a world of change where we are confronted constantly by new and threatening developments. We ought to be able to change and be open to new developments without much stress, and certainly without any despair. Harnessing the power for progressive social change in the coming years can only come through a renewal founded in the Bible and in Jesus Christ Himself.

2. Definitions of Terms

(a) Disability

According to Kilbourn, The World health Organization (WHO) defines disability as "an umbrella term for impairments, activity limitations and participation

[11] Jay Weinsten, *Social Change*, XX.

restrictions."[12] Disability as a concept is rarely found in most traditional societies because they are grouped into specific types of group like blind, deaf, lame, and dumb and so on in the society. Moreover, society also has different ways of the responding to the individual depending on what type of differentablity a person has.

(b) DABA

Dimapur Ao Baptist Arogo (DABA) is a church serving the Ao tribe of Nagaland at Dimapur. It was established on October 5, 1958. It is a member of the Ao Baptist Arogo Mungdang (ABAM) under the Nagaland Baptist Church Council (NBCC).[13]

(c) Missiology

"Missiology is the conscious, intentional, ongoing reflection on the doing of mission. It includes theories of mission, the study and teaching of mission, as well as the research, writing and publication of works regarding mission. Involvement in or doing of mission, however, preceded by several centuries the scholarly reflection on mission."[14]

3. Biblical Understanding of Disabilities

In the Old Testament, one can find two concepts of disability. The first concept portrays disability as a mark of impurity or a blemish that prohibits one from temple service. (Leviticus 21:18-21, 2 Samuel 5:9). However, the second concept depicts God as compassionate toward persons with disabilities, as in reference to opening the eyes of the blind (Isaiah 35:5, 42:16). In Leviticus 19:14 and Deuteronomy 27:18, compassion towards blind person and other person with disabilities is expected of an upright believer.[15]

The New Testament contains the same view of blindness, as in the Old Testament but it also introduces some different ideas. Jesus healed a number of blind people. Such healing is recorded in Matthew's gospel (9:27-28, 12:22, 15:30-31). Another gospel story, focusing on the blind Bartimaeus in Gospel of Mark 10:46-52, explains further the view of disability. Jesus says with compassion and supernatural understanding to the blind man,'your faith has made you whole'

---

[12] Phyllis Kilbourn, *Let All the Children Come: A Handbook for Holistic Ministry to Children with Disabilities* (Fort Washington: CLC Publication, 2013), np.

[13] Dimapur Ao Baptist Arogo Golden Jubilee Otsu 1958-2008 (Dimapur: Dimapur Ao Baptist Church, 2008), 2.

[14] Alan Neely, "Missiology," *Evangelical Dictionary of World Missions*, edited by A. Scott Moreau, HarolodNetland and Charles Van Engen (Grand Rapids Michigan: Baker Books House, 2000), 633.

[15] Samuel N. Kabue, "Church and Society's Response to Disability: Historical and Sociological Perspective," in *Disabled God Amidst Broken People: Doing Theology from Disability Perspective*, edited by Wati Longchar and Gordon Cowans (Manila: The ATESEA, 2007), 3-4.

(Mark 10:52). Ezamo Murry is of the view that the New Testament speaks of an inclusive community where there is no difference between, men or women, Jews or Gentiles, and for that matter the able-bodied or the disable-bodied.[16] Hence, we find that generally the Bible is for the inclusion and restoration of the weak, the broken, the poor, the outcast, and the stigmatized.[17]

4. Some General Perception towards Children with Special Needs

Over the years, perceptions towards disability have varied significantly from one community to another. The earliest literature in the Hebrew writings, referring to society's attitude towards disabilities, suggest that those exhibiting strange behavior were thought to be in the possession of evil spirit. In the classical world, Aristotle as cited by Young commanded that disabled child should not be spared. The Sparta, on the other hand, drowned or abandoned any deformed child unfit for citizenship and warrior status in the Taygetus Mountains. But, the collapse of Roman Empire and the advent of Christianity saw some changes in the lives of the disabled people. While St Augustine of hippo felt that the deaf were incapable of faith, since they could not hear the word of God and no divine miracle could help them, Luther as cited by Young insisted that the deaf "hear" and received the gospel since it is not ears that are important but God illumination of the heart, and since all are "spiritually deaf" apart from regeneration.[18]

Bernal states that, "Society has staggered a long way from the belief that children with special needs were the product of the Devil, or changelings. They may be hesitant and apprehensive, but progressive steps are now being taken towards such children enjoying the status of agents of change."[19] In a recent article 30th June, 2015, *The Times of India* wrote on Indian's reluctance in adopting the children with special needs. Justice Kanade as quoted by Sequiera voiced out, "Whenever there is a child with special needs in India, parents do not opt for taking these children..."[20]

Article 23 of the UNCRC[21] establishes the right of children with disabilities to be able to enjoy a "full and decent life in conditions that ensure (their) dignity, promote self-reliance and facilitate the child's active participation in society." It

---

[16] Ezamo Murry, "Disability is a Reality Even in The Divine Community," in *Journal of Tribal Studies*, xvi/1 (January-June, 2011): 34.

[17] Murry, "Disability is a Reality Even in The Divine Community," 33.

[18] Amos Young, *Theology and Down Syndrome: Reimagining Disability in Late Modernity* (Waco, Texas: Baylor University Press, 2007), 34.

[19] Catherine Bernal, "The Sociological and Historical Context of Disability," in *Meeting the Needs of Children with Disabilities: Families and Professionals Facing the Challenge Together,* edited by Helen K. Warner (Abingdon, Oxon: Routledge, 2006), 21.

[20] Sequeria Rosy, "Indians Don't Want to Adopt Kids with Special Needs: HC," *The Times of India* (30th June 2015), 1-10.

[21] United Nation Convention on the Rights of the Child.

also requires education, health, rehabilitation, recreation and employment services to be provided for children with disabilities to enable them to achieve the fullest possible social integration.

5. Differently Abled Children in Dimapur Ao Baptist Arogo

As US differently abled activist Judy Heumann (1998) as cited by Mark Priestly argues, the global struggle for differently abled people's inclusion requires the development of knowledge at national and local levels.[22] Therefore, an agenda for social change in DABA must be based on some understanding of disability from a DABA perspective and our Differently Abled studies must reflect local need, local knowledge and local experience. Churches need to be welcoming to all children; not just in providing Sunday Schools and Children's Club but in every aspect of church life- children should be involved in worship, communion and prayer. Collecting offering and stewardess is a very common practice in our local church. The DAC can feel welcomed in the church by participating in this kind of worship service. It is helpful to have a photo gallery with names of key individuals in the church council the children's advocate, Sunday school Teacher, Youth Director, etc., When we use bold print for people's names, children who are hard of hearing and have difficulty discovering people's name, could find such display helpful. Differently Abled Children will feel welcomed when they find that provision has already been made for them; it is the attention to details that matters.[23] According to the Youth Director, the church does not put any restriction in letting Differently Abled Children perform in the church services.[24] Presently the assistant choir master in DABA is a differently abled man.[25] DABA also has a special Toilet for the differently able people and sidewalks for the wheel chair user. What DABA needs today is to make awareness program through sermon, home visitation, seminars about DAC. The church should not only wait for the DAC to come to them but should welcome them by going to them and inviting them to the church.

6. The Challenges faced by Differently Abled Children

Differently abled children are subjected to multiple deprivations and limited opportunities in several dimensions in their lives. Some of the challenges they face are:

---

[22] Mark Priestly, "Developing Disability Studies Programmes: the international context," in *Disability and Social Change: A South African Agenda*, edited by Brian Watermeyer (Cape Town: HSRC Press, 2006), 18.

[23] Simon Bass, *Special Children, Special Needs: Integrating Children with Disabilities* (London: Church house Publishing, 2003), 3.

[24] Interview with Imnatoshi Longkumer, Youth Director, DABA, 5th July 2015.

[25] Interview with Jongshimanen, Music Director, DABA, 5th July 2015.

(a) Social Isolation

The social effects of the DAC create social distance between the DAC and the families, and the community.[26] This negative attitude to the DAC and parents, leads to stigma and social isolation.[27] The varying physical and developmental disabilities that effect children in this society cause them to feel different, and often times not accepted by other children. Many children suffer from the lack of inclusivity, having different ways of processing or sharing information than peers of their age.

(b) Lack of Effective Participation

One of the reasons for lack of participation by DAC is due to lack of support, parental care, encouragement and help. If they do not get support, they may experience failure and later drop-out from school. This defeats the very purpose of inclusion and consequently the inclusion process will also fail.[28] It is the lack of passion on the part of the government for the health and education of those with developmental and physical disabilities that truly and unlawfully makes them the sting of the society. With a practical government health and education plan, supported by local churches and schools, the stigma could widely erase.

(c) Community Misconceptions and Stigmas

Society's attitudes towards DAC are absolutely ruthless. There is a tendency that these children get labeled quickly which means that people may talk about their condition and make assumptions about it rather than getting to know the child. Most often, people do not look at the child's interest, strengths and personality.[29] Children are referred to as "the blind child" or "the lame child" thus erasing their personal identities, and making their disability their sole identity. This use of language is another powerful example of ignorance that prevents those with disabilities to rise above the negative societal expectations.

(d) Inferiority Complex

Inferiority complex is another challenge faced by DAC. A DAC may have a poor self-image and lack confidence because of the difference he sees between himself and his friends or because of inappropriate comments made about his lack of progress in a particular developmental area as children tend to compare themselves

---

[26] Samuel George, "Persons with disabilities in India," *in Doing Theology from Disability Perspective*, edited by Wati Longchar and Gordon Cowans (Kolkata: Atesea, 2011), 35.

[27] Prerna Sharma, "Rights of Children with disability," in *Child Safety, Welfare and Well Being: Issues and Challenges,* edited by Sibnath Deb (New Delhi: Springer, 2016), 226.

[28] Neena Dash, *Inclusion Education for Children with Special Needs* (New Delhi: Atlantic Publishers & Distributors, 2006), 72.

[29] Penny Tassoni, Kate Beith and Kate Bulman, *Child Care and Education: Cache Level 3* (London: Saffron House, 2007), 497-498.

with others.[30] This view is again reinforced by the idea that they are not a human being with ability, heart, or personality, but simply just a disabled person. They are taught from a very young age to identify themselves by their short comings, not their strengths. This negative stigmatism starts with the parents, and trickles down to the children, thus causing generations of ignorance.

(e) School Related Challenges

Education is one major area where the parents and DAC face many challenges. It is generally known that though the parents want to send their children to the school, they are not allowed to take admission in the schools because of their special needs and the negative attitude towards DAC. In many societies, the children with disabilities have traditionally been separated for education and hence there is a need to change the existing educational system so that it does not become an instrument for differentiation by separating children according to social class and above all according to their abilities or disabilities.[31] In this regard, Sparks as quoted by Allen states that the common goal is to gain acceptance in our educational system for DAC.[32] Throughout the centuries, there has been a perception and belief that DAC would not necessarily be able to lead independent lives. But today, this situation is improving, even though many children and families report that they have to fight to get equal access to education.[33]

(f) Challenges faced by the Family

It is a common fact that there are many challenges faced by family of DAC. These families experience excessive caretaking demands, financial burden, and restrictions on leisure activities and social lives, as well as disruptions of family plans.[34] In addition to that, when working in a school,[35] the presenter became aware that families often have to fight to get what they want for their children regardless of whether it's a medical, educational or social service to which they are' entitled. "Change provides challenges and uncertainty, but it also allows for opportunities and development."[36] Parents need to be confident and find

[30] Angela Dare & Margaret O'Donovan, *Good Practice in Caring for Young Children with Special Needs* (Cheltenham: Stanley Thornes Ltd, 2001), 46.

[31] M. L Dhawan, *Education of Children with Special Needs* (Delhi: Isha Books, 2005), 4-5.

[32] Ellen Allen & Glynnis Cowdery, *The Exceptional Child: Inclusion in Early Childhood Education* (Stanfort: np, 2015), 9.

[33] Tassoni, Beith & Bulman, *Child Care and Education: Cache Level 3*, 497.

[34] Jan Blacher, Bruce L.Baker, and Lauren D. Berkovits, "Family Perspectives on child Intellectual Disability: Views from the Sunny Side of the Street," in *The Oxford Handbook of Positive Psychology and Disability,* edited by Michael L. Wehmeyer (New York: Oxford University Press, 2013), 167.

[35] School name: Cherry Blossom School Kohima.

[36] Catherine Carroll-Meehan, "Introduction," in *Challenges and Change for the Early Years Workforce: Working with Children from Birth to 8,* edited by Christine Ritchie (New York: Routledge, 2015), 8.

energy to challenge a system and resources that do not always meet their children requirements.

(g) Medical Challenges

Lack of facilities and trained medical professionals, and social stigma has always been major hindrances towards the treatment of DAC. Social stigma towards disability hinders them from hassle less access to treatment.[37] It is more difficult for the parents of DAC as they find it hard to pay for medical treatment, special treatment and so on.[38] DAC often are with a variety of developmental disabilities, that are often difficult to diagnose, hard to remediate, and impossible to cure. Most of the time the Doctors are ill-trained and it becomes a challenge for the DAC and the family to wait for the right treatment and diagnose.

(h) Abuse

We know that disabled children are at an increased risk of being abused compared with their non-disabled peers. Abuse can take many forms ranging from, physical, mental, sexual, bullying and emotional, including in the family, schools, and private and public institution, and community at large. The negative attitudes regarding DAC, as being of less human, less valuable, and less potential than others gives way to abuse.[39]

7. Differently Abled Children and Ministry

Our mission should be to support and encouraged the inclusion of differently abled in the life and work of the church and society and also to reach out and help families and differently abled children.

(a) The role of the family

When a DAC is born into a family, most parents do everything they can do promote that child's well-being and life chances.[40] There is general agreement among childcare professionals that parents know their children best and every effort should be made to keep children with special needs at home with their families. But, this can be achieved only if sustained, flexible and child-centered services are provided, which allow families choice and make it possible for children

---

[37] Enakshi Ganguly Thukral, *Status of Children in India* (New Delhi: HAQ Centre for Child Rights, 2005), 71.

[38] Bharti Ali & Praveena Nair S, *Twenty Years of CRC: A Balance Sheet*, vol. I (New Delhi: CRC20BS Collective, 2011), 27.

[39] Prerna Sharma, "Rights of Children with Disability" in *Child Safety, Welfare and Well being: Issues and Challenges,* edited by Sibnath Deb (New Delhi: Springer, 2016), 227.

[40] Denis P. Hogan "Family Consequences of Children's Disabilities" (New York: Library of Congress Cataloging-in-Publication Data, 2010), 8.

to be cared for at home.[41] All children have their special interest, needs and thus, their families can in the best way work it out effectively.[42]

(b) The Role of the Pastor

The role of the pastor is to make others realize that there is a need for a ministry with DAC.[43] At the same time, they should also know if they have any DAC in their local community or church.[44] Ignorance is one of the main causes of lack of ministry to the DAC. The pastor should go to the DAC and the families instead of waiting for them to come to the church.

(c) Role of the churches and the Congregation

As with any ministry, the church leadership, as well as the rest of the congregation, needs to be made aware of the need for the ministry among DAC so that they can support the ministry, especially through prayer and provide financial and helping hands.[45] Ignorance is one of the biggest reasons churches don't have a more comprehensive ministry to families of DAC.

It is probable that not all parents have the immediate confidence or desire to be actively involved in care and management routines. In this situation, the church can play active role in working with parents to accept their God-given role as primarily faith shapers and cooperate with the work God is doing in the hearts of children.[46]

(d) Role of the government and NGO

The concept of reasonable accommodations in educational institutions is a fairly recent phenomenon. Persons with Disabilities Act, 1995, remained pretty much silent on provision of reasonable accommodation to students, especially at institutions of higher education. It was only after India signed the United Nations Convention on the Rights of Persons with Disabilities (UNCRPD) in

---

[41] Angela Dare, Margaret O'Donovan, *Good Practice in Caring for Young Children with Special Needs* (Cheltenham: Stanley Thornes Ltd, 2001), 143.

[42] Helen K. Warner "Meeting the fundamental needs of children with disabilities," in *Meeting the Needs of Children with Disabilities: Families and Professionals Facing the Challenge Together,* edited by Helen K. Warner (Madison Ave, New York: Routledge, 2006), 3.

[43] Gene Newman & Joni Eareckson Tada, *All God's Children: Ministry with Disabled Persons* (Grand Rapids, Michigan: Zondervan Publishing House, 1981), 29.

[44] David W. Anderson, "Reaching out and bringing in: Ministry and with Persons with Disabilities (Bloomington: WestBow Press, 2013), 79.

[45] Julie Bohn, "Making Christ Accessible," in *Let All the Children Come: A Handbook for Holistic Ministry to Children with Disabilities,* edited by Phyllis Kilbourn (Fort Washington: CLC Publication, 2013), np.

[46] Pat Verbal, "Why you Church Needs a Special Needs Ministry," in *Special Needs-Special Ministry: For Children's Ministry,* edited by Jim Pierson, Louise Tucker Jones, Joni Eareckson Tada (Loveland: Zondervan Publishing House, 2004), 14.

2007, ratified in 2009, that the concept of reasonable accommodation started getting discussed as demanded by the DAC.[47] To this end, in the present scenario, the efforts of UN agencies, NGO's, governments and national and international disability organizations to eliminate all forms of prejudices and discrimination against DAC are bearing fruits. In our Naga society, the NGO'S, the church, private organizations, schools and individuals are also doing relentless work in uplifting people with disabilities especially towards children. Likewise, in DABA, programs, seminars and church activities are initiated through the NGO's. However, the progress is very slow and so in this regard the church, NGO's, individual's, etc., need improve the work process to be more effective in this ministry towards DAC.

(e) Sunday school hour

Sunday school is one agency which can help in meeting the needs of the families of DAC, as most often, the challenges of raising DAC are overwhelming, and many families face those challenges without the Church's intentional, active involvement. This begins with Sunday school classes that welcome the children.[48] Usually for parents who bring their special needs child to church often feel vulnerable for themselves and for their child as it is difficult to encounter people who don't understand and who aren't always welcoming.[49] By understanding their difficulties and employing some strategies in our classrooms and at home, Sunday school classes can help these students (DAC) overcome their fear.[50]

(f) Educational provisions for DAC

In previous generations, children for whom no 'cure' was found were sent away to institutions or kept out of sight. Later, children were sent to special schools rather than to mainstream schools which meant that they had limited education, as expectations were low.[51]

It is imperative that teachers focus on the child and not on the impairment. Early childhood special educators should look for similarities between DAC and their typically developing peers, not differences. Attentions should also be focused on the children's strengths and abilities and not their disabilities.[52] So, teachers are

---

[47] Br. Mani Karott, "A Christian Perspective on Disability," in *Drishtikone: Evangelical Perspective on Mission and Ethics*, Issues. 1 (2013): 8-9. https://www.google.co.in/Webhp?Sourceid=chrome. (Access on 7th July 2015, 3:00 PM).

[48] Pat Verbal, "Why you Church Needs a Special Needs Ministry," 11.

[49] Pat Verbal, "Why you Church Needs a Special Needs Ministry," 12.

[50] Katie Wetherbee & Jolene Philo, *Every Child Welcome: A Ministry Handbook for Kids with Special Needs* (Grand Rapids: Good News Publishers, 2015), 87.

[51] Tassoni, Beith & Bulman, *Child Care and Education: Cache Level 3*, 497.

[52] Richard Gargiulo & Jennifer Kilgo, *An Introduction to Young Children with Special Needs: Birth Through Age Eight* (Belmont: Wadsworth, 2007), 29.

expected to take account of this by looking carefully at how they organized their lessons, the classroom, the books and materials they give to each child and the way they teach.[53]

(g) Working with the school

In our day to day life, one encounters many children who need to be taught many skills than how to read and write, how to draw and color, how to recall information and take test. A good teacher is expert at teaching all those things, yet, there are many children who need more than that. They need someone who has the commitment, compassion and courage to reach out and connect with them. They need someone to touch not only their minds, but to also touch their hearts and souls to break down walls and stereotypes, to look beyond the obvious and see what lies beneath.[54] A positive attitude is the single most important qualities for anyone who works with DAC.

8. Missiological Implications

Mission is holistic and inclusive and it concerns with building communities. At the same time it is contextual, rooted in the socio-cultural realities of the people. It is an effective tool for change and transformation. Therefore, doing mission is an effective tool in liberating the margins especially the DAC.

(a) Missional Theology

Missiology is an applied science. Missiological reflection focuses specifically on a set of particular issues. These issues call us to hear the cries, see the faces, understand the stories, and respond to the living needs and hopes of the persons who are an integral part of that context.[55]

Mission and development both belongs together. Mission without development is like activity in itself empty; development activity without mission is blind. Both, however, are totally incomplete without the common celebration of life, which gives thanks to God.[56] Missional theology explores and implies the missionary nature of God. It also articulates the gospel and to live faithfully in the ongoing mission of God in a particular context.[57]

---

[53] Dhawan, *Education of Children with Special Needs*, 1-2.

[54] Malesa Breeding, Jerry E. Whitworth & Dana Hood, *Let all the Children Come to Me* (Colorado Spring: David C Cook, 2006), 22.

[55] Charles Van Engen "Specialization/Integration in Mission Education," in *Missiological Education for the Twenty-first Century: The Book, the Circle and the Sanda,* edited by J. Dudly Woodberry, Charles Van Engen and Edgar J. Elliston (Eugene, Oregon: Wipf and Stock Publishers, 1997), 220.

[56] Theo Sundermeire "Theology of Mission," *Dictionary of Mission: Theology, History, Perspective*, edited by Karl Muller, Theo Sundermeler, Stephen B. Bevans and Richard H. Blies (Orbis Books: MaryKnoll, New York, 1997), 449 (429-451).

[57] Benjamin T. Conner, *Amplifying Our Witness: Giving Voice to Adolescents with Developmental Disabilities*, 17.

(b) Practical Theology

Practical theology is critical reflection on the action of the church in the world. According to Swinton as cited by Benjamin Conner, the church participates in the "continuing mission of God in, to, and for the world." Following Newbigin, Swinton states that the church is the "hermeneutic of the gospel."[58] Practical theology acts as a channel of empathies to the multifaceted relations of the weaker sections and those who are not. It also enables the weaker section to act as a channel to the people through their "woundedness," by associating with the image of the suffering, crucified God.[59] Practical theology, thus, acts on both the church and the DAC.

(c) Tribal Theology

Tribal Theology works towards making the Gospel of Jesus Christ relevant and meaningful to the people; it works towards making tribal Christian faith to be natural, contemporary, relevant and authentic in Christ.[60] The purpose of tribal theology is to articulate a living and empowering theology in the light of the given realities of the tribal people.[61] The need of the hour is doing mission among the DAC, taking the examples of the authentic Mission of Christ in tribal context.

(d) Liberation Theology

According to Gustavo Gutierrez, as cited by Deborah Creamer, liberation theology "is a theological reflection born of the experience of shared efforts to abolish the current unjust situation and to build a different society, freer and more human." Thus, when we do mission from the weaker section, it seems correct to study God and the Church from the DAC perspective and do theology for their struggle for liberation.[62]

(e) Social Model

This model acknowledge that the difficulties to be a part of the society and its institutions lies in the environment rather than in the individual and that such obstacles can and must be prevented, reduced and eliminated. Environmental obstacles come in many appearances and are found at all levels of society. They

---

[58] Benjamin T. Conner, *Amplifying Our Witness: Giving Voice to Adolescents with Developmental Disabilities* (Grand Rapids, Michigan: Wm. B. Eerdmans Publishing Co., 2012), 15.

[59] Joanna Z Ray, "Practical Theology: In search for a 'disabled' God" (NP: Lulu, 2006), 19.

[60] Yangkahao Vashum" Introducing Tribal Theology: A Case for Contextual Theology," in *A Living Legacy: Essay in Memory of Jonathan H. Thumra,* edited by Shimreingam L. Shimary & Yangkahao Vashum (Jorhat, Assam: Barkataki and Company Pvt. Ltd., 2014), 245.

[61] Yangkahao Vashum" Introducing Tribal Theology: A Case for Contextual Theology," in *A Living Legacy: Essay in Memory of Jonathan H. Thumra*, 244.

[62] Deborah Beth Creamer, *Disability and Christian Theology: Emboieded Limits and Constructive Possibilities* (New York: Oxford University Press, 2009), 75.

can be seen in policies and regulations created by governments, for example.[63] The social model thus, focuses on disability as a diversity of human condition and not as unwanted features to be fixed or cured. The subject thus, shifts from them to us, from what is wrong with them to what is wrong with the culture and environment that has been organized for them.[64] One of the examples of social model of DABA is that, it has provided for a wheelchair user to get into the church with a ramp, so that the wheelchair user is free to go into the building without any hindrance.

(f) Medical Model

Medical model states that disability is regarded as a weakness that naturally prevents full participation in the economy and the society.[65] It also views disability as having a lack or impairments that needs to be "fixed."[66] And so, it is the job of doctors, rehabilitation professionals, government bureaucrats, and social workers to take care of individuals with disabilities and to help them adjust to a society structured around the abilities and interests of the nondisabled. Thus, society's role should be paternalistic. Their action should be as a form of welfare or charity.[67]

(g) Human Rights

According to Human rights, disability is linked with violation of human right. "This method encounters the fundamental inequality."[68] Ecumenical experiences have continued to lead to new emphases in the theological discussion on human rights. Legitimacy can be bought only when human rights are set out according to the perception of the weak and the oppressed. When human rights are treated from the view of the poor, or in this case DAC, the prophetic task of the church gains a special emphasis.[69]

---

[63] Geeta Chopra, *Child Rights in India: Challenges and social Action* (New Delhi: Springer, 2015), 214.

[64] Anita Ghai "The Psychology of Disabled People" *in Psychology in India Volume: Clinical and Health Psychology, Volume 3,* edited by Misra Girishwar (New Delhi: Dorling Kindersley, 2010), 120.

[65] Jeffrey A. Schwartz, Charles D. Siegal and Michael Waterston, "Disability Policy: United States," *Encyclopaedia of Disability: A History in Primary source Documents,* edited by Gary L. Albrecht, Sharon L. Snyder, David T. Mitchell, etc. (Thousand Oaks, California: Sage Publications, Inc, 2006), 469.

[66] Geeta Chopra, *Child Rights in India: Challenges and Social Action,* 213.

[67] Jeffrey A. Schwartz, Charles D. Siegal, Michael Waterston, " Disability Policy: United States," *Encyclopaedia of Disability: A History in Primary source Documents,* edited by Gary L. Albrecht , Sharon L. Snyder, David T. Mitchell, etc. 469.

[68] Geeta Chopra, *Child Rights in India: Challenges and Social Action,* 213.

[69] Wolfgang Huber "Human Rights" Theology of Mission," *Dictionary of Mission: Theology, History, Perspective,* 195-196.

(h) Ethics and Mission

Human freedom and the immortality of the human soul are two of the basic claims of Ethics. The first claim for the responsibility whereas, the second as justification for doing good and avoiding evil at all times. The method of evangelization today should be concerned with social changes which gives importance to justice and peace, missionary dialogue, and so on. History challenges us to give importance not for only responsibility but also for compassion. Jesus fulfilled this evangelization agenda, "whose moral actions demonstrates to be a part of a social environment and yet embraced others."[70]

9. Holistic Approach

Theologian Amos Yong states, "A biblically informed and inclusive pneumatological ecclesiology emphasizes both that the church is liberated from whatever disabling barriers might exclude certain of her members from full access and participation and that the 'weaker' members are accorded more honor by God and therefore are more central to the identity of the body of Christ."[71] Yong goes on to say, "The Holy Spirit ... actually acts as the champion and advocate of all people, especially the poor, the 'weak,' and the oppressed, and initiates them into the body of Christ. The result is or should be a kind of hospitality in which us/them barriers are overcome"[72]

G.Warneck states as cited by Theo Sundermeier, "Because Christianity is not form and law but spirit and life, it may pervade the whole of human personal and social life, which may also take on the same popular, civic, social and cultural forms."[73] If it is characteristic of the Spirit to join what is old with what is new; what is past and what is to come; diversity with unity; freedom and development of the individual with responsibility for the whole of the community; if the Spirit is God's power and does not allow Godself to be limited or confined within any barriers or patterns, then it is immediately evident that the spirit is truly the power we need in order to be able to continue the worldwide work of liberation which Jesus began in the power of the same Spirit.[74] And so, mission must be Spirit filled.

Jesus, in his early ministry, often responded to the differently abled with compassion. He healed many disabled persons and restored their health. This inspired Christians to serve the differently abled all over the world. However, Jesus towards the end of his life took the alternate path, not the healing of the

[70] Dionisio Miranda "ETHICS" Theology of Mission," *Dictionary of Mission: Theology, History, Perspective*, 135-136.

[71] Amos Young, *Theology and Down Syndrome: Reimagining Disability in Late Modernity* (Waco, Texas: Baylor University Press, 2007), 204.

[72] Amos Young, *Theology and Down Syndrome: Reimagining Disability in Late Modernity*, 205.

[73] Theo Sundermeire "Theology of Mission," *Dictionary of Mission: Theology, History, Perspective*, 430.

[74] Felix Porsch, "HOLY SPIRIT," *Dictionary of Mission: Theology, History, Perspective*, 192.

differently abled, but he himself became differently abled by accepting the cross.[75] Stigma and discrimination can be removed only if we imagine ourselves as created in the image of God who is differently abled which sees a human life in relationship with God and other creatures. Such an image of God reflected in human beings can bring a wholesome understanding of the image of God.[76]

"For Jesus, God is compassionate, merciful and loving. Because Jesus understands God as love and himself as the expression of that love, he saw his mission as being sent by God to be the savior of the world. So the nature of God as love shaped Jesus' understanding of his mission as the embodiment of God's loving purpose on earth.[77]

According to C. S. Song as quoted by Hung, "God's heart aches when the world is gripped with pain and suffering."[78] He says that God came not to save the righteous, rather to save the sinners, the poor and the differently abled people. Song further says that, "we cannot do the theology in our office, but we must go out and feel the pains of the differently abled people as well as the pains of God. Then our theology may help in building the faith and courage of the differently abled people."[79] DAC do not only long for inclusion in the society but also for participation. So the society must grant them identity as persons and include them as vital parts in the network of life.[80]

Another aspect of the ministry of Jesus is to establish the kingdom of God. He was constantly surrounded by sick and disabled people; the paralyzed (Mt 12:10), deaf and dumb (Mt 12:22), the blind (Mk 10:46-52), the mentally ill (Mt 8:28-34). It is said that wherever he went, such people would crowd around him. So it was a way of life for Jesus to be constantly surrounded by Differently Abled People.[81] This indicates that the Church must be inclusive of all people who are in need and, not only the rich and able people. Through engaging in social change, the Church can establish the Kingdom of God.

A study on the missional engagement towards DAC has led to a conclusive finding that societal attitudes are significant since they determine to a large degree the extent to which the personal, social, educational and psychological needs of

---

[75] D. John Samuel, "Biblical Perspectives of the Disabled," *in Embracing the Inclusive Community: A Disability Perspective,* edited by A. Wati Longchar and R. Christopher Rajkumar (Bangalore: BTESSC/SATHRI, NCCI & SCEPTRE, 2010), 42.

[76] Samuel George, "Image of God and Disability: Stigma and Discrimination," in *Sprouts of Disability Theology*, edited by Christoper Rajkumar (Chennai: NCCI, 2012), 64-65.

[77] Walter A. Elwell "Jesus and Mission" *Evangelical Dictionary of World Missions,* edited by A. Scott Moreau, Harold Netland and Charles Van Engen (Baker Books: Grand Rapids, 2000), 517.

[78] Wong Hin Hung, "Jesus and the Disabled People: A Church Response to the Disability," in *Embracing the Inclusive Community: A Disability Perspective*, 103-104.

[79] Hung, *Jesus and the Disabled People: A Church Response to the Disability*, 104-105.

[80] Murry, "Some Aspects in Psychology of the Disabled Person," 68-69.

[81] Karott, "A Christian Perspective on Disability," 8-9.

DAC will be realized. To this end, efforts to eliminate all forms of prejudices and discrimination against DAC should be undertaken by the church. Perhaps, it is high time for us to realize that DAC are not to be shunned or discriminated. The need of the hour therefore is for the family, the Church and the Society to change its attitude towards the DAC and give them their rightful place in the life and ministry of the society.

16

The Impact of BPO Work Culture on Indian Family
A Pastoral Response

Saraswati Koirala

Introduction

Change is something that is inevitable in our society.[1] The Institution of family has seen tremendous change throughout the history. Some of the changes were constructive while some were disturbing to the life of a family. Business Process Outsourcing (BPO) work culture is one among them that has changed the family structure in India. On one hand, with the rise of BPOs there has been tremendous development in economy of India. On the other hand it has changed the entire outlook of a family pattern.

It is not uncommon for a family to go through the transition as the working pattern changes, however, this essay makes an attempt to bring out the impact that BPO work culture has made upon the lives of an individual and in turn how it has impacted his/her family. We will firstly explore the kind of social change that is taking place in India. The reasons for the change and its effect in the society will also be highlighted. In such scenario of changes, how church need to respond to the issues will also be discussed. Secondly, this paper will give an overview of Indian family and the transitions in its system. It will then try to define BPO work culture and its positive and negative impact upon an individual and his/her family. Thirdly, it will try to look into how churches have understood the issues of BPO work culture in India and also how they have dealt with the issues. Have

[1] Lacey Hall, "Changing Homes, Changing Nation," in *The Marriage Affaire: The Family Counselor*, edited by J. Allan Petersen (Illinois: Tyndale House Publishers, 1971), 235.

Church looked into this matter seriously? If they have looked into the issues, what strategies have been used to deal with the issues? Lastly, it discusses the pastoral response to the issues that have arisen due to BPO work culture in a family.

1. Social Change: Its Effects

Change, according to Joseph H. Fichter as cited by H. K. Rawat, is a "variation from a previous stage or mode of existence." Therefore, social change is a variation in a social structure,[2] social relationships and a change that is seen in all aspects of social life which include family life, work life, religion, political area, economic area, and many more.[3] Change cannot be said as modern phenomena but it is true that rate of the change in contemporary world is tremendous.[4] It is essential to know the various factors that are involved in this change.

Ram Shakal Pandey says that physical, biological, technological and cultural factors are responsible for a social change.[5] Hence, social change is analysed in different ways; economists focus this change from their economic factors, sociologists focus on social behaviour and on social structure, and political scientists view into political changes and so on.[6] Yogendra Singh has noted that during the past 50 years, western lifestyle has influenced Indian culture and society immensely.[7] The institutions such as "family, caste, kinship, village, polity and economy" are witnessing considerable change in India.[8] Dube says that if there is a change in an individual's personality, it brings change in the social system too.[9] Hence, it is clear that an individual and his/her family are deeply connected to their social system.

The change in the economy has impacted Indian family system.[10] Modernisation and westernisation has changed the outlook of Indian society[11] and this has brought tremendous change in family structure too. It is not only joint family that has been changed into nuclear family system but even nuclear

---

[2] S. S. Mathur, *A Sociological Approach to Indian Education* (Agra: Agrawal Publications, 2009), 103.

[3] H. K. Rawat, *Sociology: Basic Concepts* (Jaipur: Rawat Publications, 2010), 269.

[4] Wilbert E. Moore, *Social Change* (New Jersey: Prentice-Hall, Inc., 1974), 2.

[5] Ram Shakal Pandey, *Education in Emerging Indian Society* (Agra: Agrawal Publication, 2011), 197.

[6] Gabriele Dietrich and Bas Wielenga, *Towards Understanding Indian Society* (Thiruvalla: Christian Sahitya Samithi, 2008), 201.

[7] Yogendra Singh, *Cultural Change in India: Identity and Globalization* (New Delhi: Rawat Publication, 2008), 115.

[8] S. L. Doshi, *Postmodern Perspective on Indian Society* (Jaipur: Rawat Publications, 2010), 147.

[9] S. C. Dube, *Modernization and Development: The Search for Alternative Paradigms* (New Delhi: Vistaar Publications, 1988), 20.

[10] Rawat, *Sociology: Basic Concepts*, 280.

[11] Dietrich and Wielenga, *Towards Understanding Indian Society*, 201.

family is going through adaptive changes due to the change in the economic structure in the society.[12]

During 19th century, church faced a great challenge with the Industrial Revolution in Europe. People started to migrate to cities, hierarchical feudal system in village was lost and many social problems occurred. In India similar situation has come up with the emergence of science and technology which has increased urban life. The church on the other hand is continuing to live within the four walls expecting people to come occasionally to meet God. It is failing to respond meaningfully to the emerging concerns and the need of the people and their situation. Since our society is changing day by day, the church has to revise its worship pattern and its mission strategy. At present, new style of service, counselling and prophetic role in the socio-economic affairs of the nation is the great challenge before the church.[13]

Most churches focus exclusively on the Sunday worship service that the church is not able to attract many members. Some of the members who are working on Sunday are not able to attend this worship service. On the other hand some attend church service only on three occasions which George Ninan mentions as "hatching (baptism), matching (marriage) and despatching (burial)." He further says that most of the church sermons are irrelevant to the life of the church members because church leaders focus mainly on past events rather than giving any guidelines for their future.[14] Therefore, churches need to change their role as the outlook of Indian society mostly in urban context is changing day by day. Hence, in order to effectively engage in the lives of people, it is very important to analyse, study and understand the context in which Christians are placed.

2. BPO Work Culture and Indian Family

In India, the normative patterns of a family are either extended, i.e., joint family or nuclear family.[15] Joint family was a starting point in setting up a pattern of a family in India.[16] The psychological bond within the members is seen in joint family system.[17] But Western modernization is constantly influencing Indian family system. Growth in industrialization means more urbanization, and family is the first institution that is to be influenced.[18] Urban employment structure is

---

[12] Yogendra Singh, *Modernization of Indian Tradition* (Jaipur: Rawat Publications, 2011), 174.

[13] Ninan, *Church and Society: Challenges and Responses in the 21st Century*, 151.

[14] Ninan, *Church and Society: Challenges and Responses in the 21st Century*, 143.

[15] Murli Desai, "Family and Interventions: Curriculum Planning," in *Family and Interventions: A Course Compendium*, edited by Murli Desi (Bombay: Tata Institute of Social Science, 1994), 23.

[16] M. S. Gore, *Urbanization and Family Change* (Delhi: Sangam Books Limited, 1990), 2.

[17] P. D. Devanandan and M. M. Thomas, eds., *The Changing Pattern of Family in India* (Bangalore: The Christian Institute for the Study of Religion and Society, 1960), xii.

[18] Jacob S. Quiambao, *The Asian Family in a Changing Society* (Manila: East Asia Christian Conference, 1965), 41.

such that it compels an individual and families to leave a rural living and settle in urban centers. Hence, the traditional joint family system has shifted in a direction of the nuclear family.

M. Poster says that in traditional nuclear family, the father used to be the authoritative head and mother would devote herself to the development of the child. In a psychoanalytic language, child developed strong superego, learned independence, by battling with the authority of a father.[19] But in today's context, authority of a father is subdued by different authority figures as the father does not have time to spend with his own children. Mother is also forced to work outside the home because of expensive cost of living. Hence, this brought a distant relationship within the family members, especially with children. Child rearing practices have also changed in the context of dual career family.

(a) Meaning of BPO and Some Related Terms

BPO "refers to the rearrangement of entire business functions to some other service providers, primarily in low cost locations."[20] BPO companies are external providers that administer and manage one or more information technology.[21] It includes call centres employees who work over phones and also business process offices, those who work over webs.[22]

Outsourcing is a process where one organization hands over some part of its work to another organization "making it responsible for the design and implementation of certain business process under the requirements and specifications of the outsourcing company."[23]

Call centre is a "department within a company or a third-party organization that handles telephone sales and/or service."[24]

[19] M. Poster, "Family, History and Sociology," *Dictionary of Pastoral Care and Counselling*, edited by Rodney J. Hunter (Bangalore: Theological Publications in India, 2007), 408.

[20] K. Tamizharasi and Umarani, "Work Stress and Job Performance Evaluation of BPO Employees," *International Journal of Advanced Research in Computer and Communication Engineering* 3/1 (January 2014): 2 of 8, http://www.ijarcce.com/upload/2014/january/IJARCCE5D_A__tamizharasi_work.pdf (18 June 2015).

[21] Prathibha J. Mishra and Manglesh Kumar, "Socio-Economic Impact in India," *International Interdisciplinary Research Journal* 2/3 (March 2014): 1 of 10, http://www.internationaljournals.co.in/pdf/giirj/2014/march/8.pdf (19 June 2015).

[22] Binay Kumar Pattnaik, "Globalization, ICT Revolution and Socio-cultural Changes in India: Sociological Explorations," in *India between Tradition and Modernity*, edited by Joanna Kurczewska, Ishwar Modi and Janusz Mucha (Jaipur: Rawat Publications, 2014), 269.

[23] Kumar, "Socio-Economic Impact in India," 3 of 10.

[24] http://www.pcmag.com/encyclopedia/term/39218/call-center (19 June 2015).

(b) BPO Work Culture and its Impact

Usually social scientists say that technological advancement or industry is a great factor in bringing changes to the family.[25] Organizations function not in isolation but within the main system of society. It takes various sources from society like people, capital, and resources; and in return gives goods and services as its output which impacts the life of people.[26]

John Stott says that work is something that occupies a significant place in most people's lives. The average employees divide their day into "three more or less equal periods- eight hours' sleep, eight hours' work and eight hours' leisure."[27] Those who work on call centres "are forced to live as Indian by day and Westerners after sundown."[28] A typical BPO functions twenty four hours a day.[29] Working method of BPO sectors are very different from conventional work pattern.

The work culture of BPO sector is composed of odd timing of work schedule. Employees are forced to work during the night due to the difference in the time zone of Multinationals.[30] They work throughout the night and sleep throughout the day. This is something very new that has entered in a peaceful Indian family.

Every employee in BPO is assigned to achieve some targets. Such targets increase the work load of the employee.[31] Their daily targets are calculated in terms of number of calls and e-mails they attend successfully.[32] They are measured on their service performance. There are restricted assigned areas for the employees at their work place. Superiors keep records of their work through systems not giving them any freedom of breaks if they need any.[33] This increases physical, emotional and mental stress on the workers which leads to burnout.[34]

Usually those working in BPO do not get leave on national holidays.[35] Binay Kumar Pattnaik, mentions in his survey that insufficient holiday is one of the reasons of having stress among BPO employees.[36] This causes a disturbance in family time.

---

[25] William J. Goode, *The Family* (New Jersey: Prentice-Hall, INC, 1964), 104.

[26] Umarani, "Work Stress and Job Performance Evaluation of BPO Employees," 2 of 8.

[27] John Stott, *New Issues Facing Christians Today* (Mumbai: GLS Publishing, 2003), 185.

[28] Ramesh, "'Cyber Coolies' in BPO: Insecurities and Vulnerabilities of Non-Standard Work," 496.

[29] Ramesh, "'Cyber Coolies' in BPO: Insecurities and Vulnerabilities of Non-Standard Work," 494.

[30] Umarani, "Work Stress and Job Performance Evaluation of BPO Employees," 5 of 8.

[31] Umarani, "Work Stress and Job Performance Evaluation of BPO Employees," 5 of 8.

[32] Ramesh, "'Cyber Coolies' in BPO: Insecurities and Vulnerabilities of Non-Standard Work," 495.

[33] Madhavi Challa, "Quality of Working Life of BPO employees: Literature Review," *International Journal of Management and International Business Studies* 4/3 (2014): 2of 4, http://www.ripublication.com/ijmibs-spl/ijbmisv4n3spl_15.pdf (18 June 2015).

[34] Umarani, "Work Stress and Job Performance Evaluation of BPO Employees," 1 of 8.

[35] Ramesh, "'Cyber Coolies' in BPO: Insecurities and Vulnerabilities of Non-Standard Work," 495.

[36] Pattnaik, "Globalization, ICT Revolution and Socio-cultural Changes in India: Sociological Explorations," 270.

Employment opportunities in BPO sectors have provided good financial packages to urban youth.[37] Good image of work and high salary, have attracted many young people in this sector.[38] Thus, every new avenue has its own positive and negative impact which one cannot avoid. It depends upon an individual how well they can cope up with such impact.

(c) Some Positive and Negative Impact of BPO on Indian Family

Increase in cost of living has encouraged women folk to work outside the home. This has drastically changed the family scenario in urban cities.[39] Unlike other traditional manufacturing sectors, call centres are offering more employment opportunities for women.[40] Urban women are able to earn good amount of income and support their families which has changed their socio-economic status in their families. Even the standard of living of the middle class has improved to a great extent as BPO provides good amount of salary and quick promotions.

Unemployment in India is said to be very high. In such scenario, BPO is providing job to the jobless educated youth.[41] In a research done in the year 2014, it was found that BPO provided direct employment to almost 1.6 million professionals.[42]

Among the negative impacts, BPO employees work not in the traditional time schedule (9 am to 5 pm). Their working schedule is such that they have their lunch at mid-night and return home early morning to be woken up at 6pm to begin their work schedule again. They usually miss family and social interactions.[43] There is always difficulty in maintaining a healthy work-life balance.

There is also less time to communicate and interact with children. They also 'outsource' the caring of their children too – to babysitting or day care centres. This has led to less parental bond with the children. This creates a negative psychological impact in the adolescent phase. According to Sigmund freud, as mentioned by Abraham Scaria, at anal stage (1-3 years) of a child, parent's attitude, their consistency and their patterns of discipline is very important in achieving

---

[37] Joseph George, "The Changing Pattern of the Family in India: Contemporary Explorations," in *The Changing Pattern of the Family in India: A Renewed Version*, edited by P. D. Devanandan and M. M. Thomas (Bangalore: Christian Institute for the Study of Religion and Society, 2007), 25.

[38] Ganiger, "Women in BPO's and its Impact on Family: A Sociological Analysis," 1 of 2.

[39] Aparajita Chowdhury and Manoj Manjari Patnaik, "Understanding Indian Family Life: The Gender Perspectives," *Excel International Journal of Multidisciplinary Management Studies* 3/7 (July 2013): 4 of 10, http://zenithresearch.org.in/images/stories/pdf/2013/JULY/EIJMMS/6%20_EIJMMS_VOL3_ISSUE7_JULY2013.pdf (21 June 2015).

[40] Ramesh, "'Cyber Coolies' in BPO: Insecurities and Vulnerabilities of Non-Standard Work," 496.

[41] Ramesh, "'Cyber Coolies' in BPO: Insecurities and Vulnerabilities of Non-Standard Work," 492.

[42] Ganiger, "Women in BPO's and its Impact on Family: A Sociological Analysis," 1 of 2.

[43] Joseph George, "Marriage and Family Counselling," in *A Study Book on Counselling*, edited by George Varghese (Thiruvalla: Christian Sahitya Samithi, 2012), 89.

the developmental goal. If such conflicts are not solved, then it affects the later stage of life.[44] This may lead them to substance abuse, wrong relationship, pre-marital sex and many other issues.

Intimacy between husband and wife is disturbed. This may harm the growth of family ties and the emotional needs of family members remain unfulfilled and ignored.[45] There are marital issues leading to divorce which is rising up in the churches.

Employees have several roles to play such as in family, community, church, work place, and so on and mostly these create tension, as expectations and demands are from different people. In a research, it is proven that all these pressures results in a stress among BPO employees.[46] The employee's stress level is usually high and opportunity for their personal growth is not much seen.[47] They are more prone to stress because of their monotonous work nature and long working hours. Since most of the BPOs are located on the outskirts of cities, they get tired after the travel to and from workplace.[48]

Health has become major concern for the employees in high-tech BPO sectors. *Times of India* records that there is greater chance of heart disease to those who work more than 35 to 40 hours a week. Scientists researched and came to the conclusion that there are 33% greater risk of stroke to those who work for more than 55 hours a week.[49] In the research it is found that employees in BPO sectors do not remain in this sector for a long time because they get sleep disorder, eye-sight problem, high stress level and different kinds of sickness. In a research, it is found that near about 80% of employees of BPO sectors are suffering from such diseases.[50] Ramesh, in his research, finds that BPO employees get into several health issues such as "nervousness, chronic fatigue, body ache, insomnia, nausea, anxiety, restlessness, irritability and even depression." He further says that in order to cope up with the psychological and physical stress, employee develops poor eating habits, smoking, overeating, excessive consumption of coffee and so on. It

---

[44] Abraham Scaria, "Theories of Personality," in *A Study Book on Counselling*, edited by George Varghese (Thiruvalla: Christian Sahitya Samithi, 2012), 260.

[45] Ashwani Kumar, "The Changing Face of Family & Its Implications on the Mental Health Profession in Delhi," *Delhi Psychiatry Journal* 14/1 (April 2011): 2 of 4, http://www.delhipsychiatricsociety.com/pres-journal.pdf (21 June 2015).

[46] D. Sugumar, et al., "Addressing Health Related Challenges Faced by the Business Process Outsourcing (BPO) Employees by Stress," *African Journal of Business Management* 7/12 (28 March 2013): 4 of 9, http://www.academicjournals.org/article/article1380792753_Sugumar%20et%20%20al.pdf (11 June 2015).

[47] Challa, "Quality of Working Life of BPO employees: Literature Review," 2 of 4.

[48] Umarani, "Work Stress and Job Performance Evaluation of BPO Employees," 5 of 8.

[49] Kounteya Sinha, "Working Over 8 hrs a Day Raises Stroke Risk by 33%," *The Times of India* (20 August 2015), http://timesofindia.indiatimes.com/home/science/Working-over-8-hrs-a-day-raises-stroke-risk-by 33/articleshow/48550484.cms (2 Sep 2015).

[50] Umarani, "Work Stress and Job Performance Evaluation of BPO Employees," 1 of 8.

increases their healthcare costs too.[51] It is said that on an average one employee in a day receives 100 calls, and each call can be for 4-15 minutes. And one floor of the company receives 35,000 calls on a daily basis. *Times of India* records that such intense work leads some BPO executives to use drugs[52] and pills like *spasmo-proxyvon*.[53] Such health issues have become a great matter of concern not only to the sector but also to the family and society.

It is not only children who suffer but also elderly in the family who get affected. The care for aged people within families has declined due to the different timings of the work system of spouses. At the time when family support is needed most, they are being neglected and left on their own. Children adopt the same 'outsourcing' attitude of sending the old parents to old age homes.

The independent life that BPO is providing to employee is helping them in attractive living but it is failing to give them a balanced life.[54] BPO employees are mostly living a self-centred life, moving away from their families and community. Such kind of isolated life has led to pre-marital sex, extra marital affairs and live-in relationships.[55] The late night shifts, deadlines to finish their target and the monotonous nature of job are affecting the work life of BPO employees. Young BPO employees are mostly seen into drugs, crime, depression and suicidal tendencies.[56]

Women in the family are affected more with the rise of work pressure. Even if women are independent in terms of financial stability, most married men have patriarchal tendencies and they are expected to play both the roles, traditional as well as modern. Sonal Pathak and Anil Sarin quotes Sylvia Hewlett, President of the Center for Work-Life Policy, "if a woman takes time off to care for children or an older parent, employers tend to see these people as less than fully committed."[57] Marriage, parenthood, work, household activities are all expected to be balanced by her otherwise conflicts arise. Hence, the role of male and female are in question.[58]

---

[51] Ramesh, "'Cyber Coolies' in BPO: Insecurities and Vulnerabilities of Non-Standard Work," 496.

[52] "These drugs keep them going even when their throat goes dry due to the numerous calls they attend to." Refer to Saibal Sen and Sumati Yengkhom, "BPO Blues," *The Times of India* (10 Oct 2011), http://timesofindia.indiatimes.com/city/kolkata/BPO-blues/articleshow/10298472.cms (1 Sep 2015).

[53] Yengkhom, "BPO Blues," *The Times of India.*

[54] Sarin, "Management of Stress among Women Employees in BPO Industry in India: A Contemporary Issue," 3 of 6.

[55] Pattnaik, "Globalization, ICT Revolution and Socio-cultural Changes in India: Sociological Explorations," 274.

[56] Challa, "Quality of Working Life of BPO employees: Literature Review," 3 of 4.

[57] Sarin, "Management of Stress among Women Employees in BPO Industry in India: A Contemporary Issue," 3 of 6.

[58] Patnaik, "Understanding Indian Family Life: The Gender Perspectives," 4 of 10.

Women are struggling to maintain their work-life balance. It is more challenging when they have to take care of their children.

3. Social Change and Church Role

Most of the city churches in India have become more flexible, unlike the traditional Sunday worship, to accommodate members from the IT companies (especially those in BPO sector who work as per the US timings). Churches have started worship service on other days like Saturdays and some week days. Few years back, churches were silent in their response towards Sunday working employees. Gradually the concern arose regarding the worship service for those who work even on Sundays. Churches were rigid in their traditional pattern of Sunday worship. Sunday was not a working day for many Christians since it was considered Sabbath as people were supposed to take a break from their work and activities apart from going to the church.

The impact of globalisation has enabled the world to be a global village accessible 24/7. This has stretched the 9-5 timings and made it 24/7. The workers in the BPO sector work in shifts to facilitate this 24/7 global economy. The leisure after 5 pm where family members used to spend time with each other is lost now. Today such family time is hardly seen among the employees who are involved in late night shift or those working more than 8 hours a day. A matter of deep concern in the churches is this growing disconnect between the family members that has been brought by the lack of leisure time. Church's response to such a situation is poor and at times nothing other than just bringing a flexible worship timing. The pastors and church leaders have not fully addressed these concerns from pastoral care and counselling perspective as well as from therapeutic point of view. Church is more concerned with the spiritual aspect and other aspects are neglected. Churches in Tier-I cities like Delhi, Mumbai, Bengaluru, Chennai, Kolkata, Hyderabad and some Tier-II cities have started evening service on Sundays and week day services so that working people could get some fellowship. Such services have helped BPO employees to some extent as they take sleep the whole day after their night shift. In my observation, many of the BPO employees have difficulty in attending Sunday service, be it in the morning or in the evening unless they have week off on Monday.

In my interview with a CNI priest, I found out that in Mumbai, if a father of a family is unable to attend the church on Sundays due to the work in BPO, other family members also suffer when the person is responsible to take them to the church. In his experience as a Youth Director, youngsters working in BPO were not able to attend most of the church programmes; their attendance was low compared to the time before joining BPOs. This has become serious issue not only in Mumbai but also in other Tire-I and Tire-II cities. Good Shepherd Tamil Church in Mumbai, which is located in Dharavi, is open during the day and conducts daily service too so that believers can attend services and gather for fellowship anytime of the day and the week.[59] But in cities, it is not so easy to keep church open for the whole day. Cathedrals keep its door open so that anytime people can visit and pray. But the question I want to raise is, will the change of timings in the church service or letting the church open for whole day going to meet the need of the employee who is not only struggling spiritually but also socially, emotionally and physically? How can church provide the care and counselling that is very much needed to the stressed BPO employee struggling to balance their work-life?

Scott Floyd says that long-term stress is a crisis after which an individual finds difficult to cope with life situation.[60] The Burnt out and Stressed out employees are not able to spend quality time in prayer and meditation. They lack in spending quiet time with God. Due to the odd working hours, an individual as well as his/her entire family is deeply affected and this has impacted their spiritual life as well. It becomes very challenging to the person to stay connected with the church. On the other hand, the church too finds it difficult to provide proper pastoral care to such families as they are unable to reach even through house visits.

The married[61] BPO employees are the ones who are struggling more than the unmarried to maintain their work-life balance in terms of the marital, familial, social, and spiritual with the work. This is the challenge that the church of today is facing now: Work-life balance issue. If at all church starts to teach and provide care to their members to balance their work-life it would bring great difference and would enrich their relationships alongside their stressful job.

The BPO work culture is such that even the social connection is built within itself. Company picnics, gyms within the workplace, food courts and hangouts within the campus make sure that the employees socialise within themselves. This leads to another collateral effect of not having the fellowship among the believers. Going to church becomes outdated for them and as such the question arises – Why go to church when my needs are met in the campus? Unfortunately, the personal problems are on the rise with the rise in divorce cases, marital disputes, parental care and above all Christians have lost their faith in God due to lack of fellowship amongst believers. It is high time that the Church realise that this issue would have a cascading emotional and spiritual breakdown leading to a severe crisis that could again cripple Christianity as well as the Indian economy.

---

[59] Interview with D. S. Marian, Priest of Church of North India, Mumbai Diocese, 27 August 2015.

[60] Scott Floyd, *Crisis Counseling: A Guide for Pastors and Professionals* (Bangalore: Asian Trading Corporation, 2012), 97.

[61] It is generally found that married people have multiple responsibilities as compare to unmarried people so that it is quite difficult for them to manage their work life properly. Refer to Gupta and Sharma, "An Empirical Analysis of Work Life Balance In Corporate Employees with Special Respect to Marital Status in Moradabad Region," 1 of 6.

Due to hectic work schedules in BPOs, couples get less chance of interpersonal communication between them. This is a clear voice to the churches in cities where not only extending church services is going to solve the rising issue but there should be regular pastoral care and counselling, marriage and family enrichment programs, teachings on work-life balance and some seminars on stress management should be provided to the working BPO employees.

4. Pastoral Response

B. J. Hagedorn says that family therapy is a "way of joining and reconstructing a dysfunctional family system."[62] Family therapist helps the family in crisis by joining the family and by digging out the underlying problems and helps them in adopting the transformation in the structure.[63] It is said that pastoral therapist has a unique position from where he/she can respond to the problems related with family life.[64] Through 'Family Growth Groups'[65] and 'Conjoint Family Therapy'[66] pastor can provide effective care and counselling to the families in crisis due to BPO work culture.

(a) Family Growth Groups

Clinebell mentions Dauglas Anderson who describes family growth group as a program which involves three to five families who meet together frequently and provide mutual care It supports growth of a family and provides opportunities for family to "increase their awareness of their unique strengths and resources" and use it in family living.[67] In a case, where families are struggling due to odd working hours, family growth groups can be a great support for each other. In a church context, the pastor can make a group of families working in BPO industries. They can frequently meet with each other according to their holidays. In this way they can care for each others' need and support in the time of crisis situation.

---

[62] B. J. Hagedorn, "Family Theory and Therapy," *Dictionary of Pastoral Care and Counseling*, edited by Rodney J. Hunter (Bangalore: Theological Publications in India, 2007), 423.

[63] Salvador Minuchin, *Families and Family Therapy* (Massachusetts: Havard University Press, 1947), 110.

[64] Loy O. Bascue and Roy Lewis, "Marital and Family Therapy Skills," in *Clinical Handbook of Pastoral Counseling*, edited by Robert J. Wicks, Richard D. Parsons and Donald Capps (New York: Integration Books, 1993), 268.

[65] Douglas Anderson describes more on Family Growth Groups. Refer to Clinebell, *Basic Types of Pastoral Care and Counseling*, 303.

[66] Conjoint family therapy was developed by Don Jackson, John Weakland and Virginia Statir in the 1960s. Refer to Jacques Miermont, "Family Therapies," *The Dictionary of Family Therapy*, translated by Chris Turner, edited by Hugh Jenkins (Massachusetts: Blackwell Publishers Ltd., 1995), 157.

[67] Howard J. Clinebell, *Basic Types of Pastoral Care and Counselling: Resources for the Ministry of Healing and Growth* (Nashville: Abingdon Press, 1984), 303.

(b) Conjoint Family Therapy

The assumption of this therapy is that the "most effective way to help a troubled family member is to help the whole family change their ways of relating and communicating." The only goal of this therapy is to enhance relationship within families for better environment of healing and growth of each member.[68] This therapy provides a resource for "understanding client problems, gathering information about those difficulties, and ultimately treating them." Conjoint sessions are beneficial in the midst of marital conflict where couples are in the verge of separation and divorce.[69] This therapy helps family to see positive growth in the frustrating behaviour of family members. It resolves the conflicts of living together by helping to recognize that the growth is possible only at the point of conflict within family members. Therefore, Conjoint Family Therapy is essential to those family members whose family environment is disturbed due to work pressure and stress in BPO sectors. Church needs to be aware of such families and provide this therapy either by referring such cases to professional therapist or conduct by himself/herself if they know the process.

5. Suggestions for the Church and Pastoral Ministry

In a contemporary society, family pattern is changing at a rapid speed. At the same time it is going through many social crises which are very important to be noticed.[70] Church should come out of its conventional way of ministry. They should come up with some new strategy to provide pastoral care and minister those who are particularly working in BPOs.[71]

(a) Weekday Service

Church should be flexible enough to provide services to those who are working in BPOs. Since BPO employees hardly get leave on Sundays, they can at least attend the church service on weekdays. If it's not possible to provide a service for them on a weekly basis, the church can make sure that services are conducted twice or thrice in a month during weekdays.

(b) Cell Group Meetings/Support Groups

Cell group meetings in city context are very helpful for the members of the church. Such group meetings bring closeness among each other. This will help them to get some fellowship and a time to interact with other members of their church. Pastor

---

[68] Clinebell, *Basic Types of Pastoral Care and Counseling*, 306.

[69] Bascue and Lewis, "Marital and Family Therapy Skills," 276.

[70] Nathan W. Ackerman, *The Psychodynamics of Family Life: Diagnosis and Treatment of Family Relationships* (New York: Basic Books, Inc., 1960), 15.

[71] Paras Tayade, "Pastoral Response to BPOs with Special Reference to Select Churches in Pune" (M.Th Thesis, Senate of Serampore College, 2011).

can take an opportunity to join such meetings in order to find out and observe work related issues and accordingly he/she can plan to help an individual.

(c) Home Visitation and Counselling

H. Anderson mentions that, according to family therapist, home visitation is a part of assessment and treatment. Home visit gives an opportunity to learn about family pattern, its values, its style of living and its ways of being together as a family, which gives an idea to a counsellor regarding the particular family.[72] Pastor needs to be aware of those families whose members are under stress and who are in need of counselling help.[73]

(d) Awareness among Church Members

Pastor needs to make aware his/her congregation to provide much support to the family of BPO workers as their work pressure is high. Women groups can constantly visit and encourage wives of the employees. Since, husband works late night and is not able to give time to her and the children, she may feel isolated and their marriage may be in danger. The regular encouragement and support from church members may help her to overcome her situation.

(e) Seminars on Life, Family and Work

Church can organise family enrichment programs for those families whose members are working in BPOs. Such enrichment programs help in making marriage better and promotes individual growth and mutual fulfilment. Here, pastor can emphasize on Biblical teachings regarding marriage and give some practical steps to overcome crisis situation.

There should be practical sessions where individuals are taught to improve in balancing their life. They should be given teachings on self disciplining, sensitive towards their family member's emotion and training on communication skills. Individuals can be taught regarding their roles and their needs within the marital relationship, family structure and help them to resolve the conflicts that have arisen within his/her relationships with the loved ones.

Church can take initiative in organising seminars or stress inoculation training[74] which will help employee to understand, anticipate and prevent problems that are related to stress.[75] Stress management helps in analysing one's

---

[72] Anderson, "Family, Pastoral Care and Counseling," 416.

[73] Clinebell, *Basic Types of Pastoral Care and Counseling*, 302.

[74] "Stress inoculation training comprises an educational stage (conceptualising stress problems), a skill-building stage (e.g. relaxation exercises, coping self-statements), an application stage (exposure to a variety of stressors in order to test out skills)." Refer to "Stress Inoculation Training," *Dictionary of Counseling*, edited by Colin Feltham and Windy Dryden (New Delhi: I.K. International Pvt. Ltd., 2005), 224.

[75] "Stress Inoculation Training," *Dictionary of Counseling*, 224.

work load, also challenges one's "irrational beliefs", and helps in finding healthy balance between work, home life and other activities.[76]

Conclusion

A vast segment of Indian society is getting urbanised because of which family is always affected. The change in work ethics from agriculture to industry is being accompanied by fragmentation of joint family and adaptation of nuclear unit. Now, family is a matter of concern because traditional nuclear family is experiencing transition due to the BPO work culture among other factors. Even though, BPO is providing good standard of living, employees are being subjected to stress in terms of their work pattern which in return is affecting their family health. Family is a basic foundation to the church and society. If a family is disturbed, the whole atmosphere of the church is disturbed. Therefore, it is the task of the church to come forward and deal with the issues.

---

[76] "Stress Management," *Dictionary of Counseling*, edited by Colin Feltham and Windy Dryden (New Delhi: I.K. International Pvt. Ltd., 2005), 224.

17

Issues Faced by Sexual Minorities (LGBT) Challenges for Pastoral Ministry

Lipoklemla Pongener

Introduction

There has been an increasing interest in the theme of 'Christian engagement in social change' and particularly on how homosexual people have gained their sexual identity as LGBT (Lesbian, Gay, Bisexual, and Transgender) that brought about social change. This paper is a reflection on how the issues of sexual minorities have influenced the medical, constitutional, legal, human rights, societal and psychological spheres, thus bringing social tolerance towards sexual minorities, not just around the world but also in India where various organizations and NGOs are making efforts to uplift sexual minorities. Consequently, this has challenged the Christian understanding of sexuality, and so, Christian engagement in social change in the context of sexual minorities (LGBT) is being awakened. It has, therefore, become necessary to understand the sexual orientation as LGBT of the homosexuals, the plight of the sexual minorities and the new dimensions that social change has brought in. The paper concludes with an empirical study of the response of the church and church engagement towards LGBT community. Pastoral care and counselling models are presented along with practical suggestions.

1. Christian Engagement in Social Change

In the words of John Stott, Christian Engagement in Social Change implies, turning our faces towards all God's creatures in compassion, making our hands dirty in God's service and allowing the love of God to stir deep within us that is unlimitedly flowing.[1] Since the formation of the world council of churches (WCC) in 1948, there has been an urgency towards social change. The initial operation was characterized by engaging in activities of aid on a large scale, and also in researching of the causes of poverty and injustice.[2] In a statement by Philip Potter, "the Uppsala Assembly in 1968 called the churches to action for world development."[3] The mandate of Christian social work is derived from the Ten Commandments notion of 'love your neighbor as you love your God' which was further clarified in the parable of the Good Samaritan where Jesus asked his disciples to 'go and do likewise.' Jesus' short span of living as a human on the earth was crucial to the idea of social change because he took the side of the poor and downtrodden, raised voice against prevailing injustice and the authority of the ruling class, and as a result, Christ had to pay the price of his crucifixion.[4] In the same way, professing Christians are recognizing the problems facing humanity today, and progressively becoming involved in dynamically setting out to promote change. An increasing number of Christians believe they have a 'higher sense of duty or calling' to combat the overwhelming issues facing the inhabitants of the earth. Christians, being motivated by their faith, sense that they have a right and a responsibility to be involved in the world comprising of community, social and political action.[5] The goal of engaging in the mission of social transformation is to see lives being transformed by the power of Christ, a cross-centered and resurrection-powered life that no longer lives for self but dies daily for the kingdom mission of social change.[6] According to George Furniss, the pastoral caregiver plays an incarnational role representing the ever-present companionship of God to those in distress as the wounded healer.[7] Speed Leeas and Paul Kittlaus state that Christian Social Action has focused on reconciling groups and changing institutional structures.[8] Christians involved in social change, who see that society's leaders and the systems as inadequate, need to emphasize God's grace and goodness as well. Christians must engage in society as pastoral care givers by taking on the reality of sin and grace, good and evil in the world and in people. Thus, the ministry of holistic pastoral care believes that there is hope for positive

---

[1] John Stott, *New Issues Facing Christians Today* (London: Marshall Pickering, Revised Edition 1999), 18.

[2] Philip Potter, *Life in all its Fullness: Reflections on the Central Issues of Today's Ecumenical Agenda* (Grand Rapids: William B. Eerdmans Publishing Co., 1981), 83.

[3] Philip Potter, *Life in all its Fullness*, 115.

[4] www.directionjournal.org/7/1/social-action-christian-mandate.html. Accessed on 6/10/15.

[5] www.realtruth.org/articles/317-scba.html. Accessed on 29/9/15.

[6] www.christianitytoday.com/.../four-steps-to-community-engagement.html. Accessed on 29/9/15.

[7] George Furniss, *Sociology for Pastoral Care* (Britain: SPCK, 1994), 52.

[8] Speed Leeas & Paul Kittlaus, *The Pastoral Counselor in Social Action* (Philadelphia: Fortress Press, 1981), 12.

transformation.[9] A. Crockett and D. Voas say, "the Church is a community, but it is not in a world of its own."[10] Therefore, Christians must engage in society and bring transformations. The contemporary society is being challenged by the issue of LGBT and the urgency of the theme is seen to be a current trend in theological learning. In the light of Christian engagement in social change, we will discuss the meaning of sexual minorities, their different sexual orientation as LGBT due to their homosexual lifestyle.

2. Christian Engagement in Social Change in the Context of Sexual Minorities

Before exploring Christian engagement in social change, it is necessary to understand some key terms. Arvind Narrain clarifies that some identities of sexual minorities have been found traditionally while others have been constructed through the spread of modernity. LGB expanded to LGBT.[11] In the view of Sarasu Esther Thomas, sexual minorities are identified by the acronym LGBT which is a short form for lesbians, gays, bisexual and transgender.[12] Magdalene Jeyarathnam defines sexual minorities as people with different sexual orientation, and another commonly used term is queer (in other words, non-heterosexual sexuality).[13]

Definition of LGBT: According to D. K. Sahu, a lesbian indicates a woman who is fascinated with women emotionally/sexually/romantically and gay indicates a man who is fascinated with men emotionally/sexually/physically. A bisexual is a person who is fascinated emotionally/sexually with both men and women. Finally, a transgender indicates a person who is physically born in a certain sex but is more comfortable with the gender/sexual identity of a different gender, and may choose to go in for a sex reassignment surgery or hormonal treatment.[14] Magdalene Jeyarathnam explains that "transgender in contemporary usage includes pre-operative and non-operative transsexual people or male and

---

[9] Speed Leeas & Paul Kittlaus, *The Pastoral*, 15.

[10] Alasdair Crockett & David Voas, "A Matter of Attitude: Homosexuality and Divisions in the Church," *Modern Believing* 45/3 (July, 2004): 23.

[11] Arvind Narrain, "Queer Laws: the Laws Treatment of Sexually Minorities," *Communication for Development* 5/3 (Jan, 2002): 25. The terms lesbian, gay, bisexual, and transgender (LGBT) refer to distinct groups within the gay culture. The initial initiatives for persons who were gay focused mostly on men. Thus, in an attempt to draw attention to issues specific to gay women, 'lesbian' is listed. Persons who are bisexual or transgender have been traditionally left out of in research studies and health initiatives, and later considered standard to include these two groups along with gay men and lesbians. Refer- https://www.mentalhelp.net/articles/what-is-the-meaning-of-lgbt/ Accessed on 9/110/15.

[12] Sarasu Esther Thomas, *Law for Christians in Contemporary India* (Bangalore: BTESSC, 2014), 57.

[13] Magdalene Jeyarathnam, "Struggles of People with Different Sexual Orientation," *Religion & Society* 54/4 (Dec, 2009): 45.

[14] D.K. Sahu, "Human Sexuality-A Legal Perspective," *Religion & Society* 54/4 (Dec, 2009): 44.

female cross-dressers."[15] D. K. Sahu says that, in India transgenders are known as Hijras, and kothis.[16] Also, Sarasu Esther Thomas throws light on the fact that some traditions in India recognize the hijras as the Sexual Minorities.[17]

Sexual Orientation: The term sexual orientation denotes the direction of one's sexual attraction:[18] "the pattern of sexual arousal or the object of sexual or romantic interest is conceptualized as composed of sexual desires and fantasies, sexual behaviors and the ways an individual conceives of herself or himself as for example- homosexual, bisexual or heterosexual."[19]

Homosexuality: Homosexuality is the "disposition to seek sensory pleasure through genital bodily contact with persons of one's own sex in preference to sexual relations with the opposite sex. This behavior is generated not by sensory endings or body chemistry but by choice and conditioning, by what persons have learned as desirable."[20] Gregory M. Herek and Alan E. Kazdin state that "psychology regards homosexuality as an alternative form of sexuality that is not associated with pathology."[21] The term gay (LGBT) has been used by homosexuals to label

---

[15] Magdalene Jeyarathnam, "Struggles of LGBT Community-Experiences of a Counsellor," *Religion & Society* 55/1&2 (Mar, Jun, 2010): 81.

[16] D.K. Sahu, "Human Sexuality – A Legal Perspective", 44. Kothi term used for feminized men- Refer A.V. Ravikumar & K. Anil Kumar, "Sexual Behavior and Its Determinants among Homosexual and Bisexual Men in Mumbai, India," *Family Welfare* 57/2 (Dec, 2011): 13.

[17] Sarasu Esther Thomas, *Law*, 62. Hijra- a socio-cultural construct in which a transgender person who is biologically male takes on the gender role of a female. Hijras in India have their own form of social organization and form a parallel society. Refer- D.K. Sahu, "Human Sexuality – A Legal Perspective", 44.

[18] Magdalene Jeyarathnam, "Struggles of People with Different Sexual Orientation", 45.

[19] Ellen K. Feder & Edgardo Menvielle, "Sexual Identity," *Bioethics* 4th Edition, vol. 6, S-Z, edited by Bruce Jennings (Chicago: Gale Cengage Learning, 2014): 2936. According to Jerome Kagan, "sexual orientation refers to enduring emotional, romantic, sexual, or affectionate feelings of attraction to individuals of a particular gender. Three sexual orientations are commonly recognized: Homosexual-attraction to individuals of one's own gender; Heterosexual-attraction to individuals of the opposite gender; and Bisexual-attractions to members of either gender." Refer- Jerome Kagan, *The Gale Encyclopedia of Childhood & Adolescence* (New York: Gale, 1988), 343.

[20] J. M. Vayhinger, "Sexual Variety, Deviance and Disorder," *Dictionary of Pastoral Care and Counselling*, edited by Rodney J. Hunter (Bangalore: Theological Publication, 2007), 1150.

[21] Gregory M. Herek and Alan E. Kazdin, ed., "Homosexuality," in *Encyclopedia of Psychology* vol. 4 (Washington DC: American Psychological Association, 2000): 152. According to Gregory M. Herek and Alan E. Kazdin "homosexuality encompasses a variety of phenomena related to a same-sex sexual orientation. Homosexuality also refers to patterns of same-sex romantic and emotional bonding, identities and communities based on same-sex desires and relationships, and the shared culture created by those communities. Homosexuality is usually understood as the counterpart to heterosexuality, with bisexuality applied to individuals who manifests either heterosexual and homosexual behavior or attraction," 149.

their life style because they feel that this label has fewer negative implications than 'homosexual.'[22]

3. The Influence of Modernism towards Sexual Minorities (LGBT)

Alex Callinicos says that modernity demanded the entire course of human history as characterizing a more or less continuous forward movement.[23] R. Ahuja comments on the impact of western culture on Indian society in terms of its effect on our social system which broadened the outlook of people who started talking of their rights and freedom. These ideas were transmitted mainly through western education. The introduction of the new values, the rational and secular spirit and the ideologies of individualism, equality and justice assumed great standing.[24] J. Boswell mentions that, in the Roman realm, Christianity rose to power during a period of extreme crisis of homosexual practice. One phase of social change is perhaps related to the decline of Roman tolerance on sexual issues.[25] Centuries later, in the way that the church exercised authority on the Roman understanding of sexuality, it did the same in India. Section 377 was enacted on sodomy and homosexuality acts which were practiced by gay, Lesbian, bisexual and transgender partners.

(a) Traditional Hindu Versions and the British Colonial Regime of Section 377

Prior to the British rule in India, Hindu tradition had a tolerant view of LGBT, especially the hijras. According to a Hindu tradition, Lord Rama blessed and gave the hijras the power to confer blessings on people during certain auspicious occasions. Even today in North India, the hijras visit homes on the birth of a baby to bless the baby, and hijras are invited to dance at weddings.. Another common tradition is of the Aravanis (hijras of Tamil Nadu). The legend says that Aravan, Arjuna's son, had to be sacrificed for the Pandavas victory in kurukshetra. Being unmarried, he wanted to marry and spend his last night with a wife. The women refused because they didn't want to be widowed. So, Krishna assumed a woman 'mohini' and married Aravan. This event is celebrated every year by

---

[22] Irwin G. Sarason & Barbara R. Sarason, *Abnormal Psychology: The Problem of Maladaptive Behavior*, 7th Edition (New Jersey: Prentice-hall, 1993), 217.

[23] Alex Callinicos, *Social Theory: A Historical Introduction,* 2nd Edition (US: Polity, Reprinted 2012), 13. S. L. Doshi, states that the traditional society in Europe or any other part of the world (Britain, England, America, France) has witnessed radical forces of social changes. Refer- S. L. Doshi, *Modernity, Postmodernity and Neo-Sociological Theories* (Jaipur: Rawat, 2003), 1.

[24] Ram Ahuja, *Society in India* (Jaipur: Rawat, Reprint ed. 2011), 477.

[25] John Boswell, *Christianity, Social Tolerance and Homosexuality* (Chicago: The University of Chicago, 1980), 119.

the Aravanis.[26] Inspired by the deontological call of educating the Indians with missionary zeal, the British colonial authorities began to identify all the corrupt and immoral customs and practices that were prevailing in their colonies. This led to the imposition of sodomy laws in all British colonies. The Christian colonialists found the existing culture of tolerance towards homosexual practices conflicting to the normative Judeo-Christian understanding of sexual morality. As a result, it resolved to impose rigid rules that criminalize 'unnatural' sexual practices with an intention to save the colonized from their immoral and corrupt sexual practices. So in 1861, in India the British colonial administration imposed Sec. 377 undemocratically on the colonized to 'cure' and to 'purify' them of their 'primitive and deviant' sexual practices. In 1967, the British parliament passed the sexual offences Act which decriminalized homosexuality and acts of sodomy between consenting adults.[27]

(b) LGBT Population/Organizations and NGOs in India

According to a recent US review dated 5th, April 2015, roughly 10% of the world's population is LGBT.[28] In India, 5 to 19% of the population has a different sexual orientation apart from heterosexual.[29] In India, there is no official statistics for the LGBT population, but according to the figures submitted to the Supreme Court in 2012, about 2.5 million gays self-declared to the Ministry of Health.[30] Thus, only in the last decade of the 20th century, the LGBT movement has brought to

---

[26] Sarasu Esther Thomas, *Law*, 62. In ancient India homosexual practice was either ignored or stigmatized as inferior but not condemned as sin and oppressed as a criminal act. Kamasutra depicts homosexual practices in sensual terms. The erotic sculptures that adorn temples like khajuraho openly depict homosexual acts along with heterosexual acts. When it comes to sexuality, homosexuality practices were tolerated as long as men and women fulfilled their responsibilities to heterosexual marriage, family and procreation. Islam also tolerated homosexual activities as long as men fulfilled their marital responsibilities. This was the setting when the British came to India with the duty of conquest and evangelization. Refer- George Zachariah, "The church: A rainbow community of the beloved and equals: Reflections on Christian Responses to the Repealing of Section 377 of the IPC." *Religion & Society* 54/4 (Dec, 2009): 3.

[27] George Zachariah, "The church, 4.

[28] There are around 9 million LGBT Americans. Refer- www.belongto.org/service.aspx?contentid=2160. Accessed on 20/8/15.

[29] Magdalene Jeyarathnam, "Struggles of People," 82.

[30] A very popular gay dating Website which has about 1.8 million men registered from around the world, India has about approximately 140,000 individual males registered, a figure more than Western countries like USA (46,645), UK (41,021) and ranks 3rd in the highest number of people registered from a country and nearly 80% of them are under the age of 15-30 years. The highest numbers registered State are Maharashtra (25,564), Tamil Nadu (16,380), Karnataka (14,763), Delhi (13,441) and cities are in highest numbers are New Delhi (13,391), Mumbai (11,001), Hyderabad (10,273), and Bangalore (8,000). Refer- https://en.wikipedia.org/wiki/Homosexuality_in_India. Accessed on 20/8/15.

the front the rights of those discriminated against due to their sexuality.[31] In India several organizations, including the Naz Foundation Trust, the National AIDS Control Organization, Law Commission, Union Health Ministry, National Human Rights Commission and the Planning Commission have expressed support for decriminalizing homosexuality, and pushed for tolerance and social equality for LGBT people.[32] There are quite a few significant NGOs working for the upliftment of LGBT community such as, the Humsafar Trust,[33] Free Gay Lesbian contacts support,[34] the Equal India Alliance,[35] Mingle Mission for Indian Gay & Lesbian Empowerment,[36] and the Samapathik Trust.[37] The rights of Sexual Minorities have progressed at lightning speed through democracies in the world in the last two decades.[38] Many movements for social change fought against severe family pressure and for the freedom to make one's own choice for marital partner. Thus, the institution continues and is changing.[39]

Social change has brought in new dimensions of understanding sexual minorities (LGBT) and, with the advancement of modernism, the LGBT community has expanded and identity rights have gained support from both international and national human rights organizations and democracies.

4. Issues Faced by Sexual Minorities (LGBT)

The issues of LGBT, and its progress will be dealt both in the wider and Indian context.

(a) Medical

Developments in the understanding of LGBT in the medical world can be viewed chronologically. On December 15, 1973, the trustees of the American psychiatric association dropped homosexuality from the list of recognized mental disorders

---

[31] D. K. Sahu, "Human Sexuality, 37.

[32] www.legalservicesindia.com/.../rationale-of-lgbt-lesbian-gay-bisexual-an.Accessed on 20/8/15.

[33] The Humsafar Trust is the first NGO in India started to serve the needs of the gay community. The Trust work on the health of the community to 'Motivate Safer Sex among MSM at Selected Sites in Mumbai Metro' and it has emerged as one of India's strongest voices in support of health and human rights for lesbian, gay, bisexual and transgender (LGBT) communities. Refer- www.gayindiaforums.com › ... › Activists and Gay Organizations. Accessed on 20/8/15.

[34] The phone is attended by a counselor on Saturdays between 3pm and 7pm initiated by the Humsafar Trust. Refer- www.indiandost.com/gay_group.php. Accessed on 20/8/15.

[35] The Equal India Alliance is a non-profit working for LGBT and Queer equality in different settings such as NGOs, schools, colleges, corporates, and individuals. Refer- www.equalindiaalliance.wix.com/home#!about-us. Accessed on 20/8/15.

[36] www.Mingle.org.in/. Accessed on 20/8/15.

[37] https://www.facebook.com/pages/Samapathik-Trust.../14006143277910. Accessed on 20/8/15.

[38] J. P. Singh, "Plaint of a Gay Husband," *The Times of India* (Pune), 30 June 2015, 13.

[39] Radhakrishnan, "Feminism, Family and Social Change: Myths and Models," *Social Action* 44/4 (Oct-Dec, 1994): 50.

and named it as 'sexual disorientation disturbance.'[40] According to Christi R. Vonholdt, the American Psychiatric Association (APA) poll to normalize homosexuality was compelled by politics, not science. In 1973, there were no clinical, or scientific arguments whatsoever that would have justified a change in the assessment of homosexuality. In 1978, five years after the APA's resolution to delete 'homosexuality' from the manuel, a poll was carried out among 10,0000 American psychiatrists of the APA members. 68% of the 25,000 psychiatrists from whom the questionnaires were collected, still viewed homosexuality as a psychological disorder.[41] With regard to transgender persons, it is said that prenatal factors, either genetic or hormonal, can cause individuals to be born with imperfect formed sex organs, for example, a person with the genetic characteristics of a female can possess both ovaries and testes.[42] The perception of the gender identity (boy or girl) is different from the sexual organs and so trans-sexualism is a gender identity disorder.[43]

---

[40] Anthony Kosnik, *Human Sexuality* (London: The Catholic Theological Society of America, 1977), 70.

[41] Christi R. Vonholdt, "The Diagnosis of Homosexuality, the A.P.A., and the World Health Organization," in *Striving for Gender Identity: Homosexuality and Christian Counselling*, edited by Christi Ruth Vonholdt (Germany: German Institute for Youth & Society, Reprinted 2000), 165. It has been noted that the APA's removal of 'homosexuality' as a diagnosis has brought great disadvantages to persons who want to overcome their sexual orientation (for example, one reason is there need to have a 'real family' with children), 165. However, it has been observed that a homosexual phase is quite common in adolescence. Refer- Peter Storey, *Psychological Medicine: An Introduction to Psychiatry*, 10th Edition (Edinburgh: Longman, 1986), 224. The most frequent homosexual activity is masturbation with homosexual fantasies. Other common homosexual activities include mutual masturbation, bodily contact with ejaculation, oral-genital relations and anal intercourse. Refer- Peter Storey, *Psychological Medicine*, 225-226. In the view of Money, a person's sexual orientation is also thought to be strongly dependent on socialization after birth. Refer- Cited by Irwin G. Sarason& Barbara R. Sarason, Abnormal Psychology, 219.

[42] Frank R. Scarpitti & Margaret L. Anderson, *Social Problems* (New York: Harper & Row, 1989), 127.

[43] Nel Antonides, Lecture Notes from Diploma in Clinical Pastoral Counselling, Netherlands, 1. Klinefelter syndrome is entitled for Dr. Harry Klinefelter, who first reported its symptoms in 1942. Males usually have an X chromosome and a Y chromosome (46, XY), and females usually have two X chromosomes (46, XX). 47, XXY (or XXY) is a genetic condition caused when someone has two X chromosomes and one Y chromosome. Persons with an XXY chromosome arrangement are measured genetic males. Physical characteristics may perform around the time of puberty, when gender identity and sexual characteristics begin to take shape. XXY is normally caused by nondisjunction, when a pair of sex chromosomes fails to separate during egg (or sperm) formation. When an egg (or sperm) with an extra X chromosomes joins with a normal sperm (or egg), the resulting embryo will end up with three sex chromosomes (XXY) instead of the normal two (XX or XY). In about 10% of cases, chromosomes fail to separate when a cell divides very early in embryonic development, and only some of the baby's cells have an extra X chromosome and, 75% of XXY individuals are never diagnosed. Males who grow breast tissue or who do not develop facial or body hair may perhaps feel self-conscious. Adolescence might need support as they face gender identity issues. XXY is one of the most common genetic conditions, affecting about 1 in

In 1992, the World Health Organization (WHO) deleted 'homosexuality' from its diagnostic list.[44] In the opinion of Christi R. Vonholdt, "the WHO instead of taking its clue from the American Psychiatric Association and dropping homosexuality as a diagnosis, would have done better to study, first and foremost the social compatibility of a homosexual lifestyle and to analyze the medical facts." Hence, from a medical perspective, such life study is nothing but 'desirable.'[45] In the early 1990s, science appeared on the edge of finding a 'gay gene' or, as Mr. Kerry referred to, some inborn, biological basis for homosexuality, akin to eye color or height. However, none of the 'gay gene' studies have turned out successfully. Even a 2000 study of nearly 5,000 Australian twins revealed that, despite having identical genes, only 20% of male homosexuals and 24% of female homosexuals had a homosexual twin. To many researchers, these findings support the argument that homosexuality stems more from external influences than inborn genetics.[46]

(b) Constitutional

Several moves to accommodate the LGBT community have taken place recently. The Delhi High Court has clearly inferred constitutional provisions to reflect the evolving social traditions by decriminalizing same-sex practice and consequently promoting democracy.[47] However, the Supreme Court later reversed this, declaring only parliament can revoke the law not the courts.[48] Sex reassignment surgery by a doctor with the consent of the patient could be protected from criminal liability under one interpretation of Section 88 of the Indian Penal Code.[49] Some achievements have been made in the Supreme Court (Written Petition Civil) of 2013 decided on 15th April 2014, where 'transgender' were recognized as the 'third gender' in India.[50] On 24th April 2015, the Rajya Sabha passed the Bill protection and providing rights for transgender. The Bill created welfare

---

660 genetic males. Refer- www.learn.genetics.utah.edu/content/disorders/chromosomal/klinefelter/ Accessed on 30/9/15.

[44] Christi R. Vonholdt, "The Diagnosis of Homosexuality," 163.

[45] Christi R. Vonholdt, "The Diagnosis of Homosexuality," 166.

[46] www.washingtontimes.com/news/2004/.../20041128-121135-7392r/? Accessed on 14/9/15.

[47] Madivalappa Matolli, "Homosexuality, Human Rights & Indian Culture," *Legal News & Views* 24/8 (Aug, 2010): 9. In 1986 the US Supreme Court stated that a homosexual claim to privacy rights was inappropriate in the Bowers case. Refer- Svati P. Shah, "True Sex and the Law: Prostitution, Sodomy, and the Politics of Sexual Minoritization in India," in *Sexuality Studies* edited by Sanjay Srivastava (New Delhi: Oxford University Press, 2013), 173. Bowers v. hardwick were found by police having oral sex in the bedroom. Refer- Scarpitti, *Social Problems*, 123-124.

[48] Swaminathan S. Anklesaria Aiyar, "After Gay Rights, Is Polygamy the Next Revolution," *The Times of India*, (Pune), 12 July, 2015, 13.

[49] Aarthi Mundkur, "Unrecognized Minority: the Plight of Transsexuals Visca Vis the Law," *Communication for Development* 5/3 (Jan, 2002): 30.

[50] Sarasu Esther Thomas, *Law*, 66. According to Adler, in 1993 at the international conference on transgender law and empowerment policy issued the international bill of gender rights. Refer-

boards both in the Center and in the State level. Transgender Rights Courts, and 2% reservation in government jobs and prohibition of discrimination in employment. It also makes provisions for pensions and unemployment allowances for members of the community.[51] Social Justice Minister Thaawar Chand Gehlot and the Central government are contemplating a proposal to adopt transgender identity with surgeries in public hospitals. It has to be decided if the cost of these interventions are to be borne by the government or will be subsidized. According to the plan the government will identify public hospitals where surgeries will be made available.[52]

(c) Legal

The movement to repeal Section 377 was led by the Naz foundation India Trust, which filed a public concern lawsuit in the Delhi High Court in 2001 seeking legalization of homosexual intercourse between consenting adults. In 2003, the Delhi High Court refused, and on 7th Nov 2008, the Indian Health Minister supported this petition while the Home Minister opposed such a move. On 12 June 2009, India's Law Minister Veerappa Moily agreed that Section 377 might be outdated.[53] On July 2nd 2009, homosexuality in private was legalized. Thus, Section 377 of the Indian Penal Code, originally enacted by the British in 1860, was abolished.[54] However on 11th December 2013, the Supreme Court of India in a decision called Suresh Kumar koushal vs. Naz foundation overturned the decision on Naz foundation and upheld the validity of Section 377 of the Indian Penal Code,[55] that criminalizes homosexuality as 'against the order of nature.'[56]

(d) Human Rights

On the ground of Human Rights, it was argued before the Supreme Court in 2009 that Section 377 which criminalized Homosexuality offended different constitutional rights: right to equality under Article 14 of the Constitution and under Article 21 the right to privacy, right to life and personal liberty and right to health.[57] On 18th, July 2009 in Delhi the Commission on policy, governance and

---

Cited by Timothy F. Murphy, "Gender Identity and Society," *Bioethics* 4th Edition, edited by Bruce Jennings, vol. 3 F-I (Chicago: Gale Cengage Learning, 2014): 1252.

[51] Jatin Gandhi & Smriti Kak Ramachandran, "Bill Promises Welfare Board, Job Quotas for Transgenders," *The Hindu* (Hubballi), 25 April 2015, 12.

[52] Subodh Ghildiyal, "Transgenders can Choose Gender Soon," *The Times of India* (Pune), 1 July 2015, 13.

[53] D. K. Sahu, "Human Sexuality, 41.

[54] Somen Das, "An Ethical-Theological Perspective on Human Sexuality." *Religion & Society* 54/4 (Dec, 2009): 21.

[55] Sarasu Esther Thomas, *Law*, 65.

[56] J. P. Singh, "Plaint," 13.

[57] Madivalappa Matolli, "Homosexuality," 6.

public witness consultation listened to the views of leaders from Islam, Sikhism and Christianity including the Naz foundation. In Chennai on 28th July, 2009, the Commission on Justice, Peace and Creation in the Chennai consultation listened to inclusive community participants from the church and society including the LGBT community. In these consultations, the fear expressed was decriminalization would open a prospective Pandora box leading to same-sex marriage and the right of same-sex couples to adopt children. It would develop a threat to meaning and sanctity of marriage and related social institutions.[58]

(e) Societal

India is among countries with a social component of a third gender but mental, physical, emotional and economic violence against LGBT community in India prevails, because of a lack of support from family, society or police.[59] A more obvious issue is one of the stigma placed on the community by societal structures and systems. This then leads to the negative internalized self-perception of individuals in the community and, denial of rights and opportunities as citizens, which in turn affects the lack of resources and the livelihood of the community.[60] Struggles of LGBT are of self-identity, social acceptance, and psychological effects (depression, isolation, suicidal tendencies, self-harm).[61] Stigma and discrimination based on the ground of being a homosexual and increased vulnerability to sexually transmitted infections (STI) are two important dimensions the homosexual population are generally identified with. Many 'men sex with men' (MSM) are married and engaged in marital sex as a social duty in response to strong social norms and intense family and community pressure for procreation, and as a defense mechanism to avoid stigma and discrimination from homosexuality.[62] Transsexuals are subject to tremendous discrimination from family, society and the law.[63] Sarasu Esther Thomas says, "Christian traditions have also considered sexual relationship among sexual minorities as sinful, particularly same sex relationships."[64] According to Drumm, the church has pushed against same-sex

---

[58] D. K. Sahu, "Human Sexuality, 43. The US Supreme Court on 26th June 2015, declared same-sex couples across the country the right to wed. Refer- Chidanand Rajghatta, "Same-Sex Marriage Now Legal Across US," *The Times of India* (Pune), 27 June 2015, 13.

[59] www.legalservicesindia.com/.../rationale-of-lgbt-lesbian-gay-bisexual-an. Accessed on 20/8/15.

[60] David Selvaraj, "Theological Reflection on Human Sexuality," *NCC Review* cxxxv/6 (Jul, 2015): 64.

[61] Paper Presentation Christian Counselling Centre, P.G. Certificate in Psychological Counselling (Vellore), 2013.

[62] A.V. Ravikumar & K. Anil Kumar, "Sexual Behavior and its Determinants among Homosexual and Bisexual Men in Mumbai," *The Journal of Family Welfare* 57/2 (Dec, 2011): 12.

[63] Aarthi Mundkur, "Unrecognized Minority, 31.

[64] Sarasu Esther Thomas, *Law*, 58.

marriages and transsexual surgery.[65] The LGBT community are being ostracized and excluded from the fuller communion of the church.[66] The unrepented gay person is ostracized by the community and not allowed participation in its sacramental life.[67]

(f) Psychological

Psychology has put forward several theories for the causes of homosexuality. Psychological factors that cause homosexuality are need for the same-sex parent's love. In need of gender identification, the homosexual feels an absence of masculinity or femininity within himself or herself. Therefore, this results in the pursuit to fulfill this need through another man or woman. In the case of a female homosexual, the fear of intimacy with someone of the opposite sex is due to abuse either by her father or another significant man or men in her life.[68]

Homophobia evidently marks gays and lesbians as targets of social ostracism and contempt. Such negative stereotypes carry excessive harm to the social and psychological well-being of gay and lesbian people.[69] The homosexual inferiority complex generates self-pity and self-dramatization. The painful awareness of being different in a negative sense stimulates a wish for recognition and appreciation as of the idealized people.[70] In the case of boys who feel lonely and inferior, longing for warmth, their admiring interest in the physical appearance or personality characteristics of their own sex takes on an erotic dimension. The sensual day dreams or masturbation imaginations are centered on the adored ones of the same sex which leads to the homosexual desire.[71] With regard to women, different factors have been attributed to origin of homosexual tendency. A girl who feels homosexually attracted to other women feels an ugliness complex, feeling less feminine or less attractive as a girl. Further comparison with a sister in physical attractiveness or in other respects and inferiority among her brothers with thoughts like 'I am only a girl' may lead to imitation of boyishness. Another reason could be lack of attention by the opposite sex during adolescence. She might think 'they do not find me as attractive as other girls' and may come to admire the womanliness of other girls who are more sought after.[72] Psychological problems

---

[65] Cited by Alan Aldridge, *Religion in the Contemporary World: A Sociological Introduction*, 3rd Edition (Cambridge: Polity, 2013), 177.

[66] George Zachariah, "The church, 2.

[67] Robert J. Wicks & Richard D. Parsons, eds., *Clinical Handbook of Pastoral Counseling*, vol. 2 (New York: Integration Books, 1993), 269.

[68] Richard A. Cohen, "Healing Homosexuality," in *Striving for Gender Identity*, 118.

[69] Scarpitti, *Social Problems*, 125.

[70] Gerard Van den Aardweg, "The Homosexual Inferiority Complex," in *Striving for Gender Identity*, 103.

[71] Gerard Van den Aardweg, "The Homosexual," 104.

[72] Gerard Van den Aardweg, "The Homosexual," 111-112.

that lesbians bring in social counseling range from the social stigma of being a lesbian, social ostracism, to more severe hatred and violence.[73]

Thus, modern developments in the fields of medicine, law, government, and psychology paved the way for the social leniency towards LGBT, and the traditional rigidity against homosexual culture slowly began to diminish. The medical studies towards homosexuality removed the threat of abnormality/neurotic, and in spite of the religious taboo and societal stigma against homosexuality, it became a lifestyle and its desirability widened. The revolt for rights against sexual identity and privacy rights continued throughout centuries and currently LGBT community identity is supported in most western countries. India, due to its multi-religious and multi-cultural richness, cannot negotiate to a mutual term but transgender rights have been supported by the government. Though, human rights and democracy in the world have allowed freedom for the LGBT, they go through psychological problems such as ostracization, victimization, exploitation and discrimination from the society and family. Having said this, to most scientists, homosexuality is still a psychological disorder. As a result, Christian engagement is required in order to respond to homosexuality from a Biblical understanding and, from pastoral theology and psychology.

5. Christianity and Church's Engagement towards LGBT

With the advent of the modern gay rights movement, Christianity, from wider perspective, has raised its voice for lesbian, gay, bisexual and transgender equality. Christians have long looked at discrimination in our culture and wondered how this injustice is consistent with Jesus' message to love our neighbors as ourselves. Thus, the need arises to create support with other like-minded Christians to study, pray, struggle and grow while embarking on a mission to make our churches and communities reflective of the inclusive love that Jesus teaches.[74] A. Crockett and D. Voas says, the present crisis in the Church over homosexuality has raised many questions, such as, why have disagreements over the issue been increasing rather than decreasing?[75] George Zachariah states that, "as members of the church in India, it is our responsibility to reflect upon the implications of the Delhi high court verdict: how do we become a church to those brothers and sisters who are ostracized and excluded from the fuller communion of the church? How can the

---

[73] Robert J. Wicks & Richard D. Parsons, eds., *Clinical Handbook*, 245.

[74] www.believeoutloud.com › The Background. Accessed on 14/9/15. "In the U.S. alone, there are more than 5,000 churches that intentionally embrace the full inclusion of LGBT people. Four of the United States largest Christian denominations, representing some 10 million people, have passed inclusive policies ranging from statements of LGBT affirmation to LGBT ordination and marriage equality." Besides, other denominations are actively working to pass similar policies in the near future and, majority of the Christians contemplate that laws should protect the LGBT community from discrimination.

[75] Alasdair Crockett & David Voas, "A Matter of Attitude, 23.

church reclaim its vision of a rainbow community of the beloved and equals?[76] Alasdair Crockett and David Voas discuss that the rapidity of social change and the fact that sexuality is vital to the free expression of personal identity makes it difficult for a church to proclaim that sexual orientation could disqualify an individual from ministry or even membership[77]

Empirical Study:

Organizations: The ECI Bishop in Chennai appointed a transgender pastor Ms. Bharathi, who, however, has currently left the church and is doing other ministry. And, in Chennai some Christian Organizations are working for the LGBT community.[78]

Churches: Manna Ministry in Hyderabad, Vineyard Church and Hindustani Covenant Church in Pune, have projects for the Hijras community, such as, evangelistic discipleship, counselling, vocational training, schools for the children and few other.[79]

Individuals: According to a social worker Dora (name changed) working with hijras in Pune, the hijras say that many Christians come and visit them and take photos with them but their lives are not changed. Instead, their communication is being publicized for personal profits. The counsellor felt the need to protect them in their fragile stage.[80]

In an incident two years ago, Ms. Meena had experience encountering with two prostitute hijras in the red light area in Pune. According to their testimony, they were excommunicated by their parents at a young age because they possessed deformed sex organs and, they looked different. When they were introduced by an agent to do transgender surgeries in order to be fit for prostitution, they felt they were left with no choice. According to Meena, since society does not accept them, the church should not only rescue but employ them, give vocational training for their livelihood and even include them in the church membership.[81]

Rev. Joyson Charian, Pastor of Hope Manna Church, Pune, has had three years of experience with Manna group of ministries Hyderabad, working

[76] George Zachariah, "The Church, 2.

[77] Alasdair Crockett & David Voas, "A Matter of Attitude, 29. The Calvary Baptist Church in Washington, D.C. has ordained Allyson Robinson transgender woman (who change his sexuality due to his desirability), as per 6th Aug 2014 news. Refer- Bob Allen, "Robinson, Allyson: Baptist Calvary Church," *The Christian Century* 131/16 (Washington DC: Aug, 2014), 12.

[78] Information from Sources through Verbal Communication, Chennai, 20-25 September 2015. Ms. Magdalene Jeyarathnam runs the Centre for Counselling, an Organization which trains counsellors to work with LGBT community in Chennai. Refer- Magdalene Jeyarathnam, "Struggles of LGBT, 79.

[79] Information from Sources through Verbal Communication, Bangalore, Pune, 20-25 September, 2015.

[80] Information through Verbal Communication, Pune, 25 September 2015.

[81] Interview with Meena, Pune, 16 September, 2015.

among the hijras community 25 kms away from the city. It started in the 1990's as evangelistic discipleship, later on started vocational training and, free school education for the children. The ministry was done in four villages; one third of these villages comprised of the hijras community. Out of the field study, 90% were not hijras (transgender) but due to economic problems their identity had become a dual-identity. The hijras of Hyderabad are mostly poor farmers and only once in a year they harvest crops and the rest of the year, they remain jobless. So in their village, they act as normal farmers and after the crop harvesting is over they move out to neighboring towns and cities (especially Mumbai). They keep their hair long, so in the village they bind turban but when they go away from village, they open their long hair and dress themselves differently as hijras and travel around collecting money and even get involved in prostitution. The money that they earn helps the families or individuals to survive throughout the year. At present Rev. Joyson Charian is serving as pastor in Hope manna church Pune. In his church, he has given an orientation regarding LGBT to the youth. The youth's attitude is that they already have preconceived ideas about hijras, so, according to them, LGBT is a modern version of naming them.[82]

Renemla Ozukum a theologian, has experience of working in an NGO for a decade in social justice and peace building ministry. According to her, LGBT members are also human beings like us, more creative, relational, and less violent. Why are we stigmatizing them as sinners or categorizing them as the third gender? Where did God mandate to categorize their gender as the third, whose and what kind of sin is bigger or worst? Who has a right to excommunicate them? Why are we judging their life by their sexual affirmation/orientation alone? Her response to the Church is not to get busy in motivational activities inside the church building but go out to the place where human beings are struggling and vexed into trouble by outside forces and structural violence. Therefore, take up social justice ministry as part of church's vocation.[83]

A case study further illustrates the current attitude in the church towards LGBT. Mr. Aza (name changed) was a childhood Christian friend of mine from Nagaland, an active youth member in church youth fellowship. From adolescence, he looked like a gay, the way he spoke, walked, laughed, smiled and did things that were effeminate. Since he looked like a 'sissy' was, shy, and possessed a soft nature, girls often laughed and joked over him. Later on, as he reached adulthood, he started to wear women's clothes, and associated with women, and do knitting, weaving, interior designing, and cooking. In the process of his identity confusion,

[82] Telephonic Interview with Rev. Joyson Charian, Pune, 26 September 2015. Harassment from eunuchs especially on train touched scary heights, three Eunuchs at Daund demanded and forced passengers to give them money and robbed Rs.5000 from a laborer when he was trying to take out Rs.100 to give to them. The eunuchs pushed them out of the train, the man is in ICU. Refer- *The Times of India* (Pune), 27 August 2015, 2.

[83] Telephonic Interview with Renemla Ozukum, 25 September, 2015.

he and few of his other gay friend's formed a group. Unfortunately, they were ostracized by his villagers as not part of the community. Due to cultural and societal stigma, his family forced him into marriage later on, but his marriage was not successful. In the process, because of strong cultural and societal stigma, he began to develop a low self-image and inferiority complex leading to progressively lesser social interaction. A few years back, he died of HIV according to some sources.[84]

From this study, the hijra community (transgender) are facing dual-identity crisis and severe poverty. Christianity in general and church in particular has both positive and negative views towards LGBT. The church has responded to a great extent in its attitude and involvement towards the transgender (hijras) community. However, the LGB community still needs positive attention.

6. Understanding of Sexuality in order to Deal with the LGBT struggles of Homosexuality

A pastoral counsellor has the responsibility to make sure he/she is familiar on issues related to sexuality.[85] Somen Das states that the theological affirmations of human sexuality can be defined as the whole range of feelings and actions dominated by the intimate relationship between persons.[86] It is necessary to accept our own body with its sexual needs and deal with them creatively. The body is the temple of God, we need to have an affirmative relationship with other bodies knowing fully well our possibilities and limitations. God has created humanbeings with the body and sexuality is basic to the human structure. Adam was incomplete without Eve, she was created to be 'a helper fit for him.' According to God's purpose, woman and man are constitutive of each other.[87] Horst Klaus Hofmann opines that Biblical commands and restrictions on sexual behavior make sense only in the light of the distinction between male and female as reported in the creation story. The creator made us fundamentally different in order to make complementary partnerships in the world of human relationships possible.[88]

Although, sexuality is basic to human structure, it is not central to the human experience. John Stott writes that the teaching of the word of God supports that sexual experience is not essential to human fulfillment. It is not indispensable to humanness. Jesus Christ was single yet perfect in his humanity.[89] According to Donald Goergen, celibacy is a positive choice of the single life for the sake of

[84] Mr. A, Case Study done by the writer (Lipokla).

[85] Paper Presentation Christian Counselling Centre.

[86] Somen Das, "An Ethical," 32.

[87] Somen Das, "An Ethical," 33.

[88] Horst Klaus Hofmann, "Sexuality- a Gift of God," in *Striving for Gender Identity*, 64.

[89] Horst Klaus Hofmann, "Sexuality," 72.

Christ in response to the call of God. To choose celibate singleness, however, is to put one's life and one's freedom in the context of a particular response to God.[90]

In the light of this understanding of sexuality, there are some practical steps the church can follow to deal with the LGBT community.

Practical Steps for Church

1. There is a need for awareness and education within the church, in order to reach out to the sexual minorities. Firstly, there must be an awareness and education for the pastors, church leaders in terms of biblical understanding of sexuality that will enable to respond appropriately to the issue of LGBT.
2. It is essential for the church to appoint and send full time church counsellors for counselling training for specialization in dealing with the LGBT sexuality orientation struggles.
3. The church requires to open clinical counselling centers for LGBT community.
4. It is a necessity that the church should educate the congregation both family and adolescence through seminars for preparation within family sphere in order to identify and to prevent homosexual tendency.
5. The church should be encouraged to have an open mind and attitude to LGBT issues, by making efforts to organize integrated seminars inviting medical experts, psychiatrists and psychologists who can educate regarding LGBT sexual orientation; both secular and Christian seminar speakers from legal and social justice perspective can speak on human rights and justice issues of LGBT. Scholarly theologians can also speak on LGBT issue from biblical and ethical perspectives.
6. The church needs to take up an agenda to conduct inter-cultural seminars in order to educate Indian families irrespective of religion regarding the purpose of God's plan of human sexuality.
7. Lastly, church approach should be one of acceptance and a non-judgmental attitude towards LGBT community.

In all these, pastoral ministry has a great role to play to bring about liberation for people belonging to sexual minority who are being looked down upon and are discriminated by the church as well as the society.

7. Response from Pastoral Care and Counselling Perspective: Counselling Models and Practical Suggestions

The primary issues that counsellors seldom address are those long term issues that cannot be quickly resolved that birthed homosexuality: lack of affirmation, lack of sense of belonging, abuse/molestation, and the effect of labeling, unfairness,

[90] Donald Goergen, *The Sexual Celibate* (New York: The Seabury, 1969), 108-109. There are two major dimensions to celibate life: a positive choice of all that is implied in the single life as well as putting this choice in the context of the Christian vocation. Celibacy then requires a conscious motivation sufficient to make a wise choice, 109.

victimization and fear.[91] Jay E. Adams states "usually one who is involved in a homosexual activity develops a grossly distorted view of sex and other interpersonal relations. They start to live a double life, and transmit the problem of fear and guilt."[92] Thus, some psychological therapies, and models can be used while doing treatment with LGBT.

(a) Erik H. Erikson Psychosocial Model: Psychosocial Crisis- 5th Stage: Identity verses Role Confusion (Adolescence-12 to 18 years)

The task at adolescence stage is to achieve ego identity and avoid role confusion.[93] A person who reaches this stage with a sense of mistrust, shame and doubt or guilt and inferiority is perhaps confused and self-unsure leading to an identity crisis. This stage can cause one to feel isolated, empty, anxious and indecisive.[94] Thus, in the later school years, adolescence become overwhelmed with the physiological confusion of their genital maturation.[95] As the adolescence seeks somehow tentative forms of playful intimacy in friendship and competition, in sex play and love, in argument and gossip, the individual is pertinent to experience a peculiar tension (demanding a tense inner reservation and a carefulness in commitment). In case an adolescent does not resolve such strain, he/she may isolate and enter into stereotyped and formalized interpersonal relations. Otherwise he/she could seek intimacy with the most improbable partners due to repeated hectic attempts and depressing failures.[96]

Since LGBT community are in confusion of their identity as male or female, the Erickson's psychosocial model will help them to be aware of the developmental tasks of physical maturation, involvement in the peer group, heterosexual relationship and sex role identity during adolescence. This will help one to know group identity as well as individual identity and, to avoid alienation and role confusion.[97]

---

[91] Frank Worthen, "Helping People Step out of Homosexuality," in *Striving for Gender Identity*, 216.

[92] Jay E. Adams, *Competent to Counsel* (New Jersey: Presbyterian & Reformed, 1970), 36.

[93] C. George Boeree, *Personality Theories* (Pennsylvania: Shippensburg University, 2006), 11.

[94] Prem Prakash, *Psychological Foundation of Education* (New Delhi: Kanishka, 2007), 531.

[95] Erik H. Erikson, *Identity Youth and Crisis* (New York: W.W. Norton, 1968), 128.

[96] Erik H. Erikson, *Identity*, 167.

[97] Course Material of Post Graduate Certificate in Psychological Counselling (Vellore: Christian Counselling Centre, 2012), 81.

(b) Sigmund Freud Psychosexual Model[98] - Psychosexual Development - 5th Stage: Genital Stage (starts from early adolescence)[99]

Freud believed that every person normally passes through sexual instinct.[100] With puberty, there is re-emergence of the earlier drives. Drive energy is focused on the genitals once more but this time with an adult expression of sexuality.[101] In this phase, the psychological foundation has already been set for the determination of the direction of sexual orientation. The sense of oneself as a male or female individual is the foundation for the direction of erotic attractions.[102]

Freud's psychosexual model will help the individual to identify the psychosexual development at adolescence. This will help to resolve the identity confusion and be educated of the sexual instinct as meant for heterosexual relationship. Erickson's psychosocial and Freud's psychosexual models fall in the same adolescence stage.

(c) Rational Emotive Behavior Therapy (REBT) Albert Ellis Model

Albert Ellis developed 'Rational Emotive Behavior Therapy.'[103] The basic idea of REBT lies on one's own formation of psychological problems. As a result, a reorganization in our thoughts and statements will result in a conforming reorganization of one's behavior. In dealing with and changing the negative cognitive response to positive cognitive response, one experiences positive behavioral response.[104] Self-Limiting Beliefs are some common beliefs that get in the way of effective living such as Being Liked and Loved: 'I must always be loved and approved by the significant people in my life.' Another example is of being hurt: 'people who do anything wrong, especially those who hurt me are evil and should be blamed and punished.' Tyranny of the Past: 'what I did in the past, and especially what happened to me in the past determines how I act and feel today,' is also another example.[105] These irrational beliefs are worthless, self-downing, awfulizing, damnation, and over generalization. These derivatives collectively produce the negative feelings of anxiety, depression, misery, self-pity

---

98 Walter Mischel, *Introduction to Personality*, 6th Edition (New York: John Willy & Sons, 1999), 52.

99 Arun Kumar Singh, *The Comprehensive History of Psychology* (Delhi: Motilal Banarsidass Publishers, 1991), 340-341.

100 Walter Mischel, *Introduction*, 52.

101 Abraham Scaria, "Theories of Personality," in *A Study Book on Counselling*, edited by George Varghese (Thiruvalla: CSS, 2012), 261.

102 Angela Ludwig, "Striving for Gender Identity," in *Striving for Gender Identity*, 86.

103 David Capuzzi & Douglas R. Gross, *Counselling and Psychotherapy: Theories and Interventions* (New Jersey: Printice-Hall, Inc., 1999), 274.

104 George Varghese & Daniel Mammen, "Psychotherapies in Counselling," in *A Study Book on Counselling*, 309.

105 Course Material of Post Graduate Certificate, 79.

and worthlessness.[106] REBT helps to confront one's irrational thinking and belief system. It is very important to apply this to members of the LGBT community who have low self-esteem and inferiority complex, and, to replace with positive rational beliefs and thoughts.

(d) Thomas C. Oden (Pastoral Theologian) Model: Empathetic Understanding, Acceptance and Grace

Empathetic Understanding: Through the therapist's genuine empathy care, the troubled client experiences a profoundly liberating feeling of being known and being understood. Empathy is the requirement of all therapeutic effectiveness in dealing with the client. The client's self-awareness, self-acceptance and self-direction begins to work when he/she experiences the empathetic understanding of the therapist.[107]

Acceptance: The counsellor's relation to the client is authentically different from ordinary human relations. As in addition to the positive acceptance of feelings for the client, there is a conforming absence of any threat or judgmental quality of the therapist attitude.[108]

Grace: The client attains to actualize his/her freedom as within the context of the safety of divine accepting love under the condition of grace. The client experiences a reflective sense of divine approval to be who he/she is.[109]

In order for fear, guilt, shame to be healed, the counselee's essential interpersonal needs (the need to feel loved, accepted, respected in their uniqueness) must be met as therapeutic process.[110] Thomas C. Oden's therapeutic model will help the person struggling with sexual orientation to overcome the societal stigma and will help in the healing process of coming out of homosexuality.

(e) A Practical Treatment Plan for Healing Homosexuality of the People with Different Sexual Orientation (LGBT) Suggested by Richard A. Cohen

1. During the Transitional period, the most important characteristic for change is self-motivation, which involves one's commitment and the will power to change. They should be cut off from sexual behavior, such as, LGBT bars, pornographic magazines or movies and, disconnection from those who will tempt into homosexual activity.[111]

---

[106] George Varghese & Daniel Mammen, "Psychotherapies," 309-310.

[107] Thomas C. Oden, *Kerygma and Counselling* (Philadelphia: The Westminster John Knox Press, 1966), 49-50.

[108] Thomas C. Oden, *Kerygma*, 64.

[109] Thomas C. Oden, *Kerygma*, 68-69.

[110] Deborah Van Deusen Hunsinger, *Theology and Pastoral Counselling: A New Interdisciplinary Approach* (Grand Rapids: William B. Eerdmands Publishing Company, 1995), 182.

[111] Richard A. Cohen, "Healing Homosexuality," in *Striving for Gender Identity*, 120.

2. Develop a support network such as facilitators who has transitioned successfully from homosexuality for several years or persons who understands the process of healing homosexuality.
3. Counseling with a same-sex counselor will understand the nature of homosexuality and the process of transitioning. A counsellor needs to establish a very close relationship with the client. In the final stage or fourth stage of transitioning an opposite sex counselor will be more suitable.[112]
4. In the process of change, support from family and friends is necessary because sharing with them will build the opening for the individual. LGBT who wish to alter out of homosexuality into heterosexuality cannot change without the help of others because they need time, touch, talk and therapeutic healing.
5. It is essential to read Literatures about the process of healing and transition out of homosexuality.[113]
6. The Church community must emphasize on personal values that talk about a child of God, not sexual identity. Meditation and prayer can help to reprogram the subconscious mind by switching negative imprinting with positive loving messages.[114]
7. Identify faulty belief systems, develop new coping skills and problem-solving techniques, learn to communicate in a more assertive, positive manner, continue to emphasize personal values and develop the support network.[115]
8. Healing the homo-emotional wounds by creating healthy, healing relationships man to man and woman to woman. Identify and remove the defensive detachments toward the same-sex parent or significant other of the same sex. Fulfill the unmet homo-emotional love needs through nonsexual, non-erotic bonding with members of the same sex. Internalize and develop a masculine or feminine identity.[116]
9. Healing the hetero-emotional wounds by establishing healthy, healing relationships man to woman and woman to man. Identify and remove the defensive detachments toward the opposite sex parent or significant others of the opposite sex. Fulfill unmet hetero-emotional love needs through nonsexual, non-erotic bonding with members of the opposite sex. Develop an appreciation and understanding of the opposite sex.[117]

To instill hope is one of the most essential principles of counselling.[118] Instead of ostracizing them, the church and the pastoral care givers must make it known

---

[112] Richard A. Cohen, "Healing," 121.

[113] Richard A. Cohen, "Healing," 122.

[114] Richard A. Cohen, "Healing," 123.

[115] Richard A. Cohen, "Healing," 124.

[116] Richard A. Cohen, "Healing," 126.

[117] Richard A. Cohen, "Healing," 128.

[118] Richard A. Cohen, "Healing," 214.

to the LGBT that there is help available by showing the love and compassion of Christ.[119] In the words of A. B. Simpson, "physical deficiency are traced to the fall and sinful state of mind and…thus there is a need of redemption that will provide healing to both physical and spiritual nature of human beings."[120] David Atkinson says that at the heart of the LGBT there is a deep loneliness, the natural human hunger for mutual love, a search for identity and a longing for completeness. A Christian environment of love, understanding, acceptance and support is needed. However, there is no need to encourage LGBT people to disclose their sexual inclinations to everybody because it is neither necessary nor helpful. However, they do need at least one to confide to whom they can unburden themselves who will not despise or reject them but will support them with friendship and prayer. Probably some professional, private and confidential pastoral counsel, professional supervised therapy group could help them.[121] The question is, will Christians have a place in their hearts to love the person who practices homosexuality? Until the counselor is prepared and able to make this commitment they will continue to be outside of Christ and in bondage to this vice.[122] In the counselling setting the counsellor should establish a trusting, confidential relationship in which a LGBT person will feel safe to explore and/or discuss his/her own process of self-identification without fear of judgment.[123] According to Yip, Spirituality and sexuality are inseparable.[124] The ministry of pastoral care is indeed in a time of transition and we have to deal issues according to the context.[125] Owing to modernity, social change takes place and in the midst of this Christians have to get involved in the world with the wholistic liberative aspect of testifying the creator God. As the world evolves we are confronted by different issues such as LGBT, and the church cannot remain adamant to this issue but has to address it.

Conclusion

Out of this paper, exploration and discussions are being made on the theme of Christian engagement in social change, how increasing number of Christians in general are responding to social actions and their involvement in the society for social cause. Primarily, social change in the sphere of sexual minorities (LGBT) is due to

---

[119] David & Don Wilkerson, *The Untapped Generation* (Grand Rapids: Zondervan Publishing House, 1971), 108.

[120] A.B. Simpson, *The Gospel of Healing* (Pennsylvania: Christian Publication, 1915), 7.

[121] John Stott, *New Issues,* 417.

[122] David & Don Wilkerson, *The Untapped,* 110.

[123] Robert J. Wicks & Richard D. Parsons, eds., *Clinical Handbook,* 232.

[124] Cited by Alan Aldridge, *Religion in the Contemporary World,* 179.

[125] William A. Clebsch & Charles R. Jaekle, *Historical Epochs of Pastoral Care* (New York: Harper & Row, Publishers, 1967), 14. The ministry of pastoral care has fallen into the position of borrowing from psychology, law, medicine, education and social work, 14.

the support from human rights and democracy in the world. Since LGBT people have a homosexual propensity, the paper explained the meaning of homosexuality, sexual orientation and its influence that created progress and constraint in the medical, constitutional, legal, human rights, societal and psychological issues. Furthermore, Christians in particular have been challenged by the issue of sexual minorities and the church attitude and initiatives are normalized though still reservations arise. Thus, LGBT community is in identity confusion and, therefore they are seeking acceptance. Various counselling models such as Erik H. Erikson Psychosocial and, Sigmund Freud Psychosexual model, Albert Ellis Rational Emotive Behavior Therapy, and Thomas C. Oden Empathetic Understanding, Acceptance and Grace can be helpful in defining Adolescence identity confusion, in clearing their irrational beliefs and in approaching in a non-judgmental way through therapeutic techniques. Finally, practical church role and a practical treatment plan of healing LGBT is discussed. Therefore, Christian engagement in social change in the context of sexual minorities (LGBT) has become a thought-provoking area for pastoral ministry. The LGBT issue is a current trend, which challenges human evolution, and Christian understanding of sexuality.

18

Caring for the Senior Citizens Challenges for Christians

Lochumi Ezung

Introduction

Old age is the last stage in the life of a person. It is an age of maturity and wisdom. It is the stage of serenity and beauty.[1] Today's rapid social changes have serious implications on the status and position of the senior citizens in our society.[2] A host of factors such as the emergence of nuclear families, greater longevity, physical separation of parents from children and the changing values of the younger generation affect the lives of the senior citizens in society.[3] Our society is changing and so do the mindset and attitude of the people towards the senior citizens. Today they are being deprived and are alienated, marginalized by the children and society at large. Thus, an attempt is made to discuss about Senior Citizens and the problems or challenges they face and some educational program implemented by Churches and Government for the Senior Citizens. Furthermore, terms like Senior Citizens, Elderly, and Old Age/people will be used interchangeably.

---

[1] Paulachan Kochappilly, "Celebration of Old Age: Care of the Old People," *Jeevadhara*, XXXI/186 (November 2001): 462.

[2] James David, "Ageing in India," *Integral Liberation: Quarterly Review for Justice, Development and Social Change*, 5/3 (September 2001): 192.

[3] James David, "Ageing in India,": 192.

Social Change

Social change is common to all societies.[4] And when we talk about social change, it is something which is inevitable and is not static. It is ever changing and an ongoing process. The social structure is subject to incessant changes. Individuals may strive for stability, yet the fact remains/reminds that society is an ever changing phenomenon; growing, decaying, renewing and accommodating itself to changing conditions.[5] The change of man and society has been the central and quite dominant concern of sociology. The concern for social change is also of great importance since it not only studies past changes but also in investigating future developments.[6]

In other words, social change includes changes in nature, social institutions, social behaviors, or social relations. It refers to the notion of social progress or socio-cultural evolution. It may also refer to a paradigmatic change in the socio-economic structure, for instance a shift away from feudalism and towards capitalism.[7] Here, social change is the combination of the 'social' and 'change' meaning change in the social structure, relations and functions of the various units which form society, whether it be family, school, organization or others.[8] Changing process may differ from society to society but no society in the world can escape from change. It is eternal law of nature and the law of life.[9]

The definitions of social change vary as some confine its scope only to changes in social relationship, while others extend it also to changes in the material as well as non-material culture.[10]

According to Puja Mondal, "Change implies all variations in human societies. When changes occur in the modes of living of individuals and social relation gets influenced, such changes are called social changes."[11]

Ram Ahuja defines, "Social change is change in establishment patterns of social relations, or change in social values, or change in structures and subsystems operating in society."[12]

---

[4] Paramjit Singh and Gurpreet Bal, *Strategies of Social Change in India* (New Delhi: M D Publications Pvt Ltd., 1996), 1.

[5] Puja Mondal, "Essay on Social Change: Meaning, Characteristics and other details." www.yourarticlelibrary.com/sociology/essay-on-social-change-menaing-characteristics-and-other-details/8590/. (2/9/15)

[6] Puja Mondal, "Essay on Social Change: Meaning, Characteristics and other details." (2/9/15)

[7] Vivek Murarka, "Short Essay on Social Changes in India." http://www.academia.edu/8406166/Social_change_in_india. (6/6/15).

[8] S. Samuel Ravi, *A Comprehensive Study of Education* (New Delhi: PHI Private Limited, 2011), 429.

[9] S. Samuel Ravi, *A Comprehensive Study of Education*, 429.

[10] G. R. Madan, *Social Change and Problems of Development in India* (New Delhi: Allied Publishers Private Ltd., 1978), 1.

[11] Puja Mondal, "Essay on Social Change: Meaning, Characteristics and other details." (2/9/15).

[12] Ram Ahuja, *Society in India* (New Delhi: Rawat Publications, 2011), 436.

According to McIver and Page as cited by Pandey, "social change is a process responsive to many types of changes, to change in man-made condition of living, to change in the attitude of man and changes that go beyond human control to the biological and physical nature."[13]

Ginsberg as quoted by Pandey says, by social change I understand a "change in social structure, i.e., the size of society, the composition or balance of its parts or the type of its organization."[14] Emile Durkheim also believes that "social change is represented by transformations in the social structure of the social relations that links individuals into a coherent entity, society, laws, norms, and sanctions that regulate social life."[15]

Social change is change in establishment patterns of social relations, or change in social values, or change in structures and subsystems operating in society.[16] It is a continuous process, which may be very slow or rapid.[17] Yet the concepts overlap. Changes in human societies are not so easily investigated. Each society is unique, and any changes that take place are likely to result from a whole complex of interacting factors, i.e., environmental, technological, personal, cultural, political, religious, economic, and so on.[18] Hence, it can be understood that social change refers to the modifications and variations which take place whether desirable or not in the life patterns of an individual and community at large.

Why should Christians get involved? To answer this question, John Stott in his book *New Issues Facing Christians Today* brings out two possible attitudes with which Christians can engage in social change. One is to *Escape* and the other is *Engagement*. 'Escape' means turning our backs on the world in rejection, washing our hands, and steeling our hearts against its agonized cries for help.[19] Whereas, 'engagement' means turning our faces towards the world, getting our hands dirty, sore and wore in its service, and feeling deep within us the stirring of the love of God which cannot be contained.[20] Christ's followers, therefore, are called in one

---

[13] R. S. Pandey, *Education in Emerging Indian Society* (Agra: Agrawal Publications, 2011), 196.

[14] R. S. Pandey, *Education in Emerging Indian Society*, 196.

[15] Taner Cam and Mustafa Kayaoglu, "Social Change from the Perspective of Some Prominent Contemporary Sociologists," *Journal of International Social Research* 34/7: 628. (628-635) http://www.sosyalarastirmalar.com/cilt7/sayi34_pdf/6psikoloji_sosyoloji_felsefe/cam_taner_vd.pdf. (29/9/15)

[16] Ram Ahuja, *Society in India*, 436.

[17] Bhatia & Bhatia, *The Philosophical and Sociological Foundations of Education* (Delhi: Doaba House, 1990), 141.

[18] Fakhar Naveed. Different Theories of Social Change. http://mass.pakgalaxy.com/different-theories-of-social-change.html. (2/9/15)

[19] John Stott, *New Issues Facing Christians Today* (Mumbai: GLS Publishing, 2003), 17-18.

[20] John Stott, *New Issues Facing Christians Today*, 17-18.

way or another, not to conform to the values of society but to transform them (Rom 12:1-12, Eph 5:8-14).[21]

1. Why Senior Citizen a Social Concern?

A problem is considered social when difficulties met by a group of people result from the functioning, organization or structure of society which may endanger society at large and old age has emerged as a social problem not only because of the rising proportion of aged people in the population but also because of their declining role and status in our society. Aging becomes even more disturbing when culture spreads irreverence toward the elderly and economic competition works to their disadvantage. Physical, social and emotional changes at this age require adjustments in interpersonal relations with the members of one's immediate family as well as the wider society.[22] When the situation changes, and when there is a transition in the social structure, the main sufferers are the elderly people who once were an integral part of the family and society. But now the elderly parents find no place in the home and the society, since everyone in the industrialized society are busy and hardly find time even to think about the elderly people in the home. And it is only in this situation that some concerned people have began to think of ways and means how to take care of the elderly.[23]

2. Definition and Understanding of Senior Citizens

(a) Senior Citizens

A senior is term as older or elderly people. On the other hand, it is defined as being any member of the community who is of advanced years.[24] 'Senior Citizen' or 'elderly' as the person who is of age 60 years or above can be termed as Senior Citizen.[25] "Old age" is also associated with declining faculties, both mental and physical and a reduction in social commitments of any person. In India, those who have attained the age of 60 years and above are defined as elderly for the purpose of availing old age benefits.[26]

---

[21] Wheaton, "Transformation: The Church is Response to Human Need," eds., Vinay Samuel and Christopher Sugden in *The Church in Response to Human Need* (Grand Rapids, Michigan: William B. Eerdmans Publishing Company, 1987), 255-256.

[22] James David, "Ageing in India,": 199.

[23] S. K. Parmar, "Indian Society and Senior Citizens," *NCC Review*, CXXIX/10 (October 2009): 6.

[24] Bob Orrick, "What is a Senior Citizen?" http://www.senioryears.com/citizen.html. (4/8/15)

[25] General Knowledge Today. "India's Elderly Population: Some Fundamentals." 8th March 2013. http://www.gktoday.in/indias-elderly-population-some-fundamentals/ (4/8/15).

[26] *National Human Rights Commission, Know Your Rights: Elderly People* (New Delhi: Veerendra Printers, 2011), 1. http://nhrc.nic.in/Documents/Publications/KYR%20Elderly%20English%20 Final.pdf. (1/10/15).

(b) Understanding of Senior Citizens

The old age is the last phase of the life span of an individual human being. It consists of ages nearing or surpassing the average life span of human beings, this stage is called as senior citizens or elderly. The age 60 in India, 65 in the USA, the United Kingdom and many other countries considered old age which became eligible to retire. Hence it is the beginning of old age. Senior citizen is a common polite designation for an elderly person which means that the person is retired. "Senior citizen" is replacing the term old age and the term was apparently coined in 1938.[27]

(c) Senior Citizens in India

As report released by the United Nations Population Fund and Help Age India which says, of the 90 million seniors, 30 million are living alone.[28] Over two-thirds of elderly people in India are neglected by their family members while one third of the elderly claimed to have suffered physical or verbal abuses.[29]

(d) Senior Citizens and Indian Constitution

The constitution of India recognizes the duty of the state towards the elderly. According to Article 41 "the state shall, within the limits of its economic capacity and development, make effective provisions for securing the right to work, to education, and to public assistance in case of unemployment, old age, sickness and disablement and in other cases of undeserved want."[30] The Maintenance and Welfare of Parents and Senior Citizen Act 2007, which is also known as "Senior Citizen's Act" was enacted. Maintenance of parents is included in section 125 of Criminal Procedure Code 1973. Under the above acts, parents can claim maintenance from their children.[31]

(e) Initiatives taken by Government for the Senior Citizens

The ministry of social justice and empowerment, which is the nodal ministry for this purpose, focuses on policies and programs for the senior citizens in collaboration with State Governments, NGO's and Civil Society. The programme

---

[27] Andrew B. Natarajan, "Senior Citizens-Society and Religion," *NCC Review*, CXXIX/10 (October 2009): 13.

[28] Aarti Dhar, "Concerns Over an Aging India." *The Hindu* October 7, 2012. http://www.thehindu.com/news/national/concerns-over-an-aging-india/article3972671.ece. (4/8/15).

[29] *The Times of India*. "Over 65% Elderly Face Neglect In Old Age: Study." July 21, 2015. http://timesofindia.indiatimes.com/india/Over-65-elderly-face-neglect-in-old-age-Study/articleshow/48040965.cms. (10/8/15).

[30] A. B. Bose, "Policies and Programmes for the Aging in India," in *The Aging in India*, edited by A. B. Bose, K. D. Gangrade (New Delhi: Shakti Malika Abhinav Publications, 1988), 60.

[31] General Knowledge Today. "India's Elderly Population: Some Fundamentals." 8th March 2013. http://www.gktoday.in/indias-elderly-population-some-fundamentals/ (4/8/15).

aims at their welfare and maintenance, especially for indigent senior citizens, by supporting old age homes, day care centers, mobile Medicare units etc.[32]

(i) National Policy on Older Persons (NPOP) 1999[33]

- To encourage families to take care of their family members
- To provide care and protection to the vulnerable elderly people
- To provide adequate health care facility to the elderly
- To create awareness regarding persons to help them lead productive and independent lives

(ii) National Policy for Senior Citizens 2011

The foundation of the new policy, known as the "National Policy for Senior Citizens 2011" is based on several factors. These include the demographic explosion among the elderly, the changing economy and social milieu, advancement in medical research, science and technology and high levels of destitution among the elderly rural poor. This policy addresses issues concerning senior citizens living in urban and rural areas, special needs of the 'oldest old' and older women.[34]

(iii) Schemes Implemented for the welfare of Senior Citizens[35]

In Implementation of existing policies, several schemes for senior citizens were formulated under the 12th plan. These include: (a) a scheme for awareness generation for the maintenance of parents and senior citizens act, 2007, (b) setting up a helping for senior citizens, (c) establishing a national commission for senior citizens and (d) establishing a national trust for the aged.

The committee has also recommended the following new policies and laws:[36]

- A comprehensive law for the social security of senior citizens must be enacted.
- An integral action plan must be evolved involving various stakeholders and departments of the government.

---

[32] "Essay: Issues Concerning Elderly People." The Calibre: Current Affairs & Analysis 2nd Oct 2012. http://thecalibre.in/in-depth-current-affairs/essay-issues-concerning-elderly-people/102012/?p=1561/. (21/8/15)

[33] "Essay: Issues Concerning Elderly People." The Calibre: Current Affairs & Analysis 2nd Oct 2012. (21/8/15).

[34] National Policy for Senior Citizens March 2011. http://socialjustice.nic.in/pdf/dnpsc.pdf. (15/9/15).

[35] PRS Legislative Research, Report Summaries: Implementation of Schemes for the Welfare of Senior Citizens. 2015. http://www.prsindia.org/parliamenttrack/report-summaries/implementation-of-schemes-for-the-welfare-of-senior-citizens-3155/. (15/9/15).

[36] PRS Legislative research, report summaries: implementation of schemes for the welfare of senior citizens. 2015. (15/9/15).

- A new national policy on older persons must be formulated. While a national policy on older persons was launched in 1999, it has not been implemented effectively. A draft national policy on senior citizens was published in 2011 but has not been finalized and implemented either.

3. Some Challenges Faced by Senior Citizens

The elderly population in India is continuously increasing and also the problems faced by these people are increasing simultaneously. The most important problems that the senior citizens are facing today are deteriorating health, malnutrition, lack of shelter, fear, depression, senility, isolation, boredom, non-productivity, and financial incapacity.[37] Some of the challenges are as follows:

(a) Economic Problems

With age, the activity of man shrinks and comes to a near halt at a certain stage.[38] The economic factor plays an important role for the well being of the aged. Money becomes a cause of anxiety as one gets older.[39] The economic problem is enhanced because of retirement and shrinking of funds which are to be used for monthly expenses.[40] In a country like India, where two-fifths of the population is below the poverty line, a large number of persons in old age are left with very inadequate incomes. Some studies have indicated that within about five years after retirement, a large number among them exhaust their savings and become dependent on their children or relatives.[41]

(b) Psycho-Social Problems

Psycho-social perspectives refer to generation particulars, living arrangement, religiosity, social participations adjustment with the environment, talents and life style of the aged as perceived by them.[42] They suffer from psychological problems of loneliness, dementia, senility, depression, anxiety, worry, isolation, adjustment, etc. The psychological problems are mostly interlinked with other social issues like lack of housing facilities, achievement skills, family care, and leisure time activities, lack of involvement in family responsibility.[43] The psychological

---

[37] Andrew B. Natarajan, "Senior Citizens-Society and Religion," *NCC Review*, CXXIX/10 (October 2009): 14.

[38] G. C. Mathur, "Housing for the Aging," in *The Aging in India*, edited by A. B. Bose, K. D. Gangrade (New Delhi: Shakti Malika Abhinav Publications, 1988), 41.

[39] James David, "Ageing in India," 193.

[40] Usha Bambawalwe, *Growing Old in Young India* (Pune: Snehavardhan Publishing House, 1993), 41.

[41] G. C. Mathur, "Housing for the Aging," 41.

[42] K. Pappathi, *Ageing: Scientific Perspective & Social Issues* (New Delhi: A.P.H Publishing Corporation, 2007), 56.

[43] K. Pappathi, *Ageing: Scientific Perspective & Social Issues*, 56.

problems faced by the elderly can be a matter of great concern. Failing health, continuing ailments, poor financial situation and humiliation in the family can all add up to feelings of helplessness, hopelessness, depression and anxiety.[44]

(c) Health Problems

It is a biological fact that when one becomes old, health and vigor decline.[45] And caring for the senior citizen whether in health or disease, is different from doing the same for an adult or a child.[46] There are, however, individual differences here. Some individual continue to enjoy good health even in old age whereas others have poor health even in their 40's and 50's. In every old age, difficulties are experienced in carrying out day-to-day activities.[47]

(d) Negative Attitude

Older people are seriously neglected in a sense they are the "lost generation" of today.[48] Unfortunately, our society has typically devalued older people. This devaluation has been characterized by negative stereotypes about this population (i.e., ageism/prejudice against older people), fear of aging and misconceptions about what it means to be old.[49] Furthermore, our society typically holds negative attitudes towards disability because older people are likely to have one or more disabling conditions; they may have risk factors for being devalued. Negative attitudes can, and do, influence behaviors toward an individual or a group of people.[50]

(e) Loneliness

Loneliness is a state in which one feels incomplete and the primary affect is longing.[51] All of us, regardless of age, have pangs of loneliness. But the difference in the loneliness of senior citizens is that it is ever present.[52] An emotional and psychological problem tormenting the elders is loneliness. This is due to the

---

[44] G. C. Mathur, "Housing for the Aging," 49.

[45] G. C. Mathur, "Housing for the Aging," 48.

[46] O. P. Jaggi, "Health Care for the Ageing," in *Understanding Greying People of India*, edited by Arun P. Bali (New Delhi: Inter-India Publications, 1999), 125.

[47] G. C. Mathur, "Housing for the Aging," 48.

[48] Paul B. Maves and J. Lennart Cedarleaf, *Older People and the Church* (New York: Abingdon-Cokesbury Press, nd), 27.

[49] Charlene M. Kampfe, *Counseling Older People: Opportunities and Challenges* (USA: American Counseling Association, 2015), np.

[50] Charlene M. Kampfe, *Counseling Older People: Opportunities and Challenges*, np.

[51] Paramjeet Kaur Dhillon and Geeta Poduval, "Attitude towards Institutionalization of the Aged," in *Psycho-Social Aspects of Aging in India*, edited by Paramjeet Kaur Dhillon (New Delhi: Ashok Kumar Mittal, 1992), 219-220.

[52] J. Paul Brown, *Counseling with Senior Citizens* (Philadelphia: Fortess Press, 1968), 74.

growing "emptiness syndrome." The children go away to far-off countries in search of economic betterment. Even if they live within the country, due to the spread of western ideas such as "spacing, privacy, individualism and non-interference," the nuclear families are becoming the norm even in villages. The younger generation generally lacks sensitivity towards elders' need for emotional support. All these factors have contributed to the psychological trauma called "loneliness."[53]

(f) Family

Senior citizens are facing problems like lack of care, emotional and economic support from the family, etc. Our culture recognized the status of the parents as that of God. But now what is observed in our society is that the children are not willing to take care of their parents, they do not want to spend money on them, they are treating them as aliens, and they do not want to share an emotional bound with parents. This is because of fast life, industrialization, money oriented minds, and inflation, etc., children have no time to look after their parents because of their busy schedule and they left or kept at care homes or hospitals. As a consequence of this situation the elders are getting neglected and secluded from families.[54] Old people are being considered as a burden on the economic resources so that the young can maintain their desired standard of living.[55] Iqra Rehman also further adds that many senior citizens are suffering from the family problems. He gives some points which are related to family problems that senior citizens face they are:[56]

- No respect from the family to the senior citizens
- No help, no love and no care
- There is also property dispute among family

(g) Crime against Senior Citizens

Increasing urbanization has led to a rise in crime against the elderly. The criminals pick on the old people because they are easy targets. The protection which was offered to them when living in the joint family system is missing and they now have no security. Crime against the elderly fall under the categories of violent

---

[53] Rameeza A. Rasheed, "When Loneliness Stalks the Senior Citizens." *The Hindu* May 16th 2010. http://www.thehindu.com/opinion/open-page/when-loneliness-stalks-the-senior-citizens/article431016.ece. (4/8/15)

[54] Shweta Durge, "Old Age Problem in India." *The Viewspaper.* February 21, 2011. http://theviewspaper.net/old-age-problem-in-india/. (4/8/15)

[55] Mahalakshmi Ganapathy, "Is there no place for the old?" *Youth Ki Awaaz.* August 17th 2011. http://www.youthkiawaaz.com/2011/08/elderly-abuse-india/ (21/8/15).

[56] Iqra Rehamn, Anwaar Mohyuddin, Social Issues of Senior Citizens. The Explorer Islamabad. file:///C:/Users/Jesus/Downloads/EJSS_66_SOCIAL_ISSUES_OF_SENIOR_CITIZENS.pdf. (15/9/15)

crimes, including murder, sexual assault and burglary; financial crimes, such as property disputes and fraud; elder abuse, both physical and emotional.[57]

Recently a 18 year old boy was inspired by a Bollywood thriller movie which made him to kill a 90 year old man and his 64 year old daughter in law in their apartment. This happened just because he needed money to buy a fancy cell phone.[58] Thus, the lives of the elderly people are also at high risk.

(h) Marginalized

With the emerging dominant trend of nuclearization of family and the self-centeredness of kin and siblings both in rural and urban areas in India, the elderly people have become marginalized in their being whole-heartedly accepted in the family of their children and grandchildren. Thus in the absence of joint family, the modernization process is heading to a state where elderly people are becoming physically, socially and emotionally uprooted, irrespective of their caste, religion and gender background. Hence, reflecting their marginalized status.[59]

(i) Social Isolation

Social isolation is a process in which persons, group, or culture lose or do not have communication or cooperation with one another, which results to open conflict. When a person gets old and attained the status of senior citizens, they suffer social isolation. It is noted that senior citizens are becoming the victim of social isolation maybe because of the varying trends in the lifestyle and change in a family structure. The social isolation makes the senior citizens increase the process of aging and it is the major issues in the social factor.[60] Emile Durkheim is of the view that the social bond is the thing which fibers the class, age and race of the people and senior citizens feel fast aging due to the less social bond.[61]

(j) Grief and Loss

Most of the senior citizens have the notion that when the longer he/she lives, the more friends and family members may pass away ahead of them and losing the

---

[57] Mahalakshmi Ganapathy, "Is there no place for the old?" *Youth Ki Awaaz*. August 17th 2011. (21/8/15).

[58] "Bollywood thriller inspired teen to kill two senior citizens." *Times of India Delhi*. 23/7/2015. http://timesofindia.indiatimes.com/city/delhi/Bollywood-thriller-inspired-teen-to-kill-two-senior-citizens/articleshow/48180452.cms. (21/8/2015)

[59] Nandu Ram, "Marginalized Groups and the State of Human Rights in India: An Overview," in *Marginality, Exclusion and Social Justice*, edited by Ashish Saxena (Jaipur: Rawat Publications, 2013), 39-40.

[60] Iqra Rehamn, Anwaar Mohyuddin, Social Issues of Senior Citizens. The Explorer Islamabad. file:///C:/Users/Jesus/Downloads/EJSS_66_SOCIAL_ISSUES_OF_SENIOR_CITIZENS.pdf. (15/9/15)

[61] Iqra Rehamn, Anwaar Mohyuddin, Social Issues of Senior Citizens. The Explorer Islamabad. (15/9/15).

people they care about specially their spouses can leave senior feel abandoned and vulnerable.[62]

4. Help Age NGO in India

India is today home to 100 million senior citizens. The pity is that today's rapid urbanization has overtaken the traditional value system of the society and has shifted their socio-economic priorities. Now sons and daughters and their children find no time for the senior citizens in their family. The elderly, who have provided their services and support to the society, feel unloved and neglected at this phase of their lives. Their deteriorating physical strength and other geriatric illness adds more to their difficulties.[63] There is often poor financial condition, lack of affordable health care and the general neglect by society has propelled HelpAge India to step in and bring in elder welfare programs and advocate for elder friendly policies over 36 years. It was established in 1978, and HelpAge India is a leading charity platform in India working with and for disadvantaged elderly and has become the representative voice for India's elderly. It has also dedicated in improving the status for India's senior citizens, and it works in 23 states providing medical services, poverty alleviation and income generation schemes both in urban and rural India.[64]

A report by the United Nations population fund found the number of people over 60 years in India will increase from around 100 million today (approx) to more than 324 million by 2050. The organization has further warned the government to prepare for the additional strain this will put on families and health and welfare services.[65] It also predicted the number of people over 80 years will increase sevenfold. Officials have said that they were particularly concerned about the impact of elderly women, who will outnumber men, and be more vulnerable in Indian society. We need to support senior citizens because:[66]

- India has the second largest aged population in the world
- 75% of persons of age 60 and above reside in rural areas
- One third are below the poverty line and majority of them are illiterate
- 90% have to continue to work if they have to survive
- 1 out of 8 elderly feels no one cares whether they exist or not.
- 12 million people in India are blind 70-80% of these are elderly 62.6% are blind due to cataract

[62] Mack Fritch, The Psychological and Social Impacts of Aging. http://www.seniorhomes.com/p/impacts-of-aging/. (15/9/15).

[63] HelpAge- NGO India, http://www.helpageindia.org/. (14/9/15).

[64] HelpAge- NGO India, http://www.helpageindia.org/. (14/9/15).

[65] http://www.helpageindia.org/why-support-elders.html. (14/9/15)

[66] http://www.helpageindia.org/why-support-elders.html. (14/9/15)

- Only about 11% of India's workforce participates in any sort of guaranteed retirement income
- More than two third of the oldest old (80+) are financially dependent on others.

5. Psycho-Social Development by Erik H. Erikson

A psycho-analyst and theorist, Erikson was born in Germany in 1902. He had concerned for social elements in human growth. Erik Erikson presents 8 stages of growth on psycho-social development.[67] The 8 stages are as follows:

1st stage: Infancy, **2nd stage**: Early Childhood, **3rd stage**: Play Age, **4th stage**: School Age, **5th stage**: Adolescence, **6th stage**: Young Adulthood, **7th stage**: Adult and **8th stage**: Old Age.[68] For better understanding on senior citizens the last stage will be dealt briefly.

The stage (approximate age-65 years and above) is characterized by an adult accepting oneself, allowing the acceptance of death, or else falling into despair. The highest virtue in this stage is 'wisdom.'[69] This stage is either the stage of integrity or despair. Integrity in simple meaning is a sense of coherence and wholeness resulted from the positive living in the earlier stages. Means such person "has taken care of things and people and has adapted oneself to the triumphs and disappointed of being, by necessity, the originator of others and generator of things and ideas."[70] And he/she has inherited the fruit of the previous stages. Such a gradually mature person has the matured fruit-that is integrity. The opposite experience is despair that reveals an often unconsciousness fear of death. The person experiencing despair will feel time is short, too short for the attempt to start another life and to try out alternative roads to integrity.[71] We should remember that senior citizens are in different stage of life and their 'aspirations and experiences' are different. They respond to a situation with their 'emotional, intellectual, physical, spiritual and all other aspects of their personality. They bring their total experience to every learning situation.[72]

6. Role of Church towards Senior Citizens

The role of the church is to provide opportunities for spiritual growth at all periods of life but many churches are concerned about educating the children and youth, which leaves educating senior citizens undone.[73] Christian education

---

[67] Akheto Sema, *Understanding the Nature and Purpose of Christian Religious Education* (Delhi: ISPCK, 2011), 94-95.

[68] Akheto Sema, *Understanding the Nature and Purpose of Christian Religious* Education, 95-99.

[69] Akheto Sema, *Understanding the Nature and Purpose of Christian Religious Education*, 99.

[70] Ezamo Murry, *An Introduction to Pastoral Care and Counseling* (Delhi: ISPCK, 2011), 240.

[71] Ezamo Murry, *An Introduction to Pastoral Care and Counseling*, 240.

[72] Samson Prabhakar, *Essays on Christian Education and Liturgy* (Bangalore: SATHRI, 2003), 68.

[73] J. Paul Brown, *Counseling with Senior Citizens*, 26.

is not restricted to the spiritual development of men and women only. It is also concerned about the total well-being of a person in terms of physical, mental and emotional aspect of life.[74] The role laid before the Christian educators is to cater to the needs of the aged people by molding and gearing the younger generation to take up their responsibility towards the old people; to develop true care for them physically, mentally, emotionally, spiritually and to be sensitive in handling them.[75]

Throughout history the church has maintained this charitable tradition where the church has been the forefront of providing care for the poor, the sick, the mentally impaired, the orphans and the elderly.[76]

Today, with people living longer and remaining healthier the church must also turn its attention to meet the needs of the numerous elderly people who needs special attention and care. To mention few mental health, Spiritual growth, and Physical well-being- these are the needs of the elderly which the church must now address.[77] Senior citizens can be a living witness to Christian values and attitudes in certain aspects of church life and to do so the church can help its old people in their physical, emotional, spiritual and social needs, but especially by trying to keep open the paths of personal communication, friendship and guidance.[78] In caring for the old people, the community is a great support. This is what the family members, the Christian community and society can and should extend to the aged.[79] In the mutuality of friendship, the prayer of the elderly can also become a model for others: the prayer of the elderly person rise from the depths of need, and it is the model for the prayer of every man and women.[80] Hence, there is a proper need to develop a church program that relates to the needs of the senior citizens.

7. Some Christian Educational Programs

The advents of new technology, life-saving drugs, better knowledge of health and nutrition, and effective treatment of diseases have increased life expectancy and care.[81] Though, different churches and different NGO's are at work to bring a

---

[74] Akheto Sema, *Understanding the Nature and Purpose of Christian Religious Education*, 112.

[75] Akheto Sema, *Understanding the Nature and Purpose of Christian Religious Education*, 104.

[76] Jean E. Thompson, "Life Care Ministry: The Church as part of the Elderly Support Network," in *The Role of the Church in Aging*, edited by Michael C. Hendrickson (New York: The Haworth Press Inc., 1986), 65-66.

[77] Jean E. Thompson, "Life Care Ministry: The Church as part of the Elderly Support Network," 66.

[78] Old Age and Christian Growth. http://dce.oca.org/resource/255/. (4/8/15)

[79] Paulachan Kochappilly, "Celebration of Old Age: Care of the Old People," 462.

[80] Sarah M. Moses, *Ethics and the Elderly: The Challenge of Long-Term Care* (New York: Orbis Books, 2015), np.

[81] M. S. Pai, "Senior Citizens and their Care," in *The Aging in India*, edited by A. B. Bose, K. D. Gangrade (New Delhi: Shakti Malik Abhinav Publications, 1988), 36-37.

change about, it is felt that more emphasis and importance should be given with regard to senior citizens issues. Hence, in this scenario, Senior citizens are ought to be helped, taken care and make them feel important in family and society at large. It is important for every Christian or church to take the issue of senior citizens seriously for a social change. Thus, few educational programs have been listed down in order to create awareness with regard to senior citizens in society, family and churches.

(a) Programming

Placing senior events on the church calendar states publicly that the church takes the theology of aging seriously. Should publicize and magnify the contributions of people over sixty-five years of age. Prepare messages and studies on aged saints who are prominent in the scriptures.[82] Churches should keep in mind that the program for older adults should be different from that of other age-groups. Their activities and interests should help them to understand their particular situations.[83]

(b) Educating the Younger People

The problem of senior citizens does not concern only the senior citizens but it should be a concern for the whole society.[84] The church should be the place where the young bring their strength, enthusiasm and idealism and join forces with the old who offer their wisdom.[85] It is also important to have a positive attitude towards the senior citizens as they are also a part of the society. Hence, it is the need of an hour for the church to educate the younger generation to be more sensitive and have an attitudinal transformation towards senior citizens.

(c) Ministry for Senior Citizens

David Oliver, as cited by Pakiam Samuel, says that the church should not think primarily of ministry for or to the elderly but ministry with the elderly and even ministry from the elderly.[86] Thus, the church should always have concern for its older people[87] and must also prepare itself to enlarge its ministries.

---

[82] Howard G. Hendricks, "Reaping the Rewards of Senior Ministry," *Bibliotheca Sacra*, 157/628 (October-December 2000): 389-390.

[83] Randolph Crump Miller, *Education for Christian Living* (USA: Prentice-Hall, Inc., 1956), 315.

[84] Paul Tournier, *Learn to Grow Old* (New York: Harper & Row Publishers, 1972), 36.

[85] Beth E. Brown, "Spiritual Formation in Older Adults," in *The Christian Educator's Handbook on Spiritual Formation*, edited by Kenneth O. Gangel & James C. Wilhoit (USA: Victor Books, 1994), 264.

[86] Pakiam Samuel, "The Bible and the Aged," *NCC Review*, CXXIX/10 (October 2009): 24.

[87] Earl F. Zeigler, *Christian Education of Adults* (Philadelphia: The Westminster Press, 1952), 116.

(d) Visiting Program

It will be a wise step for the church if they can also provide a vital function in caring for people who cannot attend services by visiting those senior citizens.[88] House visitation through prayers, sharing, encouraging and also listening to their needs and struggles will be of great help for the senior citizens. Churches can also make those children of aging parents to be more responsible towards their parents. It should be a collective responsibility for every individual to let senior citizens feel that they are being valued, cared and have concerns for them.

(e) Role of Family

It is the duty of every family to look after its aging members and make them feel they are not unwanted but are an integral part of the family. The elderly members, if convinced of this intention and attitude on the part of the younger members of the family, would really feel relieved and consoled.[89] Elderly people, too, need to be educated about their changing role due to the stress of modern living and the contribution that they can and should make rather than adopt the traditional Indian role of only receiving attention and care.[90] Thus, the first and the foremost step to help the elderly people should be the family.

(f) Neighborhood and Society

The neighborhood in particular and society in general, can play an important role in the life of the senior citizen and make it worth living. The society or neighborhood can form groups and develop common hobbies and recreational activities of common interest for the senior citizens.[91] Thus, in this way the senior citizens will feel that they are needed and valued in society.

(g) Preparation for Old Age

Preparation for old age should begin while one is still an earner. This would imply advice not only on various savings schemes but also on security of investment of sums received after retirement.[92] It is also equally important to educate and help the senior citizens to deal the conflicts, crisis, pains, etc., in life. Because when ones get old they become too stubborn, criticizes children, grandchildren and times fails to adjust with the society around. Thus, it is very important to prepare the senior citizen with regard to the life situations.

---

[88] "How churches can support immobile and confined senior citizens." 24/7/2015. http://family.custhelp.com/app/answers/detail/a_id/26101/-/how-churches-can-support-immobile-and-confined-senior-citizens. (21/8/2015)

[89] M. S. Pai, "Senior Citizens and their Care," 37-38.

[90] A. B. Bose, "Policies and Programmes for the Aging in India," 82.

[91] M. S. Pai, "Senior Citizens and their Care," 38.

[92] A. B. Bose, "Policies and Programmes for the Aging in India," 82.

The older population is one of the fastest growing groups and this groups is widely diverse; consequently, and educators cannot expect that one older person will be the same as another. Christian Educators will need to examine their own attitudes towards aging and older people and take steps to ensure that these attitudes are appropriate.[93] In 1982 in Vienna, the world Assembly on Aging selected the "banyan" tree as the official logo because it symbolizes longevity, self-reliance, continuing growth and a community meeting place. In the Indian context especially, this will only be possible when the old are treated with dignity and love in their families- a task that should be equally shared by the family and society.[94]

Even from the biblical perspectives, its emphasis is not on reaching its prime physically in old age, but rather spiritually, psychologically and mentally. Old age was not a defeat but a victory, not a punishment but a privilege.[95] And respect for the elderly was to begin at home as in Proverbs 23:22 says: "listen to your father, who gave you life, and do not despise your mother when she is old."[96] Bible also identifies old age in relation to "the seasons of life" and transitions in role: old age is marked by "maturity and leadership" within the society and a transition from the primary years of work, reproduction and parenting.[97] However, a distinctive aspect of the biblical teachings concerning respect for elders is the insistence on respect for older persons as a sign of righteous faith in God. For instance, Leviticus 19:32 states, "you shall rise before the aged, and honor the presence of an old man; and fear your God: I am the Lord."[98] Thus, it underlines the importance of respect and obedience toward elderly parents and members of society by suggesting that it is a moral commandment as central to respect and fear of God.[99] In New Testament, some verses also support the commandment to honour our elders, including Mark 7:9-13 and Ephesians 6:1-3. Thus, it is our prime duty that we ought to give them a special place in our lives by treating them with love, and gratefulness.[100]

Every responsible and sensible society should give every care, concern and consideration to senior citizens when they have played their innings and

---

[93] Charlene M. Kampfe, *Counseling Older People: Opportunities and Challenges*, np.

[94] James David, "Ageing in India," 200.

[95] Abraham J. Heschel, *The Insecurity of Freedom* (New York: Schocken Books, 1972), 72.

[96] Marvin R. Wilson, *Our Father Abraham: Jewish Roots of the Christian Faith* (Grand Rapids: William B. Eerdmans Publishing Company, 1989), 228.

[97] Sarah M. Moses, *Ethics and the Elderly: The Challenge of Long-Term Care*, np.

[98] Sarah M. Moses, *Ethics and the Elderly: The Challenge of Long-Term Care*, np.

[99] Sarah M. Moses, *Ethics and the Elderly: The Challenge of Long-Term Care*, np.

[100] Henry Holstege and Robert Riekse, *Complete Guide to Caring for Aging Loved Ones* (Illinois: Tyndale House Publishers, 2002), 18.

contributed their share for the growth and welfare of their society in every age.[101] Senior citizens deserve our respect, recognition, love, and care in their life. For that the church, society and individual should try to be more sensitive and create awareness for this prevailing issue.

Conclusion

In today's society, the senior citizens are often marginalized, deprived, excluded, abused, and humiliated in every angle of their lives. Negative attitude from children and society is causing a huge impact in the life of the senior citizens and are now considered as outdated. Christians ought to participate in helping the Senior citizens who deserve respect because they are valuable and important in society. We must also try to understand them and meet their challenges. The church should also be responsible enough to educate and develop with proper educational guidance for the upliftment of the senior citizens in our society. Let us try to be more sensitive to the elders around us and also try to understand and address to their needs. Thus, senior citizens must be given a definite opportunity and place in society and should make them useful and needed in society.

---

[101] Macdonald Singh, "Senior Citizens-Honoured Denizens," *NCC Review*, CXXIX/10 (October 2009): 11.

19

Christian Engagement in the Context of Human Trafficking
Perspectives from Christian Education

Nukshijungla

Introduction

Of all the organized crimes across the world, human trafficking is perhaps the most serious one. Its prime targets remain women and children who are trafficked for various illegal purposes such as prostitution, slavery, sexual abuse, forced labour and possibly for all kinds of violence and all kinds of abuse that one can imagine and contemplate against women and children.[1] The seriousness of the crime lies in the fact that women and children who are from lower strata of society and who are highly oppressed and exploited are the victims. This paper shall look into human trafficking, the issues and the several factors associated with it and bring about possible means of tackling human trafficking by Christian participation through Christian education.

1. Definition of Human Trafficking

The concept of Human trafficking refers to the criminal practice of exploiting human beings by treating them like commodities for profit. Even after being trafficked, victims are subjected to long term exploitation.[2]

---

[1] Amit Bhaskar, "Human Trafficking Law in India: An Overview," *Social Action,* vol. 63/4 (Oct-Dec, 2013): 388.

[2] Anita.Kanaiya, "Human Trafficking – A Modern day Slavery?," *EFICOR,* vol. 3 (June, 2012): 71.

Human trafficking is the practice of people being tricked, lured, forced or otherwise removed from their home or country, and then compelled to work with no or low payment or on terms which are highly exploitative. The practice is considered to be trade or commerce in people, which has many features of slavery, and which is illegal in many Countries.[3]

Human trafficking is a group of crimes involving the exploitation of men, women and children for financial gains which is violation of fundamental human rights. Victims are lured or abducted from their homes and subsequently forced to work against their wish through various means in various establishments, indulge in prostitution or subjected to various types of indignities and even killed or incapacitated for the purposes of begging and trade in human organs.[4]

2. The Importance of Christian Engagement in Social Change today

We are living in a time of great spiritual yearning and widespread social change. Christian ministers, educators, and congregations have much to offer in this context—but we are often shaken by change and torn apart and carried away by the demands of life in a fast-changing culture.[5] In this context, we desperately need to discuss the theme 'Christian engagement in Social change' and need to ask how we can build up one another in a way of life that is good for ourselves, for others, and for all creation, a way of life that has meaning and coherence because it is grounded in God and oriented towards God.[6]

Our present world has changed almost beyond recognition with the coming of industrialization, scientific inventiveness, materialist, humanist, and secularist fashions of thought, and social revolution. New problems constantly challenged old principles, and found scripture inadequate, tradition confused, and the Christian conscience unprepared.[7]

The Churches should encourage to participate more actively in the mission of God in their local communities. In Corinthians (5:18), we are reminded that through Christ we have been given the "ministry of reconciliation" not just with Church attenders but to assist God's mission towards the "reconciliation and renewal which is the end in view for the whole creation."[8] Reconciliation requires relationship, justice and forgiveness; renewal requires openness to new

---

[3] Yogendra Nath Mann, "Illegal Trafficking of Women and Children: Causes, Malady and Resolution," in *Trafficking in Women and Children in India: Emerging Perspectives, Issues and Strategies,* edited by Awadesh Kumar Singh and Atul Pratap Singh (New Delhi: Serials Publications, 2012), 251.

[4] Anita.Kanaiya, "Human Trafficking – A Modern day Slavery?," 72.

[5] http://www.caritas.org/includes/pdf/coatnet/ChristianCommitment.pdf. (18/9/15).

[6] http://www.caritas.org/includes/pdf/coatnet/ChristianCommitment.pdf. (18/9/15).

[7] http://www.caritas.org/includes/pdf/coatnet/ChristianCommitment.pdf. (18/9/15).

[8] http://www.fciv.org/downloads/Mary%20Leary.%20Religion%20and%20Human%20 Trafficking.pdf. (13/7/15).

ways of thinking, relating and acting. For the Christians to participate in the transformation of our society, including promotion of justice and equity for the poor and marginalised, encouraging social values such as fairness, compassion and collaboration rather than competition and modelling, an alternative way of living, congregations need to be encouraged and equipped.[9]

Community engagement and action for social change are an integral part of Christian discipleship. Throughout the Old and New Testament, God makes it clear that caring and speaking up for the voiceless, challenging injustice, and refusing to submit to the values of Empire are what God desires of us, and indeed the basis of how we will be judged. Christians are supposed to impact and permeate society like salt and light or shine like stars. Christian engagement in the political system can help bring integrity and service back to the heart of democracy. Every Christian can make a difference somewhere.[10]

A change in the attitude and mindset of the people may bring about changes in the social structure. The problem of social change is one of the central foci of sociological inquiry. It is so complex and so significant in the life of individual and of society that we have to explore the 'why' and 'how' of social change in all its ramifications.[11]

3. How the Issue of Human Trafficking will help to understand the theme 'Christian engagement in Social change' better

We all know that human trafficking is one of the serious crime. We need a change in the attitude and mindset of the people. Until and unless we lay the responsibility upon the people and make the society aware that there is a serious social evil prevailing in our doorstep and in our backyard, the society will never engage with it.

We cannot afford to live in a society where human trafficking exists. It is not a matter of achieving a certain level of human rights standards or reaching a higher level of development. Rather, it is a matter of having a society which is free from human trafficking and thus a society where development can be achieved. And as long as people will be trafficked, our communal wellbeing will be at risk, individual growth will be threatened, human rights principles will never be achievable and finally social development will be jeopardized.

---

[9] http://www.fciv.org/downloads/Mary%20Leary.%20Religion%20and%20Human%20 Trafficking.pdf. (13/7/15).

[10] http://wcd.nic.in/INTEGRATEDPLANOFACTION.htmhttp://stophumantrafficking-mha.nic.in/writereaddata/PRESENTATION%20ON%20HT%20FOR%205TH%20RTF. pdf. (15/9/15).

[11] http://wcd.nic.in/INTEGRATEDPLANOFACTION.htmhttp://stophumantrafficking-mha.nic.in/writereaddata/PRESENTATION%20ON%20HT%20FOR%205TH%20RTF. pdf. (15/9/15).

As we read stories of victims of human trafficking in our daily newspapers, we become aware of how human trafficking experience damages people's lives. However, we rarely realize how trafficking of persons affects the whole society. It is this impact on the society that creates a negative effect. In other words, we are all indirectly victimized by the presence of human trafficking. As human trafficking affects each and every society around the world, we need to identify actors who are primarily responsible for counteracting this negative and dangerous phenomenon and thus to engage Christians in bringing about social change in this area.

4. Human Trafficking in India

In India Human trafficking has acquired a dangerous proportion in the last few decades, the reason being that India is a source, transit and destination for the crime. Bordering alongside Nepal and Bangladesh, India becomes the right place for the traffickers. The abundance of poor population in the country is a boon for traffickers.[12] In India, the trafficking is done for almost all illegal and immoral purposes such as sexual abuse, pornography, forced labour and slavery. The root cause of the problem is poverty, unemployment, etc., Hence, the problem is social as well as legal. The government has failed to address the issue of poverty effectively.[13]

In regard with Human Trafficking, the area of the greatest concerns are poverty-stricken areas such as Andhra Pradesh, Bihar, Karnataka, Uttar Pradesh, Maharashtra, Madhya Pradesh, Rajasthan, Orissa, Assam and West Bengal.[14] Only 10 percent of Human Trafficking in India is International, while almost 90 percent is inter-state. According to a report by the National Human Rights Commission of India, nearly 40,000 children are abducted every year of which 11,000 remain untraced and possibly fall prey to the traffickers.[15]

5. Different types of Human Trafficking:

(a) Trafficking of Children

Trafficking of human beings, especially of women and children is one of the fastest growing trades, generating unaccountable profits annually. The reasons for the increase in this global phenomenon are multiple and complex, affecting both rich and poor countries alike.[16]

---

[12] Amit Bhaskar, "Human Trafficking Law in India: An Overview," *Social Action,* 387.

[13] Amit Bhaskar, "Human Trafficking Law in India: An Overview," *Social Action,* 389.

[14] http://www.coe.int/t/dghl/monitoring/trafficking/Docs/News/OrganTrafficking_study.pdf. (10/7/15).

[15] http://www.coe.int/t/dghl/monitoring/trafficking/Docs/News/OrganTrafficking_study.pdf. (10/7/15).

[16] Kailash, Satyarthi, "Trafficking of Children: Causes and Possible Solutions," in *Human Trafficking: The Stakeholder's Perspective*, edited by Veerendra Mishra (New Delhi: Sage Publications Pvt, Ltd., 2013), 101.

Trafficking of children is a worldwide phenomenon affecting large numbers of boys and girls everyday. Children and their families are often lured by the promise of better employment and a more prosperous life far from their homes. Others are kidnapped and sold. Trafficking violates a child's right to grow up in a family environment and exposes him or her to a range of dangers, including violence and sexual abuse.[17] Trafficking of children often involves exploitation of the parent's extreme poverty. Parents may sell children to traffickers in order to pay off debts or gain income, or they may be delivered concerning the prospects of training and a better life for their children.[18] The main purpose of this kind of trafficking is for child labour, slavery and for sexual exploitation.[19]

(b) Trafficking of women

Women in terrible circumstances are particularly targeted by traffickers, especially for sex industry. Criminals exploit lack of opportunities and promise good jobs or opportunities for work or study, and then force the victims to become prostitutes.[20] Through agents and brokers who arrange the travel and job placements, women are escorted to their destinations and delivered to the employers. Upon reaching their destinations, some women learn that they have been deceived about the nature of the work they will do, most have been lied to about the financial arrangements and conditions of their employment and find themselves in coercive, helpless and abusive situations from which escape is both difficult and dangerous.[21]

(c) Trafficking for Organ Trade

Human trafficking is most commonly known for the severe forms of violence but human trafficking does not stop with human beings as an individual.[22] All over the world, the organs of human beings are being trafficked, sometimes with, and sometimes without, the consent of those to whom they belong.[23] People are directly, or indirectly, being forced to sell their own organs for a low price, often to middlemen, who make lots of money from the poor vulnerable persons.

---

[17] Sunil Salankey Rao, *Trafficking of Children for Sexual Exploitation* (New Delhi: Oxford University Press, 2013), 315.

[18] Yogendra Nath Mann, "Illegal Trafficking of Women and Children: Causes, Malady and Resolution," in *Trafficking in Women and Children in India: Emerging Perspectives, Issues and Strategies,* 252.

[19] Anoop Kumar Bhartiya & Anvita Verma, "Child Trafficking in India," in *Trafficking in Women and Children in India: Emerging Perspectives, Issues and Strategies,* 404.

[20] Sankar Sen, *Trafficking in Women and Children in India* (New Delhi: Orient Longman, 2005), 148.

[21] Sankar Sen, *Trafficking in Women and Children in India,* 148.

[22] http://www.coe.int/t/dghl/monitoring/trafficking/Docs/News/OrganTrafficking_study.pdf. (10/7/15).

[23] http://www.coe.int/t/dghl/monitoring/trafficking/Docs/News/OrganTrafficking_study.pdf. (10/7/15).

Organized crime groups lure people abroad with false promises and convince or force them to sell their organs for a low price. The recipients of the organs pay a much higher price than the donors receive. This part benefits the traffickers who are part of an organized criminal network.[24] The trafficked organs can be acquired in many different and terrible ways. People may be kidnapped, killed and sold, especially children, for their organs. Other ways for the brokers to procure the organs are through deception or coercion. There have been cases where a victim will go to a doctor or hospital for an unrelated illness or accident, but in the hospital, the person's kidney is removed without their knowledge or consent.[25]

6. Factors Responsible for Human Trafficking

Trafficking in India is a violent, complex issue fuelled by a range of factors: economic injustice and social inequality, harmful cultural attitudes and regional gender imbalances, with corruption among government officials and police allowing trafficking of children and women to continue and expand, illegal brothels to flourish and traffickers to go unpunished. Some of the factors leading to human trafficking are discussed below.

(a) Poverty

Poverty is a crucial contributing factor for the rise in human trafficking in India.[26] Despite 65 years of independence, the benefits of economic development have not trickled down to the marginalized section of the society and millions of people still live below the poverty line.[27] Poverty and hunger makes children and women belonging to the poor sections of the society highly vulnerable to human trafficking.

Poverty often cited as a major reason responsible for trafficking of children, is not the only cause. Loss of traditional sources of livelihood, growing unemployment, forced migration, the commodification of children and growing and changing consumerism resulting from globalization have all contributed to the increase in trafficking.[28]

---

[24] http://www.coe.int/t/dghl/monitoring/trafficking/Docs/News/OrganTrafficking_study.pdf. (10/7/15).

[25] http://www.coe.int/t/dghl/monitoring/trafficking/Docs/News/OrganTrafficking_study.pdf. (10/7/15).

[26] R. Venkatamuni Reddy, "A Comparative Analysis of Various Factors Influencing Human Trafficking in India," in *Trafficking in Women and Children in India: Emerging Perspectives, Issues and Strategies*, 204.

[27] R. Venkatamuni Reddy, "A Comparative Analysis of Various Factors Influencing Human Trafficking in India," 204.

[28] Ram Ahuja, *Social Problems in India* (Jaipur, Rawat Publications, 2011), 47.

(b) Social attitudes, Cultures and Practices

Women and girls are more prone to trafficking because of social norms that marginalize their value and status in society.[29] Some religious beliefs also lead people to believe that the birth of girls are a result of bad karma, further cementing the belief that girls are not as valuable as boys.[30] Various social norms contribute to women's inferior position and lack of agency and knowledge, thus making them vulnerable to exploitation such as sex trafficking. Women also face many forms of gender based violations, such as domestic violence, sexual violence and genital mutilation; which are linked to social and cultural structures that contribute to the vulnerability of women to human trafficking.[31]

Children are also vulnerable to trafficking in persons due to their parents and families' socio-economic situation. Girls are particularly vulnerable to trafficking because in many societies, parents often choose to send girls to work because they believe that education is not as important to girls who will one day marry and leave the parents.[32]

(c) Impact of Globalization

Globalization of sexual slavery has created a million dollar business, riding on the tender bodies of young women.[33] There is an increase in the feminization of poverty, as women's employment opportunities have diminished and globalizing economic forces have increased. Although, the free market economy is presented as offering a path out of such poverty cycle but without active investment in basic needs, women are unable to develop their capabilities and they cannot participate fully in the economic domain.[34]

(d) Commercial demand for Sex

In this model, male demand for prostitutes leads to a market of sex work, which, in turn, fosters sex trafficking, the illegal trade and coercion of people into sex work, and pimps and traffickers become 'distributors' who supply people to be

---

[29] Ram Ahuja, *Violence Against Women* (Jaipur: Rawat Publications, 2009), 11-12.

[30] Ram Ahuja, *Violence Against Women,* 42.

[31] Ram Ahuja, *Violence Against Women,* 262.

[32] Bharti Ali, "Child Trafficking: The Alarm that fails to Ring a Bell," in *Human Trafficking: The Stakeholder's Perspective*, 117.

[33] Samar Kumar Biswas & Somenath Bhattacharjee, "Women Trafficking: An Emerging Social Problem in India," in *Trafficking in Women and Children in India: Emerging Perspectives, Issues and Strategies*, 149.

[34] Samar Kumar Biswas & Somenath Bhattacharjee, "Women Trafficking: An Emerging Social Problem in India," in *Trafficking in Women and Children in India: Emerging Perspectives, Issues and Strategies*, 150.

sexually exploited.[35] The demand for sex trafficking can also be facilitated by some pimps' and traffickers' desire for women whom they can exploit as workers because they do not require wages, safe working circumstances, and agency in choosing customers.[36]

The children trafficked are young as "the younger the child the more money he/she will fetch."[37] Therefore, whether trafficking is for prostitution or for domestic work or camel racing or begging or pornography, whatever the purpose maybe, the younger children are preferred to their older counterparts.[38]

(e) Media exposure

The sex business is global, fuelled by multinational corporations who own or co-own different venues like hotels, clubs, fashion and modelling industry, etc., that support this business. By channelling funds into the sex industries, new job opportunities are created which are ultimately disempowering the women and the society altogether. It seems that, often in many developing countries, the government views prostitution as a necessary part of promoting tourism as a means of development.[39] Pornography has become increasingly visible throughout the developing world and over the internet, which may create an adverse circumstances for the women or enforce them to sell their body for a fold of rice for herself and for her dear ones.[40]

(f) Lack of Good Governance

The lack of proper administrative awareness has created the situation of woman trafficking more alarming.[41] Although, a number of constitutional provisions are there to prevent this crime,these are not implemented properly by the

---

[35] Atul Pratap Singh, "Trafficking of Women and Children in India: Causes, Consequences and Intervention Strategies," in *Trafficking in Women and Children in India: Emerging Perspectives, Issues and Strategies*, 99.

[36] Atul Pratap Singh, "Trafficking of Women and Children in India: Causes, Consequences and Intervention Strategies," in *Trafficking in Women and Children in India: Emerging Perspectives, Issues and Strategies*, 100.

[37] D. K. Singh, "Child Trafficking: Issues and Strategies," in *Trafficking in Women and Children in India: Emerging Perspectives, Issues and Strategies,* 397.

[38] D. K. Singh, "Child Trafficking: Issues and Strategies," in *Trafficking in Women and Children in India: Emerging Perspectives, Issues and Strategies,* 397.

[39] Samar Kumar Biswas & Somenath Bhattacharjee, "Women Trafficking: An Emerging Social Problem in India," in *Trafficking in Women and Children in India: Emerging Perspectives, Issues and Strategies*, 150.

[40] Samar Kumar Biswas & Somenath Bhattacharjee, "Women Trafficking: An Emerging Social Problem in India," in *Trafficking in Women and Children in India: Emerging Perspectives, Issues and Strategies*, 150.

[41] Gopal Bhargava, *Human Rights: Concern Future* (New Delhi: Kalpaz Publications, 2001), 160.

administration. Due to the sorry state of our prosecution and law and other mechanism, the traffickers know very well that their chance of getting arrested or being prosecuted is very minimal.[42]

7. Impacts of Human Trafficking

The menace of the human trafficking is very large and there are physical, social, moral and economic impacts. Human trafficking is a crime against individuals and its consequences are most directly felt by those who are its victims. The effects of victimization strike particularly hard at the poor, the powerless, the disabled and the socially isolated.[43] Victims of trafficking often experience abuse, exploitation, poverty and poor health prior to being trafficked. These conditions are only worsened by their experiences as victims of crime.

Every stage of the trafficking process can involve physical, sexual and psychological abuse and violence, deprivation and torture, the forced use of substances, manipulation, economic exploitation and abusive working and living conditions.[44] Unlike most other violent crimes, trafficking usually involves prolonged and repeated trauma. Below are some of the impacts of human trafficking upon women and children.

(a) Impact of trafficking on Individual

Trafficked persons are reportedly traumatised by their experiences. Depression and suicidal thoughts are commonly reported. The mental and emotional state of the survivors may include malevolence, helplessness, withdrawal, dissociation, self-blame and identification with the aggressor.[45] Some of the observed psychiatric disorders among survivors of trafficking are post-traumatic stress disorder, depressive disorder, dissociative disorders, psychotic disorders and eating disorders. Women who are made to bear the responsibility of holding their family honour through their sexual purity/chastity face additional stress because of the prevalent morality.[46]

Besides being stigmatised as outcastes and facing moral and legal isolation, trafficked people are vulnerable to HIV/AIDS infections, drug addiction, high-risk abortions and teenage pregnancies, which may affect their reproductive health for life. Trafficking victims are compelled to lead illegal lives. Illegality spoils every dimension of their lives, making them criminals. Their criminalisation severely

---

[42] Gopal Bhargava, *Human Rights: Concern Future,* 161.

[43] Bir Pal Singh & Gargi Rajvanshi, "Trafficking in Human Beings: A Critical Analysis," in *Trafficking in Women and Children in India: Emerging Perspectives, Issues and Strategies,* 183.

[44] Bir Pal Singh & Gargi Rajvanshi, "Trafficking in Human Beings: A Critical Analysis," in *Trafficking in Women and Children in India: Emerging Perspectives, Issues and Strategies,* 183.

[45] Sankar Sen, *Trafficking in Women and Children in India,* 15.

[46] Sankar Sen, *Trafficking in Women and Children in India,* 15.

stigmatises them and deepen their victimization, and leaves them with no option or alternative for restoration.[47]

(b) Social Consequences

Trafficking involves the violation of a whole range of laws and human rights. It becomes a threat to society because traffickers operate across borders with exemption from punishment with the growing involvement of organised criminals and by generally undermining the rule of law.[48] Trafficking threatens the very fabric of society because it involves not only criminals but also law enforcers. It manifests and perpetuates patriarchal attitudes and behaviour, which undermine and weaken efforts to promote gender equality and eradicate discrimination against women and children.[49]

(c) Economic Consequences

The costs of the crime of trafficking in persons incorporates many elements, including the value of all resources devoted to its prevention, the treatment and support of victims and the anxiety and prosecution of offenders. These costs may be offset in part by the recovery of criminal proceeds and assets of the traffickers.[50] Trafficking in persons also results in loss of human resources and reductions in tax revenue.[51] Further, trafficking in persons redirects the financial benefits of migration from migrants, their families, community and government or other potential legitimate employers to traffickers and their associates. All indications are that the income generated by related organized crime is significant and global. Given the ongoing nature of exploitation, human trafficking generates a stable and regular source of income for criminal networks, with a consequent impact on other forms of criminal activity as well as legitimate business.[52]

(d) Health Related Consequences

Women and children located in the commercial sex-sector either trafficked or otherwise, face higher risk of contracting sexually transmitted diseases (STDs), HIV/AIDS, tuberculosis and other diseases. Increased incidence of HIV/AIDS is also believed to have led to an escalating demand for younger commercial sex workers, who have higher probability of being free of diseases.

---

[47] Sankar Sen, *Trafficking in Women and Children in India,* 16.

[48] Bir Pal Singh & Gargi Rajvanshi, "Trafficking in Human Beings: A Critical Analysis," in *Trafficking in Women and Children in India: Emerging Perspectives, Issues and Strategies,* 183.

[49] Sankar Sen, *Trafficking in Women and Children in India,* 16.

[50] K. C. Abraham, "Women Struggling against Violence," *Voices from Third World Country,* vol. 126/16 (June, 1994): 7.

[51] K. C. Abraham, "Women Struggling against Violence," *Voices from Third World Country*: 7.

[52] Jessy Kurian, "Trafficking of Persons," *New Leader,* vol. 126/16 (August, 2013): 16.

There have also been reports of myths circulating that having sex with a virgin will actually cure STDs. Tragically these false notions are creating a demand for younger girls, even below 12 years of age.[53] Conditions such as inhumane living conditions, poor diet and hygiene, ongoing physical abuse, and lack of access to health care and protection can result in long-term health problems. Unsafe sexual practices also contribute to health issues such as unplanned pregnancies, dangerous abortion practices and sexually transmitted diseases.[54]

8. Christian Response towards Human Trafficking

Although more brutal than ever, modern-day slavery is not as obvious as it was centuries ago. Today human trafficking isn't limited to race, class or gender. Victims are not just the poor. They come from every socio-economic group.[55] Human trafficking is the dirty secret that has been hidden too long in our country. It is in every state of this great country, from large cities to small towns to rural areas. It's in our backyard whether we live in the city or the countryside.

To combat trafficking, the efforts both at the levels of respective State Governments, NGO's and Churches have been taken. Ministry of Women and Child Development has formulated a National Plan of Action to combat Trafficking and commercial sexual exploitation of women and children in 1998, with the objective to mainstream and to reintegrate the women and child victims of commercial sexual exploitation in society.[56] There are some networks and organizations which are doing great service for the humanity to save children and women from trafficking and providing them appropriate measures of rehabilitation with dignified life and living such as End Child Prostitution in Asian Tourism (ECPAT), Action Against Trafficking and Sexual Exploitation of Children (ATSEC), Action aid, etc.[57] But in spite of all this efforts and measures, trafficking is still prevalent and perhaps it is increasing day by day. Women and children are still deprived of their human rights and are used as object.

The Bible records that, when God created humans, He created them in His own image (Genesis 1:26-27). Every life is of great value, and God loves all individuals. This is one of the key source to place Human Rights within the framework of Christian thought.[58] As a result, God teaches love for our neighbour

---

[53] Jessy Kurian, "Trafficking of Persons," *New Leader*: 16.

[54] K. C. Abraham, "Women Struggling against Violence," *Voices from Third World Country*, 9.

[55] http://www.fciv.org/downloads/Mary%20Leary.%20Religion%20and%20Human%20 Trafficking.pdf. (13/7/15).

[56] Bir Pal Singh & Gargi Rajvanshi, "Trafficking in Human Beings: A Critical Analysis," in *Trafficking in Women and Children in India: Emerging Perspectives, Issues and Strategies*, 183.

[57] Bir Pal Singh & Gargi Rajvanshi, "Trafficking in Human Beings: A Critical Analysis," in *Trafficking in Women and Children in India: Emerging Perspectives, Issues and Strategies*, 184.

[58] Shimreingam Shimray, *Theology of Human Rights: A critique on Politics* (Jorhat, Assam: Barkataki & Company Pvt. Ltd., 2002), 187.

(Matthew 19:19) as well as love for those in need (Luke 10:25-37). Jesus was the one who taught the Golden Rule: "So in everything, do to others what you would have them do to you, for this sums up, the Law and the Prophets" (Matthew 7:12).[59] Further, Proverbs 31:8-9 teaches us to "Speak up for those who cannot speak for themselves, for the rights of all who are destitute. Speak up and judge fairly; defend the rights of the poor and needy." These principles certainly all apply to those hurt through the illegal practice of human trafficking.[60]

How can Christians today practice these biblical principles of helping those in the bondage of slavery? First, we must pray for those in bondage. As James 5:16 notes, "The prayer of a righteous person is powerful and effective." Human trafficking is a clear need that requires God's power for any adequate change to occur.[61]

Second, we must speak out on behalf of those in need (Proverbs 31:8-9). Those in our schools, businesses, churches, and community often are unaware of the problem of human trafficking and how to help. Perhaps God is calling us to be one of the people who would speak out and help, provide justice to those who are helpless and voiceless.[62]

Third, we must act to help those in bondage. These actions can involve a variety of means, ranging from volunteering in an anti-trafficking organization to financial giving. A growing number of organizations have emerged in recent years that provide new opportunities for Christians to serve in this area.[63]

Learning to recognize the signs of human trafficking is not as difficult as it may sound. In short, as Christians each one of us can and should help to protect our children and others from this horrific crime in our backyard. Whether by prayer, being aware, or giving time or money, faith means taking action.[64] James put it well, "In the same way, faith by itself, if it is not accompanied by action, is dead" (James 2:17).

In summary, human trafficking is a disgusting indignity against men, women, and children who have been created in God's image.[65] As followers of Christ, we have a responsibility to pray, to speak out against human trafficking

[59] Shimreingam Shimray, *Theology of Human Rights: A Critique on Politics,* 191.

[60] Shimreingam Shimray, *Theology of Human Rights: A Critique on Politics,* 192.

[61] http://www.fciv.org/downloads/Mary%20Leary.%20Religion%20and%20Human%20 Trafficking.pdf. (13/7/15).

[62] http://www.fciv.org/downloads/Mary%20Leary.%20Religion%20and%20Human%20 Trafficking.pdf. (13/7/15).

[63] http://www.fciv.org/downloads/Mary%20Leary.%20Religion%20and%20Human%20 Trafficking.pdf. (13/7/15).

[64] http://www.fciv.org/downloads/Mary%20Leary.%20Religion%20and%20Human%20 Trafficking.pdf. (13/7/15).

[65] http://www.fciv.org/downloads/Mary%20Leary.%20Religion%20and%20Human%20 Trafficking.pdf. (13/7/15).

and modern slavery, and to live in ways that will help to create a change in the lives of those impacted by this tragic crime. Law cannot be the only instrument to take care of all problems. It would be better if the problem of human trafficking can be curbed with a co-ordination and co-operation of all the members of the society.

9. Initiatives taken by Government of India for Anti-Trafficking

In view of the complexity of problem, a multi-sectorial approach is needed to arrest trafficking especially in vulnerable areas, and sections of population. The Government of India, under the Ministry of Women and Child Development, has launched in 2007 a central comprehensive scheme for prevention of trafficking for rescue, rehabilitation and reintegration of victims of trafficking for commercial sexual exploitation. The scheme has been conceived primarily for the purpose of preventing trafficking on the one hand and rescue and rehabilitation of victims on the other. The main objectives of the scheme are:[66]

1. To prevent trafficking of women and children for commercial sexual exploitation through social mobilization and involvement of local communities/awareness generation programmes, workshops, etc.
2. To facilitate rescue of victims from the place of exploitation and place them in safe custody.
3. To provide rehabilitation services both immediate and long terms to the victims by providing basic amenities.
4. To facilitate reintegration of the victims into the family and society at large.
5. To facilitate repatriation of cross-border victims to their country of origin.

The Ministry has adopted a multi branched approach to prevent and combat trafficking.

Article 23 of the Indian Constitution prohibits trafficking in human beings and beggars. The principal legislation-Immoral Trafficking (Prevention) Act, 1956' lays down provisions of providing stringent punishment to the perpetrators of crime.[67]

The Indian Penal Code also provides provisions for crimes related to trafficking.[68]

---

[66] Awadhest, *Trafficking in Women and Children in India: Emerging Perspectives, Issues and Strategies*, 484.

[67] Awadhest, *Trafficking in Women and Children in India: Emerging Perspectives, Issues and Strategies*, 485.

[68] Awadhest, *Trafficking in Women and Children in India: Emerging Perspectives, Issues and Strategies*, 485.

India is signatory with the UN Convention against Transnational Organization Crime with its protocol to prevent Suppress and Punish Trafficking especially Women and Children.

SAARC Convention on Prevention and Combating Trafficking of Women and Children in Prostitution.[69]

In 2012, 7 states in India have established a network of government agencies, police and NGO to collaborate in combating the trafficking of women and children. These states have also agreed to work closely in helping to rescue and rehabilitate the trafficked girls and to send them back to their home states.[70]

These are some of the government programmes and schemes that have been initiated to combat the growing trafficking of women and children. While there are few others which are not mentioned in the paper.

10. Educational Steps to make an impact against Human Trafficking

By far, the most effective means of combating human trafficking are education and awareness. Below are 10 safe educational steps that can be taken and considered in order to making an impact against human trafficking in our own society:[71]

1. Educate the society on human trafficking.
2. Educate the children and youth, in age-appropriate ways, on sex and sexuality.
3. Adopt a Safe Church Policy and do proper background checks on individuals working with children and youth.
4. Find out about local resources (shelters, centers, organizations) in one's area, caring for human trafficking victims and to volunteer ones time.
5. To work with area schools on anti-bullying, self-esteem and girls' empowerment programs to reduce the number of cases of desperate young people.
6. Start a small group, interested in this issue in order to keep the congregation informed about changing trends in trafficking and ways people can continue to stay vigilant.
7. Advocate for law enforcement, medical professionals and airport employees to be trained on identifying human trafficking in one's area.
8. Pay attention, follow ones instincts and speak up!

---

[69] Awadhest, *Trafficking in Women and Children in India: Emerging Perspectives, Issues and Strategies*, 485.

[70] "Commercial Sexual Exploitation," www.articles.timesofindia.indiatimes.com/keyword/commercial-sexual-exploitation. (15.01.2014).

[71] Lindsay C. Comstock, "What your Church can do about Human Trafficking," http://globalfreedomcenter.org/EducatingOurWayOutofTrafficking.pdf. (13/7/15).

9. Talk to the children and youth and educate them about the dangers of human trafficking.
10. Host a fundraiser or awareness campaign at ones church.

11. Enhancing the Role of Christian Education in Bringing about Social Change

Stopping or eradicating human trafficking completely will be an admittedly slow process, but with education and awareness and with great efforts from society as a whole, we can really begin to tackle the issue of human trafficking, in order to bring about a social change. If we do not pay attention to these social issues now, as responsible Christians, future generations will be at greater risk. In short, the world needs a more united and effective strategy and a well-developed educational steps to address human trafficking.

(a) Educating the People

So, how can people be educated regarding this issue and how can education stop Human Trafficking? It can stop trafficking at the point of contact because the traffickers' stories are not believed. It can stop trafficking at the point of need because an educated person is more likely to get a decent job and no longer need to migrate for work. It can stop trafficking because an informed worker knows his rights and does not hand them over upon arrival in a foreign land. It can stop trafficking as an informed public no longer turns a blind eye to the trafficking around them. An informed masses recognize that trafficking victims are human beings with the same needs and rights as themselves and they say, "No more. Not one more victim.[72]

(b) Education for Awareness

However, there is a new way in which to potentially improve this trafficking situation. By increasing public awareness and education about trafficking, underprivileged citizens can become more aware of the options they have, in seeking help, rather than thinking that trafficking is their only choice.[73] In strengthening law enforcement and public law education, people will know the serious consequences of trafficking. More organizations that protect trafficking victims are needed. This would provide medical and psychological treatment to

[72] Lindsay C. Comstock, "What your Church can do about Human Trafficking," http://globalfreedomcenter.org/EducatingOurWayOutofTrafficking.pdf. (13/7/15).

[73] Lindsay C. Comstock, "What your Church can do about Human Trafficking," http://globalfreedomcenter.org/EducatingOurWayOutofTrafficking.pdf. (13/7/15).

help victims overcome fear. It would also allow victims to share their stories to others in an effort to resist human trafficking.[74]

In general, people can help prevent human trafficking through public awareness, outreach, and education. For instance students can start human trafficking awareness groups at school.[75] Activities could include poster making, pamphlet designing, bumper sticker production, T-shirt designing, and bracelet making with a slogan or major design that says, "Stop Human Trafficking," which can be sold in our community. Any profits made can be turned to organizations that are working to help victims of human trafficking. For example, The Coalition to Abolish Slavery and Trafficking (CAST) is one of several worldwide organizations that help fight human trafficking and assist its victims. Their aim is in making everyone aware of the problems of human trafficking and encouraging countries to take measures to stop this illegal practice.[76]

Therefore, educating the mass on evils of Human Trafficking is a major means of tackling human trafficking which is also needed in Christian homes, institutions and the Church.

(c) Education for Participation

Education is for all and so every human has the right to be educated. Until and unless an individual is educated and made aware, there will be no participation and positive response from the people. Education therefore should not end with passing of information alone, rather it should encourage participation. Therefore, education must in response bring about Christian participation in eradicating Human Trafficking.

(d) Paulo Friere's method of Critical Consciousness or Conscientization as the tool for Transformation

Oppression breeds fear and suppresses potentiality. It makes people powerless and negative. when this negativism is internalized, a feeling of uselessness and hopelessness emerges and they lose confidence in themselves. This in turn makes people to accept the oppressive condition as inevitable. When this acceptance becomes part and parcel of culture we have a situation, which Friere calls 'the culture of silence'.[77] The most important means to overcome 'the culture of silence' is to develop a critical consciousness. Deepening of a critical awareness of the situation is aimed at bringing liberation and transformation. It is a way of

---

[74] Lindsay C. Comstock, "What your Church can do about Human Trafficking," http://globalfreedomcenter.org/EducatingOurWayOutofTrafficking.pdf. (13/7/15).

[75] http://www.unicefusa.org/sites/default/files/assets/pdf/Toolkit_End-Trafficking_Oct_2012.pdf. (13/7/15).

[76] http://www.unicefusa.org/sites/default/files/assets/pdf/Toolkit_End-Trafficking_Oct_2012.pdf. (13/7/15).

[77] Samson Prabhakar, *Essays on Christian Education and Liturgy* (Bangalore: SATHRI, 2003), 116.

looking at the world, not as a spectator or as a passive recipient, but as one who strives for change in the world, as one who would not accept the reality as given. It is the breaking of silence about one's own condition and speaking and acting out as one who has the right to speak and act.[78]

Critical consciousness is brought about not through an intellectual effort alone, but through the combination of action and reflection, which Friere calls 'Praxis'. He refers to it as 'critical transitivity' to suggest the dynamism between critical thought and critical action. He believed that once a person perceives and understands a situation as a problem and recognizes the possibilities of a response, he/she will act according to the nature of their understanding. The whole process of inculcating the critical consciousness is known as 'conscientization.'[79]

(e) Thomas Groome's Shared Praxis Approach

Christian religious education by shared praxis can be described as a group of Christians sharing in dialogue their critical reflection on present action in light of the Christian story and its vision towards the end of lived Christian faith.

Shared praxis takes place in a situation of group dialogue. Shared in the dialogue is an articulation of critical reflection upon one's present active engagement in the world as a Christian. That present engagement is in fact the embodiment of one's own story and vision, and critical reflection upon it takes place in the light of the Christian communities' story and the response which that story invites. This require that the story and its vision be made available in the pedagogical context. There are five main components in Christian education by shared praxis, each requiring some detailed explanation. These are- 1. Present action, 2. Critical reflection, 3. Dialogue, 4. The story, 5. The vision that arises from the story.

Immoral trafficking in women and children is a problem which is rooted in the socio-cultural norms. Therefore, any attempt made to tackle it through the instrumentality of law would not be sufficient. One of the major problems in the prevention and rehabilitation of such victims is the social stigma attached to them and absence of social acceptability.[80] Therefore, it requires multi-sectoral alliance like women activist groups, NGO's and other agencies to look into matters concerning their shelter, education, vocational training and over all personality development.

---

[78] Samson Prabhakar, *Essays on Christian Education and Liturgy,* 117.

[79] Juma E. Nyirenda, "The Relevance of Paulo Friere's Contribution to Education," http://archive.lib.msu.edu/DMC/African%20Journals/pdfs/africa%20media%20review/vol10no1/jamr010001002.pdf. (10/9/15)

[80] Samar Kumar Biswas & Somenath Bhattacharjee, "Women Trafficking: An Emerging Social Problem in India," in *Trafficking in Women and Children in India: Emerging Perspectives, Issues and Strategies*, 140-141.

Efforts to raise public awareness are needed to reduce demand for services of women. If people understand and are made aware that visiting prostitutes is regarded by the society as an immoral conduct and unsafe, and it is not only disgusting to the social norms and traditions and customs of society but also involves serious health implications for them, they will think twice before visiting brothels. It should be remembered that law alone is not sufficient enough to reduce the demand for services of women in prostitution.[81] Social sanctions should therefore be strengthened and applied if prostitution is to be curbed.

To successfully combat and suppress trafficking, which has been equated with modern day slavery and constitutes one of the greatest human rights challenges of our time an effective strategy is to be evolved. There should be enactment of a proper comprehensive legislation to target the traffickers and provide for proper rescue and rehabilitation programmes for the victim survivors.[82] New norms take roots only when there is the power of enforcement behind them. Purposive action need to be taken by the Church, NGO's, Educators, Governments as well as Civil Society to empower the vulnerable and restore the trafficked women and children their dignity and worth as human beings. We cannot embrace our dignity as human beings unless we champion the dignity of others.

Law should provide for the spread of moral and value education among people, both young and old. A thorough repair of the moral values of the society, through proper education, sex education, awareness programmes and removing the above mentioned drawbacks of the existing anti-trafficking legislation may be the answer to the problem of human trafficking.

Conclusion

The immoral trafficking of women and children as discussed in the paper, has been prevalent from the time immemorial and the menace of the evil has been known to almost all the sensible across the world. Sometimes this had been used as a source of fun and enjoyment at the cost of the victims. The reasons behind this evil practise may be monetary, financial or social compulsions.

The innocent victim of this social evil need strong support from all walks of society as despite the various enactments worldwide, the menace has grown manifold and the immoral trafficking has been increasing day in and day out. Every culprit should be given severe punishment, the cases of such a crime be disposed of expeditiously. At the same time, adequate measures also need to be taken for the help and rehabilitation of the victims. It is high time that the governments at centre and the states as well as the church, society and the judicial authorities try their level best to contribute in resolution of this issue.

---

[81] Sankar Sen, *Trafficking in Women and Children in India,* 167.

[82] Sankar Sen, *Trafficking in Women and Children in India,* 167.

Prevention of trafficking involves interventions at various levels to combat the initiation of trafficking. Prevention has to be a combined effort of both governmental and non-governmental agencies. It has to be a strategy to make the public aware of trafficking in persons as a mode of modern-day slavery and to sensitize them about it. The policies must be directed, particularly, to those sections of population who form the source and are most vulnerable to trafficking. The Government must make certain that good quality education, opportunities of employment and income generation programmes are put into operation to provide good quality life to highly susceptible persons. It should carry out routine programmes to educate and sensitize parents, teachers, and community workers about trafficking. Government should include gender centred education curricula in schools and introduce subjects of child sexual abuse and trafficking. Police advocacy is an important intervention that has to be fine-tuned. Awareness is the magnanimity and prevalence of the problem has to be done at the level of National Planning Commission, politicians and bureaucrats too. Their attention is to be drawn to this pertinent problem to invite policy changes. More stringent laws and better implementation are required to curb the problem. Stricter punishments shall act as a deterrent to other traffickers. Policies are required to be framed in the direction of creation of rehabilitation facilities for victims rescued. Victims need special medical and psychological care to move past the physical cruelty inflicted and trauma suffered.

NGOs can contribute by spreading awareness in community members about the prevalence of trafficking in humans. Awareness at the local level, in the community through workshops, songs, drama, meetings, leaflets and posters especially in the rural areas is also required. They should also remain vigilant and report missing persons who may be victims of trafficking. This can be helpful in identifying traffickers and their hideouts. NGOs working in rural area may carry out workshops to ensure that people are aware of safe migration practises and report inconsistent migration offers. Training programmes and activities highlighting the importance of gender equity can be organised to promote gender sensitization. Awareness is the key to prevention. The use of media helps garner attention of several hundred thousand viewers. This is an excellent medium of sensitization of people. Media should be used to transmit appropriate message to victims that legal and social help is available to them to get out of the slavery they are subjected to. Victims can be made aware of places and institutions where they can seek help. Media can help provide information to widespread viewer base about penal provisions against trafficking and the modus operandi of the traffickers through radio, television, etc. Media campaigns have proven to be a powerful tool to draw attention of both the government and the people to specific issues in the past. This power can be harnessed to create awareness about the inappropriate and illegal nature of the act and the cruel consequences thereof. The phenomenon of trafficking in humans is widespread across the country. It is a socio-economic offence and greatly affects the society. It makes people question their safety and the efficacy of the state machinery. It is the combined duty of the state and society to fight trafficking and protect the vulnerable groups. Awareness of occurrence of such crimes, effective criminal justice system and vigilant citizens can help check trafficking.

20

Pastoral Care to the Migrant Families Experiencing Loneliness in Mumbai

Marian Susi Dharmaraj

"The whole being of each person is social. To abstract a person from his or her concrete social relationships is to remove him or her from being a person."[1]

Dietrich Bonhoeffer

Introduction

Urbanization and Industrialization in modern India is the primary reason for large-scale migration of people from rural to urban areas. This migration impacts the migrants, their families and the entire society in many ways. In this chapter, the problem of loneliness as a negative impact of migration on migrant families in Mumbai will be discussed in order to suggest effective pastoral care. But before we go further, we need to ask few basic questions like what is social change and why should the Church be concerned about it.

Social change by definition means "changes in the social structure and social relationship of the society." Social change is also "variations in, or modifications of, any aspects of social processes, social patterns, social interaction or social organization."[2] Thus, it means changes in any or all aspects of society like the structure, the function, the pattern, the relationship and interactions among different social institutions.

---

[1] Lavonne Zwart Schaafsma, "The Impact of Lay Pastoral Telecare on the Spiritual Well-Being of Church Attenders," *The Journal of Pastoral Care* 54/1 (2000): 63.

[2] Pascual Gisbert, *Fundamentals of Sociology* (New Delhi: Orient Longman Limited, 1950), 270.

In contemporary India, social change is primarily a planned one. It started with national freedom movements, the launch of Indian constitution, and subsequent five year plans.[3] Planned social change continued due to the formation of important institutions and policies for industries, agriculture, education, medical research, and separate efforts for weaker section of society.[4] Heavy urbanization and industrialization directly resulted in large scale migration of people from rural to urban centers like Mumbai. However, migration is not a new phenomenon in human history.[5] People have been migrating since the beginning of human civilization for different reasons like better livelihood, better living conditions, safety, and so on. But today the society is witnessing increased number of migration as never before.

To the question what has social change got to do with the church?, Some evangelical Christians would try to argue that church has nothing to do with social concerns. They would say that church is a community of believers which should be concerned only with saving the perishing souls. However, evangelical thinker John Stott disagrees and insists that Christians should be involved in social concerns. He shows that Jesus Christ was not only preaching but also doing good and healing the sick (Mt. 4:23).[6] In fact Ivan Illich states that the church has always contributed in social change either by promoting it or by condemning it.[7]

The church needs to be concerned about migration as well. It is noticed that large and uncontrolled migration creates immense socio-economic, cultural, and psychological problems in the lives of those who are affected by migration (the migrants, their families, the people in the place of residence and also place of destination). Psychologically the migrants undergo lot of stress, anxiety, frustration, and even loneliness.

In this chapter, attempt will be made to understand the process and impact of migration as a social change. Further the psychological problem of loneliness experienced by migrant families in Mumbai will be discussed in detail. In conclusion, the present engagement of the church with the issue of loneliness in Mumbai will be briefly assessed in order to discuss what kind of pastoral care should be given by the church in Mumbai to effectively help the migrant families fight loneliness.

---

[3] Yogendra Singh, *Social Change in India: Crisis and Resilience* (New Delhi: Har-Anand Publications, 1993), 22.

[4] Yogendra Singh, *Social Change in India*, 26–27.

[5] Hector Andrade, "Theology in a Pluralistic Context: Migration as a Trope," *Janadeepa* 5/1 (2002): 45.

[6] John R. W. Stott, *New Issues Facing Christians Today* (Mumbai: GLS, 2003), 3.

[7] Ivan Illich, *Church, Change and Development* (New York: Hreder and Herder., 1970), 20.

1. Migration

(a) Definition of Migration

The term migration comes from the Latin root word *migro* from which *migratie* is derived meaning movement of large number of people or tribe from one to another place.[8] R. N. Sharma in his book *Urban Sociology* defines migration "as a process of movement of people from their areas of residence to other areas in search of better living conditions."[9] The UNO declared migrant worker as a "person who is currently or is going to be employed in a remunerative activity within the state of which he is not a citizen."[10]

(b) Migration: A Process of Social Change

Migration, when studied in the light of the definition of social change, certainly can be seen as a social change because migration alters the structures, patterns, and relationship between individuals and social institutions.

It can be said that migration from the cultural perspective brings social change because it influences the caste, class, resources, and way of life. For Emile Durkheim (one of the prominent founding fathers of sociology) migration "is a necessary social condition to push the process of social evolution from one type of social order to another."[11] Thus, it is noticed that the high caste rich people in villages often do not have control over people who leave the villages for employment in the cities. Such social change is also experienced in the place of destination.

Migration also generates high and steady income flow from cities to villages. This helps in replacing the traditional method in agriculture with modern equipment.[12] In cities, the rise in industrialization and urbanization causes weakening of the traditional society.[13] Moreover, in developing countries like India, migration to urban cities is high because of the shift in focus from agriculture to industrial sectors.[14] Thus, the advancement in technology and industrialization not only modernizes agriculture but also causes migration of agricultural labourers to work in factories.

---

[8] "The Concept of Migration: Linguistic and Sociological Coordinates," http://cis01.central.ucv.ro/revista_scol/site_ro/2013/LEXICOLIGIE/PORUMBESU.pdf (26 July, 2015).

[9] R. N. Sharma, *Urban Sociology* (Delhi: Surjeet Publications, 1993), 213.

[10] "The Concept of Migration."

[11] "Sociological Perspectives," http://www.sociologyguide.com/migration/sociologicalperspectives.php (26 June, 2015).

[12] "Social Impact of Migration," http://www.sociologyguide.com/migration/socialimpactofmigration.php (26 June, 2015).

[13] Yogendra Singh, *Social Change in India*, 153–154.

[14] Gian Singh and Shruti Mehra, "Migration: A Propitious Compromise," *Economic and Political Weekly* 49/15 (3 April, 2014): 24.

Finally, migration from the demographical perspective brings social change because people experience change in "attitudes and behaviour . . . material and social status . . . [also] change in the circle of interaction." Migrants are influenced by city life and adopt late marriage and family planning.[15] Yogendra Singh says that migration is one type of "major-structural phenomena" that brings social change in India.[16] Further Kuppuswamy from the Indian context points out that "much of contemporary social change is associated with the dominance of the urban social structure and the migration of rural people to urban areas."[17]

(c) Causes of Migration

(i) Pull Factors

R. N. Sharma observes that people migrate to cities for better living conditions.[18] Further, R. Ramachandran says that not just the poor and illiterate people migrate, but equally large number of educated and rich people migrate to cities in search of better employment.[19] Yogendra claims that urbanization has opened greater employment opportunities.[20] Thus, these positive factors like better employment and life, which encourage migration, are called pull factors.[21]

(ii) Push Factors

It is also noticed that people migrate due to push factors[22] like unemployment and starvation in their villages. Yogendra claims that rural to urban migration in India is mainly because of the socio-economic difficulty in villages rather than attraction of the cities.[23] Similarly, Awanish Kumar points out that migration to cities is because of high rate of poverty, lower employment opportunities, the social backwardness and oppression due to caste system in villages.[24] It is also due to decreased agricultural outcome, rise in rural population, and adverse

---

[15] "Social Impact of Migration."

[16] Yogendra Singh, *Social Change in India*, 149.

[17] B. Kuppuswamy, *Social Change in India* (Delhi: Vikas Publishing House, 1972), 14.

[18] R. N. Sharma, *Urban Sociology*, 213.

[19] R. Ramachandran, *Urbanization and Urban System in India* (Delhi: Oxford University Press, 1989), 92.

[20] Yogendra Singh, *Modernization of Indian Tradition: Systematic Study of Social Change* (Jaipur: Rawat Publications, 1986), 110.

[21] "What Is Human Migration?," (2005), 2, http://www.nationalgeographic.com/xpeditions/lessons/09/g68/migrationguidestudent.pdf (10 July, 2015).

[22] "What Is Human Migration?," 2.

[23] Yogendra Singh, *Modernization of Indian Tradition*, 108.

[24] Awanish Kumar, "A Class Analysis of the 'Bihari Menace,'" *Economic and Political Weekly* 44/28 (7 November, 2009): 126-127.

environmental impacts,[25] draught and famine. These negative conditions in the place of residence that compels migration are called push factors.

However in India, migration of women is primarily because of marriage.[26] They also at times migrate to support their dependent families or when the husband is not there or is an alcoholic.[27]

2. Migrant Families in Mumbai

(a) Overview of Mumbai City

Mumbai, the capital city of Maharashtra is most conducive to several trading and business opportunities due to its strategic geographical location. It is also referred to as financial capital of India.[28] As per a recent international survey, Mumbai is ranked as the costliest city in India.[29] On the one hand Mumbai is listed as one of the top trading centers of the world, but on the other hand, there is also much social, economic and developmental disparity.[30] Approximately 15% of Mumbai's population are migrants.[31] Further, more than half of its population is living in slums.[32] However, in recent times some stagnation or decline in migrant population is noticed due to closure of industries (textiles) in Mumbai and growing job opportunities in other parts of India.[33] But it should be noted that Mumbai witnesses migration not only from outside Maharashtra but also from

---

[25] T. Lakshimanasamy, "Family Survival Strategy and Migration: An Analysis of Returns to Migration," *The Indian Journal of Social Work* 51/3 (July 1990): 474.

[26] Arpita Banerjee and Saraswati Raju, "Gendered Mobility: Women Migrants and Work in Urban India," *Economic and Political Weekly* 44/28 (7 November, 2009): 115.

[27] Sunita Kumari, "Tribal Migrant Women as Domestic Workers in Mumbai," *Economic and Political Weekly* 50/16 (18 April, 2015): 85.

[28] M. H. Suryanarayana, "Human Development Challenges of Metropolis: Mumbai" (The International Policy Centre for Inclusive Growth, October 2013), http://www.ipc-undp.org/pub/IPCOnePager223.pdf (12 September, 2014).

[29] PTI, "Mumbai Continues to Be Most Expensive City in India: Survey," *India Today*, (17 June, 2015), http://indiatoday.intoday.in/story/mumbairemainsmostexpensivecityofindiasurvey/1/445178.html (17 June, 2015).

[30] "Mumbai Human Development Report 2009" (Mumbai: Municipal Corporation of Greater Mumbai, 2010), http://mhupa.gov.in/w_new/mumbai%20hdr%20complete.pdf (12 September, 2014).

[31] Zeeshan Shaikh, "Mumbai's Population Growth Rate Is Twice that of the State," *The Indian Express*, (6 January, 2014), http://indianexpress.com/article/cities/mumbai/mumbais-population-growth-rate-is-twice-that-of-the-state/ (10 June, 2015).

[32] D. P. Singh, "Poverty and Migration," in *India: Urban Poverty Report 2009* (New Delhi: Ministry of Housing and Urban Poverty Alleviation, 2009), 61.

[33] Madhavi Rajadhyaksha, "70% Migrants to Mumbai Are from Maharashtra - The Times of India,", http://timesofindia.indiatimes.com/city/mumbai/70-migrants-to-Mumbai-are-from-Maharashtra/articleshow/16428301.cms (10 July, 2015).

rural parts of Maharashtra that are affected by draughts and poor employment opportunities.

(b) Problems Faced by Migrants

In India, migration due to industrialization and urbanization help migrants progress in their social status (women and lower castes), income generation, and so on. However, it comes with a high cost. Most migrants work in hazardous conditions and suffer serious health problems. They are often taken on contract basis and suffer exploitation.[34] They also face housing, water and sanitation problem.[35] There is also problem of transportation (overcrowded public trains and buses) and limited health facilities.[36] Further, in cities there is a decline in family role and function[37] like "procreation . . . occupation, education, leisure and recreation."[38] Similarly, there is weakening of family ties because of urbanization.[39] The role and authority of the elderly has declined in the affairs of the family. Women who work outside are also expected to meet the household needs. However, women in cities particularly have greater say in the family affairs. They also now have the right to hold properties. Migrants further encounter challenges of multiple cultures, languages, and religions in cities.[40] They are often looked down as outsiders and discriminated against by the local people.[41] Migrants at times, are subjected to hate and violence by locals "sons of soil." The north Indian migrants in Mumbai were targeted by regional political parties like Shiv Sena and Maharashtra Navanirman Sena.[42] This kind of violence and hostility creates fear of social insecurity in migrants.[43]

Further, it should also be noted that constant flow of migrants to cities has increased urban unemployment.[44] In cities, it is reported that the juvenile delinquency among adolescents are common in families with socio-economic problems and disturbed family relationship.[45] Rapid urbanization, unemployment,

---

[34] Gian Singh and Shruti Mehra, "Migration," 25.

[35] B. Kuppuswamy, *Social Change in India*, 285.

[36] "Mumbai Human Development Report 2009."

[37] R. N. Sharma, *Urban Sociology*, 17.

[38] Yogendra Singh, *Modernization of Indian Tradition*, 125.

[39] B. Kuppuswamy, *Social Change in India*, 296–297.

[40] R. Ramachandran, *Urbanization and Urban System in India*, 103.

[41] Gian Singh and Shruti Mehra, "Migration," 25.

[42] Krishna Thevar, "MNS Attacks North Indian Hawkers at Jogeshwari in Mumbai," (29 April, 2015), http://articles.economictimes.indiatimes.com/2015-04-29/news/61653071_1_hawkers-mns-vibhag-pramukh-mns-workers (7 July, 2015).

[43] Gian Singh and Shruti Mehra, "Migration," 24.

[44] T. Lakshimanasamy, "Family Survival Strategy and Migration," 474.

[45] Gurumukh Ram Madan, *Indian Social Problems: Social Disorganization and Reconstruction: V. 1. Social Disorganization* (New Delhi: Allied Publishers Private Limited, 1989), 71.

and poverty are causing serious mental health problems like anxiety and depression[46] resulting into increased rate of suicide and divorce cases.[47]

Apart from the above issues, the migrants also often encounter the problem of loneliness. Let us study in detail the causes and impact of loneliness on migrants.

3. Understanding the Problem of Loneliness

John Cacioppo a psychologist and a leading researcher working on the problem of loneliness, defines loneliness as a "debilitating psychological condition characterised by a deep sense of emptiness, worthlessness, lack of control and personal threat."[48] So, loneliness is not physical isolation but a psychological condition. Further, Ira Tanner argues that loneliness is commonly suffered by all and it is not absence of friends but lack of quality relationship.[49] Tanner points out that loneliness "is not separation from people in a physical sense but separation from them emotionally."[50] B. W. Grant says that loneliness "is an unpleasant affect, combining sadness and anxiety, a felt response to the absence of sufficient relational contact."[51] Thus, loneliness is also lack of relationship not in terms of number of contacts but it has to do with the kind of contacts and the quality of relationship that a person has.

Further, Cacioppo clarifies that "loneliness becomes an issue of serious concern only when it settles in long enough to create a persistent, self-reinforcing loop of negative thoughts, sensations, and behaviors."[52] The same view is attested by the authors in the book *Loneliness, Stress and Wellbeing: A Helper's Guide* where they say that some level of loneliness is alright but chronic loneliness is dangerous.[53] So, the earlier it is dealt with the less is the impact.

(a) Causes of Loneliness

The migrant population is more prone to suffer loneliness in urban cities. There are many factors that trigger loneliness in a person. However, these factors are

---

[46] Jitendra K. Trivedi, Himanshu Sareen, and Mohan Dhyani, "Rapid Urbanization - Its Impact on Mental Health: A South Asian Perspective," *Indian Journal of Psychiatry* 50/3 (September 2008): 3–4.

[47] R. N. Sharma, *Urban Sociology*, 2.

[48] Homa Khaleeli, "Britain's Loneliness Epidemic," *The Guardian*, (22 Jan 2013), http://www.theguardian.com/society/2013/jan/22/thelonelinessepidemic (20 January, 2015).

[49] Ira J. Tanner, *Loneliness: The Fear of Love* (New York: Harper & Row, 1973), 1.

[50] Ira J. Tanner, *Loneliness*, 48.

[51] B. W. Grant, "Loneliness and Isolation," *Dictionary of Pastoral Care and Counseling*, edited by Rodney J. Hunter (Nashville: Abingdon Press, 2005), 663.

[52] John T. Cacioppo and William Patrick, *Loneliness: Human Nature and the Need for Social Connection* (New York: W. W. Norton, 2009), 7.

[53] Philip M. Murphy and Gary A. Kupshik, *Loneliness, Stress and Well-Being: A Helper's Guide* (London: Routledge, 1992), 62.

not unique to Mumbai city alone but can be noticed in any urban and industrial centers with varying degrees. Some of the major causes for loneliness among migrants in Mumbai are briefly mentioned below.

(i) Lack of Healthy Communication

The foremost thing for people is to have healthy social interaction and engage in positive activities to fight loneliness.[54] But in urban centers, it is noticed that due to over population, people are physically near, but they lack intimacy.[55] Similarly, loneliness in teenagers is found when they do not have the same kind of close relationship with their parents as in childhood. Further, loneliness is also found in housewives due to lack of interaction with the outside world and in parents who neglect communication with one another while devoting their maximum time for the upbringing of children.[56] It is also found in married couples who neglect quality time together.[57]

In Mumbai people are often busy running for work and travelling in overcrowded transportations. There is lack of quality time spent with family. Moreover, the apartment system of housing leaves less opportunity for contact with neighbours. Often in cities unlike the villages people hardly interact with their neighbours. They live in the same building as complete strangers without knowing the name and family details of their immediate neighbours. There are many incidents where people have come to know the death of their neighbour only after few days due to the stench of decomposed body. The interaction of migrants with local people is often difficult when they do not know the local language. In fact, inability to communicate in the local language severely affects the social wellbeing of the migrant families. They become more prone to social isolation and loneliness. Moreover, they do not have their families in Mumbai to provide emotional support. This results into poor communication and fellowship which triggers and aggravates loneliness among migrants in Mumbai.

(ii) Feeling of Insecurity

Loneliness may be felt in the context of families not having emotional adequacy. It is also experienced by couples with disturbed marital relationship. People also experience loneliness while working with new colleagues and in a new work place. Further unemployment and retirement causes feeling of insecurity and often

---

[54] Sukhada Tatke, "Don't Ignore Signs of Loneliness," *The Times of India*, (17 April, 2011), http://timesofindia.indiatimes.com/city/mumbai/Dont-ignore-signs-of-loneliness/articleshow/8002030.cms (17 July, 2015).

[55] Craig W. Ellison, "Loneliness : A Social-Developmental Analysis," *Journal of Psychology & Theology* 6/1 (1 December, 1978): 12.

[56] Ira J. Tanner, *Loneliness*, 17–19.

[57] Edgar N. Jackson, *Understanding Loneliness* (Philadelphia: Fortress Press, 1980), 90-91.

creates loneliness.[58] This leads to experience of emptiness and meaninglessness in migrants.[59] In the elderly, loneliness strikes when they feel left out by family[60] due to migration of children. They may feel lonely also due to death of a spouse/ longtime friend and immobility due to old age.[61] Loneliness in people may be felt due to isolation, separation, fear, deprivation, anxiety, stressful situations, competition, and need for adjustments.[62] It is also because of absence of loved ones.[63] This is true for migrant workers in Mumbai particularly who do not have their families with them. Moreover, the work culture in Mumbai is very stressful. People often experience social isolation. All these factors trigger deep sense of loneliness in migrants who are in a new place away from home.

(iii) Change in Family System

The transition from traditional joint family to modern nuclear family system due to large scale rural to urban migration causes emotional stress. In urban nuclear, family the relationship tends to be mechanical and the elderly tend to become out of place.[64] Thus, the weakening of support found in traditional joint families generate emotional disturbance in migrants.[65] Cacioppo, while talking from the western perspective, cites Robert Weiss to say that "nuclear families, relocating in and out of faceless suburbs, necessarily focus inward, a situation that places intense emotional demands on family members to be 'all' for one another."[66] So, there is lack of share and care as a community in cities where people can confidently share about their personal concerns with one another.[67] Migrants generally are forced to adopt this modern nuclear family system due to lack of housing and finance. It results into change in the role and authority of family members. The women have to help the family by working outside. Children experience parental neglect. These things become a major factor that causes loneliness.

(iv) Routine Work Culture

Tanner observes that people are very much occupied daily with the structured time in institutions like "schools, work, and church". The problem they face is

---

[58] Edgar N. Jackson, *Understanding Loneliness*, 38–41.

[59] L. Stanislaus, "The Concerns of Migration and the Local Church," in *Migration and Mission in India*`, edited by L. Stanislaus and Jose Joseph (Delhi: ISPCK, 2007), 233.

[60] Ira J. Tanner, *Loneliness*, 19.

[61] Ira J. Tanner, *Loneliness*, 110–111.

[62] Edgar N. Jackson, *Understanding Loneliness*, 15–19.

[63] Edgar N. Jackson, *Understanding Loneliness*, 44–45.

[64] Edgar N. Jackson, *Understanding Loneliness*, 64–66.

[65] James P. Alter, et al., *Community Development in Indian's Industrial Urban Areas* (Bangalore: The Committee for Literature on Social Concerns, 1958), 25.

[66] John T. Cacioppo and William Patrick, *Loneliness*, 251.

[67] John T. Cacioppo and William Patrick, *Loneliness*, 252.

how to utilize the spare times that is found apart from these structured times. Thus, routine activity or even inability to pass the free time results into boredom and also may produce depression and loneliness.[68] Migrants spend large amount of their spare time in front of the T.V. or on social networking sites like Facebook. They further become socially isolated and suffer loneliness.

(v) Change of Place

Migrants who come from closely related and familiar village life find the city life mechanical and alienating.[69] Today people are moving to different places having strange culture and context, as a result more number of people are experiencing anxiety and despair.[70] They also find difficulty in sharing their emotions and personal concerns.[71] Migration also generates stress and acute feeling of loneliness in single persons due to lack of companionship.[72] In cities, migrants live in a multicultural and pluralistic religious context,[73] unlike the simple and less pluralistic context of a village.[74] This isolation from their cultural roots causes anxiety[75] and loneliness. The following case study would reveal how change from familiar place to new place can trigger loneliness in a person.

> Katie grew up in a very close knit family always surrounded by relatives and friends. She was always part of all the family and church events in her community. After completing her college she got a job in the city far away from her home and family. Her job demanded lot of traveling from one city to another. She still managed to be in touch with her family especially her mother weekly through phone calls. Her entire routine was changed. After six months into the new job Katie started feeling physically drained. In her spare times she spent most of the time watching T.V. and eating junks. Eventually she realized that she had gained a lot of extra weight. Her relation with her office and the neighbourhood also became strained. All this made her question herself and her ability to relate with the larger society. She suffered from loneliness.[76]

---

[68] Ira J. Tanner, *Loneliness*, 81.

[69] James P. Alter, et al., *Community Development in Indian's Industrial Urban Areas*, 58.

[70] Edgar N. Jackson, *Understanding Loneliness*, 66.

[71] James P. Alter, et al., *Community Development in Indian's Industrial Urban Areas*, 17.

[72] Judson J. Swihart and Gerald C. Richardson, *Counseling in Times of Crisis* (Waco, Tex: Word Books, 1987), 80.

[73] Hector Andrade, "Theology in a Pluralistic Context," 46.

[74] R. N. Sharma, *Urban Sociology*, 21.

[75] Hector Andrade, "Theology in a Pluralistic Context," 46.

[76] John T. Cacioppo and William Patrick, *Loneliness*, 3-4.

Cacioppo cites this case study for analyzing the problem of loneliness from a different perspective. However, we can notice how Katie who migrated from a small and familiar community to a new city for work started to experience loneliness. It highlights how migrants push themselves into social isolation. Moreover, the lack of familiar environment triggers depression and loneliness.

(b) Impact of Loneliness

Loneliness in urban center is causing serious health issues like dementia, obesity, and even more chances of heart attack.[77] It can also lead to increased consumption of alcohol, lack of proper sleep, fatigue, and premature aging.[78] Often people experiencing loneliness develop a sedentary lifestyle and are prone to consume lot of fatty foods as per a study.[79] In young people loneliness may result into "depression, the use of drugs, delinquency, failure in school, and sometimes suicide."[80] It "can also awaken latent mental disorders," which might have been inactive due to care by family.[81] This is because, in loneliness a person is threatened with increased and irrational feeling of fear and anxiety. Tanner says that loneliness affects all aspects of our life, "our hopes, ambitions, dreams, vitality, desires, wants . . . our actual physical bodies. Eating and sleeping are frequently affected." Tanner however clarifies that these symptoms may be noticed even in people not suffering loneliness.[82] The urban routine work culture and lifestyle of Mumbai is very stressful. Moreover, the migrants relatively lack the social support and care to counter the impact of such stressful living. Thus, the impact of loneliness on them is more severe.

Human beings are interdependent and when this kind of intimacy is absent, people experience loneliness. There is increase in the rate of suicide and attempted suicide in modern society because of loneliness.[83] It "becomes a spiral downward that diminishes a person's capacity to relate to others and to envision a hopeful future."[84] LeShan as cited by Jackson "equate[s] acute loneliness with a loss of meaning for life, a loss of direction and purpose, and a loss of some life-sustaining

[77] Homa Khaleeli, "Britain's Loneliness Epidemic."

[78] Kendra Cherry, "Loneliness Causes, Effects and Treatments," http://psychology.about.com/od/psychotherapy/a/loneliness.htm (20 January, 2015).

[79] John T. Cacioppo and William Patrick, *Loneliness*, 45.

[80] Ira J. Tanner, *Loneliness*, 17-18.

[81] "Busy Lives and Lonely Hearts," *The Telegraph*, (15 November, 2005), http://www.telegraphindia.com/1051115/asp/atleisure/story_5476475.asp (18 July, 2015).

[82] Ira J. Tanner, *Loneliness*, 11.

[83] Paul. E. Johnson, *Person and Counselor* (Nashville: Abingdon Press, 1967), 152-154.

[84] L Gregory Jones, "My Facebook Friends," *Christian Century* 125/14 (15 July, 2008): 35.

attachment that gave life security and significance."[85] Tanner says "uncaring attitude" of others also adds to the severity of loneliness.[86]

G. R. Madan points out that the mechanical life in industrial cities, long working hours, pathetic working and housing conditions, low wages, and job insecurity results into problem of drinking.[87] He adds that loneliness might also lead to drinking in workers who are away from their families.[88] Majority of contract workers in Mumbai are migrants. They work in poor and hazardous working conditions. They live in slums due to high cost of living. They also have no proper access to health care. Moreover, the public health care facilities are limited and overburdened due to increasing population in Mumbai.

As seen earlier, problem of loneliness is not unique to migrants in Mumbai but is suffered by others as well. However, the migrants in Mumbai and elsewhere often are more socially isolated. They also lack the needed support system of family and friends. This makes them vulnerable to loneliness and depression.

4. Pastoral Care to Migrant Families

(a) Defining Pastoral Care

It is apt to mention the definition by J. W. Fowler as quoted by Holger who sees pastoral care as "sponsoring the individual through the community of faith in the sense of an ecology of care and of vocation."[89] This highlights the community aspect of pastoral care and reveals that this community of faith is interdependent "ecology." Further, the definition of William Clebsch and Charles Jaekle highlight the major areas of help covered under the arena of pastoral care. They say it "consists of helping acts, done by representative Christian persons, directed towards the healing, sustaining, guiding, and reconciling of troubled persons whose troubles arise in the context of ultimate meanings and concerns."[90] It is interesting to note that pastoral care is not a general helping act but it is in the context of ultimate meaning and purpose of human existence that is God. To this definition Howard Clinebell adds the aspect of nourishment to pastoral care.[91] The phrase "representative Christian person" in this definition is not just referring to the pastor but the whole church.[92] In this sense, pastoral care is a

---

[85] Edgar N. Jackson, *Understanding Loneliness*, 52–53.

[86] Ira J. Tanner, *Loneliness*, 15.

[87] Gurumukh Ram Madan, *Indian Social Problems*, 155–156.

[88] Gurumukh Ram Madan, *Indian Social Problems*, 162.

[89] Holger Eschmann, "Towards a Pastoral Care in a Trinitarian Perspective," *The Journal of Pastoral Care* 54/4 (Winter 2000): 422.

[90] William A. Clebsch and Charles R. Jaekle, *Pastoral Care in Historical Perspective: An Essay with Exhibits* (New York: Jason Aronson, 1974), 4.

[91] Howard John Clinebell, *Basic Types of Pastoral Care and Counseling: Resources for the Ministry of Healing and Growth* (Thiruvalla: SuVartha Bhavan, 1984), 44.

[92] William A. Clebsch and Jaekle, *Pastoral Care in Historical Perspective*, 4.

helping act to enable a troubled person to overcome the hurdles and experience wholeness in life.

(b) Biblical Basis for Pastoral Care to Migrants

God liberating his people from Egyptian slavery becomes the central theme in the history and theology of the people of Israel. In the Exodus event, we see that Yahweh sides with the exploited Hebrew migrants in Egypt and leads them in their struggle for freedom and justice.[93] Bastian Wielenga makes a critique that the Bible refers to Egypt not as a developed civilization but as house of bondage because it was built by exploiting the Hebrew migrant workers for military purpose and building tombs (pyramids).[94] But one most important implication of Egyptian slavery is that God commanded Israelites to remember their past as aliens in order to show hospitability to strangers and aliens who are with them (Lev. 19:34).[95]

In the New Testament, we see Jesus' Parable of the Good Samaritan primarily teaching us to care for the strangers.[96] Further we see the Son of Man identifying himself with the needy strangers. He says "I was hungry and you gave me food, I was thirsty and you gave me drink, I was a stranger and you welcomed me ..." (Mat. 25:35-36). Jesus equates service to the needy with service to God. He experienced forsakenness and loneliness on the cross and through his death opened the way for us to have true fellowship with God and humans.[97] It is interesting to note in Mt. 25: 35 that welcoming a helpless and distressed stranger was equated by Jesus to welcoming the Son of Man.

In conclusion, we see Dhyanchand Carr who while talking about God's command to extend hospitality to strangers clarifies that God stands not just for the Israelites but also for the dependent strangers (Deut. 10:17-19). Thus, from the Bible we see that God expects the Church to engage in the issues of migrants who are strangers in the land. The church is commanded to provide pastoral care not just to Christian migrants but to all.[98]

(c) Present Engagement of the Church with Migrants in Mumbai

Internationally, the Roman Catholic Church has established the Pontifical Council for the Pastoral Care of Migrants and Itinerant People, basically to

---

[93] Hector Andrade, "Theology in a Pluralistic Context," 48.

[94] Bastian Wielenga, *Labour: Serving God or Mammon?* (Delhi: ISPCK, 1987), 4–5.

[95] Christine D. Phol, "Biblical Issues in Mission and Migration," *Missiology* 31/1 (January 2003): 5-6.

[96] L. Stanislaus, "The Concerns of Migration and the Local Church," 228.

[97] Roger F. Hurding, *The Bible and Counselling* (London: Hodder & Stoughton, 1984), 135-136.

[98] Dhynanchand Carr, "Towards a Proper Christian Response to the Problems Faced by Refugees and Migrant Workers," in *Uprooted People in Asia* (Hong Kong: Christian Conference of Asia, 1995), 81.

address the different issues of the migrants and refugees.[99] However, its activity is not much heard of in Mumbai. In general, the church has no designated approach to engage with the migrants in Mumbai. However, the church plays an important but informal role in extending fellowship and social identity to migrant Christian families. This can be witnessed by the fact that the migrant Christians in Mumbai get to meet their relatives and friends from home towns mainly in the church on Sundays. Also, those migrants who are staying single in Mumbai feel a sense of family in churches having relatives or people from their native place.

Further it can be seen that the caste system which may be rigidly adhered to in villages often becomes dormant in urban churches enabling functional relationship and fellowship, even if caste is not completely eradicated. Importantly church shares in the joy and sorrows of migrant Christians by way of pastoral visits, care and support during crisis, and spiritual nurture. However, pastoral care is mostly benefiting those who attend the church. But it is not adequately reaching lonely people who often do not come forward seeking help. They are socially isolated due to the apartment system of living in Mumbai where individuality and anonymity exists.

Overall pastoral care by the church to non-Christian migrants is negligible in comparison to large migrant population in Mumbai. Whatever little general care is received by them is indirectly through charity and outreach programs. However, Christian NGOs are actively involved in addressing the problem of migrants. They are mainly engaged in community care, running day care centers (child care), old age homes, and orphanages, capacity building of women through education and vocation training, rescue and rehabilitation of girls forced into prostitution, health care, awareness and medical care to HIV/AIDS patient and their families, working among youths struggling with addiction, and the like. Most of the work by Christian NGOs is done in the urban slums where migrant families are mainly found.

Those NGOs which are engaged in community work encourage greater participation of all involved and enable free and open communication and fellowship. This has been very effective in breaking the social isolation of migrant families. There are many small house churches in different slum pockets of Mumbai. They are instrumental in fostering healthy fellowship among poor migrant families. It provides a sense of spiritual care and belongingness to the migrants.

However, considering the severity of loneliness and growing number of migrant population in Mumbai, the present engagement of Church and Christian NGOs is very minimal.

---

[99] http://www.vatican.va/roman_curia/pontifical_councils/migrants/s_index_generaldocuments/rc_pc_migrants_gendocuments.htm

(d) Pastoral Care Addressing Loneliness

People suffering from loneliness rarely confess to a counsellor that they are lonely. However, symptoms of loneliness like depression, anxiety, anger can be seen in such people. Further, before extending help it is important but equally difficult to ascertain whether a person is indeed suffering from loneliness and if so what is it that they are lonely about?[100] The form and level of pastoral care to migrants experiencing loneliness depends on many factors like the degree of loneliness whether momentary or chronic. Pastoral care also depends on factors like migrant's place and type of work, whether staying with family or single, their marital status, and so on. The following are some of the effective ways in which church in Mumbai can involve in providing pastoral care to migrant families who often suffer loneliness.

(i) Church Must be Open and Welcoming Community

The Church is not just to help the community members to reconcile with God, but also with one another. It is also not an additional communal organization in the society.[101] Howard Clinebell, as cited by Howard Stone, is of the view that unlike other counsellors the pastor is in an advantageous position to help people in crisis. In addition, the pastor has the church as the resource to assist in this endeavor.[102] Christian Phol argues that the church must understand that hospitality to migrants is not an outreach program but a Christian way of life. So it should live and relate with migrants and their families.[103] This is indeed a challenge to the church in Mumbai because it is easy to plan few outreach programs, but it takes serious commitment as a church in order to be an open and welcoming community of Christ. The church must become a welcoming community and help migrants participate in the community life.[104] It should welcome migrants to become friends and not guests,[105] and share in the fellowship based on kingdom values[106] of love, forgiveness, and justice.

Church must also promote interfaith dialogue and provide pastoral care to migrants in order to help grow mutually in faith.[107] This is relevant to the pluralistic context of Mumbai. Church as a community must nourish the faith of the migrants and stand with them for their rights and justice.[108] As a result, migrant

---

[100] Philip M. Murphy and Gary A. Kupshik, *Loneliness, Stress and Well-Being*, 62.

[101] James P. Alter, et al., *Community Development in Indian's Industrial Urban Areas*, 128–129.

[102] Howard W. Stone, *Crisis Counseling* (Philadelphia: Fortress Press, 1980), 8.

[103] Christine D. Phol, "Biblical Issues in Mission and Migration," 11.

[104] L. Stanislaus, "The Concerns of Migration and the Local Church," 233.

[105] Christine D. Phol, "Biblical Issues in Mission and Migration," 13.

[106] Christine D. Phol, "Biblical Issues in Mission and Migration," 10.

[107] L. Stanislaus, "The Concerns of Migration and the Local Church," 236–237.

[108] L. Stanislaus, "The Concerns of Migration and the Local Church," 234.

families (Christians and non-Christians) will be encouraged to positively interact and overcome loneliness. Even the aspect of coming together as a congregation regularly ensures the mental and physical wellbeing of those who are part of a congregation in contrast to those who do not partake in church life. It is revealed by Cacioppo based on an extensive study done by sociologist Lynda Powell and others.[109] This must encourage the church in Mumbai to become centers of rich fellowship where the lonely person can find help and healing.

(ii) Special Care to Elderly

Elderly in cities find difficulty in adjusting with modern nuclear family system. Loneliness among elderly is one major problem in India.[110] Psychiatrists say that elderly do not need medicines to fight loneliness but proper counselling, therefore the society should collectively respond to it.[111] Churches should plan regular visits to the elderly and provide religious devotional books and other resources which will be of immense help in fighting loneliness.[112] Pastors must assist the elderly in coming out from their sufferings of loneliness and find hope for their living. This is possible through treatment and proper pastoral care.[113]

Churches can intervene to help the elderly resolve their relationship crisis with the children and other family members. It will restore relationship and allow healthy communication in the families. Also, migrant elderly are considered as unemployable after retirement and are forced to remain idle irrespective of the fact that many of them may be fit for work. One way to address this unemployment issue among migrant elderly is by generating light employment opportunities for them in order to keep them physically and mentally active. It to a large extent will help them fight loneliness.

(iii) Educative Counselling

Pastors must make use of educative counselling wherein people are provided relevant information on particular issues in order to help them learn how to cope with crisis situations. It is also essential when people (migrants) want to choose vocation, plan for marriage and retirement.[114] The educative program of

[109] John T. Cacioppo and William Patrick, *Loneliness*, 260–261.

[110] Kounteya Sinha, "Loneliness, Not Obesity, Biggest Killer of Elderly," *Times of India*, (18 February, 2014), http://timesofindia.indiatimes.com/home/science/Lonelinessnotobesitybiggest killerofelderly/articleshow/30589605.cms (20 January, 2015).

[111] Dwaipayan Ghosh, "Killer Loneliness Stalks Elderly Citizens," *Times of India*, (6 April, 2014), http://timesofindia.indiatimes.com/city/kolkata/Killerlonelinessstalkselderlycitizens/articleshow/33303457.cms (20 January, 2015).

[112] Dosia Carlson, "'Help! I'm Lonely!' : A Look at the Causes of Loneliness in Older Adults, and Some Responses," *Church & Society* 89/3 (1 January, 1999): 86.

[113] William E. Hulme, *The Pastoral Care of Families: Its Theology and Practice* (Nashville: Abingdon Press, 1962), 172.

[114] Howard John Clinebell, *Basic Types of Pastoral Care and Counselling*, 337–338.

the church must also include "social skills training" to improve the conversation and interpersonal relations.[115] It will help to create awareness about the problem of loneliness. Moreover, it can guide the young migrants in Mumbai who, in order to avoid the pain of loneliness and rejection, become addicted to drugs, alcohol, prostitution, social networking sites like Facebook, pornography and the like. Educative counselling can also create awareness and help the people to make positive changes in their lifestyle and eating habits. Lastly, the church can organize informal short term language (local) course for the migrants. This will enable the migrants to improve their relationship with others.

(iv) Small Support Groups

The concept of small support group is adaptive to any situation and groups. It is seen that the support groups formed by the pastors to visit the needy not only help people in times of crisis, but also signals "a sense of belonging that can offset loneliness and isolation."[116] Further, in group counselling, the participants are enabled to help themselves.[117] Such groups can be easily started by church members in their work places and in their localities as these are informal friendly care groups which can invite even the non-Christians. The friends from other faiths will find such fellowship groups very welcoming without any threat of religious tags to it. Such groups can encourage mutual sharing and caring. This will also reduce feelings of insecurity and of social isolation often experienced by migrants in cities.

(v) Lay Pastoral Telecare

Telephone helpline is successfully used by many government and non-government agencies. In the same way, pastoral care by church can be provided to people by using telephone. In this, the pastor trains the congregation members to provide pastoral care to people through telephone.[118] It is very helpful to effectively reach maximum number of people. Pastors should use this in addition to their individual service as it is impossible for them to cover everyone.[119] Telecare in the context of Mumbai is suitable, because almost everyone has mobile phones. Moreover travelling, which is time consuming often, becomes a hindrance for pastoral care because people are geographically scattered in Mumbai. Telecare will make the lonely person feel that he/she has someone in the city who can listen to his/her feelings of fear and anxiety.

Telecare to be more effective should be both ways that is the team of church members should call the people and at the same time the people should be able to

---

[115] Philip M. Murphy and Gary A. Kupshik, *Loneliness, Stress and Well-Being*, 64.

[116] Howard W. Stone, *Crisis Counseling*, 8.

[117] Howard John Clinebell, *Basic Types of Pastoral Care and Counselling*, 367–368.

[118] Lavonne Zwart Schaafsma, "The Impact of Lay Pastoral Telecare," 66.

[119] Lavonne Zwart Schaafsma, "The Impact of Lay Pastoral Telecare," 64.

call the church in times of crisis. For this, basic counselling skill should be part of the training. This telecare is primarily possible in the context of a congregation, but it can immensely benefit others in the neighbourhood. However, in order to extend this telecare to suffering people in the society, proper planning and implementation along with a dedicated team in the church is must.

(vi) Logotherapy

Earlier we have seen that loneliness results into a deep sense of emptiness and worthlessness. People suffering from severe loneliness fail to see the meaning and purpose of existence. Further, pastors are theologically equipped to respond to the "questions of meaning" in life, so they must help people to find ultimate meaning in life by developing relationship with God in the midst of loneliness.[120] In this process, pastors can also use Logotherapy developed by Viktor Frankl. Logotherapy by definition means "analysis of human existence and the search for its meaning . . . ."[121] So, it basically helps people in searching for real meaning and purpose for their existence, even in the midst of painful struggles.[122]

Logotherapy, even though is secular in content, uses many deep theological insights which are closer to the Christian faith.[123] This therapy is said to be effective for those who face severe social problems like unemployment,[124] because it is of the view that life has unconditional meaning even in the most hostile conditions.[125] In Logotherapy, a person is helped to face even the most difficult situations in life and is redirected to find life's meaning.[126] Frankl as cited in the book *Abnormal Psychology and Modern Life* opines that there are three types of values used in Logotherapy to search for meaning in life. First is "*creative values*" attained as a result of doing or accomplishing a duty. The second is "*experiential values*" attained by experiencing life, the beauty, and love. The third is "*attitudinal values*" which enables a person to see the unavoidable pain and sufferings in life with a positive attitude.[127]

---

[120] Howard W. Stone, *Crisis Counseling*, 8.

[121] Raoul Shindler, "The Development of Psychotherapy in Austria Since 1945," in *Progress in Psychotherapy*, ed. Frieda Fromm-Reichmann and J. L. Moreno, vol. 1 (New York: Geunw & Stratton, 1956), 270.

[122] Viktor E. Frankl, *Man's Search for Meaning: An Introduction to Logotherapy* (Allahabad: St. Paul Society, 1977), 106.

[123] Roger F. Hurding, *Roots and Shoots: A Guide to Counseling and Psychotherapy* (London, 1985), 135.

[124] Harold Ernest Hatt, "Existential Analysis and Logotherapy : The Contribution of Viktor E Frankl," *Encounter* 26/3 (1 June, 1965): 335.

[125] Reuven P. Bulka, "Logotherapy as a Response to the Holocaust," *Tradition* 15/1-2 (1 March, 1975): 90.

[126] Viktor E. Frankl, *Man's Search for Meaning*, 106.

[127] *Abnormal Psychology and Modern Life* (Bombay: D. B. Taraporevela Sons & Co. Pvt. Ltd., 1969), 593.

Logotherapy to migrants who are experiencing loneliness can enable them to realize that their family's future depends on them and nothing can replace their role and responsibility towards them (creative value). In Mumbai, where life is mechanical and monotonous, people can be guided to see the beauty of life, the loving memory of a daughter back in the village, the mercy of God (experiential value). It will help overcome the stress and tension of work. Finally, Logotherapy in pastoral care can help a person in changing his/her attitude even though the situation may be grim.

(vii) Referral Counselling

Last but equally important is providing referral counselling to people suffering from acute loneliness. Referral counselling involves guiding and directing the needy person to experts in other professions.[128] It is advisable because migrants often face not just social isolation but also face health problems, legal conflict or financial issues in work which are beyond the scope of pastors. Moreover, the problem of loneliness hinders normal thinking capacity of people. So, pastors can play an important role in helping the person to assess the seriousness of the condition and encourage him/her to go for the relevant professional services. Most importantly pastors should refrain from offering spiritual solution to anything and everything.

7. Recommendations for Churches in Mumbai

Having so far sufficiently dealt with the issue of loneliness among migrant families and also studying different kinds of pastoral care to this problem, this section will try to offer some of the practical steps that the church in Mumbai can use to help people suffering from loneliness particularly the migrant families.

- A visitor's book can be maintained at the entrance of the church and ushers from the congregation can be assigned to welcome new comers with warmth to provide their names, contact details, and prayer points if any in order to visit them as soon as possible. This should be done only after knowing their willingness in advance for such a pastoral visit. This will also help in reaching out to non-members and non-Christians who visit the church.
- Take initiative to personally invite new visitors to join the coffee fellowship after the church and give them company to ensure that they are not feeling left alone or neglected.
- Form a team comprising of youths, elderly, men, and women with the task of looking for new people in the church and try building individual rapport. This will convey a sense of belonging in the visitors.

[128] Howard John Clinebell, *Basic Types of Pastoral Care and Counselling*, 324.

- Conduct seminars and retreats for families, students, working people, and elderly to create awareness on loneliness, addiction, relationship conflicts, parenting, stewardship and other relevant issues.
- Church should provide free career guidance to young people from the neighbourhood. It will help extend pastoral care to non-Christian young adults experiencing loneliness.
- Train interested church members to form and facilitate small informal fellowship groups in their locality and work place. It also can become an effective way to share love and care to non-Christian migrants experiencing loneliness.
- Have a committed team of lay people from the church to periodically telephone members and other people as per the book of visitors in the church. Ideally, there should be certain dedicated telephone numbers which will enable the lonely migrants to call the church in order to share their problems, prayer concerns, and seek guidance.
- Network with other agencies like NGO's, educational institutions, and hospitals in order to deal with mental health problems and suicidal tendencies among students affected by migration and also to cater to large number of migrants experiencing loneliness.
- Pastors should help lonely people to search for meaning and purpose in life by using techniques of Logotherapy while providing pastoral care to them.
- Church should engage the elderly and retired people in the church life by providing them small tasks like writing stories for Sunday schools, write up for church bulletin, supervision work, coordinating the men and women fellowship groups.
- Provide financial and medical help to the elderly from migrant families who are lonely and in need of help.
- Involve the Sunday school and youth fellowship while visiting old age and orphanage homes, and also while visiting lonely elderly and disabled members of the church.
- Maintain a small library in the church having books, CDs on devotional music, teachings and informative materials. It can be run by women fellowship or others.

Conclusion

Migration is as old as human history. People migrate for various reasons. However, the process of migration creates certain problems for the migrants and their families. It impacts not only the place of origin but also the place of migration. The migrants encounter imbalance in their physical, psychological, social, economic, cultural, and spiritual life. This imbalance is primarily because migration involves uprooting people from their familiar surroundings to putting them in a new place with strange culture, language, and people.

Mumbai which is a cosmopolitan center is home for people from diverse background. It as a trade and business center provides job opportunities. However, the city is over populated and congested which burdens the housing, sanitation, and health facilities. Migrants who work in chemical factories and construction sites are exposed to dangerous working condition. Migrants due to high cost of living cannot afford to bring their families to Mumbai. The slums with poor sanitation and water facilities are the only place poor migrants can often afford to stay. One common line across migrants in Mumbai both rich and poor, educated and illiterate, single and those with family is that they all suffer greater level of loneliness. This does not mean that only migrants suffer loneliness in Mumbai. In fact loneliness is common to all at some point of time in life, but the living and working conditions of migrants easily trigger loneliness in them, moreover they lack the familial and social support unlike the local people in Mumbai.

God in the Bible commands his people to extend hospitality to the strangers (migrants). This calls the church in Mumbai to proactively engage in building the migrants who are walking alone in the valley of loneliness. But the present engagement of the church is very negligible and indirect. The church in Mumbai should become a community that is open and welcoming strangers in its fellowship. Special care needs to be extended to the helpless elderly suffering loneliness. The migrants particularly the youths in order to overcome loneliness get hooked to drugs and other forms of addiction. This calls for the church to create awareness by way of educative counselling. Sustaining the wellness of migrant families can be achieved by encouraging them to join small supportive care groups in neighbourhood and work place. Pastoral care should make use of Logotherapy to help the lonely person search for meaning and purpose in life. In the context of Mumbai the use of telephone for providing pastoral care by the church will have wider reach and benefit. The pastors should also do referral counselling to appropriately help the lonely person who may need additional and expert help.

Thus, it can be said that unlike any other helping profession the pastors not only have knowledge of counselling but also possess theological insights, and also the rich resource in the form of congregation. This community aspect of pastoral care by the church is of immense support to the pastors in helping the migrant families struggling with the problem of loneliness in Mumbai.

Some Further Readings

- Abraham, K. C. “A Theological Response to Ecological Crisis.” *Bangalore Theological Forum* 25/1 (March, 1993).
- Abraham, K. C. et al. *Global Warming: Implication for South Asia and the Role of Churches.* Bangalore: SATHRI, 1994.
- Abraham, K. C. “Women Struggling against Violence.” *Voices from Third World Country* 126/16 (June, 1994).
- Abrecht, Paul. *The Church and Rapid Social Change.* New York: Doubledry & Company, 1961.
- Adogame, Afe, Janice McLean and Anderson Jeremiah, eds. *Engaging the World.* Oxford: Regnum, 2014.
- Anderson-Rajkumar, Evangeline. “Decoding ‘Silence-Voice-Speech’ As an Epistemological Tool for a Theology of Engagement.” In *God of Life, Lead Us to Justice and Peace: A Theological Reflection in the Context of India Today.* Edited by H. Vanlaluva (West Bengal: Department of Research/SATHRI.
- Bennett, John. *When Christians Make Political Decisions.* New York: Association Press, 1964.
- Boff, Leonardo. *Ecology and Liberation, a New Paradigm.* New York: Orbis Books, 1995.
- Bosch, David J. *Transforming Mission: Paradigm Shifts in Theology of Mission.* New York: Orbis Books, 1996.
- Boswell, John. *Christianity, Social Tolerance and Homosexuality.* Chicago: The University of Chicago, 1980.
- Bradbury, John P. *Perpetually Reforming: A Theology of Church Reform and Renewal.* Liverpool: T & T Clark, 2013.
- Bretherton, Luke. *Christianity and Contemporary Politics: The Conditions and Possibilities of Faithful Witness,* Wiley Blackwell, 2010.
- Bucar, Elizabeth M. Barbara Barnett, *Does Human Rights Need God?* Michigan: Eerdmans, 2005.
- Carr, Dhynanchand “Towards a Proper Christian Response to the Problems Faced by Refugees and Migrant Workers.” In *Uprooted People in Asia.* Hong Kong: Christian Conference of Asia, 1995.

- Chase-Dunn, Christopher and Salvatore J. Babones, ed. *Global Social Change: Historical and Comparative Perspectives*, The Johns Hopkins University Press, 2006.
- Cherian, M. T. *Hindutva Agenda and Minority Rights.* Bangalore: Centre for Contemporary Christianity, 2007.
- Chopra, Geeta. *Child Rights in India: Challenges and Social Action.* New Delhi: Springer, 2015.
- Coleman, John A. ed. *Christian Political Ethics*, Princeton University Press, 2008.
- Cox, Harvey *the Secular City.* New York: Macmillan, 1965.
- Cox, Harvey. *Religion in the Secular City.* New York: Simon and Schuster, 1984.
- Das, Somen. "An Ethical-Theological Perspective on Human Sexuality." *Religion & Society* 54/4 (December, 2009).
- David, James. "Ageing in India," *Integral Liberation: Quarterly Review for Justice, Development and Social Change* 5/3 (September, 2001).
- Dennison, Jack. *City Reaching: On the Road to Community Transformation.* Pasadena: William Carey, 1999.
- Dhawan, M. L. *Education of Children with Special Needs.* Delhi: Isha Books, 2005.
- Dietrich, Gabriele and Bas Wielenga. *Towards Understanding Indian Society.* Thiruvalla: Christian Sahitya Samithi, 2008.
- Evans, James H. *We Shall All Be Changed: Social Problems and Theological Renewal.* Minneapolis: Fortress Press, 1987.
- Forell, George W. *Christian Social Teaching.* Minnesota: Augsburg, 1971.
- Forell, George W. *Christian Social Teachings: A Reader in Christian Social Ethics from Bible to the Present.* Minneapolis: Fortress, 2013.
- Furniss, George. *Sociology for Pastoral Care.* Britain: SPCK, 1994.
- George, Samuel. "Persons with Disabilities in India." In *Doing Theology from Disability Perspective.* Edited by Wati Longchar and Gordon Cowans. Kolkata: Atesea, 2011.
- Granberg-Michaelson, Wesley. *Redeeming the Creation.* Geneva: Risk Book Series, 1992.
- Hunter, James Davidson. *To Change the World: The Irony, Tragedy, and Possibility of Christianity in the Late Modern World.* Oxford: Oxford University Press, 2010.
- Hunter, James Davison. *To Change the World: The Irony, Tragedy, and Possibility of Christianity in the Late Modern World.* New York: Oxford University Press, 2010.
- Johnstone, Patrick. *The Church is Bigger than You Think.* Great Britain: Christian Focus, 1998.
- Joy, K. P. *Greening of Minds.* Thiruvalla: Christava Sahitya Samithi, 2001.

- Kabue, Samuel N. "Church and Society's Response to Disability: Historical and Sociological Perspective," In *Disabled God Amidst Broken People: Doing Theology from Disability Perspective.* Edited by Wati Longchar and Gordon Cowans. Manila: The ATESEA, 2007.
- Kirby Sandra and Kate Mckenna. *Experience, Research, and Social Change: Methods from the Margins.* Toronto: Garaband, 1989.
- Kuppuswamy, B. *Social Change in India.* Delhi: Vikas, 1972.
- Kuruvilla, Philip & Wati Longchar, eds. *HIV & AIDS: Towards Inclusive Communities.* Nagpur: NCCI, 2013.
- Kuruvilla, Philip, ed., *HIV/AIDS: A Handbook for the Church in India.* Delhi: ISPCK, WCC & NCCI, 2004.
- Lemtur, Maong. *Christ in the Changing Context.* Dimapur: Tribal Development and Communication Centre, 2008.
- Leppert Sue and Francis Sullivan. *Church and Civil Society: A Theology of Engagement.* Hindmarsh: ATF, 2004.
- Lotsuro, Angeline. "Contribution of Catholic Women Missionaries to the Socio-Cultural Change among the Tribes of Northeast India," In *Christianity and Change in Northeast India.* Edited by Tanka Bahadur Subba, Joseph Uthenpurakal and Shaji Joseph Puykunnel. New Delhi: Concept, 2009.
- Madan, Gurumukh Ram. *Indian Social Problems: Social Disorganization and Reconstruction: V. 1. Social Disorganization.* New Delhi: Allied, 1989.
- Mann, Ran Singh. *Social Change and Social Research: An Indian Perspective.* New Delhi: Concept, 1988.
- Markham, Ian S. *A Theology of Engagement.* Oxford: Blackwell Publishing House, 2003.
- Mathur, S. S. *A Sociological Approach to Indian Education.* Agra: Agrawal, 2009.
- Mattam, J. SJ and P. Arockiadoss, eds. *Hindutva: An Indian Christian Response.* Bangalore: Dharmaram Publications, 2001.
- Messer, Donald E. *Breaking the Conspiracy of Silence.* Delhi: ISPCK, 2007.
- Morkuniene, Jurate. *Social Philosophy: Paradigm of Contemporary Thinking.* Washington: The Council for Research in Values and Philosophy, 2004.
- Moses, Sarah M. *Ethics and the Elderly: The Challenge of Long-Term Care.* New York: Orbis Books, 2015.
- Murray, John Courtney. *We Hold These Truths.* Maryland: Rowman & Littlefield, 2005.
- Murry, Ezamo. "Disability is a Reality Even in The Divine Community," *Journal of Tribal Studies* 16/1 (January-June, 2011).
- Nalunnakkal, George Mathew. *Green Liberation: Towards an Integral Ecotheology.* Delhi: ISPCK/NCCI, 1999.
- Natarajan, Andrew B. "Senior Citizens- Society and Religion." *NCC Review* 129/10 (October, 2009).

- Neuner, Josef "A New Theology of Proclamation." In *The Future of the Asian Churches.* Edited by James Kroeger and Peter Phan. Quezon City: Clareetian, 2002.
- Newlands, George. *Christ and Human Rights: The Transformative Engagement,* 2006.
- Niebuhr, Reinhold. *The Children of Light and the Children of Darkness.* Chicago: University of Chicago Press, 2011.
- Ninan, A. George. *Church & Society: Challenges & Responses in the 21st Century.* Edited by Rajendra K. Sail and Akshay Sail. Mumbai: BUILD & RCDRC, 2001.
- Pachuau, Lalsangkima. "Ecumenical Missiology: Three Decades of Historical and Theological Development (1952-1982)." In *Ecumenical Missiology: Contemporary Trends, Issues and Themes.* Edited by Lalsangkima Pachuau. Bangalore: The United Theological College, 2002.
- Pandey, R. S. *Education in Emerging Indian Society.* Agra: Agrawal, 2011.
- Parappally, Jacob "Witnessing to the Gospel: A Gift and a Task in the Present Day India." *VJTR* 79 (2015).
- Ralte, Rodinmawia. *Hindu and Hindutva: Hindu Tolerance, Hindu Exclusivism, Emergence of Assertive Hinduism.* Tainan: Programme for Theology and Cultures in Asia, 2014.
- Rao, Sunil Salankey. *Trafficking of Children for Sexual Exploitation.* New Delhi: Oxford University Press, 2013.
- Rauschenbusch, Walter. *Christianity and the Social Crisis in the 21st Century,* New Edition, Edited by Paul Rauschenbusch, HarperCollins, 2008.
- Rawat, H. K. *Sociology: Basic Concepts.* Jaipur: Rawat, 2010.
- Satyarthi, Kailash. "Trafficking of Children: Causes and Possible Solutions." In *Human Trafficking: The Stakeholder's Perspective.* Edited by Veerendra Mishra. New Delhi: Sage, 2013.
- Schmalzbauer, John. "Whose Social Justice? Which Evangelism?: Social Engagement in a Campus Ministry," In *The New Evangelical Social Engagement.* Edited by Brian Steensland and Philip Goff. New York: Oxford University Press, 2014.
- Selvaraj, David. "Theological Reflection on Human Sexuality." *NCC Review* 135/6 (July, 2015).
- Sema, Akheto. *Understanding the Nature and Purpose of Christian Religious Education.* Delhi: ISPCK, 2011.
- Sharma, K. L. *Indian Social Change.* Jaipur: Rawat Publications, 2008.
- Shaw, Alfred J. *Christianity and Social Change in India.* Lucknow: Lucknow Publishing House, 1983.
- Sheth, Pravin. *Environmentalism; Politics, Ecology and Development.* Jaipur: Rawat, 1997.

- Shimray, Shimreingam. *Theology of Human Rights: A Critique on Politics.* Jorhat: Barkataki, 2002.
- Shimrey, Shimreingam "Understanding Conflict Situation in North East India." In *Peacemaking in North East India: Social and Theological Exploration.* Edited by Yangkahao Vashum and Woba James. Jorhat: Tribal Study Centre, 2012.
- Singh, Paramjit and Gurpreet Bal. *Strategies of Social Change in India.* New Delhi: M D Publications, 1996.
- Singh, Yogendra. *Cultural Change in India: Identity and Globalization.* New Delhi: Rawat, 2008.
- Singh, Yogendra. *Modernization of Indian Tradition: Systematic Study of Social Change.* Jaipur: Rawat, 1986.
- Singh, Yogendra. *Social Change in India: Crisis and Resilience.* New Delhi: Har-Anand, 1993.
- Sinha, Raghuvir. *Social Change in Indian Society.* New Delhi: Naurang Rai, 1978.
- Snaitang, O. L. "Christianity and Change among the Hill Tribes of Northeast India," In *Christianity and Change in Northeast India.* Edited by Tanka Bahadur Subba, Joseph Uthenpurakal and Shaji Joseph Puykunnel. New Delhi: Concept, 2009.
- Stott, John. *Christian Mission in the Modern World.* Illinois: InterVarsity, 1975.
- Stott, John. *New Issues Facing Christians Today.* Mumbai: GLS, 2003.
- Swamy, Muthuraj. "Imagining Christian Identity in Relation to Reformed Secularism." *NCC Review* 136/9 (October, 2016): 525-543.
- Swamy, Muthuraj. *The Problem with Interreligious Dialogue: Plurality, Conflict and Elitism in Hindu-Christian-Muslim Relations.* London: Bloomsbury, 2016.
- Thomas, M. M. *The Acknowledged Christ of Indian Renaissance.* Madras: CLS, 1976.
- Thomas, M. M. *The Secular Ideologies of India and the Secular Meaning of Christ.* Bangalore: CISRS, 1976.
- Thomas, Sarasu Esther. *Law for Christians in Contemporary India.* Bangalore: BTESSC, 2014.
- Troeltsch, Ernst. *The Social Teachings of the Christian Churches.* Louisville: Westminster John Knox Press, 1992.
- Verbal, Pat. "Why you Church Needs a Special Needs Ministry." In *Special Needs-Special Ministry: For Children's Ministry.* Edited by Jim Pierson, Louise Tucker Jones, Joni Eareckson Tada. Loveland: Zondervan, 2004.
- Vischer, Lukas. "Climate Change, Sustainability and Christian Witness." *Ecumenical Review,* 49/2 (April, 1997).

- Volf, Miroslav "Faith, Pluralism and Public Engagement: A Response." *Political Theology* 14/6 (2013): 813-834.
- WCC. *Facing AIDS: The Challenge, the Church's Response.* Geneva: WCC Publications, 1997.
- Weinsten, Jay. *Social Change.* United Kingdom: Rowman & Littlefield, 2010.
- Wendler, Klaus. "Ministry to Patients with Acquired Immunodeficiency Syndrome: A Spiritual Challenge." *The Journal of Pastoral Care* 41/1 (March, 1987).
- Wielenga, Bastian. *Labour: Serving God or Mammon?* Delhi: ISPCK, 1987.
- Wilfred, Felix. *Asian Public Theology.* Delhi: ISPCK, 2010.
- William Carey Library, 1999.
- Wood, Ralph C. *Contending for the Faith: The Church's Engagement with Culture*, Baylor University Press, 2003.
- Zachariah, George. "Musings on Climate Justice: A Subaltern Perspective." *Journal of Lutheran Ethics,* 9/4 (April, 2009).

Contributors

Marian Susi Dharmaraj (MTh, Senate of Serampore College [University]) is an ordained minister in the Diocese of Mumbai, Church of North India. He has specialized in the area of Christian Ministry (Pastoral Counselling). He has several years of experience in church ministry, pastoral care and counselling.

Lochumi Ezung has recently done her MTh in Christian Education under the Senate of Serampore College (University), and she is currently involved in ministry (part-time) with her church, Lotha Baptist Church, Dimapur, Nagaland.

Z. Malsawmlien Gangte (MTh, Senate of Serampore College [University]) is Lecturer in the department of New Testament at the Asia Antioch Seminary, Guwahati, Assam, where he also serves as the Academic Dean. He has previously taught in the Evangelical College of Theology in Churachandpur, Manipur.

Reji George (MTh, Senate of Serampore College [University]) is Lecturer in the department of New Testament at the Indian Theological Seminary, Avadi, Chennai where he also serves as the Registrar.

Holika has received her MTh in New Testament from the Senate of Serampore College (University) and is currently involved in church ministry among young people in Nagaland.

Watirenla Jamir has received her MTh (Missiology) from the Senate of Serampore College (University). Currently, she is a volunteer with Yajang 'B' Baptist Church, Mangkolemba district, Nagaland. She also works in the mission field for building bamboo churches among the tea-labourers in this region. She has experience in missionary training with Youth with a Mission (YWAM), and has worked as a missionary teacher in Sikkim.

John Jebaseelan is a priest in the Methodist Church of India in Mumbai. He is interested in and writes about Ancient Greek Philosophy, Rhetoric and Patristic Theology. He holds an MPhil in Philosophy from the University of Mumbai.

Rachel Katty (MTh, Senate of Serampore College [University]) is Lecturer in Old Testament at the India Bible College and Seminary, Tiruvella, Kerala.

Saraswati Koirala (MTh, Senate of Serampore College [University]) is currently doing PhD in Pastoral Counselling at the Sam Higginbottom University of Agriculture, Technology and Sciences (SHUATS), Allahabad. She is also a coordinator and a faculty of MDiv. Extension Studies at *Hariyo Kharka* in Kalimpong (West Bengal). She is involved in counselling young people and is working with different NGOs, and churches.

Asish Thomas Koshy (DTh, Federated Faculty for Research in Religion & Culture) is Assistant Professor of New Testament at the Union Biblical Seminary. His interest lies in Johannine literature and biblical hermeneutics. He is currently preparing his doctoral work on *Resurrection and Family of God in the Gospel of John* for publication.

H. Lalnunmawia is an ordained Pastor of the Mizoram Presbyterian Church presently working at Champhai, Mizoram, pastoring four local churches. Ordained in 2005, he served as a missionary Pastor in Nepal for four years. He has completed MTh (Missiology) under the Senate of Serampore College (University) in 2016.

Nukshijungla Longkumer (MTh, Senate of Serampore College [University]) is Lecturer at the Calcutta Bible Seminary in the field of Christian Ministry (Christian Education).

Wilson Paluri (DTh, North India Institute of Post Graduate Theological Studies) is an ordained priest of Church of North India and is currently serving as an Assistant Professor of Religion and Cultural Studies at the Union Biblical Seminary, Pune. He has contributed several articles in the area of Indian Philosophy, Indian Christian Theology, Global Ethics, Ecology and Globalization. He is also on the editorial board of UBS Journal and the Publication of Ecumenical Research Forum.

Mary Grace Z. Pangamte has recently completed her MTh in New Testament from the Senate of Serampore College (University), and now is preparing for her enrolment in doctoral programme. Her research interest and focus is in feminist biblical studies.

Lipoklemla Pongener is the Assistant Chaplain at the Christian Medical College & Hospital, Ludhiana. She is trained in Christian Ministry (Counseling) and has recently completed her MTh under the Senate of Serampore College (University).

Nicky N. Sangma is serving as an Assistant Pastor in charge of Missions at Tura Baptist Church in the state of Meghalaya. He has done his MTh (Senate of

Serampore College [University]) in the field of Christian Theology specializing in Systematic Theology. His research interest lies primarily in the field of systematic theology, implications of Christian doctrine and Philosophy of Religion, Science and cosmology. His particular areas of focus are in the theologies of Søren Kierkegaard, Friedrich Schleiermacher, and the Reformed tradition.

Muthuraj Swamy (PhD, University of Edinburgh) is the Dean, Faculty of Theology and Formation at the Union Biblical Seminary. He is the author of several articles in the fields of Religion, Society and Theology, and a book, *The Problem with Interreligious Dialogue: Pluralism, Conflict and Elitism in Hindu-Christian-Muslim Relations* (London: Bloomsbury, 2016). He is the General Editor of the Mission Theology in the Anglican Communion series (publishing services by SPCK), London.

Richie Varghese (BD, Union Biblical Seminary, Pune) has special interests in the area of ethnic/religious nationalism, especially Hindutva in India. He is also interested in political economy and developmental issues in Asia with a special focus on India. He is engaged in social work and in Christian youth ministry.

S. James Wesly (MTh, Senate of Serampore College [University]) is Assistant Professor in the Christian Ministry Department at the Bishop's College, Kolkata, where he also serves as the Dean of Studies. His area of specialisation is Pastoral Care and Counselling and Practical Theology.

Index